MW01274127

Running QuickBooks® 2006
Premier Editions

Kathy Ivens

CPA911 Publishing, LLC
Philadelphia PA

Running QuickBooks 2006 Premier Editions

ISBN Number 0-9720669-7-7

Published by CPA911 Publishing, LLC December 2005

Copyright 2005-2006 CPA911 Publishing, LLC

CPA911 is a Registered Trademark of CPA911 Publishing, LLC.

All rights reserved. No portion of the contents of this book may be reproduced in any form or by any means without the written permission of the publisher.

The publisher and author have used their best efforts to make sure the information in this book is reliable and complete. They make no representations or warranties for the accuracy or completeness of the contents of this book, and specifically disclaim any implied warranties. The publisher and author disclaim any responsibility for errors or ommissions or the results obtained from the use of the information in this book.

QuickBooks is a registered trademark of Intuit Inc., and is used with permission. Screen shots reprinted by permission of Intuit Inc.

Windows, Microsoft Excel and Microsoft Word are registered trademarks of Microsoft Corporation, and are used with permission. Screen shots reprinted by permission from Microsoft Corporation.

Contents

Acknowledgements

Cover Design: Matthew Ericson

Production: InfoDesign Services (www.infodesigning.com)

Indexing: AfterWords Editorial Services (www.aweditorial.com)

I owe a great debt of gratitude to Shane Hamby and Roger Kimble of Intuit, Inc. for their diligent attention to my questions, and their unfailing generosity and expertise in providing explanations.

Introduction

Intuit offers several Premier editions of QuickBooks, which have features not available in other version of QuickBooks. This book provides explanations and instructions for the features of interest to users of the Premier editions of QuickBooks 2006.

For coverage of QuickBooks basics, read QuickBooks 2006: The Official Guide, from McGraw-Hill Publishing. A copy of the book is in your QuickBooks Premier edition software package.

Chapter 1

Getting Started

Updating existing company files

Creating a new company file

Using the EasyStep interview

Setting up your company file manually

Configuring the QuickBooks window

QuickBooks Premier editions offer features not available in other versions of QuickBooks. If you previously worked with QuickBooks Pro, you'll find that your Premier edition of QuickBooks has all the features available in QuickBooks Pro, plus the advanced features built into the Premier editions.

Most of the advanced features are in both the generic Premier Edition and all the industry-specific Premier editions. However, each of the industry-specific Premier editions has additional features and tools that are helpful for running QuickBooks for that specific industry. If you have the Accountant Edition, you also have many of the tools that are in the industry-specific editions. This makes it easier to support clients who install QuickBooks Premier editions.

In this chapter, I'll cover the tasks you face as you set up and configure your company file in QuickBooks Premier.

Company File Setup

You have several options available for setting up your company file in QuickBooks 2006 Premier. If you upgraded from an earlier version of QuickBooks (any edition), you must update your existing company file.

If you're new to QuickBooks, you need to create a company file, either by going through the EasyStep Interview, or creating the file manually.

Opening an Existing Company File

If you installed QuickBooks 2006 Premier in the same folder that held your previous version of QuickBooks, the first time you launch QuickBooks the software opens the company file that was open when you last closed QuickBooks (using the previous version). Then the system begins the process of updating the file to Premier 2006 (see the section Performing the Update).

If you installed QuickBooks 2006 Premier in a new folder (in order to preserve the previous version), and you want to continue to use your existing company file in the old version, but also use it in QuickBooks 2006, you have the following choices:

- Back up your company file, using the new QuickBooks 2006 folder as the target location. Then restore the file (see "Restoring a Backup File", later in this chapter).
- Back up your company file to its usual backup location, and then copy that backup file to the new QuickBooks 2006 folder. The file has a .QBB extension. Then restore the file.
- Copy the company file (the file with the .QBW extension) to the folder that holds QuickBooks 2006. Then open in from the Welcome to QuickBooks Window (discussed next).

If you installed QuickBooks 2006 into a new folder, no existing company file opens (because there is no "last-used" file. The first time you open QuickBooks Premier you see the Welcome to QuickBooks window seen in Figure 1-1.

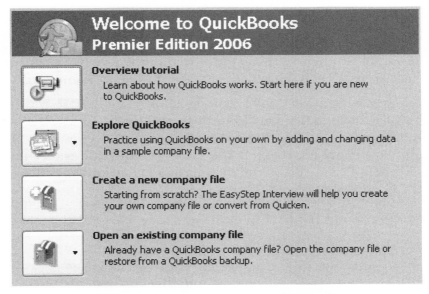

Figure 1-1: You need to open a file to begin using QuickBooks.

If you copied the company file (with a .QBW extension) to the QuickBooks 2006 folder, click the icon next to Open An Existing

Company File. Then select Open An Existing File from the command list that's displayed.

In the Open A Company dialog, double-click the file to open it and let QuickBooks begin updating it (see the section "Performing the Update").

Restoring a Backup File

If you have a backup of a company file in your QuickBooks 2006 folder, you can restore it and then update it. Choose File → Restore from the QuickBooks menu bar, or click Open An Existing Company File in the Welcome to QuickBooks window, and then choose Restore A Backup File from the drop-down menu.

Use the following guidelines to retrieve and update a backup file in the Restore Company Backup dialog:

- If you have the backup file in your QuickBooks 2006 folder, select it.
- If the backup file is in another location, use the Browse button to navigate through your computer to find the file. (QuickBooks backup files have the filename pattern *CompanyName*.QBB.)

When the fields at the top of the dialog are filled in with the data identifying the backup file, QuickBooks automatically fills in the bottom of the dialog with data identifying the restored file (see Figure 1-2). The name of the company file remains the same, but the extension changes to .QBW. The default location is the installation folder for QuickBooks.

If you prefer to keep company data files in their own subfolder, click the Browse button at the bottom of the dialog to open the Restore To dialog.

- If the subfolder exists, double-click its icon and then click Save. You return to the Restore Company Backup dialog.
- If the subfolder doesn't exist, click the New Folder icon on the Restore To dialog, enter a name, press Enter to save the new subfolder, and then double-click its icon and click Save. You return to the Restore Company Backup dialog.

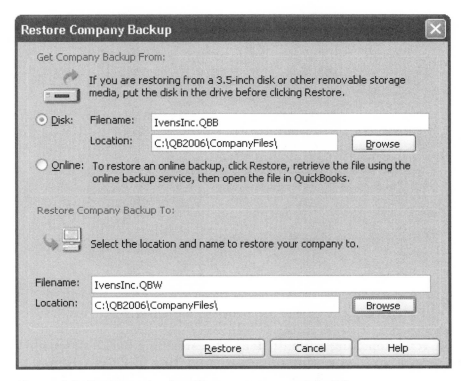

Figure 1-2: Restore a backup file so you can update it for
QuickBooks 2006 Premier.

Click Restore. QuickBooks restores the backup (which takes a few seconds or a few minutes, depending on the size of your company file), and then begins the update process to convert the file to Premier Edition.

Performing the Update

Instead of immediately loading your company file (whether you restored a backup or selected an existing file) QuickBooks opens the Update File To New Version dialog seen in Figure 1-3.

Confirm the conversion by typing Yes and clicking OK. (Even though the dialog shows all capital letters, you can use lowercase letters.) Another message appears to warn you that you can't use this file in an older version of QuickBooks after it's updated.

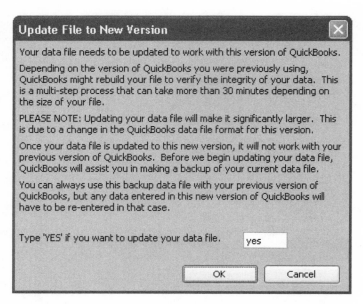

Figure 1-3: Convert your company file to Premier 2006.

If you're opening a file (instead of restoring a backup), QuickBooks has to back up the existing file before updating it. Click OK, and in the QuickBooks Backup dialog, specify a filename and location for the backup file. Use the Browse button if you want to select a different location.

If you select your hard drive as the backup location, QuickBooks issues a warning about the dangers of hard drive back ups, and asks you to click OK to confirm your decision. Of course, you'd backed up the existing file during your regular backup procedure, so it's okay to save this extra backup to your hard drive.

If you're using a multi-user version, a warning dialog appears to remind you that network users won't be able to use the file until they've updated their version of QuickBooks. Click Yes to confirm you want to continue updating the file.

QuickBooks creates the backup, and then converts the file. Depending on the size of the file, this can take a minute, or several minutes. When the file is converted, it opens in your QuickBooks Premier edition window.

Creating a New Company File

If you're just starting with QuickBooks, you need to create a company file. You can either use the Easy Step Interview (a wizard that walks you through all the processes involved in setting up your company's books), or create your company file manually.

Using a Predefined Company File

Some of the industry-specific Premier editions have predefined templates of company data files. You can turn one of these predefined files into your own company file.

NOTE: *In QuickBooks 2006, unlike QuickBooks 2005, no list of predefined files appears during company setup, but they're there—they're just hidden.*

A predefined file makes the process of creating your company file less onerous, because many of the elements and configuration settings are pre-configured for you. The predefined company files usually include the following components:

- Chart of accounts suitable for the type of business
- Preferences settings configured to match the type of business
- Items (the products and services you sell)
- Lists that are prepopulated with commonly used entries for the type of business (Customer Type, Vendor Type, Job Type, Customer Messages, and so on)

Don't confuse the pre-configured company data files with the sample files that are available. Sample files give you a chance to see how QuickBooks transaction windows and reports work, but you can't use the sample files for your company.

You can select a predefined company data file during the company setup process, whether you use the EasyStep Interview or create the file manually. During setup, QuickBooks asks you to choose the industry that comes closest to your own business.

Unlike the industry listings that were clearly identified in QuickBooks 2005 Premier editions, none of the industry listings are identified as predefined company files.

However, some of the industry listings are predefined files—they're just hidden (not identified as predefined company files). Table 1-1 lists the predefined company files that are buried innocuously in the list.

Industry	Subcategory
Construction	All subcategories
Retail	All subcategories
Consulting, Professional and Technical Services	Advertising Architecture Building Inspection Consulting-Professional Consulting-Personal Drafting Engineering Graphic Design Industrial Design Interior Design Legal Services Other Consulting, Professional and Technical Services Other Design Services Surveying & Mapping

Table 1-1: Industry choices that are really predefined company files.

TIP: If you're an accountant and you help clients set up QuickBooks Pro, the same predefined company files are available in the Industry list. Previous to QuickBooks 2006, predefined company files were available only in Premier editions.

EasyStep Interview

The EasyStep Interview is a wizard that walks you through all the processes involved in setting up your company data file.

TIP: *Each task the wizard walks you through can be accomplished manually, using the QuickBooks menus, commands, and configuration dialogs. See the section "Manual Company Setup", later in this chapter.*

If you've used the EasyStep Interview in previous versions of QuickBooks, you'll be pleasantly surprised at the new version of this feature. The whole process is streamlined, shorter, less complicated, and easier to complete.

The first window welcomes you to the wizard. Click Start Interview to begin. (If you want to set up your company file manually, click Skip Interview, and read the section "Manual Company Setup".)

Company Information Section

In the first window, enter your company information. Notice that there are two fields for your company name:

- The Company Name field is for the company name you use for doing business (your d/b/a name), and that name (along with your address) is used on printed transaction forms, and the reports you generate in QuickBooks.
- The Legal Name field is used only if the legal name of your company differs from the company name you use for doing business. That name is used for government forms (if you do your own payroll, or you export your QuickBooks files to a tax preparation application).

For many companies, both entries are identical, and when you type the data in the Company Name field and press the Tab key, QuickBooks automatically duplicates it in the Legal Name field. Change it if necessary.

Enter your Tax Identification Number. This may be an EIN number, or your Social Security number, depending on the type of business organization your company has. When all the information is filled in, click Next.

Creating an Administrator

In the next window, you can assume the role of administrator, just by virtue of the fact that you're the person setting up the company file, and the decision about the password is yours to make.

If you're ready to set up an administrator for this company, enter a password, and then retype it to confirm it. This does not have to be done during company setup, and most people wait until later to set up the administrator and additional users. If your computer is in a secure place (not in a public place where other people can easily use it), and nobody else works on your QuickBooks files, you probably don't need an administrator. Click Next to move on.

Saving the File

The next window is an announcement that you're about to save your information in a QuickBooks company file. Click Next again to get to the Filename For New Company dialog, in which you save the data file. QuickBooks automatically uses the company name for the filename, but you can change the filename if you wish.

By default, QuickBooks saves the company file in the folder in which the software is installed. However, I prefer to save company files in a discrete subfolder, and if you want to do the same, follow these steps:

1. Enter the filename, but do not click Save.
2. Click the Create New Folder icon at the top of the window to create a New Folder.
3. Enter a name for the new folder (e.g. CompanyFiles), and press Enter.
4. Double-click the new folder's listing to open it.
5. Click Save to save your file in this subfolder.

It takes a few minutes to save the file, and then the wizard presents the next windows.

Customizing Your Company File

The ensuing wizard windows are designed to help you set up your company file to suit your business and accounting needs. Whatever data you enter in these windows can be changed at any time in the future. This interview is just a quick way of making sure you cover all the important topics before you start creating transactions in QuickBooks.

Selecting an Industry

The wizard displays a list of industries, and subcategories for each industry, as seen in Figure 1-4. Scroll through the list to find the industry in which your business fits, and then find the subcategory that matches (or comes closest to) your own business.

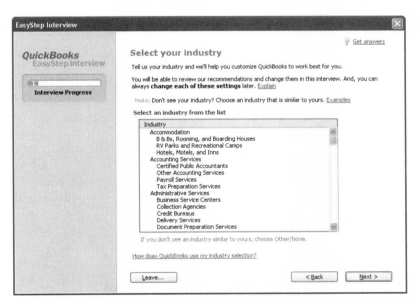

Figure 1-4: Select the industry and subcategory that matches your business.

If one of the predefined files listed in Table 1-1 (presented earlier in this chapter) matches or almost matches your business, select that listing to save yourself a lot of time and effort in setting up the components you need to run your company in QuickBooks.

In the following windows, the wizard asks a series of questions about the way your business operates. You must indicate whether you sell products or services or both, whether you collect sales tax for any sales, create estimates for your customers, make cash sales, track accounts payable, and so on. Go through all the windows, indicating your answers and clicking Next.

Nothing you select is immutable; you can change any Yes to No (or the other way around) at any time in the future, using the Preferences dialog.

Creating a Chart of Accounts

After you complete all the questions about the types of transactions you'll use in QuickBooks, the wizard displays a page indicating it's time to establish the accounts you need.

When you click Next, the wizard wants to know your start date for using QuickBooks. This is your "go live" date, and it means that every financial transaction before that date is historical, and every financial transaction after that date must be created in QuickBooks. QuickBooks uses this date to manipulate some of the information in the following wizard windows.

For example, the next window asks if you want to set up a bank account. If you select No, you can add the bank account as you configure your chart of accounts. I recommend you select No, because of the way QuickBooks uses the information it asks for if you select Yes.

If you select Yes, you're actually creating the bank as an account in your chart of accounts. The wizard asks for the bank name (the name you want to use in the chart of accounts, such as Operating Account), and optionally, the account number. You're also asked to indicate whether you opened this bank account before your QuickBooks start date.

If you indicate that the bank account existed before your start date (a highly likely scenario), in the next window you're asked to enter the last statement date, and the reconciled bank balance as of that date. Don't enter any amount in the bank balance field, leave it as zero.

Don't Enter Opening Balances for Bank Accounts

When you enter an opening balance for a bank account, whether in the EasyStep Interview or when you're adding bank accounts later, QuickBooks automatically posts that amount to the bank, and to an account named Opening Bal Equity.

The Opening Bal Equity account is something QuickBooks invents to hold prior equity (and not all opening balances can be posted to prior equity). Most accountants don't want to see a balance in the Opening Bal Equity account, so you should avoid entering an opening balance. You can post the opening balance later, using an Opening Trial Balance journal entry (covered in Chapter 2). Chapter 11 has information for accountants about clearing the Opening Bal Equity account.

After asking about your bank account(s), QuickBooks displays the expense accounts that have been selected for your chart of accounts, based on the industry type you selected (see Figure 1-5). This is not a complete chart of accounts, but you can create additional accounts as needed (covered in Chapter 2).

The next window displays the income accounts that have been automatically placed in your chart of accounts. These expense and income accounts that QuickBooks automatically selects are useful and relevant, so you should accept them.

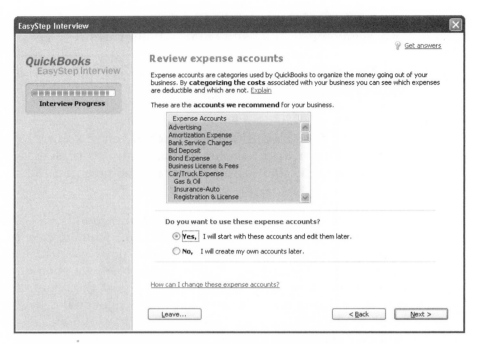

Figure 1-5: A bare-bones set of expenses for your chart of accounts is automatically created for your type of business.

Manual Company Setup

If you click the Skip Interview button when the EasyStep Interview opens, the Creating New Company dialog opens, and you can enter the basic information quickly (see Figure 1-6).

Enter the company name the way you want it to appear on reports, invoices, and other forms. If the company's legal name differs from the "Doing Business As" name, enter it in the Legal Name field.

Enter the other contact information if you want to display it on forms. The e-mail address is used if you send invoices, estimates, statements, and other customer documents by e-mail instead of printing them. QuickBooks provides a feature for e-mailing these documents as PDF files, and you can learn how it works in Chapter 3 of *QuickBooks 2006: The Official Guide.*

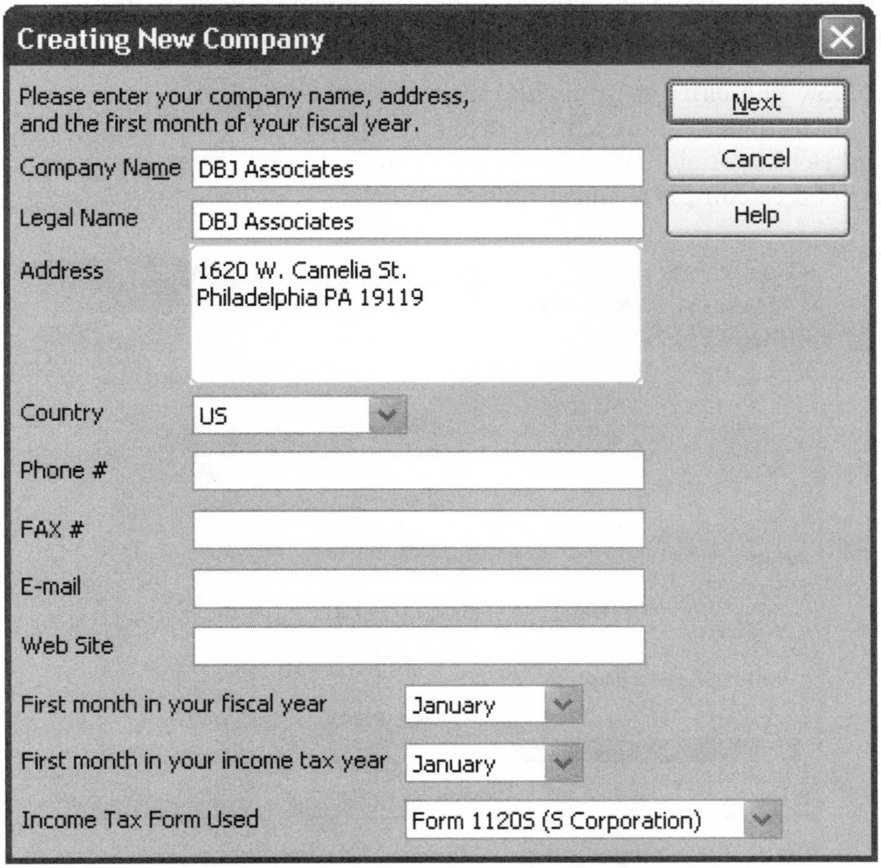

Figure 1-6: Enter company information in the Creating New Company dialog

Click Next and select a type of business so QuickBooks can install the appropriate chart of accounts (see Figure 1-7). The list that's displayed includes some of the subcategories that provide a predefined company file, and if one of them matches your business, select it to save yourself a lot of setup work. See Table 1-1 earlier in this chapter for the subcategories that produce a predefined company file.

You can also choose the option (No Type) to enter or import your own chart of accounts. Then click Next to save the company file in the Filename For New Company dialog.

Now you can set up a full chart of accounts, enable features, add entries to lists, and do all the other configuration tasks required to use QuickBooks efficiently. The chapters in this book cover the information you need to complete those tasks.

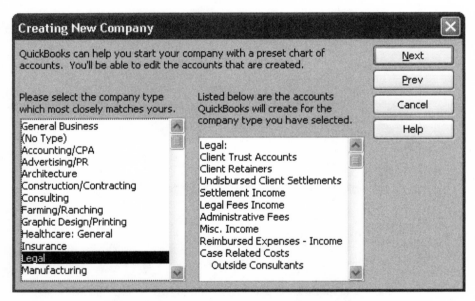

Figure 1-7: Select the type of business that matches your own company.

Configuring the QuickBooks Window

If you've used QuickBooks before, the QuickBooks 2006 software window is a surprise—lots of changes! It's more than just a new look—some menu commands have moved, some menu commands have disappeared, some old elements have disappeared (navigators), and new elements have been introduced.

NOTE: *When QuickBooks opens, you see the QuickBooks Learning Center. Before you use or close this window, deselect the option Show This Window At Startup, so you don't have to wait for it to load every time you want to work in QuickBooks.*

In this section I'll go over the components in the QuickBooks software window, which contains the following components by default:

- Menu bar
- Icon bar
- Home page

Menu Bar

If you're new to QuickBooks, the menu bar is unremarkable; it looks like any menu bar from any Windows software. Each menu item has a list of commands, and some commands have an arrow pointing to the right, indicating the availability of subcommands.

However, if you're an experienced QuickBooks user, and you've upgraded to QuickBooks 2006 from a previous version, the menu bar is full of surprises. Most of the menu lists are shorter (QuickBooks has removed a lot of the "Buy A Service From Intuit) menu items).

More important, some menu items have disappeared, and since some of the newly nonexistent commands were probably those you used often, it'll take you a little time to get used to the new interface.

The menu commands you'll probably miss the most (according to the people in my office, and client users, who have been working on the QuickBooks 2006 version since it was first released) are the missing lists on the Lists menu. The following lists are no longer available on the Lists menu:

- Customers:Jobs
- Vendors
- Employees

These lists are also missing from their respective menus, e.g. the Vendors List menu item is no longer on the Vendors menu. All of the lists are now available in the new Customer, Vendor, and Employee Centers (discussed later in this chapter).

Icon Bar

If you're new to QuickBooks and created a new company file, the Icon bar is rather sparse. If you updated to QuickBooks 2006 from an earlier version, and opened an existing company file, the icons that were available before appear now.

Customizing the Icon Bar

The icons that appear on the Icon bar may not include the features you use most frequently, so you should change the Icon bar to make it more useful. You can also change the way the Icon Bar and its icons look. Choose View → Customize Icon Bar to open the Customize Icon Bar dialog, which displays a list of the icons currently occupying your Icon bar (see Figure 1-8)

NOTE: *If you log in to QuickBooks, the settings you establish are linked to your user name. When you make changes, you're not changing the Icon bar for other users.*

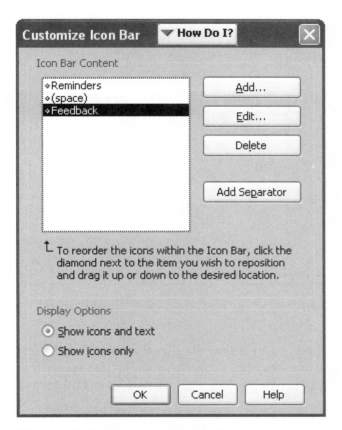

Figure 1-8: Design your own Icon bar.

Adding an Icon

You can add an icon to the Icon bar from the Customize Icon Bar dialog, or by automatically adding an icon for the QuickBooks window you're currently using.

Adding an Icon in the Dialog

To add an icon from the Customize Icon Bar dialog, click Add to open the Add Icon Bar Item dialog seen in Figure 1-9. When the Add Icon Bar Item dialog opens, scroll through the list to select the task you want to add to the Icon bar. Then choose a graphic to represent the new icon (QuickBooks selects a default graphic, which appears within a box). You can also change the name (the title that appears below the icon) or the description (the text that appears in the Tooltip when you hold your mouse pointer over the icon).

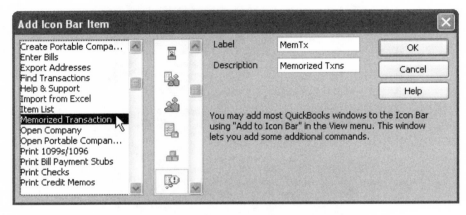

Figure 1-9: Select your oft-used features for placement on the Icon bar.

To position your new icon at a specific place within the existing row of icons (instead of at the right end of the Icon bar), first select the existing icon that you want to sit to the left of your new icon and then click Add.

Adding an Icon For an Open Window

If you're currently working in a QuickBooks window, and you think it would be handy to have an icon for fast access to that window, it's easy to add an icon to the Icon bar.

While the window is open, choose View → Add *<Name of Window>* To Icon Bar. A dialog appears so you can choose a graphic, a title, and a description for the new icon.

Changing the Order of Icons

The list of icons in the Customize Icon Bar dialog reads top-to-bottom, representing the left-to-right display on the Icon bar. Moving an icon's listing up moves it to the left on the Icon bar, and vice versa.

To move an icon, click the small diamond to the left of the icon's listing, hold down the left mouse button, and drag the listing to a new position.

Displaying Icons Without Title Text

By default, both icons and text display on the Icon bar. Select Show Icons Only to remove the title text under the icons. This makes the icons smaller, and you can fit more icons on the Icon bar. Position your mouse pointer over a small icon to see a Tooltip that describes the icon's function.

Changing the Icon's Graphic, Text, or Description

To change an individual icon's appearance, select the icon's listing and click Edit. Then choose a different graphic (the currently selected graphic is enclosed in a box), change the Label, or change the Description (the Tooltip text).

Separating Icons into Groups

You can insert a separator between two icons, which is a way to create groups of icons. (Of course, you must first move icons into logical groups on the Icon bar.) The separator is a gray vertical line.

To accomplish this, in the Customize Icon Bar dialog select the icon that should appear to the left of the separator bar and click Add Separator. QuickBooks inserts "(space)" to the listing to indicate the location of the separator.

Removing an Icon

If there are icons you never use, or use so infrequently that you'd rather replace them with more useful icons, you can remove them. Select the icon in the Customize Icon Bar dialog and click Delete. QuickBooks does not ask you to confirm, the icon just disappears from the Icon bar.

NOTE: You cannot remove the icons for Home page, Customer Center, Vendor Center, Employee Center, or Report Center.

Home Page

New in QuickBooks 2006 is the Home page, which is a central access point for commonly used QuickBooks functions. The page has multiple sections, and each section has a set of icons (see Figure 1-10).

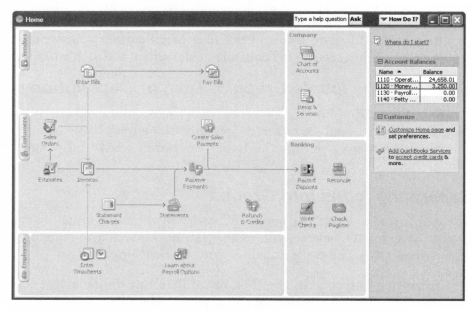

Figure 1-10: The Home page provides quick access to the most common functions.

The sections of the Home page, as well as the icons that appear in each section, change depending on the way you set up and customize your company file.

If you used the EasyStep Interview to create a new company, the configuration options you chose determine the contents of the Home page you see. For example, if you indicated you didn't have employees, the Home page has no Employees section.

As you enable features (such as estimates, progress billing, inventory management, and so on) QuickBooks adds the appropriate icons to the Home page.

Customizing the Home Page

You can customize the Home page in the Desktop View section of the Preferences dialog (on the Company Preferences tab). To open the dialog,

click the Customize Home Page link on the right side of the Home page, or choose Edit → Preferences, and select the Desktop View icon in the left pane.

This dialog (see Figure 1-11) lets you select and deselect some icons, and provides links to other Preferences dialogs that you can visit to enable or disable features. As you enable features, QuickBooks adds the related icons to the Home page.

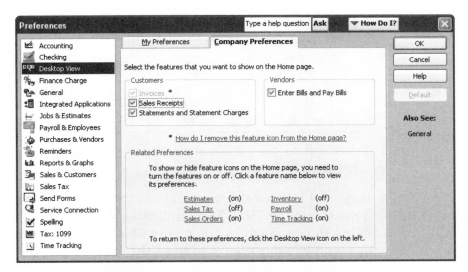

Figure 1-11: Customize your QuickBooks features and the Home page icons that provide access to those features.

Removing the Home Page

If you don't like having the Home page in your software window all the time, you can close it by clicking the X in the top right corner. To open it, click the Home icon on the Icon bar

If you close the Home page, it opens again the next time you open QuickBooks, or change companies. That's because by default, QuickBooks displays the Home page when a company file is opened.

You can change this behavior in the My Preferences tab of the Desktop View category in the Preferences dialog (see Figure 1-12).

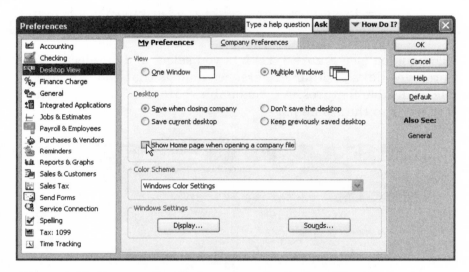

Figure 1-12: You can disable the automatic display of the Home page.

The option is named incorrectly; it should say "Show Home Page When Opening **This** Company File". The implication is that you're enabling or disabling the option for all company files. If you work in multiple company files, and you don't want to have the Home page appear automatically, you must open the Preferences dialog in each file and make this change.

TIP: If you disable the Home page, be sure to put icons for your oft-used functions on the Icon bar, to avoid the extra mouse clicks needed to access functions from the menu bar.

QuickBooks Centers

QuickBooks centers are windows that display data about specific areas of your company. You can see current data, analyze that data, and manipulate the way the data is presented. The following centers are available:

- Customer Center
- Vendor Center
- Employee Center
- Report Center

Open each center from its associated icon on the Icon bar. You can also open all but the Report Center by clicking the button on the left side of the appropriate section on the Home page.

It's important to note that the only place you can see the Customer List, Vendor List, and Employee List is by opening the appropriate Center.

Customer Center

The Customer Center, seen in Figure 1-13, contains information about your customers, jobs, and the sales transactions you've created. It's also the only place you can view your list of customers and jobs.

Figure 1-13: Everything you need to know about customers and jobs is available in the Customer Center.

When you select a customer or a job in the Customers & Jobs pane, you can change the view of that customer's history by selecting different options in the drop-down lists in the right pane.

You can also use the buttons in the right pane to edit the customer's information, create a QuickReport, and perform other tasks. The buttons on the top of the window provide quick access to common tasks.

The Transactions tab (see Figure 1-14) provides information about all the types of sales transactions in your QuickBooks system. You can filter the way the information is displayed by changing the options in the drop-down lists in the right pane.

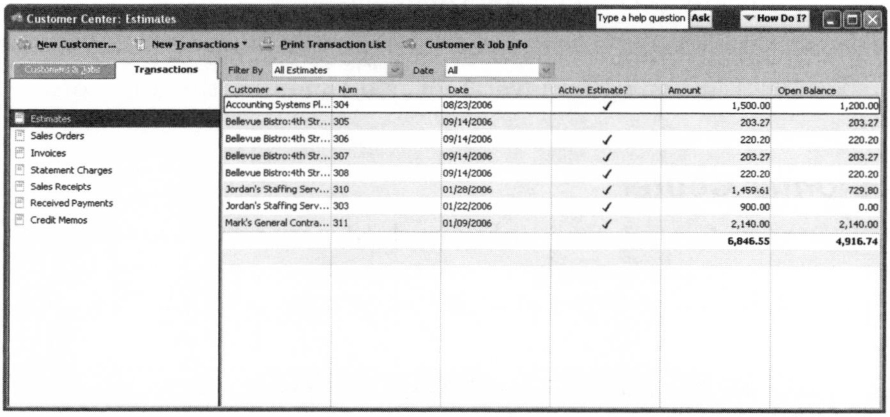

Figure 1-14: Check the current status of your sales transactions.

Vendor Center

Like the Customer Center, the Vendor Center is the location of all the information relating to vendors (see Figure 1-15). It's also the only place to view the Vendor List.

Use the buttons at the top of the window, and in the right pane, to work with vendor information, and to create transactions.

Open the Transactions tab to view information about transactions related to vendors (bills, payments, purchase orders, and so on).

Figure 1-15: Select a vendor and then choose what you want to display about that vendor.

Employee Center

The Employee Center, seen in Figure 1-16, operates similarly to the Customer and Vendor Centers. You can select an employee's name to view information, and filter that information by changing options.

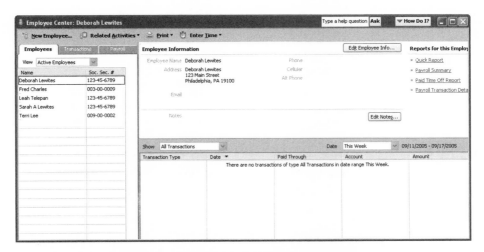

Figure 1-16: Track employees and payroll data in the Employee Center.

The Transaction tab lets you view information about the transactions connected to payroll (liabilities payments, company contributions to pensions and insurance, and so on).

The Payroll tab (which doesn't appear until after you've begun using QuickBooks payroll services, provides quick links to payroll functions.

Report Center

The Report Center provides one-click access to all the reports that are available in menus and submenus in the Reports menu system on the menu bar. In addition, as you can see in Figure 1-17, the Report Center provides easy-to-understand explanations of report contents.

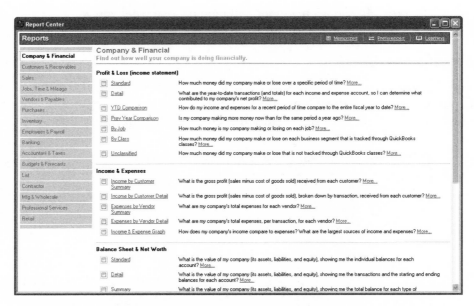

Figure 1-17: Use the Report Center instead of drilling down through the Reports menu structure.

Chapter 2

The Chart of Accounts

Designing a chart of accounts

Creating accounts

Using subaccounts

Manipulating accounts

Importing a chart of accounts

Entering opening balances

Managing equity account balances

The most important step in your company setup is the creation of your chart of accounts. QuickBooks may have created some accounts for you during the initial setup of your company file, but you'll need many additional accounts in order to keep books accurately. In this chapter, I'll discuss creating the chart of accounts, as well the various ways in which you can manipulate the accounts you've created.

It's easier to configure your company file if you create the chart of accounts before you create other lists. Some of the lists you create require you to link the items in the list to accounts. For example, service and product items are linked to income accounts.

Designing a Chart of Accounts

If you're designing your own chart of accounts, be sure to do so carefully, because you have to live with the results every time you use QuickBooks. Discuss the design with your accountant, who can help you design a scheme that works for the transactions you have to enter, and the reports you need.

You have several decisions to make about the general scheme you'll use for your chart of accounts. You need to decide whether you'll use numbered accounts, and if so, how many digits to use for each account. You should also design a scheme for using subaccounts. Subaccounts make it possible to post transactions in a way that makes it easier to identify the components you're tracking. In addition, you must create a protocol for account naming, and make sure everyone who works with the QuickBooks data files understands the protocol and applies it.

Using Account Numbers

By default, QuickBooks does not assign numbers to accounts, and you should switch your QuickBooks configuration options to correct that oversight. A chart of accounts with numbers is easier to design, and easier to work with. Numbered accounts also have account names, of course, but you can categorize accounts by number, which makes the chart of accounts easier to work with.

Enabling Account Numbers

To switch to a number format for your accounts, you have to change the QuickBooks preferences as follows:

1. Choose Edit → Preferences from the menu bar to open the Preferences dialog.
2. Select the Accounting icon in the left pane.
3. Click the Company Preferences tab.
4. Select the Use Account Numbers check box (see Figure 2-1).

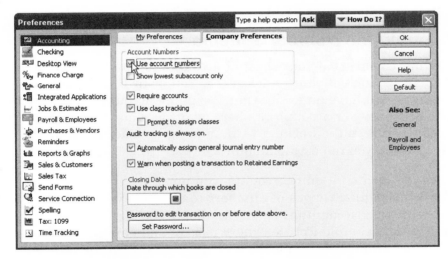

Figure 2-1: Change the accounting options to add numbers to your accounts.

If you selected a predefined chart of accounts when you set up your company file, all the accounts included in the predefined chart of accounts are automatically switched to numbered accounts. You may want to change some of the numbers to maintain consistency in your account categories. You can do so by editing the accounts (see "Editing Accounts" later in this chapter).

When you select the option to use account numbers, the option Show Lowest Subaccount Only becomes accessible (it's grayed out if you haven't opted for account numbers). This option tells QuickBooks to display only the subaccount on transaction windows instead of both the parent account and the subaccount, making it easier to see precisely which account is receiving the posting. (Subaccounts are discussed later in this chapter in the section "Using Subaccounts.")

QuickBooks does not automatically number accounts you added manually, so you must edit those accounts to add a number to each account record. If some accounts lack numbers, and you select Show Lowest Subaccount Only, when you click OK, QuickBooks displays an error message that you cannot enable this option until all your accounts have numbers assigned. After you've edited existing accounts that lack numbers, you can return to this preferences dialog and enable the option.

Designing the Number Scheme

After you've converted your chart of accounts to numbered accounts, you have a more efficient chart of accounts. You, your bookkeeper, and your accountant will have an easier time assigning accounts to transactions. That's because your account numbers give you a quick clue about the type of account you're working with, making it easier to select the right account when you're posting amounts.

As you create (or edit) accounts, you must use the numbers intelligently by assigning ranges of numbers to account types. You should check with your accountant before finalizing the way you use the numbers, but the example I present here is a common approach. This scheme uses four-digit numbers, and the starting digit represents the beginning of a range:

NOTE: *You can have as many as seven numbers (plus the account name) for each account.*

- 1xxx Assets
- 2xxx Liabilities
- 3xxx Equity
- 4xxx Income
- 5xxx Expenses (of a specific type)
- 6xxx Expenses (of a specific type)
- 7xxx Expenses (of a specific type)

- 8*xxx* Expenses (of a specific type)
- 9*xxx* Other Income and Expenses

You can, if you wish, have a variety of expense types and reserve the starting number for specific types. Many companies, for example, use 5*xxx* for sales expenses (they even separate the payroll postings between the sales people and the rest of the employees), then use 6000 through 7999 for general operating expenses, and 8*xxx* for other specific expenses that should appear together in reports (such as taxes).

Some companies use one range of expense accounts, such as 7000 through 7999 for expenses that fall into the "overhead" category. This is useful if you bid on work and need to know the total overhead expenses so you can apportion them to appropriate categories in your bid.

If you have inventory and you track cost of sales, you can reserve a section of the chart of accounts for that account type. Some companies use 4300 through 4999 for cost of sales; other companies use the numbers in the 5000 to 5999 range.

Also, think about the breakdown of assets. You might use 1000 through 1099 for cash accounts and 1100 through 1199 for receivables and other current assets, then use 1200 through 1299 for tracking fixed assets such as equipment, furniture, and so on.

Follow the same pattern for liabilities, starting with current liabilities and moving to long term. It's also a good idea to keep all the payroll withholding liabilities together.

Usually, as you create new accounts, you should increase the previous account number by ten, so that if your first bank account is 1000, the next bank account is 1010, and so on. For expenses (where you'll have many accounts), you might want to enter the accounts in intervals of five. These intervals give you room to squeeze in additional accounts that belong in the same general area of your chart of accounts when they need to be added later.

Understanding the Accounts Sort Order

You have to create a numbering scheme that conforms to the QuickBooks account types because QuickBooks sorts your chart of accounts by account type. If you have contiguous numbers that vary by account type, your reports won't be in the order you expect. QuickBooks uses the following sort order for the chart of accounts:

Assets:

- Bank
- Accounts Receivable
- Other Current Asset
- Fixed Asset
- Other Asset

Liabilities

- Accounts Payable
- Credit Card
- Other Current Liability
- Long-Term Liability

Equity

Income

Cost Of Goods Sold

Expense

Other Income

Other Expense

Non-Posting Accounts

NOTE: Non-posting accounts are created automatically by QuickBooks when you enable features that use those account types, namely Estimates, Purchase Orders, and Sales Orders.

Account Naming Protocols

You need to devise protocols for naming accounts, whether you plan to use numbered accounts, or only use account names. When you're posting transactions to the general ledger, the only way to know which account should be used for posting is to have easy-to-understand account names.

Your protocol must be clear so that when everyone follows the rules, the account naming convention is consistent. This is important because without rules it's common to have multiple accounts for the same use. For example, I frequently find expense accounts named Telephone, Tele, and Tel in client systems, and all of those accounts have balances. Users "guess" at account names, and if they don't find the account the way they would have entered the name, they invent a new account (using a name that seems logical to them). Avoid all of those errors by establishing protocols about creating account names, and then make sure everyone searches the account list before applying a transaction.

Here are a few suggested protocols—you can amend them to fit your own situation, or invent different protocols that meet your comfort level. The important thing is to make sure you have absolute rules so you can achieve consistency.

- Avoid apostrophes
- Set the number of characters for abbreviations. For example, if you permit four characters, telephone is abbreviated "tele"; a three-character rule produces "tel"; utilities is abbreviated "util" or "uti".
- Decide whether to use the ampersand (&) or a hyphen. For example, is it "repairs & maintenance" or "repairs-maintenance"? Do you want spaces before and after the ampersand or hyphen?

Creating Accounts

After you've done your homework, made your decisions, designed your protocols, and checked with your accountant, you're ready to create accounts. Start by opening the Chart of Accounts list, using any of the following actions:

- Press Ctrl-A
- Click the Chart of Accounts icon on the Home page
- Choose Lists → Chart of Accounts from the menu bar

Press Ctrl-N to open a New Account dialog, and select an account type from the Type drop-down list. The dialog for creating a new account changes its appearance depending on the account type you select, because each account type contains particular fields to hold relevant information. Figure 2-2 shows the New Account dialog for an expense account.

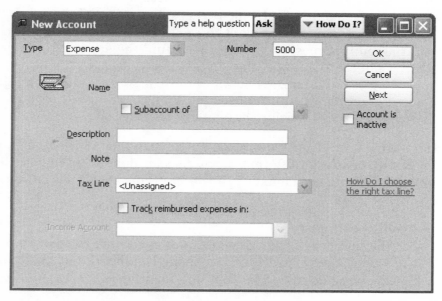

Figure 2-2: The only required entries for a new account are a number (if you're using numbers) and a name.

If you've configured QuickBooks for account numbers, there's a field for the account number. The Description field is optional. The Note field, which only appears on some account types, is also optional, and I've never come up with a good reason to use it.

The Tax Line field is useful if you're planning to prepare your own business tax return. (If you didn't specify a tax return form in the

Company Information dialog, the Tax Line field doesn't appear on the New Account dialog.)

If you don't want anyone to post transactions to the account now, you can select the Account Is Inactive option, which means the account won't be available for posting amounts while you're entering transactions. See the section "Hiding Accounts", later in this chapter.

As you finish entering each account, click Next to move to another blank New Account dialog. When you're finished entering accounts, click OK and then close the Chart of Accounts list by clicking the X in the top-right corner.

Avoid Opening Balances

Some account types have a field for an opening balance. Don't enter a balance while you're creating new accounts. The best way to put the account balances into the system is to enter an opening trial balance as a journal entry or by entering historical transactions (see the section "Entering Opening Balances" later in this chapter).

The account types that offer an opening balance field (remember, this is the field to ignore and avoid) are the following:

• Asset accounts except Accounts Receivable
• Liability accounts except Accounts Payable
• Equity accounts

Creating Subaccounts

Subaccounts provide a way to post transactions more precisely, because you can pinpoint a subcategory. For example, if you create an expense account for insurance expenses, you may want to have subaccounts for vehicle insurance, liability insurance, equipment insurance, and so on.

Post transactions only to the subaccounts, never to the parent account. When you create reports, QuickBooks displays the individual totals for the subaccounts, along with the grand total for the parent account.

To create a subaccount, you must first create the parent account. If you're using numbered accounts, when you set up your main (parent) accounts, be sure to leave enough open numbers to be able to fit in all the subaccounts you'll need. If necessary, use more than four digits in your numbering scheme to make sure you have a logical hierarchy for your account structure.

For example, suppose you have the following parent accounts:

- 6010 Insurance
- 6050 Utilities

You can then create the following subaccounts:

- 6011 Vehicles
- 6012 Liability
- 6013 Equipment
- 6051 Heat
- 6052 Electric

You can have multiple levels of subaccounts. Using the same 6010 insurance account as an example, create these subaccounts:

- 6011 Vehicles (subaccount of 6010)
- 6012 Cars (subaccount of 6011)
- 6013 Trucks (subaccount of 6011)

Of course, to make this work you have to widen the numerical interval between Vehicles and Liability, or use more than 4 numbers in your account numbering scheme.

When you view the Chart of Accounts list, subaccounts appear under their parent accounts, and they're indented. When you view a subaccount in the drop-down list of the Account field in a transaction window, it appears with colons between each account level:

ParentAccount: Subaccount

Or

ParentAccount:Subaccount:Subaccount.

For example, using the two-level structure I just created, the drop down list in the Account field in transaction windows shows the following:

6010 Insurance:6011 Vehicles

Because many of the fields in transaction windows are small, you may not be able to see the subaccount names without scrolling through the field. This can be annoying, and it's much easier to work if only the subaccount to which you post transactions is displayed.

That annoyance is cured by enabling the preference Show Lowest Subaccount Only, discussed earlier in this chapter. When you enable that option, you see only the last part of the subaccount in the transaction window, making it much easier to select the account you need. Using the example I cited, you'd see only

6011 Vehicles

QuickBooks offers two methods for making an account a subaccount: the New Account dialog, or dragging an account listing to an indented position.

Creating Subaccounts in the New Account Dialog

To use the New Account dialog for creating subaccounts, create the parent account, and then take the following steps:

1. Open the Chart of Accounts list.
2. Press Ctrl-N to create a new account.
3. Select the appropriate account type.
4. Enter an account number
5. Name the account
6. Click the Subaccount check box to place a check mark in it.
7. In the drop-down box next to the check box, select the parent account.
8. Click OK.

The new subaccount appears indented below its parent account in the Chart of Accounts window.

Creating Subaccounts by Dragging Account Listings

You can omit the extra steps of selecting the Subaccount check box and selecting the parent account. Create all the accounts you need, as if they were all parent accounts. However, be sure you assign account numbers with subaccounts in mind.

After you create all your accounts, open the Chart of Accounts window (if it isn't still open), and position your mouse pointer on the diamond symbol to the left of the account you want to turn into a subaccount. Your pointer turns into a four-way arrow.

Drag the diamond symbol to the right to indent it. QuickBooks automatically configures the account as a subaccount of the unindented listing immediately above this account. If you open the account's dialog, you'll see that the Subaccount Of option has a check mark, and the parent account referenced is the account name of the unindented listing above the subaccount. Repeat the action for the remaining listings under the parent account.

After you've created a subaccount, if you drag an account listing below that subaccount further to the right, creating another level of indentation, QuickBooks makes that account a subaccount of the subaccount above it.

Using Subaccounts for Easier Tax Preparation

One clever way to design your parent accounts and subaccounts is to design your chart of accounts around your tax return. This saves your accountant time, and that means you save money.

For example, the tax return you use may have a line into which you enter the total for office expenses. However, for the purpose of analyzing where you spend your money, you prefer to separate office expenses into multiple accounts, such as Computer Ribbons & Toner, Paper & Other Consumables, and so on. Office Supplies becomes the parent account, and any specific subcategories you care about become the subaccounts.

In fact, to save even more money on accounting services, arrange the order of your income and expense accounts and subaccounts in the order in which they appear on your tax return.

You can obtain a copy of a blank tax return at www.irs.gov. Enter the name of your tax form in the search box labeled Search Forms And Publications. Then, from the list of search results, select the form you need. Most of the forms are PDF files, and require Acrobat reader (available free at www.adobe.com).

Go through the return to see the order in which income, expenses, and other totals are required. If you see references to other forms, such as a direction to insert the total from Line 21 of Form XXXX, download those forms, too.

Manipulating Accounts

You can edit, delete, hide, and merge accounts, and you'll probably perform some or all of these actions as you tweak your chart of accounts into a state of perfection. Tinkering with the chart of accounts is an ongoing process, because you'll find things you want to change as you use transaction windows and create reports.

Editing Accounts

If you need to make changes to an account, open the chart of accounts window, click the account's listing to select it, and press Ctrl-E. The Edit Account dialog appears, which looks very much like the account dialog you filled out when you created the account.

Adding and Changing Account Numbers

One of the most common reasons to edit an account is to add or change account numbers for existing accounts. After you enable the account number feature, QuickBooks automatically attaches numbers to any existing accounts that came from a predefined chart of accounts, but fails to attach numbers to any accounts you created manually. Therefore, you must add the missing numbers. In addition, if you don't like the numbering scheme that QuickBooks used, you can change the account numbers.

If you want to make wholesale changes in the numbering system QuickBooks used, it's easier to export the chart of accounts to Excel, make your changes with the help of the automated tools in Excel, and then import the changed chart of accounts into your company file. This works as long as you make no changes to anything except the account numbers, because QuickBooks will use the account name to accept the accounts properly (they won't appear to be duplicates).

The automated tools in Excel include the ability to search and replace text, and the ability to drag your mouse down a column and automatically increment the numbers in the column. For example, suppose QuickBooks automatically numbered your expense accounts starting with 6000, and incremented each account by ten, so that the second expense account number is 6010, the next is 6020, and so on.

You may prefer to use numbers that start in the 5000 range for some (or all) of the expense accounts. If a range of expense accounts starts with 6110 (6110, 6120, etc.), and you want those accounts in the 5000 range, just replace 61 with 50 (or 51, or whatever). You could also change the first two numbers, select those two cells, and then drag your mouse down the column as far as appropriate. Excel changes the numbers in each cell to match the interval pattern you created in the first two cells.

Be sure to back up your company file before trying this, in case something goes awry. To learn how to export/import the chart of accounts, see Appendix A (importing Excel files) and Appendix B (importing IIF files).

Editing Optional Account Fields

You can edit any field in the account, including (with some exceptions) the account type. For example, you may want to add, remove, or change a description. For bank accounts, you might decide to put the bank account number in the dialog, or select the option to have QuickBooks to remind you to order checks when you've used a specific check number. If you want to change the account type, the following restrictions apply:

- You cannot change A/R or A/P accounts to other account types
- You cannot change other account types to be A/R or A/P accounts
- You cannot change the account type of accounts that QuickBooks creates automatically (such as Undeposited Funds).

- You cannot change the account type of an account that has subaccounts. You must make the subaccounts parent accounts (it's easiest to drag them to the left), change the account type of each account, and then create the subaccounts again (drag them to the right).

Editing the Tax Line Field

If you're going to do your own taxes, every account in your chart of accounts that is tax-related must have the right tax form information in the account's tax line assignment. The Tax Line field doesn't exist unless you specified an income tax form when you set up your company file. You can rectify the omission by choosing Company → Company Information, and selecting the right form from the drop-down list in the Income Tax Form Used field.

To see if any tax line assignments are missing, choose Reports → Accountant & Taxes → Income Tax Preparation. When the report appears, all your accounts are listed, and each account either has its assigned tax form or the notation "Unassigned".

QuickBooks assigns the tax line for tax-related accounts that exist in a predefined chart of accounts. However, the accounts you manually add don't automatically have a tax line assigned, so you must perform that step yourself. If you created your own chart of accounts from scratch, or added a great many accounts to a predefined chart of accounts, the number of accounts that you neglected to assign to a tax form is likely to be quite large.

If you don't know which form and category to assign to an account, here's an easy trick for getting that information:

1. Choose File → New Company and choose the option to create a new company yourself (click Skip Interview on the first page of the EasyStep Interview wizard).
2. Fill out the Company Informatin dialog, using a fake company name. You can skip the general information such as the company address, phone number, tax identification number, and so on.
3. Select the income tax form you use for tax returns.

4. Choose a company type that's the same as the one you chose for your company file.

5. When prompted, save the new company file.

When the new company file opens, open the chart of accounts and press Ctrl-P to print the list. The printed list has the tax form information you need. Open your real company, open the chart of accounts, and use the information on the printed document to edit accounts so they contain tax form information.

Deleting Accounts

To delete an account, select its listing in the Chart of Accounts window, and press Ctrl-D. QuickBooks displays a confirmation message, asking if you're sure you want to delete the account. Click OK to delete the account (or click Cancel if you've changed your mind).

Some accounts cannot be deleted, and after you click OK, QuickBooks displays an error message telling you why you cannot complete the action. Any of the following conditions prevent you from deleting an account:

- The account is linked to an item
- The account has been used in a transaction
- The account has subaccounts

If the problem is a link to an item, find the item that uses this account for posting transactions, and change the posting account. Check all items, because it may be that multiple items are linked to the account. (When you open the Items list, you can view the posting accounts in the Account column.)

If the problem is that the account has been used in a transaction, you won't be able to delete the account. QuickBooks means this literally, and the fact that the account has a zero balance doesn't make it eligible for deletion. I know users who have painstakingly created journal entries to move every transaction out of an account they want to delete, posting the amounts to other accounts. It doesn't work.

If the problem is subaccounts, you must first delete all the subaccounts. If any of the subaccounts fall into the restrictions list (usually they have transactions posted), you can make them parent accounts in order to delete the original parent account.

An account that was created automatically by QuickBooks can be deleted (as long as it doesn't fall under the restrictions), but a warning message appears to tell you that if you perform actions in QuickBooks to warrant the use of the account, the system will automatically create the account again. For example, if QuickBooks created an account for Purchase Orders, you can delete it if you haven't yet created a Purchase Order. When you create your first Purchase Order, QuickBooks automatically recreates the account.

If you're trying to delete an account because you don't want anyone to post to it, but QuickBooks won't delete the account, you can hide the account by making it inactive. See the next section "Hiding Accounts".

If you're trying to delete an account because transactions were posted to it erroneously, you can merge the account with the account that should have received the postings. See the section "Merging Accounts".

Hiding Accounts

If you don't want anyone to post to an account but you don't want to delete the account (or QuickBooks won't let you delete the account), you can make the account inactive. In the Chart of Accounts window, right-click the account's listing and choose Make Inactive from the shortcut menu.

Inactive accounts don't appear in the account drop-down list when you're filling out a transaction window, and therefore can't be selected for posting. By default, they also don't appear in the Chart of Accounts window, which can be confusing. For example, you may have money market bank accounts that you don't want anyone to use during transaction postings. However, if you don't see the account in the Chart of Accounts List window, you won't know its current balance. In fact, you might forget it exists.

To view all your accounts in the Chart of Accounts window, including inactive accounts, select the option Include Inactive at the bottom of the window. A new column appears on the left side of the window, with a column heading that's a large black X. Inactive accounts display a large black X in this column. To make an inactive account active, click the black X (it's a toggle).

TIP: *If the Include Inactive option is grayed out, there are no inactive accounts.*

Using a Hidden Account in Transactions

Sometimes, in an office with multiple QuickBooks users, the bookkeeper or owner wants to prevent other users from posting transactions to a certain account. For example, it's not unusual for equity accounts (such as Draw) to be misused, and it's rather common to see inappropriate postings to Miscellaneous Expenses. It's better if only people with some expertise post transactions to these account types.

You can hide an account (make it inactive), and still use it. When you're entering data in a transaction window, don't use the drop-down list in the Account field (because of course, the account won't appear). Instead, enter the account name or number manually.

QuickBooks displays a message asking if you want to use the account just once, or reactivate the account. Click the option to use the account just once. (You can use the account "just once" as many times as you want to.)

Merging Accounts

Sometimes you have two accounts that should be one. For instance, you may be splitting postings inappropriately, and your accountant suggests that one account would be better. Perhaps there's no reason to post some revenue for consulting work to an account named Income-Consulting, and other revenue to an account named Income-Fees.

Often, you may find that accidentally, two accounts were created for the same category. As I discussed earlier in this chapter, I've been to client sites that had accounts named Telephone and Tele, with transactions posted to both accounts. Those accounts badly need merging. Accounts must meet the following criteria in order to merge them:

- The accounts must be of the same type
- The accounts must be at the same level (parent or subaccount)

If the accounts aren't at the same level, move one of the accounts to the same level as the other account. After you merge the accounts, you can move the surviving account to a different level.

Take the following steps to merge two accounts:

1. Open the Chart of Accounts window.
2. Select (highlight) the account that has the name you *do not* want to use anymore.
3. Press Ctrl-E to open the Edit Account dialog.
4. Change the account name and number to match the account you want to keep.
5. Click OK.

QuickBooks displays a message telling you that the account number/name you've entered already exists for another account, and asking if you want to merge the accounts. Click Yes to confirm that you want to merge the two accounts. All the transactions from both accounts are merged into the account you chose to keep.

If you're doing some serious housekeeping on your company file, and you find three (or perhaps more) accounts that should be merged into a single account, merge the first two, then merge the surviving account with the third account.

Importing the Chart of Accounts

Importing a chart of accounts is an efficient way to get exactly the chart of accounts you need without going through all the work of entering accounts one at a time. Of course, to import a chart of accounts, you have to have an import file. You can import data into QuickBooks from either of these source file types:

- An Excel worksheet with a file extension .xls or .csv.
- A tab-delimited text file, with a file extension .iif.

If you're an accountant, creating import files that you can take to clients provides a valuable service for your clients, and also makes your own work easier—the chart of accounts is configured properly for your tax, planning, and analysis services. Many accountants create import file templates to create a customized chart of accounts for each QuickBooks client.

The steps required to import an Excel file are in Appendix A, and the steps required to import an IIF file are in Appendix B. Because you can import a variety of QuickBooks lists, I thought it was more efficient to put the import instructions in one place, instead of repeating the rather lengthy, complicated, steps in every chapter of this book that discusses imported files.

In the following sections, I'll discuss the steps you need to take to prepare a file so it can be imported for the chart of accounts.

TIP: When properly prepared an import file for the chart of accounts can be used for earlier (or later) versions of QuickBooks.

Exporting Information from Other Software

You can create an import file from scratch, but if you're already storing the chart of accounts in another software application, you can export the data. You can create an import file from a database report, a spreadsheet document, or from another accounting software application. If the export feature of your database or software offers a variety of file types, you can select any of the following:

- Excel file
- CSV file (a delimited text file with comma-separated values)

- Delimited text file (can use any character for separating values, but usually the tab character is the default separator)

Delimited text is plain, readable, text that is separated into categories with a delimiter. The delimiter is a character that indicates the end of the characters for a category, so that the text following the delimiter is recognized as being in the next category. The delimiter character, which is known to the software application that is using the file, is not part of the text. CSV files use a comma as the delimiter; other delimited files either ask you to select a delimiter, or automatically default to a Tab character.

In QuickBooks, as in all databases, a category is a field or a record. One delimiter indicates the end of a field, and a different delimiter indicates the end of a record. A record is a set of information about an entity. For example, if you have an address book, a particular person's information is a record. A field is an element within a record, so an address book usually has fields named LastName, FirstName, Street, City, State, Zip, Telephone, etc.

If your exported file is an Excel file, you can open it by double-clicking its listing in Windows Explorer or My Computer. If Excel is open, you can use the File → Open command, or click the Open icon on the toolbar, and select the file.

If your exported file is a delimited text file, you can open it in Excel using either method. However, if you open the file from within Excel you face a few extra steps—you must walk through the process of confirming the delimiter

Use the following steps to open the file from Windows Explorer or My Computer:

1. Navigate to the folder that holds your exported file.
2. Right-click the file's listing and choose Open With from the shortcut menu, and then choose Microsoft Excel from the Open With dialog that appears.
3. Excel opens with your export file in the software window.

To open the file from within Excel, take the following steps:

1. Click the Open icon on the Excel toolbar, or choose File → Open from the menu bar.
2. In the Open dialog, click the arrow to the right of the Files Of Type field at the bottom of the dialog, and select All Files (*.*).
3. Navigate to the folder that holds your exported file.
4. Double-click the listing for your exported file. Excel recognizes the fact that the file is a delimited text file, and launches the Text Import Wizard.
5. Click Next to view the way the wizard interprets the delimiter as it attempts to place each field in a column, and each record in a row.
6. Click Next to see the columns the wizard is importing, and the format for each column. Leave the data type format as General. You can remove any columns you don't need.
7. Click Finish to open the file in the Excel window.

After you've loaded the file, save it as an Excel file (with the .xls extension). Once your chart of accounts data exists as an Excel file, you're almost ready to import it directly from Excel into QuickBooks. Your last step is to prepare the file so QuickBooks can handle it properly.

Using an Existing QuickBooks Account List

The best way to create an import file for a chart of accounts is to export a chart of accounts from an existing QuickBooks company file. Then, open the file in a spreadsheet application to see the contents (for this discussion, I'm assuming you use Excel). The contents and the format of the spreadsheet document are a template, because they contain the appropriate elements of an import file.

It doesn't matter which company you use to export the chart of accounts, and you could even use one of the sample companies that QuickBooks includes. The idea is to get a basic chart of accounts, manipulate it, and save it as an import file. To export the chart of accounts from a QuickBooks company file, use the following steps:

1. Open the company you want to use for your template chart of accounts.
2. Choose File → Utilities → Export → Lists To IIF Files, to open the Export dialog.

3. Click the check box next to the listing for Chart of Accounts to insert a check mark.
4. Click OK to open the Export dialog for saving a file.
5. Select a location, and enter a filename for the export file. QuickBooks automatically adds the extension .iif to the filename.
6. Click Save.

Manipulating the Exported QuickBooks Data

When the exported file is loaded in Excel (or any other spreadsheet application), it may seem complicated and mysterious. As you can see in Figure 2-3, QuickBooks exports a lot of information that doesn't resemble the data you see when you create or edit an account.

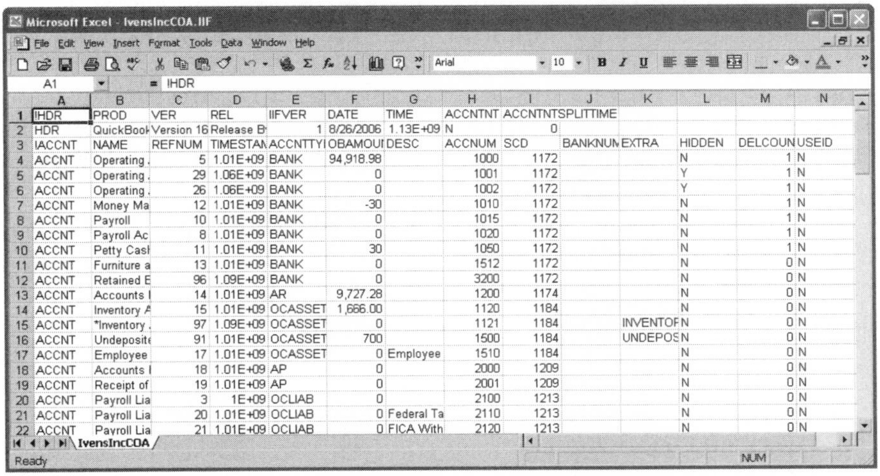

Figure 2-3: QuickBooks exports data you don't need for an import file.

The first cell in the third row (A3) contains the text !ACCNT. This is a list keyword, and it indicates that the contents of the file from this point down, until the next keyword, are part of a chart of accounts list. In this case, because you exported only the chart of accounts, no other keywords are found in this file. However, if you export multiple lists, each list starts with a row that contains its own list keyword.

All the cells in the first column, below the list keyword, have the word ACCNT (without the exclamation point), indicating that the data in each row is part of a chart of accounts list. ACCNT is a record keyword.

Starting with the second column, all the text in the row that contains the list keyword (!ACCNT) are headings that represent field names.

All of the rows beneath the row of field names are account records—each row represents an account in the chart of accounts.

Deleting Extraneous Data

The first two rows of the QuickBooks export file don't belong in an import file for the chart of accounts. Delete them by right-clicking the row numbers in the leftmost column, and choosing Delete from the shortcut menu. The remaining rows move up, and what had been Row 3 is now Row 1.

Many of the columns contain extraneous data, and those columns don't belong in an import file. To delete columns in Excel, right-click the column's letter in the top row, and select Delete from the shortcut menu.

Delete the following columns (I'll identify them by the heading text that was in Row 3, but is now in Row 1 if you've deleted the first two rows). These columns all contain internal references to the company file from which the chart of accounts was exported.

- REFNUM
- TIMESTAMP
- DELCOUNT
- USEID

In addition, you can delete the following columns, which contain information specific to the company from which you exported the chart of accounts:

- SCD (the tax form for the account)
- OBAMOUNT (the opening balance)
- BANKNUM (the bank number for bank accounts)

If you want to use these columns, you must replace the data with data that's specific to the company file that will receive the import.

Creating an Excel Import File

If you want to import the chart of accounts directly from an Excel file, save your file with the extension .xls or .csv. The data in your file must follow a set of conventions and rules in order to be recognized as an import file by QuickBooks. In this section, I'll go over the rules. (Appendix A contains the instructions for performing the import.)

Don't Mix Lists in a Worksheet

The list of accounts must be the only data in the worksheet (or in a spreadsheet). Other lists you want to import, such as customers, must be in their own, discrete, worksheets or spreadsheets. (You can find information about creating import files for other lists in the appropriate chapters of this book.)

Header Row Keywords

The top row must contain headers that categorize the data in each column. You can enter the header text that QuickBooks requires (keywords), or leave the header text from the export file you created, and map that text to the QuickBooks keywords during the import procedure.

Mapping the Header Row Keywords

A QuickBooks mapping is a set of data that links the text in the heading row of your import file to category names that match the fields of the list being imported. For example, if you're importing an Excel or CSV file that has a column named AccntName (because that's what your previous application used for account names), you must map that text to the QuickBooks text "Name".

If your Excel file doesn't have a header row, insert a blank row at the top of the worksheet, and enter the QuickBooks column heading keywords. Alternatively, you can skip the heading row and specify the column letters when you perform the import. For example, if the data in Column B is account names, you can map Column B to the Name keyword when you import the file. The steps for performing these import tasks are in Appendix A.

Following are QuickBooks keywords for the column headings of commonly imported data (other keywords exist, such as those required for special types of accounts, but I'm covering only the common and necessary keywords). You can enter these keywords at the top of each column, matching the keyword to the appropriate column of data. If your export file created header rows with different text for the column headings, you don't have to change that text; instead, you can map your text to the QuickBooks keywords when you import the file (covered in Appendix A). For example, QuickBooks uses the keyword "Name" for the account name, but your export file from another software application may use the keyword "Acctname".

NAME

(Required field) The name of the account. If you want to create subaccounts, after you create the account name for the parent account, use the following format for subaccounts:

ParentAccountName:SubaccountName (the colon tells QuickBooks this is a subaccount).

TYPE

(Required field) The type of account. The data in this column must match the QuickBooks keywords for account types (see Table 2-1). For example, if your data text is AR (for Accounts Receivable), you must replace that text with the text "Accounts Receivable"

DESCRIPTION

(Optional field) The description of the account. You can use up to twenty-nine characters (including spaces).

NUMBER

(Optional field) The account number, needed if you're using numbered accounts.

IS INACTIVE

(Optional field) This field specifies whether the account is hidden (inactive) by default. The data is N or Y (for No or Yes). If you omit this column, QuickBooks assumes all accounts are active, and not hidden.

Bank
Accounts Receivable
Other Current Asset
Fixed Asset
Accounts Payable
Credit Card
Other Current Liability
Long Term Liability
Equity
Income
Cost of Goods Sold
Expense
Other Income
Other Expense

Table 2-1: QuickBooks required keywords for account types.

BANK ACCT. NO/CARD NO./NOTE

The account number of the account. This is used for bank, credit card, and other current liability (loan) accounts.

OPENING BALANCE

The opening balance of the account. It's not a good idea to use this field. See the section on creating opening balances later in this chapter.

AS OF (DATE)

The date of the opening balance (which you aren't going to import, right?).

REMIND ME TO ORDER CHECKS

The check number you want to use to trigger a reminder to order checks. If you're creating a generic, boilerplate, import file, don't use this field.

TRACK REIMBURSED EXPENSES

For expense accounts. The data is Yes or No to indicate whether the expense account is tracked for collecting reimbursed expenses. You must create a discrete income account for each expense account that you track for reimbursed expenses.

INCOME ACCOUNT FOR REIMB. EXPENSES

The name of the income account that you use to track the reimbursed expense for this expense account. Be sure these accounts are included in your import file.

Figure 2-4 represents an Excel file that's ready to be imported. Notice that not all the available fields are used. Read the instructions in Appendix A to import your file.

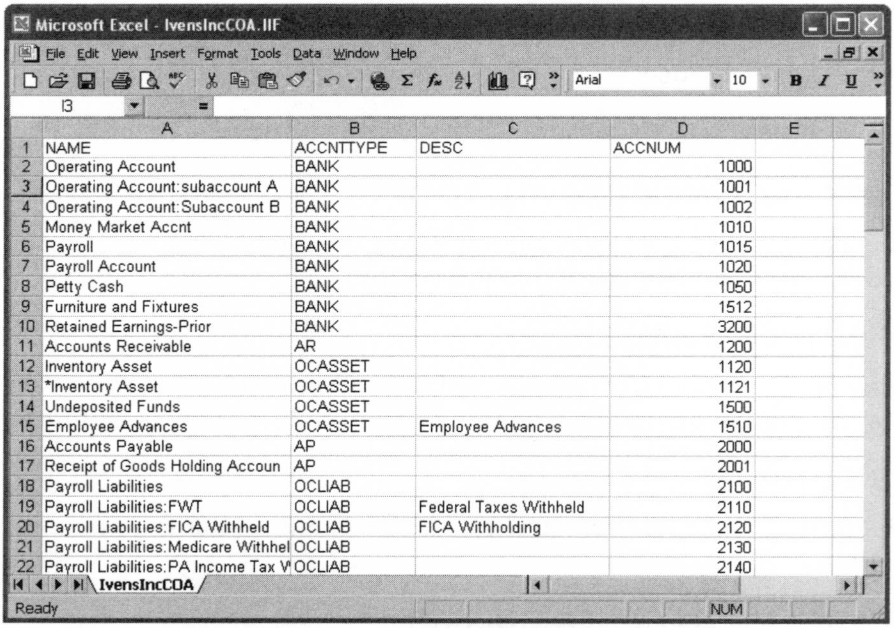

	A	B	C	D	E
1	NAME	ACCNTTYPE	DESC	ACCNUM	
2	Operating Account	BANK		1000	
3	Operating Account:subaccount A	BANK		1001	
4	Operating Account:Subaccount B	BANK		1002	
5	Money Market Accnt	BANK		1010	
6	Payroll	BANK		1015	
7	Payroll Account	BANK		1020	
8	Petty Cash	BANK		1050	
9	Furniture and Fixtures	BANK		1512	
10	Retained Earnings-Prior	BANK		3200	
11	Accounts Receivable	AR		1200	
12	Inventory Asset	OCASSET		1120	
13	*Inventory Asset	OCASSET		1121	
14	Undeposited Funds	OCASSET		1500	
15	Employee Advances	OCASSET	Employee Advances	1510	
16	Accounts Payable	AP		2000	
17	Receipt of Goods Holding Accoun	AP		2001	
18	Payroll Liabilities	OCLIAB		2100	
19	Payroll Liabilities:FWT	OCLIAB	Federal Taxes Withheld	2110	
20	Payroll Liabilities:FICA Withheld	OCLIAB	FICA Withholding	2120	
21	Payroll Liabilities:Medicare Withhel	OCLIAB		2130	
22	Payroll Liabilities:PA Income Tax W	OCLIAB		2140	

Figure 2-4: This Excel worksheet is ready to be imported into QuickBooks (as described in Appendix A).

Creating an IIF Import File

If you don't have Excel, you can use another application to store your chart of accounts data. The data file must be delimited, categorizing the data as described in the preceding sections. Use the QuickBooks keywords on the header row and the first column as described in the following sections.

Even if you do use Excel, there are several advantages to an .IIF import file. The file is smaller than a spreadsheet document, and is therefore easier to e-mail, or copy to a floppy disk. In fact, you can store multiple .IIF files on a single floppy disk. This is useful if you're an accountant and want to take boilerplate chart of account files to client sites, using different import files for different types of clients. For example, you can create boilerplate charts of accounts for corporations, proprietorships, partnerships, product-based businesses, service-based businesses, and so on. Additionally, importing an IIF file is much easier than importing an Excel/CSV file.

Column A Keywords

The first column must contain QuickBooks keywords that represent the type of list being imported. Insert a blank column as Column A and enter the keywords.

- Cell A1 holds the keyword that describes the file's contents. For a chart of accounts import file, that keyword is !ACCNT (must have an exclamation point as the first character).
- The rest of column A contains the keyword for each row of data, indicating the type of QuickBooks list. For a chart of accounts import file, that keyword is ACCNT.

Column Heading Keywords

Each field in a QuickBooks account record is a column in your document. Starting with Column B, each column heading must be a keyword representing a QuickBooks field. The order in which the columns appear doesn't matter, because QuickBooks imports the data into the appropriate field, using the column heading keyword. The following sections describe the column heading keywords and the type of data in each column.

NAME

Name is a required field, which means that you must have data in this column for every account. The data, of course, is the account name. You can use up to thirty-one characters (including spaces).

ACCNTTYPE

The account type is a required field, and the column must contain data for each account. The text you use for the data must match QuickBooks keywords. Table 2-2 contains the keyword for each QuickBooks account type.

Type of Account	Keyword
Bank	BANK
Accounts Receivable	AR
Other Current Asset	OCASSET
Fixed Asset	FIXASSET
Other Asset	OASSET
Accounts Payable	AP
Credit Card	CCARD
Other Current Liability	OCLIAB
Long-Term Liability	LTLIAB
Equity	EQUITY
Income	INC
Cost of Goods Sold	COGS
Expense	EXP
Other Income	EXINC
Other Expense	EXEXP
Non-Posting	NONPOSTING

Table 2-2: Keywords for QuickBooks account types in IIF files.

DESC

This optional field is for the account description. You can use up to twenty-nine characters (including spaces).

ACCNUM

This field is for the account number, and is only required if want to use numbers for the chart of accounts. For data in this column, enter the account number for each account.

You can design a scheme for account numbers that matches the way you want to work with the chart of accounts. Account numbers can have up to seven digits in the account number, and only numbers are permitted. Unlike some other accounting software, QuickBooks does not support a divisionalized chart of accounts, so you cannot use dashes to separate an account into divisions.

If you use account numbers, it's terribly important to base your numbering scheme on the QuickBooks sort order for accounts (covered earlier in this chapter). If you don't, the account list will appear to be sorted out of order (if you think of numbers as the sorting standard).

Remember that you have to start a numbering system for each account type. For example, assume you're using the following design for asset account types (the list is in the proper sort order):

- 1000-1099 Bank Accounts
- 1100-1199 Accounts Receivable
- 1200-1299 Other Current Assets
- 1300-1399 Fixed Assets
- 1400-1499 Other Assets

You could, of course, assign a larger span of numbers to any asset account type, or use fewer or more than four digits for your numbering scheme.

If the chart of accounts you're working on has only one or two accounts for each account type, you can enter the numbers manually. However, if any account type has more than three or four accounts, it's easier to create account numbers using Excel's automatic numbering feature (technically called the *Autofill* feature). For example, use the following actions to number bank accounts with intervals of ten:

1. Enter the first account number in the ACCNUM column, in the row occupied by the first bank account.

2. Enter the next account number (incremented by ten, if that's the increment you prefer) in the next row.

3. Position your cursor in the cell in which you entered the first account number and drag down to select both that cell and the cell below it (which has the second account number you entered). This "teaches" Excel the interval.

4. Position your cursor in the lower right corner of the bottom cell so the cursor appears as intersected vertical and horizontal lines.

5. Drag down to automatically fill in account numbers in the remaining bank accounts.

Perform the same actions on each account type, and remember to restart the numbering for each account type to match your numbering scheme.

EXTRA

This optional field specifies a balance sheet account that's automatically added by QuickBooks if it is needed. If you create a column for this field, the data specifies the account(s) using the following keywords:

- OPENBAL for Opening Balance Equity
- RETEARNINGS for Retained Earnings
- SALESTAX for Sales Tax Payable
- UNDEPOSIT for Undeposited Funds

HIDDEN

This optional field specifies whether the account is hidden (made inactive) by default. The data is N or Y (for No or Yes). If you omit this column, or omit any data in the column, QuickBooks assumes the accounts are active and not hidden.

SCD

This optional field holds the data for the tax form information for each account. The data is a code, which is derived from data in the file named bustax.scd (installed in the QuickBooks software folder).

You only need this information if you're planning to do your own taxes in TurboTax. To fill in the data, you can use the technique for obtaining the tax form information described earlier in this chapter.

OBAMOUNT

This optional field is available for inserting an opening balance for those accounts that can manage opening balances. However, this approach forces an offset balancing entry in an equity account. Don't use this field, it's not a good idea to import accounts with opening balances. See the section "Entering Opening Balances" later in this chapter.

Saving the IIF Import File

You turn your worksheet into an import file for QuickBooks when you save it. Use the following steps in Excel (or another spreadsheet application) to save the file properly:

1. Choose File → Save As to open the Save As dialog.
2. Navigate to the folder in which you want to save the file.
3. In the Save As Type field at the bottom of the dialog, select Text (Tab Delimited).
4. In the File Name field, enter a name for the file and replace the .txt extension with iif.
5. Click Save.

TIP: If your spreadsheet application won't let you change the .txt extension to .iif, save the file with the .txt extension, and then rename the file in My Computer or Windows Explorer to <filename>.iif.

Excel displays a message telling you that some features in the file may not be compatible with tab-delimited files. However, since those features involve special formatting for text (e.g. bold or italics) and other "bells and whistles" available in Excel, you don't have to worry about losing them (it doesn't affect the accuracy of the imported data). Click Yes to save the file. If you continue to work in the file, every time you save the file you'll see the same message, so just continue to click Yes.

You can send the file via e-mail, or save the file to a floppy disk and mail it (or deliver it in person and perform the import yourself). To import the file, use one of the following commands:

- In QuickBooks 2006, choose File → Utilities → Import → IIF Files.
- In versions of QuickBooks earlier than 2006, choose File → Import → IIF Files.

(see Appendix B for details).

Entering Opening Balances

If you're creating a new company, you need to enter the opening balances for your balance sheet accounts (called the *opening trial balance*). Then you can add all the transactions that took place since the beginning of the year to create a thorough history of transactions while you're posting the current year's activity to the general ledger. (Although you can enter opening balances during the EasyStep Interview or when you create accounts manually, I always advise clients to skip that step).

QuickBooks does not have an item or feature called the "opening balance," per se. However, every account register is sorted by date, so using the first day of your fiscal year creates an opening balance automatically. Confer with your accountant to develop the opening balance, and then enter it as a journal entry (see Chapter 5 to learn about General Journal Entry features in the Premier Editions).

Workarounds for QuickBooks Limitations

When you work with journal entries, especially when you're trying to enter an opening trial balance, you run into a couple of QuickBooks idiosyncrasies. In this section, I'll explain those quirks, and the workarounds you can apply.

A/R and A/P Entries Can't Exist in the Same JE

In QuickBooks, a journal entry can contain only the A/P account or the A/R account; you cannot use both of those accounts in the same journal entry (and the odds are good that both accounts have balances in your opening balance). You'll get an error message that says, "You cannot use more than one A/R or A/P account in the same transaction" (which is not a clear explanation).

Unfortunately, QuickBooks doesn't issue the error message until after you enter all the data and try to save the journal entry, which is very annoying (I've seen people throw things as a response to all that wasted time). Incidentally, this restriction does not have its roots in accounting standards; it's an arbitrary rule that QuickBooks built into its software.

A/R and A/P Entries are Limited to One Entity

Another problem with opening balances for A/R and A/P is that QuickBooks insists you attach a single customer or vendor name to the entry if you're making a journal entry that involves either the A/R or the A/P account. You can't just enter an A/R or A/P balance against your previous equity (or against income or expenses, for that matter). If you're keeping customer info outside of QuickBooks (perhaps you have a retail business and keep customer charges elsewhere), you're out of luck.

If you decide that's OK, and you're willing to enter customer opening balances in your JE, you have another problem: You can't enter A/R for more than one customer. Before you say "Okay, I'll just enter a separate A/R line for each customer in the journal entry", get this—QuickBooks won't permit more than one A/R line in the journal entry (the same restrictions apply to A/P).

You see, QuickBooks' approach is to enter the opening balance when you create a customer or vendor. Both the New Customer and New Vendor windows have a field for this purpose. Those totals are posted to A/R and A/P as of the date you enter, which should be the first day of the fiscal year if you're trying to create an opening trial balance.

Neither of these data entry methods—A/R lines or opening balances during customer setup—is a good idea. The entry is only a total, and you cannot enter discrete invoices or bills, saddling you with several annoying drawbacks, such as:

- You can't easily deal with disputes over specific invoices or bills (you'll have to find the original paperwork).
- Customer payments have to be applied as partial payments against the total you entered. This makes it more difficult to have conversations with customers about their accounts.

- You don't have the opportunity to enter memos on invoices or bills.
- It makes it difficult to track those amounts that are for reimbursed expenses.

The solution is to enter your opening trial balance without the A/R and A/P entries. Adjust the equity account if your accountant preconfigured the opening trial balance for you. Then, use QuickBooks transaction windows to enter the open invoices for customers and the open bills from vendors, using dates earlier than your opening balance date for the transactions. Let QuickBooks post the totals to the general ledger.

You can create one comprehensive invoice per customer/vendor and pay it off if you don't want to bother with the individual invoices that created the opening balance. The equity account will automatically adjust itself back to your accountant's original totals as you enter the transactions.

Managing Equity Balances

Regardless of the number of equity accounts you create, QuickBooks only posts to two equity accounts: Retained Earnings, and Opening Bal Equity. The following sections discuss workarounds you can adopt to make it easier to manage these accounts.

Retained Earnings

QuickBooks posts profit (or loss) to the Retained Earnings equity account, which is a running total. It's a good idea to create a separate equity account for your previous equity to separate the current equity from the previous equity. At the end of each year, you can create a journal entry to move the current year's equity change into the account you create for previous equity.

In previous versions of QuickBooks, if you tried to open the register, the following message was displayed: "This account is a special automatically created account. It does not have a register." In addition, when you view the chart of accounts, the Retained Earnings account is the only balance sheet account that doesn't display the current balance.

However, you could always post transactions to the Retained Earnings account. If fact, like many other business owners, I performed a journal entry at the end of each year to move the balance in the Retained Earnings account into the Previous Earnings account.

Starting with QuickBooks 2005, you can open the register of the Retained Earnings account. When you double-click the account's listing, an Account Quick Report opens, displaying all postings to the account. You can easily distinguish QuickBooks' automatic postings of profit (or loss) from transaction postings.

Automatic postings have the following characteristics:

- The Type column displays the text Closing Entry.
- The Date column displays the last day of your fiscal year.
- You cannot drill down into the transaction (hovering your mouse over the listing does not change your mouse pointer to a "zoom" (a Z enclosed in a magnifying glass).

Transaction postings have the following characteristics:

- The Type column displays the transaction type (e.g. General Journal, or Invoice).
- You can drill down to see the original transaction. Hover your mouse over the listing, and when your mouse pointer changes to a "zoon", double-click to open the transaction window.

The Accounts category of the Preferences dialog contains the option Warn When Posting To Retained Earnings. Enabling this option means that when anyone tries to post an amount to the Retained Earnings account, QuickBooks displays a warning message. The message explains that the Retained Earnings account is designed to track profits, and the amounts that are posted to the account should be generated automatically, not manually posted through a transaction.

The warning message doesn't prevent the user from continuing with the transaction, and posting to the Retained Earnings account. However, if this is a user who doesn't understand the account (or inadvertently chose the account from a drop-down list), the warning message might prevent the user from going on (which is usually a good thing).

Opening Bal Equity Account

The Opening Bal Equity account you see in the chart of accounts is a QuickBooks invention. It doesn't have any connection to the phrase "opening balance" the way that term is usually applied in accounting.

QuickBooks uses the Opening Bal Equity account as the offset account when users enter opening balances during setup. Those opening balances might have been entered during the EasyStep Interview, or when users entered an opening balance as they manually created accounts, customers, or vendors.

> TIP: In my books, articles, and seminars, I always advise users and accountants to avoid filling in any opening balance fields during setup. Instead, I suggest they create transactions that predate the QuickBooks start date to establish those balances (and post the amounts to the appropriate accounts).

You can (and should) ask your accountant to move the balance in the Opening Bal Equity account to Retained Earnings, or Previous Earnings, or to another appropriate account (not necessarily an equity account).

However, after you clear out the balance in the Opening Bal Equity account, you can't relax. Any of the following actions will put funds back into the account:

- Entering an opening balance when creating a new account.
- Entering an opening balance when creating a new customer.
- Entering an opening balance when creating a new vendor.
- Entering an opening balance when creating a new inventory item.
- Telling QuickBooks to make an adjustment when bank reconciliation doesn't work.

Read the section on managing the Opening Bal Equity account in Chapter 11 to learn more about this account, its annoyances and dangers, and how to resolve the problems it can cause.

Chapter 3

Customizing QuickBooks

Enabling and disabling features

Configuring default settings

Setting up sales tax

Customizing templates

QuickBooks doesn't automatically enable every feature that exists in the software, because many companies don't need the entire range of available functions. For example, some QuickBooks users are running service businesses, so they don't need inventory functions. Businesses that aren't required to collect and remit sales tax don't want to be bothered with sale tax fields on the transaction windows.

In addition to enabling or disabling features, some preferences let you set a default pattern for tasks, saving you from the boredom of repetitious selections when you're working in transaction windows.

The Preferences dialog contains all the options you need to set up your company file for accuracy, convenience, and ease-of-use.

NOTE: *If you chose an industry and business that included a predefined company file, many of the preferences required for your type of business are automatically enabled, but you still must configure default settings for some functions. See Chapter 1 to learn about the predefined company files.*

The settings you configure impact the way you enter data, as well as the way data is kept and reported. It's not uncommon for QuickBooks users to change these preferences periodically. In fact, the more you use QuickBooks, the more you'll find yourself opening the Preferences dialog to see if you can adapt a setting to make your work faster and easier.

Understanding the Preferences Dialog

Choose Edit → Preferences from the menu bar to open the Preferences dialog. The categories are listed in the left pane of the dialog, and each category has two tabs: My Preferences and Company Preferences.

My Preferences Tabs

The My Preferences tabs offer options that are user preferences, and are applied on a user-by-user basis as each user logs in to QuickBooks (if you set up logins for multiple users). Each user can set his or her preferences without affecting any other user's preferences.

Unfortunately, if you use QuickBooks for multiple company files, the My Preferences settings aren't globally applied. You have to reset these options for each company file. This tab should probably be named *My Preferences For Working In This Company File*.

Company Preferences Tabs

The Company Preferences tabs offer options for the currently opened company, and QuickBooks remembers the preferences you set for each company. If you run multiple companies in QuickBooks, it's an advantage to have a "company only" array of settings, because you may not need the same features in every company. For example, you may have inventory tracking enabled for one company file, and not for another.

If you're using logins to access your QuickBooks company files, only the administrator, or a user with administrator permissions, can set the options in the Company Preferences tabs.

NOTE: *The majority of categories in the Preferences dialog have options for the Company Preferences tab only.*

In this chapter, I'm not going to cover all of the preferences; instead, I'll concentrate on those that seem to be missed, or misunderstood, by users (according to the e-mail queries I receive, and the questions I'm asked at seminars). *QuickBooks 2006: The Official Guide* (a copy of which is in your Premier Edition software package) discusses all the preferences categories.

General Preferences

The General Preferences category has several options that control the general behavior of QuickBooks, and let you set some of those behavior patterns to suit your needs.

My Preferences for the General Category

The options in the My Preferences tab of the General category (see Figure 3-1) are designed to let you control the way QuickBooks behaves while you're working in transaction windows. Because the options you select here have no effect on any other user who runs QuickBooks, you're free to tweak the settings to your own advantage.

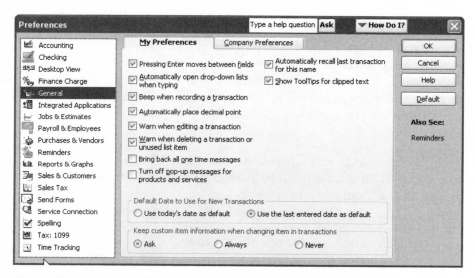

Figure 3-1: Configure QuickBooks to respond to your actions according to your personal preferences.

Pressing Enter Moves Between Fields

This option exists for people who always forget that the Tab key is the default (usual) key for moving from field to field in any Windows software application. When these people press Enter instead of Tab, the record they're working on is saved, even though they haven't finished filling out all the fields.

If you fall in this category, QuickBooks gives you a break from the need to force yourself to get used to the way Windows works. If you select this option, when you press the Enter key, your cursor moves to the next field in the current window. To save a record, click the appropriate button (usually labeled Save or OK).

Beep When Recording A Transaction

For some transactions types, QuickBooks provides sound effects to announce the fact that you've saved the transaction. Besides a beep, you might hear the chime of a bell (well, it's more like a "ding"), or a ka-ching (the sound of an old fashioned cash register). If you don't want to hear sound effects as you work in QuickBooks, you can deselect the option.

Automatically Place Decimal Point

This is a handy feature, and I couldn't live without it (my desktop calculator is configured for the same behavior). It means that when you enter characters in a currency field, a decimal point is automatically placed to the left of the last two digits. Therefore, if you type 5421, when you move to the next field the number changes to 54.21. If you want to type in even dollar amounts, type a period after you enter 54, and QuickBooks automatically adds the decimal point and two zeros (or you can enter the zeros, as in 5400, which automatically becomes 54.00).

Warn When Editing A Transaction

This option, which is selected by default, tells QuickBooks to flash a warning message when you change any existing transaction and try to close the transaction window without explicitly saving the changes. This means you have a chance to abandon the edits. If you deselect the option, the edited transaction is saved automatically, unless it is linked to, and affects, other transactions (in which case, the warning message appears).

It's not a good idea to disable this option, because there are times when you make changes to a transaction, and you don't want to save the changes. The most common occurrence is when you want to print a packing slip for an invoice. After you save the invoice, you can bring it back into the Create Invoices window and select a packing slip template. That template lacks many of the fields that are important for an invoice, such as the financial information. After you print the packing slip, and close the window, you can click No when QuickBooks asks if you want to save the change you made to the invoice.

Warn When Deleting A Transaction Or Unused List Item

When selected, this option produces a warning when you delete a transaction or an item that has not been used in a transaction—it's a standard message asking you to confirm a delete action. (QuickBooks doesn't permit you to delete an item that has been used in a transaction.)

Bring Back All One-Time Messages

One-time messages are those dialogs that include a Don't Show This Message Again option. If you've selected the Don't Show option, select this check box to see those messages again (although you'll probably once again select the Don't Show option).

Automatically Recall Last Transaction For This Name

This option means that QuickBooks will present the last transaction for any name (for instance, a vendor) with all the fields filled with the data from that last transaction. Most of the time, you merely have to change the amount, and any other information (for instance, text in a memo field), can often be retained for the current transaction.

This feature is useful for transactions that are repeated occasionally, or irregularly. (Repeating transactions that are scheduled regularly are best managed with memorized transactions.). One problem that occurs with this option is that users don't remember to check the text in the memo field, which often contains the invoice number from the vendor. The current transaction is usually linked to a different invoice, so if you enable this option you need to get into the habit of checking all fields to make sure they're appropriately filled out.

Show ToolTips For Clipped Text

This option (enabled by default) means that if there is more text in a field than you can see, hovering your mouse over the field causes the entire block of text to display. Very handy!

Default Date To Use For New Transactions

Use this option to tell QuickBooks whether you want the Date field to show the current date or the date of the last transaction you entered when you open a transaction window.

If you frequently enter transactions for the same date over a period of several days (for example, you start preparing invoices on the 27th of the month, but the invoice date is the last day of the month), select the option to use the last entered date so you can just keep going.

If you need to record a transaction with a different date, just change the date in the transaction window.

Keep Custom Information When Changing Item In Transactions

This option determines what QuickBooks does when you change the description text or enter a different price after you enter an item in a sales transaction form, and then change the item in the item column.

This option is new in QuickBooks 2006, and when I queried QuickBooks personnel about it, they explained it to me as follows:

Let's say you select an item named Widget, and then in the Description field, you type text to describe this widget, changing the default description that displayed when you selected the item. (Or, perhaps this widget item had no default description, so you typed one.)

Then, you realize that you didn't really mean to sell the customer a Widget, you meant a Gadget, and the descriptive text you just typed was meant for the item named Gadget (which you thought you'd selected in the Item column).

You return to the Item column (on the same line), click the arrow to see your item list, and select Gadget. Now, you think you have to type all that descriptive text again, because Gadget has its own descriptive text, and it will automatically replace your work.

This option prevents that typing you did from going to waste. If you select Always, QuickBooks will keep the descriptive text you wrote, even though you changed the Item. This descriptive text is linked to this different item only for this invoice; no changes are made to any item's record.

If you select No, QuickBooks just fills in the description that goes with the new item you selected.

If you select Ask, as soon as you change the item, QuickBooks asks if you want to change only the item and keep your customized description on the invoice. You can answer Yes (or No) and you can also tell QuickBooks to change this Preferences option permanently to match your answer.

The same thing happens if you entered a different price (instead of, or in addition to, the description), and then changed the item.

The people at QuickBooks who provided this explanation told me this chain of event occurs frequently. Okey dokey.

Company Preferences for the General Category

The Company Preferences tab in the General section has the following three configuration options:

- Time Format, which lets you choose the format you want to use when you enter data related to time. Your choices are Decimal (for example, 11.5 hours) or the Minutes, which uses the standard HH:MM format (e.g., 11:30).
- Always Show Years As 4 Digits, which you can select if you prefer to display the year with four digits (01/01/2005 instead of 01/01/05).
- Never Update Name Information When Saving Transactions.

The last option is important. By default, QuickBooks asks if you want to update the original information for a name when you change it during a transaction entry. For example, if you're entering a vendor bill and you change the address, QuickBooks offers to make that change back on the vendor record. If you're entering a customer invoice, you may change the terms, or the sales tax rate, and QuickBooks asks if you want to see the new information the next time you use this customer in a transaction.

If you don't want to be offered this opportunity, select this option to tell QuickBooks you never want to update records.

Accounting Preferences

In the Accounting category, there are options on both the My Preferences tab and the Company Preferences tab. This category is important, because it sets configuration options that have a significant influence on your company file, and on the way you do your work in QuickBooks.

My Preferences for the Accounting Category

The My Preferences tab has only one option, Autofill Memo In General Journal Entry. This Premier-only feature is incredibly useful.

Have you ever opened an account register and seen a journal entry you don't understand? No text appears in the memo field, so you have to double-click the transaction line to open the original transaction window, where (hopefully) one of the lines has an entry in the memo field that will explain the transaction. With any luck, you're not going through this time-consuming and annoying process while your accountant or <gasp> an IRS auditor is sitting next to you.

"Mystery journal entries" are commonplace in account registers because, frankly, it's a lot of trouble to enter a comment in each memo line of a journal entry that includes many accounts.

In QuickBooks Premier Editions, an AutoFill Memo check box appears on the GJE window. If you select the option in this Preferences dialog, that check box is selected by default every time you open a GJE transaction window.

Then, whatever you type in the Memo field on the first line of the JE is automatically entered in the Memo field of every line. Of course, you can change the text in any individual Memo field, but you'll find that most of the time the text on the first line is appropriate for all the lines.

> **NOTE:** *The Premier editions have other advanced options for journal entries, which are covered in Chapter 5.*

Company Preferences for the Accounting Category

The Company Preferences tab, seen in Figure 3-2, has several important options that affect the configuration of your company file, as well as the way you perform basic accounting processes in QuickBooks.

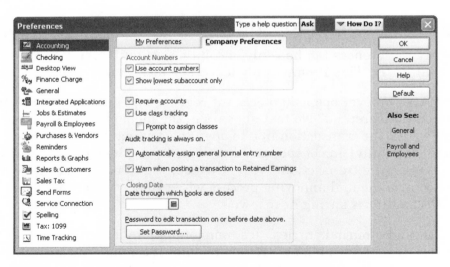

Figure 3-2: Set the basic accounting and posting procedures you prefer.

Specify whether you want to use account numbers in your chart of accounts (your accountant will probably tell you that numbered accounts are always a better idea). When you enable account numbers, a Number field appears in the New Account dialog, and in the Edit Account dialog. Account numbers also appear in the drop-down list in the Account field in transaction windows, and in reports.

If account numbers are enabled, the option Show Lowest Subaccount Only becomes available. Selecting this option means that only the subaccount number and its name are displayed in the drop-down list for the Account field of a transaction window. That makes it easier to select accounts when you're creating transactions, because you don't have to scroll through the account name to get to the subaccount name.

You can specify whether an account is required for every transaction, which means users won't be able to save a transaction unless an account has been assigned to each transaction (or each line of a transaction). This option is enabled by default, and it's foolish to disable it. If you choose to disable it, QuickBooks permits users to save transactions without assigning an account, which is a ridiculous way to run accounting software (and I know of no other accounting software that permits unposted transactions).

If you disable this option, and a user enters a transaction without specifying an account, QuickBooks automatically assigns transaction amounts to the Uncategorized Income or Uncategorized Expense account. Having balances in those uncategorized accounts is not very useful when you're trying to prepare taxes, or analyze your business.

You can enable class tracking if that's appropriate for your company (see Chapter 4 for more information on class tracking). If you select the Use Class Tracking option, the Prompt To Assign Classes option becomes available. Select that option if you want QuickBooks to remind users to assign a class to each transaction, or to each line of a transaction.

However, if the user ignores the reminder, QuickBooks will still save the transaction, so you could end up with unclassified transactions. If classes are important to your financial reporting (for instance, you need divisional Profit & Loss reports), you need to find a way to convince users that the class assignment reminder cannot be ignored. Good luck!

The Closing Date options represent the QuickBooks method for closing books. You can opt to assign a password to see previous year transactions, so a user that doesn't know the password can't make changes to transactions that occurred before the closing date. Chapter 17 of

QuickBooks 2006: The Official Guide has information about the way the QuickBooks Closing Date feature works.

Chapter 7 of this book covers the Closing Date Exception report, which is a Premier-only feature. You can use the report to see transactions that were changed in the closed period. This is sometimes the only way to reconcile an opening balance for the next year that doesn't match the closing balance of the previous year.

This dialog also contains the statement Audit Tracking Is Always On. In previous versions of QuickBooks, turning on the audit trail was an option. Few users selected the option, but now you have no choice.

The audit trail records everything that happens in QuickBooks. When you create a transaction, modify a record, modify a transaction, etc, the details are recorded. You can view the audit trail by choosing Reports → Accountant & Taxes → Audit Trail.

Checking Preferences

Click the Checking icon in the left pane of the Preferences dialog to configure your preferences for check writing. There are options on both the My Preferences and the Company Preferences tabs.

My Preferences for the Checking Category

The My Preferences tab, seen in Figure 3-3, lets you pre-select the bank account you want to use for specific transaction types. This is useful if you have multiple bank accounts, and you use a specific bank account for a specific purpose.

For example, you may deposit revenue to an interest bearing account, such as a money market account, and then transfer the necessary funds to your operating account when it's time to pay your bills. In that case, field for the Open The Make Deposits Form should contain the name of your interest bearing account.

Even though you can always select a bank account when you're working in a transaction window, pre-selecting the appropriate account eliminates the possibility of error. You've probably noticed that a payroll account isn't listed in this dialog—payroll account information is configured in the Company Preferences tab (discussed next).

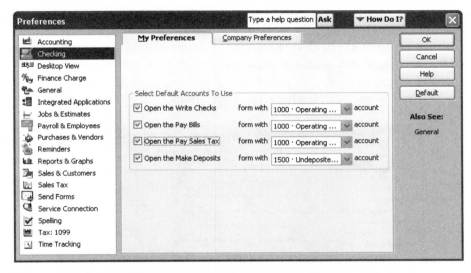

Figure 3-3: Automatically assign transaction types to a specific bank account.

If you have multiple bank accounts and you don't set default options in this dialog, the first time you open a transaction window you must select an account. Thereafter, QuickBooks will default to the last-used account for each transaction type.

Company Preferences for the Checking Category

In the Company Preferences tab, seen in Figure 3-4, you can choose the default options for check writing procedures.

The option Print Account Names On Voucher tells QuickBooks to add account information to the voucher (check stub). By default, if you use check forms with vouchers, QuickBooks prints the payee, date, memo, and amount on the voucher. If you enable this option, the following information is added to the voucher:

- For A/P checks, the name of each account to which you posted amounts to create this check, along with the amount posted to each account. This option is useful if you're using check forms that have vouchers, and you tear off and save the vouchers (I don't imagine the vendors to whom you send the checks care about your internal account postings).
- For payroll checks, the name of each payroll item included in the check, along with the amount assigned to each item.
- For checks used to purchase inventory items, the name of each inventory item included in this check.

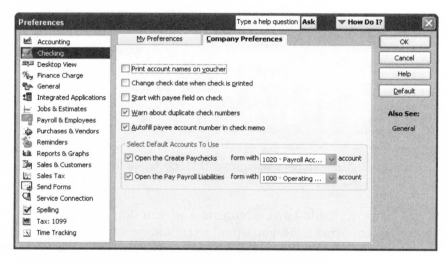

Figure 3-4: Set the default options for check writing.

The option Change Check Date When Check Is Printed determines the date that appears on the checks you print. This is useful if you don't print checks the same day you create them, and you always want the check date that's printed on the check to be the actual date on which you print the check. For example, you may run the Pay Bills process, or create direct disbursement checks, every Monday, but you wait until later in the week to print and mail the checks.

The option Start With Payee Field In Check applies to transaction windows connected to vendors. If you enable the option, when you open the transaction window your cursor is automatically placed as follows:

- For the Write Checks window, your cursor is in the Payee field instead of the Bank Account field at the top of the window. The Bank Account field is automatically populated with the default bank account for writing checks (if you selected one in the My Preferences window), or the bank account you used the last time you worked in the Write Checks window.
- For the Enter Bills window, your cursor is in the Vendor field instead of the Accounts Payable field at the top of the window. However, the Accounts Payable field doesn't appear in the window unless you have multiple A/P accounts in your chart of accounts. If you don't have multiple A/P accounts, the default cursor placement becomes the Vendor field anyway.
- For the Enter Credit Card Charges window, your cursor is in the Purchased From field instead of the Credit Card field at the top of the window. This is only meaningful if you set up your credit cards as liability accounts and enter credit chard charges as you incur them, instead of paying the credit card bill as a regular vendor account. (If you opt to track your credit cards as liabilities, you must perform a reconciliation.)

The option Warn About Duplicate Check Numbers, enabled by default, makes sure you don't use the same check number twice (unless you're silly enough to ignore the warning, because QuickBooks only warns, and won't actually prevent you from using a check number twice). Disabling this option can cause extreme stress when you're trying to reconcile your bank account, go over your finances with your accountant, or deal with a disputed bill payment.

The option Autofill Payee Account Number In Check Memo, also enabled by default, is another useful feature. Most of your vendors h ave assigned you a customer account number, and it's common to write that number in the lower left portion of a check (the check's Memo field in QuickBooks). When you create a vendor in QuickBooks, the Additional Info tab of the vendor record has a field named Account No. QuickBooks will copy the data from that field into the Memo field.

The last items on this dialog are for setting default accounts for payroll checks, if you do payroll in-house. Select the account to use for payroll checks, and the account to use for paying liabilities (withholding and employer payments).

Finance Charge Preferences

Finance charges can be an effective method for speeding up collections. Don't think of this as a way to garner "found money", because the finance charges you collect almost certainly won't cover the cost of tracking and chasing overdue receivables.

To apply finance charges to late customers, you have to establish the rate and circumstances under which the charges are assessed. Those configuration options are in the Company Preferences tab of the Finance Charge category, seen in Figure 3-5. Here are some guidelines for setting finance charge options:

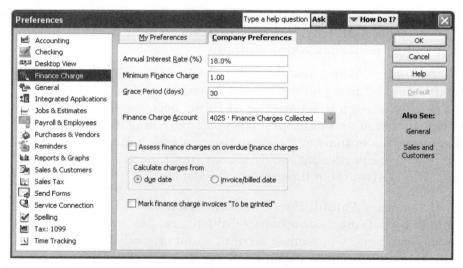

Figure 3-5: Set up finance charge options to improve collections.

- The interest rate is annual, and QuickBooks automatically converts the rate you enter to a monthly rate when you assess finance charges. For example, if you want to assess a finance charge of 1.5 percent per month, enter **18%** in the Annual Interest Rate field.

- You can assess a minimum finance charge for overdue balances. QuickBooks will calculate the finance charge for each customer, and if the amount of the finance charge is less than the minimum you specify, the amount is rolled up to meet your minimum.
- Use the Grace Period field to enter the number of days of lateness you permit before finance charges are assessed.
- During setup, QuickBooks probably created an account for finance charges. If so, it's displayed in this window. If not, enter (or create) the account you want to use to post finance charges (it's an income account).
- The issue of assessing finance charges on overdue finance charges is a bit sticky, because the practice is illegal in many states. Selecting this option means that a customer who owed $100.00 last month and had a finance charge assessed of $2.00 now owes $102.00. As a result, the next finance charge is assessed on a balance of $102.00 (instead of on the original overdue balance of $100.00).
- Specify whether to calculate the finance charge from the due date (which depends on the terms you set for the customer), or the invoice date. Usually, the due date is the trigger for finance charges.
- You can opt to have the finance charge invoices printed, which you should do only if you're planning to mail them to nudge your customers for payment. QuickBooks creates an invoice when finance charges are assessed, but by default these invoices aren't printed—they exist only to record the transaction. Finances charges appear on the statements you send to customers.

After your finance charge options are set, you can assess finance charges every month. Perform this task just before you configure and print customer statements. Detailed instructions for assessing finance charges and creating statements appear in Chapter 5 of *QuickBooks 2006: The Official Guide*.

Jobs & Estimates Preferences

Use the Company Preferences tab for this category to turn on the estimates feature, and configure the way estimates work in your company.

As seen in Figure 3-6, you can customize the way you create estimates, as well as the way you invoice customers against estimates.

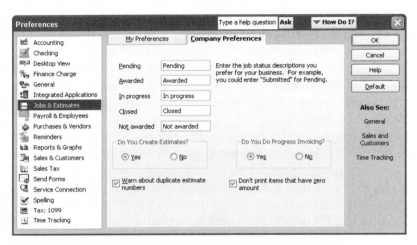

Figure 3-6: Configure the way you prepare and use estimates.

Estimates are de rigueur for some business types, such as construction and contractor businesses, and are advantageous for service-based businesses that approach customer work on a project (job) basis. The QuickBooks Premier editions provide some very productive functions for estimates, including a way to turn an estimate into a purchase order, a sales order, or an invoice. Those functions are covered in Chapter 6 of this book.

Estimates don't affect your financials—nothing is posted to income or expense accounts. When you create your first estimate, QuickBooks creates a non-posting account named Estimates in your chart of accounts. You can open the account register to see the estimates you've created. (QuickBooks treats purchase orders in the same manner.)

To enable estimates, select the Yes button under the option Do You Create Estimates? You can also create the phrases you want to use for describing the status of estimated jobs, changing the text to match the jargon you use in your company. The status is tracked in the job record, and the text doesn't appear in any transactions (such as invoices or purchase orders). This is an internal function.

When estimates are enabled you can select the option to do progress invoicing, which means sending invoices for the job as progress proceeds. For example, you can invoice the customer for 50% of the job's total when 50% of the job is completed. QuickBooks automatically does the calculations to make it easy to create accurate progress invoices. If you select the option to create progress invoices, you can tell QuickBooks to skip line items that have a zero amount.

The option to warn you about a duplicate estimate number is enabled by default, and since two estimates with the same number could be confusing, it's best to leave it enabled. Having QuickBooks examine your data to check for an existing number causes a slight delay in processing, but unless you're working with a very large company file (in the many millions of bytes), the delay isn't long enough to be annoying.

Payroll & Employees Preferences

If you're doing your own payroll processing in QuickBooks, use the Company Preferences tab of the Payroll & Employees category to configure the options for creating employees and printing paychecks.

You can configure the default settings for employee records, the information that appears on transaction windows, the information that appears on reports, and default settings for printing paychecks. Chapter 8 of *QuickBooks 2006: The Official Guide* takes you through the basic payroll tasks.

Purchases & Vendors Preferences

Use this dialog to configure the way you purchase products, and manage vendor bills. You can turn on inventory tracking and purchase orders, but as you can see in Figure 3-7, you have to enable both features; you can't pick only one. However, if you only need the inventory features, just don't ever create a purchase order and QuickBooks won't notice or care.

This dialog also provides a way for you to make sure you don't use duplicate purchase order numbers, and to warn you about insufficient quantities of inventory items when you're creating an invoice or a sales order. QuickBooks does not prevent you from completing the invoice or sales order if your stock levels aren't high enough to fill the order. See Chapter 6 to learn more about this subject, and to learn how to create and manage backorders.

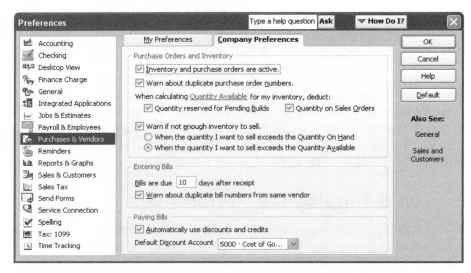

Figure 3-7: Set the default configuration options for managing vendors and purchases.

The option to warn you about stock levels by calculating the inventory items currently assigned to sales orders, and subtracting that total from the quantity on hand, is a Premier Edition-only feature, and is very handy.

The Entering Bills section of the dialog offers the opportunity to set the default terms for vendor bills. These terms are automatically applied to vendors as you create them, but you can (and almost certainly will) change vendor records so they reflect the actual terms you have with each vendor. QuickBooks uses 10 days as the default, and you should change that if the most common vendor terms you have is a different number of days.

QuickBooks calculates due dates for vendor bills by adding the number of days in the vendor's terms to the bill date you enter when you're entering vendor bills. The due dates are used to display bills to pay when you use the Pay Bills window, and when you establish reminders for bill payment.

The option to warn you if you enter a vendor bill with the same number as a previously entered bill is enabled by default. Don't disable it unless you enjoy paying the same bill twice. Actually, even with this warning enabled, you should have a protocol for marking bills when they've been entered in QuickBooks. Get a stamp that says "Entered", or put a large check mark on the bill, to indicate you've entered the bill in your QuickBooks company file.

The option Automatically Use Discounts And Credits means that when you pay vendor bills, QuickBooks will display information about discounts and credits due you, so you can make the appropriate adjustments. QuickBooks tracks discounts, and you must assign a default discount account when you enable this option. Most discounts are for timely payment of a bill connected to buying inventory items, so it makes sense to create a discount account as a Cost of Goods Sold account type. Name the account appropriately, such as Discounts Taken.

NOTE: *QuickBooks 2006: The Official Guide has extensive information on entering and paying vendor bills, using purchase orders, and taking discounts and credits. See Chapters 6 and 7.*

Sales & Customers Preferences

This dialog, seen in Figure 3-8, is where you establish your preferences for the way you sell to, ship to, invoice, and receive payments from, your customers.

If you use one shipping method more than any other, you can select a default shipping method in the Usual Shipping Method field. This default method appears automatically on sales transaction forms that contain the Via field. In some Premier editions, QuickBooks prepopulates this field with one or more shippers, and you can add your own shipping methods to the Ship Via list (covered in Chapter 4).

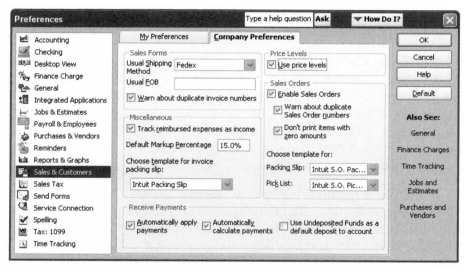

Figure 3-8: Set the default options for transactions related to sales.

In the Default Markup Percentage field, you can preset a markup for items for which you have recorded a cost (inventory items). Enter the markup percentage as a number (QuickBooks automatically adds the percent sign).

QuickBooks uses the percentage you enter here to automate the pricing of inventory items. When you're creating an item, as soon as you enter the cost QuickBooks automatically adds this percentage and displays the result as the price. If your pricing paradigm isn't consistent, you'll find this automatic process more annoying than helpful, because you'll constantly find yourself deleting and re-entering the item's price as you create items. If that's the case, don't use this field.

In the Usual FOB field, set the FOB language you want to appear on sales transactions that have an FOB field. FOB (Free On Board) is the location from which the shipment is determined to be the customer's responsibility. This means more than just paying for freight; it's a statement that says, "At this point you have become the owner of this product." The side effects include assigning responsibility if goods are lost, damaged, or stolen.

For instance, if your business is in Philadelphia, Pennsylvania, then Phila.PA is probably your FOB entry. If you drop ship, use the location of the vendor's warehouse as the FOB point. Incidentally, don't let the size of the text box fool you; you're limited to 13 characters.

NOTE: *FOB settings have no impact on your financial records.*

Use the Track Reimbursed Expenses As Income field to change the way your general ledger handles payments for reimbursements. When this option is enabled, the reimbursement can be assigned to an income account that you create for this purpose.

To establish this paradigm, QuickBooks adds a field for reimbursed expenses to the account record dialog for all the expense accounts in your chart of accounts. You must select an income account to track the reimbursed income for any expense that you're charging back to customers.

- When you invoice a customer for a reimbursable expense, QuickBooks posts the amount to the income account you select in the expense account's record.
- When the option is not enabled, the reimbursement is posted to the original expense account, washing the expense.

My e-mail indicates that many users find this confusing, and I can understand why. It's not the concept that's confusing, because posting the money due from customers for an expense you incurred on their behalf to an income account is very logical. Without this, you'd "wash" your expenses, and if you mark up reimbursed expenses to cover handling, you could open a P & L report that shows a negative expense for some accounts.

The confusion is in the setup. QuickBooks does not permit you to create an income account called "reimbursements for customer expenses". Instead, you must create a specific income account for each expense account that might incur a reimbursable expense.

This can add a lot of income accounts to your chart of accounts, all of which display totals in the income statements you print. My solution is to "pretend" reimbursements are going to one income account by creating an income account named Customer Reimbursements. All the other income accounts I have to add because of QuickBooks' rule are subaccounts of this account. When I print reports, I can glance at the total, or collapse the report so it displays only the totals in parent accounts.

See Chapter 6 of *QuickBooks 2006: The Official Guide* to learn how to enter and invoice reimbursable expenses.

The field Warn About Duplicate Invoice Numbers tells QuickBooks to warn you if you're creating an invoice with an invoice number that's already in use.

The Use Price Levels option turns on the Price Level feature, which lets you customize prices for customers, jobs, and items. You can create as many price levels as you need (covered in Chapter 4).

NOTE: *QuickBooks Premier editions add even more power to the use of price levels by letting you apply price levels to items in addition to customers and jobs.*

The Choose Template For Packing Slip field lets you select a default packing slip template for product shipments. The drop-down list in this field actually contains all the built-in sales templates (e.g. invoice templates), not just packing slip templates. The list varies depending on the industry-specific version of QuickBooks Premier editions you're using, and the industry you selected when you used the EasyStep Interview.

The Automatically Apply Payments option determines whether the default behavior is to apply customer payments automatically rather than manually. This really means that if the feature is turned on, customer payments are applied as follows:

- If the amount of the payment matches an invoice amount, the payment is automatically applied to that invoice.
- If more than one invoice has the same amount, the payment is automatically applied to the oldest invoice with that amount.

• If the amount of the payment is less than any invoice, the payment is applied as a partial payment to the oldest invoice.

TIP: *If you don't apply payments by invoice and instead you use balance-forward billing, it's okay to leave the automatic application feature turned on.*

The Automatically Calculate Payments lets you skip entry of the amount of the payment in the Amount field, and head directly for the list of invoices in the Receive Payments window. As you select each invoice for payment, QuickBooks calculates the total and places it in the Amount field. If your customers' checks always match the amount of an open invoice, this saves you some data entry.

If the option is disabled, selecting an invoice listing without entering the amount of the payment first generates a QuickBooks error message.

Because the option is automatically enabled, the first time you select an invoice before entering the payment amount in the Amount field, QuickBooks displays a message explaining the option, and asking if you'd like to disable it.

The option Use Undeposited Funds As A Default Deposit To Account means all received funds are posted to the Undeposited Funds account. If you enable this option, the Receive Payments and Enter Sales Receipts windows lack a bank account field where you can select the account into which you want to deposit the money. All receipts are automatically posted to the Undeposited Funds account.

If you disable this option, those cash receipts transaction windows display two options for depositing your payment:

• Group With Other Undeposited Funds (the Undeposited Funds account)
• Deposit To <a specified bank account>

In the Sales Order section, you can enable or disable the sales orders feature. When the feature is enabled, two additional options are available:

- You can opt to receive a warning when you use a sales order number that's already in use
- You can prevent zero amount line items from printing on sales orders.

You can also choose a default template for Sales Order packing slips, and pick slips. When would you use a packing slip for a sales order?

Sales Tax Preferences

If you collect and remit sales tax, you need to configure the sales tax features in QuickBooks. Sales tax is becoming a complicated issue and has created an enormous administrative burden for small businesses.

In recent years, many states have created multiple sales tax authorities within the state (by county, city, town, or even a group of zip codes), and each location has its own tax rate.

Businesses in some of those states must remit the sales tax they collect to both the state and the local sales tax authority (or to multiple local sales tax authorities).

In some states, businesses remit all the sales tax to the state, but must report taxable/nontaxable sales on a location-by-location basis.

As a result, tracking sales tax properly (which means in a manner that makes it possible to fill out all the forms for all the authorities) has become a very complicated process.

One of the significant changes in state sales tax rules is a change in the "source" rule, (the source of the rate). In most states, the source rule has always been "origin-based", which means the location of the business that's collecting the tax determines the rate.

Many states are adopting new sales tax laws that change the rate source to "destination-based", which means the tax rate changes depending on the location of the customer. As more and more states create different rates for discrete jurisdictions, businesses have to create complicated solutions to track each rate. At the time of this writing, there are more than 7,600 sales tax rates in the United States (even with several states that have no sales tax).

Because of the complications, and because of the importance of accurate reporting of sales tax (to avoid audits, fines, and annoying communications from your state tax authority), I'm going to present a rather lengthy detailed discussion of the issues and tasks involved in setting up sales taxes properly.

In fact, even though Chapter 4 is dedicated to explaining how to set up lists for your company file, I'm going to cover the lists attached to sales tax reporting in this section, so all the information about setting up the sales tax feature is in one place.

If your state hasn't instituted new, complicated, sales tax structures, you can skip most of the following discussion. But don't relax—your time (and attendant paperwork headache) is probably coming.

Enabling the Sales Tax Feature

Start by setting the basic options for sales tax in the dialog shown in Figure 3-9. You must set up sales tax codes to link to your customers, so you know whether a customer is liable for sales tax. You must also set up sales tax items, so you can set a rate (a percentage), and you must link the sales tax item to a taxing authority.

Enable the sales tax feature by selecting the Yes option under the label Do You Charge Sales Tax? Then, in the Owe Sales Tax section, specify whether you remit sales taxes when you invoice your customers, or when you receive payments from your customers. The information that arrived with your sales tax license should clearly state which option is applicable in your state.

In the Pay Sales Tax section, indicate the frequency of your remittance to the taxing authority. You don't get to choose—the notice that arrived with your sales tax license and reporting forms indicates the schedule you must use.

Many states base the frequency on the amount of tax you collect, usually looking at your returns for a specific period—perhaps one specific quarter (the period they examine is usually referred to as the *lookback* period).

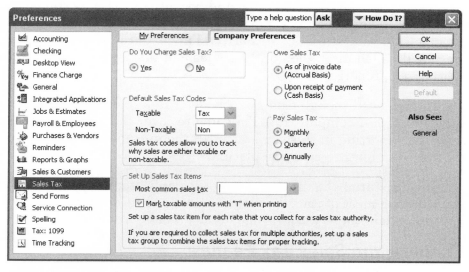

Figure 3-9: Check your sales tax license for the information you need to configure sales tax remittances.

If your sales tax liability changes dramatically during the lookback period, you may receive notice from the state that your remittance interval has changed. If that occurs, don't forget to return to the Preferences window to change the interval.

The Sales Tax Codes and the Most Common Sales Tax fields in this dialog are discussed in the following sections.

Understanding Tax Codes and Tax Items

QuickBooks has two discrete entities for configuring sales tax: Sales Tax Codes and Sales Tax Items. Many QuickBooks users get them confused, so I'll attempt to clarify everything, and I'll start by defining each entity:

- A sales tax **code** indicates tax liability, which means the entity to which it's linked (a customer or an item) is deemed taxable or nontaxable, depending on the code. Tax codes contain no information about the tax rate or the taxing authority; they just offer a Yes or No answer to the question "taxable?"

- A sales tax **item** contains information about the tax rate and the taxing authority to which you remit taxes and reports. Like all items, the sales tax item appears on sales forms. The amount of tax due is calculated when you add the sales tax item to the taxable line items (products and services) on an invoice or sales receipt.

Working with Sales Tax Codes

Linking a sales tax code to customers and items lets you (and QuickBooks) know whether sales tax should be calculated for that item for this customer. A customer's sales tax liability is like a light switch; it's either on or off.

However, if a customer is liable for sales tax, it doesn't mean that every item you sell the customer is taxable, because some items aren't taxable—like customers, items have a tax liability switch that operates as an on/off switch.

For sales tax to kick in, both the item and the customer must have their tax liability status set to "taxable".

I can't give you a list of taxable/nontaxable categories, because each state sets its own rules. For example, in Pennsylvania, food and some other necessities of life aren't taxable, but some types of consulting services are. Other states don't tax services at all, reserving the sales tax for products. Some states seem to tax everything—California comes to mind.

QuickBooks prepopulates the Sales Tax Preferences dialog with the following two sales tax codes:

- Tax, which means liable for sales tax
- Non, which means not liable for sales tax

For many of us, that's enough; we don't need any additional tax codes for customers or for items. We can move on to creating sales tax items so tax rates can be calculated on sales forms.

However, for some companies, those two tax codes aren't enough. Some taxing authorities care about the "why"—most often they want to know why a customer *isn't* liable for sales tax.

If your state sales tax report form wants to know why a customer is taxable, it's probably asking about the tax rate for that customer. Many states are setting up multiple sales tax rates, basing the rate on location (county, city, town, or zip code). Identifying a customer as "taxable because he's in the Flummox County of our state" means the tax charged on sales to that customer are the tax rates assigned to Flummox County. (Tax rates are configured in sales tax items, not sales tax codes. See the section "Working with Sales Tax Items".)

Most taxing authorities are only interested in the "why not" question. Is a customer nontaxable because it's out of state and the rules say you don't have to collect taxes for out-of-state sales? Is the customer nontaxable because it's a nonprofit organization, or a government agency? Is the customer nontaxable because it's a wholesale business and collects sales tax from its own customers? If your state requires this information, you must create tax codes to match the reporting needs required by your state.

Creating Sales Tax Codes

If you want to create codes to track customer sales tax status in a manner more detailed than "taxable" and "nontaxable," follow these steps to add a new sales tax code:

1. Choose Lists → Sales Tax Code List.
2. Press Ctrl-N to open the New Sales Tax Code window.
3. Enter the name of the new code, using up to three characters.
4. Enter a description to make it easier to interpret the code.
5. Select Taxable if you're entering a code to track taxable sales.
6. Select Non-taxable if entering a code to track nontaxable sales.
7. Click Next to set up another tax code.
8. Click OK when you've finished adding tax codes.

This procedure works nicely for specifying different types of nontaxable customers. For example, you could create tax codes similar to the following for nontaxable categories:

- NPO for nonprofit organizations
- GOV for government agencies
- WSL for wholesale businesses
- OOS for out-of-state customers (if you aren't required to collect taxes from out-of-state customers)

For taxable customers, the permutations and combinations are much broader, of course. If you're required to collect and remit sales tax for some additional states, just create codes for customers in those states, using the postal abbreviations for each state.

The problem is that QuickBooks' tax code setup doesn't work well for categorizing taxable customers if you do business in a state with complicated multiple tax rates. Those states issue codes for each location and its linked rate, and the codes are almost always more than three characters—but three characters is all QuickBooks permits for a sales tax code.

The workaround for this lies in the ability to assign a sales tax item to a customer, as long as the customer's configuration indicates "taxable" (using the built-in Tax code, or any other "yes it's taxable" based code you created). Sales tax items, which can hold the information about the specific tax locations and rates, are discussed next.

Working with Sales Tax Items

A sales tax item is a collection of data about a sales tax, including the rate and the agency to which the sales tax is remitted. QuickBooks uses sales tax items to calculate the amount on the Tax field in sales forms, and to prepare reports for tax authorities.

Creating the Most Common Sales Tax Item

The Sales Tax Preferences dialog has a field named Most Common Sales Tax, and you must enter a sales tax item (not a sales tax code) in that field. This is the tax item that's automatically assigned to customers, but you can change any customer's tax item as needed.

This step is required, but you haven't yet created any sales tax items, because you can't create sales tax items until you've enabled the sales tax preference. This "chicken or the egg" situation can be complex.

The drop-down list in the Most Common Sales Tax field contains the entry <Add New>, so all you have to do is create your most common sales tax item, and it becomes the default sales tax item (it's linked to all the customers you create from here on).

If you do business in a state that has a single sales tax, the sales tax item you create here works fine. However, if you do business in a state that requires you to report multiple rates, you may need to assign customers a sales tax group item, not a single sales tax item.

You can't create a group item in this dialog, so you can invent any sales tax item you wish in this dialog (it's a placeholder). After you've enabled sales tax collection, you can create your sales tax items and groups. Then, you can return to this dialog and change the most common sales tax item to the one that really is the most common sales tax item.

Click the arrow next to the Most Common Sales Tax field, and choose <Add New> from the drop-down list to open the New Item dialog. Follow these steps to create the new sales tax item:

1. Select Sales Tax Item as the item type.
2. In the Tax Name field, enter a name for the item.
3. Enter a description to describe this sales tax on your transaction forms.
4. Enter the tax rate. QuickBooks knows the rate is a percentage, so it automatically adds the percent sign to the numbers you type (for instance, enter 6.5 if the rate is 6.5%).
5. Select the tax agency (the vendor) to which you pay the tax from the drop-down list, or create the vendor by choosing <Add New> (see Chapter 2 for information on adding vendors).
6. Click OK.

In the future, when you need to enter additional sales tax items, click the Item icon on the Icon Bar, or choose Lists → Item List from the menu bar. Press Ctrl-N to open the New Item dialog and create the new sales tax item.

When you create new sales tax items, you can use the Tax Name field to enter those complicated, pesky tax rate codes if you're in a state that has codes you couldn't use because of the three-character limitation of the tax code in QuickBooks. In fact, even if you'd created tax codes for multiple tax venues and attached them to customers, you'd still have to create these tax items in order to calculate rates and assign the tax authorities.

When you've finished configuring sales tax, click OK to close the Sales Tax Preferences dialog. QuickBooks displays a message offering you the opportunity to assign a tax status to existing customers and existing non-inventory and inventory parts (see Figure 3-10). (This tax status query is about a tax code, the Yes or No taxable status, not about applying a tax item to customers and items.)

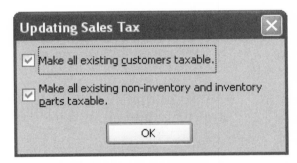

Figure 3-10: Automatically apply a tax status to existing entities in your company file.

Select or deselect the options as needed. QuickBooks marks all existing customers and inventory/non-inventory parts items taxable or nontaxable, depending on your selection. If you have existing service items, they aren't marked taxable, and if they are taxable, you'll have to edit your service items to change their tax status.

The default you set doesn't just apply to existing customers and items. As you add new customers and items, they are automatically marked with a tax code of taxable or nontaxable, matching the selection you made in this dialog.

Unfortunately, the automatic application of the tax status to newly created items isn't limited to inventory and non-inventory parts; it includes new Service items and Other Charges items you create. If your services are not taxable, you'll have to make sure you change the tax status of each service item you create in the future.

This is the same function that did *not* mark service items taxable when you were offered the opportunity to mark customers and inventory/non-inventory parts taxable. Now, new service items you create are automatically marked as taxable. Sigh! Well, a foolish consistency is the hobgoblin of little minds (according to Ralph Waldo Emerson).

Sales Tax Groups

In some states, the tax imposed is really two taxes, and the taxing authority collects a single check from you, but insists on a breakdown in the reports you send. For example, in Pennsylvania, the state sales tax is 6%, but businesses in Philadelphia and Allegheny Counties must charge an extra 1%. The customer pays 7% tax on taxable items, and a check for 7% of taxable sales is remitted to the state's revenue department.

However, the report that accompanies the check must break down the remittance into the individual taxes (the subtotals for the 6% tax and the 1% tax, and the total for both taxes).

In some other states, the customer pays a single tax, but the business that collects the tax remits two reports and two checks: the portion of the tax that represents the basic state sales tax is remitted to the state, and the locally added tax is remitted to the local taxing authority.

Your challenge is to display and calculate a single tax for the customer on your invoices and sales receipts, and yet be able to report multiple taxes to the taxing authorities. Sales tax groups meet this challenge.

A sales tax group is a single tax entity that appears on a sales transaction, but behind the scenes, it's really multiple sales tax items. QuickBooks creates the tax amount on the transaction by calculating each of the multiple entries in the group and displaying the total (the customer is being charged the "combo" rate). When you prepare sales tax reports and checks, QuickBooks breaks out the individual totals.

A sales tax group is an item, and you create it the way you create a sales tax item (in the Items list). The sales tax items that are included in

the group must be created first. For example, in Pennsylvania, businesses in Philadelphia County create the following items:

- A Sales Tax item named PABasic (or something similar), configured for 6%, and specifying the vendor named Pennsylvania
Department of Revenue as the tax agency.
- A Sales Tax item named Phila (or something similar), configured
for 1%, and specifying the same vendor, Pennsylvania Department
of Revenue, as the tax agency.
- A Sales Tax Group item named PA Tax (or something similar),
which consists of both of the previously created items (see Figure
3-11).

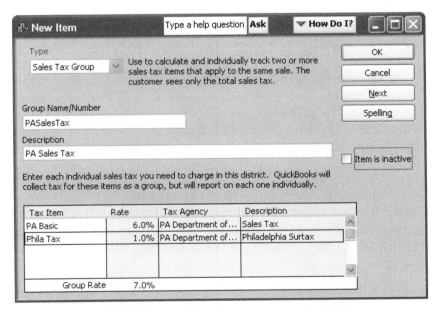

Figure 3-11: A Sales Tax Group is a combination of multiple sales tax
items.

If your sales tax reporting rules are to send the basic state sales tax
to the state, and remit the local sales tax to a local taxing authority, use
the same system described here, but specify the appropriate vendor codes
for the tax agencies connected to each tax item. QuickBooks will respond
correctly when you run reports and create the checks.

When all your sales tax configuration options, sales tax codes, and sales tax items are recorded in your company file, you can perform all the tasks related to reporting taxable and nontaxable sales, and remitting payments to the proper authorities. Read Chapter 7 of *QuickBooks 2006: The Official Guide* to learn how to manage sales tax reporting and remittances.

TIP: To learn how to troubleshoot very complex sales tax rules in transaction windows, see Appendix C. The section on applying sales tax includes workarounds that have been created by me, and by accountants I've worked with on these pesky problems.

Linking Customers to Sales Tax Items

All customer records contain both a sales tax code and a sales tax item. When you create a new customer, assuming you opted to make customers taxable, the sales tax code Tax is automatically applied, and the sales tax item you specified in the Most Common Sales Tax Item in the Sales Tax Preferences dialog is also automatically applied.

If you're in one of those states that adopted multiple tax rates depending on the customer's location, you can go through all your customer records and change the Tax Item field (on the Additional Info tab) to the sales tax item you created for the rate and authority that the customer falls under.

If that sounds incredibly boring, you can wait until the next time you create a sales transaction for each customer. When you open a sales transaction form and enter a customer name, a field labeled Tax appears right under the line items. This is the customer's sales tax item assignment. (The customer tax code appears below the sales form, at the bottom of the form's window.)

If you change the sales tax item on the sales form, after you save the transaction QuickBooks offers to change the customer record to match the change in the sales tax item. Very handy!

Customizing Templates

QuickBooks Premier editions provide a wide range of templates for sales forms. In addition to the standard Invoice, Estimate, and Sales Receipts templates, you'll find useful templates such as Quotes, Work Orders, Proposals, Time & Expense Invoices, and more.

Not all the new templates are available in all Premier editions, but since many of these templates are really customized versions of QuickBooks standard templates, you can create the template you need.

Editing Predefined Templates

QuickBooks uses the term *predefined templates* for those templates that are built-in, and are also locked against major changes. When you edit a predefined template, you can tweak its appearance, or remove your company address information, but you cannot change the contents of the form.

(You can use a predefined template as the basis of a new template, in which you're not limited to minor tweaks—covered in the next section, "Creating New Templates".)

If you're satisfied with the contents (the existing fields and columns) of a predefined template, but you want to change its appearance, you can edit the template.

Open the template when a transaction window is open by clicking the Customize button over the Template field. The list of templates available for this transaction form appears. Select the form you want to work with, and click Edit.

Alternatively, you can choose Lists → Templates to open the list of all the available templates. Then double-click the template you want to use.

When you're editing a predefined template you perform your work in the Customize dialog seen in Figure 3-12.

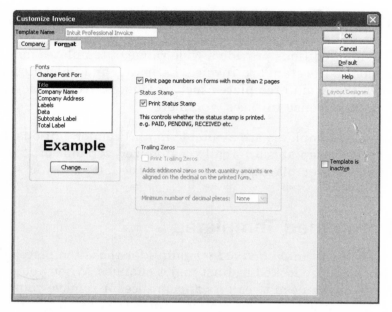

Figure 3-12: You can tweak the appearance and format of a predefined template.

The Format tab is the place to change the appearance of the text that appears in the form, and the most common alteration is a change of font for the elements in the template.

Select an element (such as labels—the text that appears on each field in the transaction form), and click Change. Then select a font, size, and style (bold, italic, etc.).

In the Company tab, you can deselect the company address information (if you use pre-printed forms), or add a company logo (useful if you use blank paper to print your transaction forms).

Creating New Templates

You can use a predefined template as the basis of a new template. Essentially, you're creating a copy of the original template, and building a new form by adding, removing, and relocating elements. You can start the process from the transaction window, or from the Templates List.

Choosing a Template in a Transaction Window

If you're working in a transaction window, click the Customize button above the Template field and select the appropriate template from the drop-down list. The list of available templates is limited to those that match the type of transaction window.

Select the template you want to use as the basis of your new template, and click New. When the Customize dialog opens, enter a name for this new template, and begin customizing your new template.

Choosing a Template from the Templates List

You can also create a new template from any template installed by QuickBooks. Choose Lists → Templates to open the Templates list window, which displays all the templates available in this company file.

Right-click the template you want to use, and choose Duplicate from the shortcut menu. In the Select Template Type dialog (see Figure 3-13), choose the type of template you want to create.

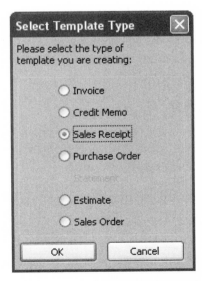

Figure 3-13: Select the type of template you want to create.

Most of the time, you'll create a template of the same type you selected as the basis of your new template. (It wouldn't make sense to try to create a purchase order from a sales receipt.) However, sometimes one predefined template may come very close to the template you want to create, even if you're creating a template of a different type. For example, you can use an invoice template to create a sales receipt template or a sales order template.

If a template type is grayed out and therefore inaccessible, it means the company file you're working in isn't configured to use that type of template. For example, in Figure 3-13, the Statement template is unavailable, because sending statements isn't enabled in this company's configuration options.

After you select the template type for your new template, the listings in the Template List include the template you duplicated, in the format DUP: <Template Name>.

Double-click the listing to open it, and enter a name for your new template in the Template Name field at the top of the dialog. Now you can begin creating your new template.

Whether you started in the transaction window, or in the Templates List, when you indicate to QuickBooks that you're creating a new template, the Customize template dialog that opens displays all the tabs needed to redesign the original template (see Figure 3-14).

Customizing the Template Header

The template header contains the fields you see at the top of the template window when you're creating a transaction. You can add or eliminate fields, and change the text that appears in the header.

Each field has a check box for Screen and Print, so you can determine whether a field (along with its contents) is available on the screen when you're creating the transaction and also in the printed version.

For example, in the original sales receipt template that I used as the basis of a new template in Figure 3-14, both of the Ship To field check boxes are deselected. However, if you're using a sales receipt template in a retail environment, and the customer wants you to ship the purchases, you'll need to select those fields for both the screen and printed versions of the transaction document.

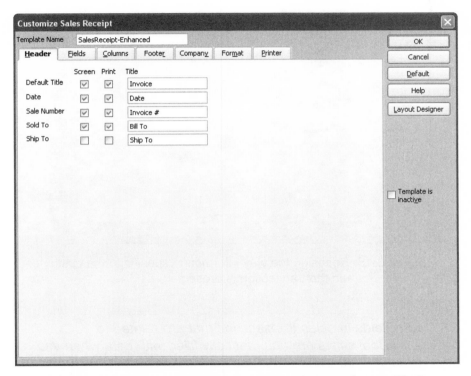

Figure 3-14: Every element of the original template can be modified and customized.

Customizing the Template Fields

In the Fields tab (see Figure 3-15), you can select and deselect the fields that appear on the screen and print versions of the template, and you can change the text that's used as the label for a field.

For example, if you pay commissions to sales people, select the Rep field for the screen version of the template, so you can track the sales rep. If you ever ship products to cash customers, select the fields relating to shipping.

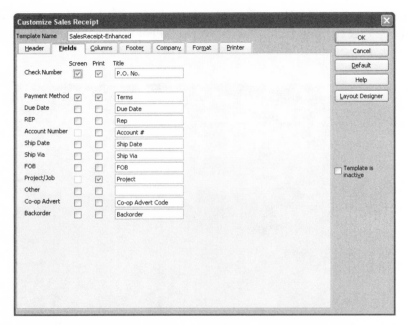

Figure 3-15: Redesign the way information specific to the customer and the transaction is presented.

TIP: Fields in sales transactions that are related to QuickBooks lists are automatically filled with data when you select the customer in the transaction window. The data is taken from the customer's record. Rep and Account Number are examples of list-based fields.

QuickBooks provides a field named Other, which you can add to the template, giving it a label that suits your purposes. Perhaps you want to track the way this order is received, labeling the field Source (or something similar), and entering data such as InternetSale, PhoneSale, or so on.

If you created custom fields in the Names lists, QuickBooks automatically adds those to the Fields tab. You can enable those fields, and enter appropriate data. (Not all custom fields are suitable for all types of transactions).

Customizing the Template Columns

In the Columns tab (see Figure 3-16), you can design the column headings that appear in the line item section of the transaction form.

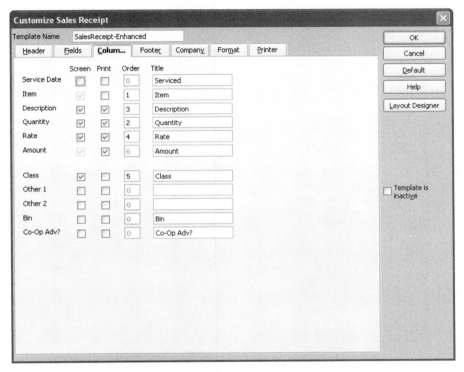

Figure 3-16: Customize the data that's used when you enter line items in transactions.

You can select and deselect the columns that appear on the screen, the printed transaction document, or both. In addition, you can determine the order in which columns appear (the numbers indicate a left-to-right pattern, so column 1 is the furthest left column).

QuickBooks provides two columns named Other that you can use to create labels, and then enter the appropriate data. In addition, if you created custom fields for items, they appear as available columns.

Customizing the Template Footer

In the Footer tab, seen in Figure 3-17, you can determine what appears at the bottom of the transaction.

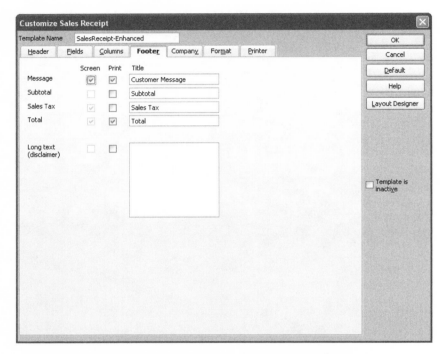

Figure 3-17: Most of the fields in the footer are too important to remove.

Some of the fields can't be removed from the Screen version of the transaction, and even though they can be removed from the print version, it's not a good idea to deselect them. It's hard to imagine the circumstances in which you'd want to eliminate financial totals from a transaction document.

If you don't use Customer Messages (e.g. "Thank you for your business"), deselect the field from both versions.

The bottom box is a text box that you can use to print a message (the text you enter does not appear in the transaction window). This is the place to enter disclaimers, information about returns, or other substantial amounts of text.

The text you enter appears on every transaction you print when you use this template, so if you need one type of disclaimer for some sales (such as return policy information), and other text for different types of sales (such as warranty information for certain types of products), you'll have to customize two templates, one for each type of text.

By default, the long text appears in the lower left part of the transaction document, but you can move it in the Layout Designer (covered later in this chapter).

Customizing Company Information

In the Company tab (see Figure 3-18), select the company data that you want to print on the transaction document. If you use pre-printed letterhead, you can deselect all the company information.

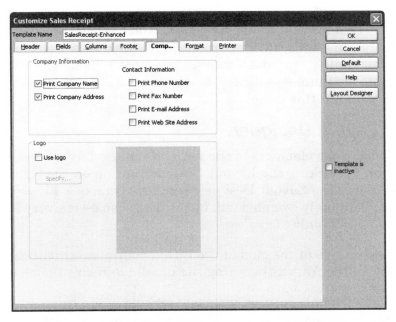

Figure 3-18: Select or deselect company information, depending on whether you use blank paper or preprinted forms.

TIP: If you deselect the company information because you print the transaction on a preprinted form, QuickBooks leaves the space blank. If your preprinted text doesn't fit in the blank space, use the Layout Designer to move the elements in the transaction document.

If you use blank paper, you can add any of the fields in the Contact Information section of this dialog. The data that appears in the fields is taken from the Company Information dialog (choose Company → Company Information to make sure the data you want to print actually exists).

Customizing Fonts and Printing

The Format tab is the same dialog discussed earlier in this chapter in the section discussing the ability to change fonts for the elements in the transaction document.

The Printer tab offers the option to customize the settings for the printer you selected for this transaction type. You can change the paper size, the orientation (landscape or portrait), and the number of copies that are automatically printed. Of course, you must remember to put paper that matches those specifications into the printer when you print a transaction created in this template.

Using the Layout Designer

You can reposition the elements of the template in the Layout Designer, which you open by clicking the Layout Designer button on the right side of the dialog. When the Layout Designer window opens (see Figure 3-19), it seems overwhelmingly complicated, but it really isn't—it's very logical and therefore not difficult to use.

To change the size of the element, position your pointer on one of the sizing handles on the frame, then drag the handle to resize the element.

To move an element, position your pointer inside the frame and when your pointer turns into a four-headed arrow, drag the frame to a different location on the form.

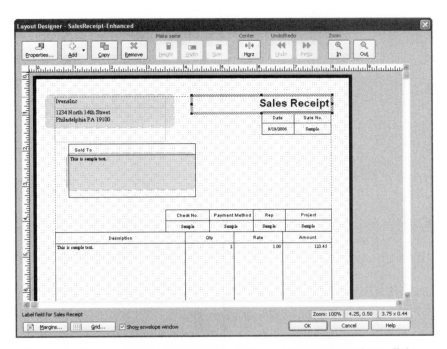

Figure 3-19: Use the Layout Designer to make your template slick and professional.

Double-click an element's frame to see a Properties dialog that permits all sorts of option changes for the selected element. Figure 3-20 shows the Properties dialog for the Description field.

If you use window envelopes to mail your documents, you need to be careful not to relocate or overlap the address areas, which are preconfigured to be in the right place for standard window envelopes.

By default, the Show Envelope Window option at the bottom of the Layout Designer is selected, so the areas of the form that are designed to print correctly (where the envelope windows are) have a green highlight.

If you use single-window envelopes, you only need to worry about the Sold To field, which contains the recipient's name and address.

The button labeled Undo at the top of the Layout Designer window is a lifesaver.

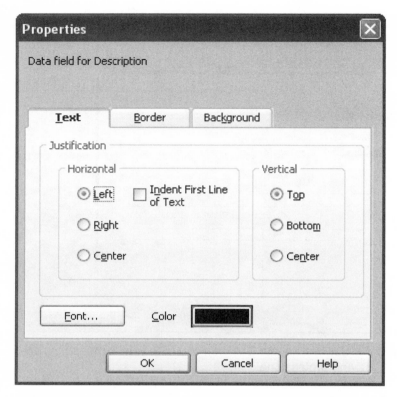

Figure 3-20: You can enhance the appearance of specific elements.

When you finish with the Layout Designer, click OK to return to the Customize Invoice dialog, and save your new template. This new template name appears on the drop-down list when you create the appropriate transaction type.

TIP: *You can also use this new template as the basis for other customizations.*

Detailed information about using the Layout Designer is in Chapter 3 of QuickBooks 2006: The Official Guide, which is in your Premier edition product box.

Chapter 4

Lists and Classes

Creating lists

Creating custom fields in lists

List limits

Creating classes

Lists are mini-files within your QuickBooks data file, and they contain the data you use when you create transactions. For example, the names of your customers and vendors are held in QuickBooks lists. (Database developers usually refer to these files-within-the-file as *tables*.)

Most of the fields in the QuickBooks transaction windows require you to make a selection from a drop-down list. If the selection you need isn't there, you can create it while you're creating the transaction (which is called *on the fly* data entry). However, that interrupts the process of creating a transaction, which makes you less productive. Take the time now to get this basic data into your system.

Creating your lists is one of those "which came first, the chicken or the egg" exercises. Some lists have fields for other list items, such as the Customer:Job list, where each dialog contains fields for data that's contained in auxiliary lists (Terms, Price Level, Type, and so on).

In this chapter, I'll go over the lists, describing their use. The instructions for creating, editing, merging, and deleting list items are in Chapter 2 of QuickBooks 2006: The Official Guide, a copy of which is included in your QuickBooks Premier edition software package.

I'll start with the auxiliary lists, which QuickBooks calls the Customer & Vendor Profile Lists. After you create items for these lists, you can choose data from a drop-down list when you're creating data for the larger lists.

Customer & Vendor Profile Lists

Some of the Customer & Vendor Profile lists let you filter, sort, and categorize information about your customers, jobs, and vendors. Other lists in this category are for maintaining information that makes it easier to manage transactions.

When you create customers and vendors, you can pre-assign the entries in some of these profile lists as default settings, and the data will appear in transaction windows involving those customers and vendors.

The default settings you specify aren't etched in stone; you can change any field's data in any transaction window.

To access these lists choose Lists → Customer & Vendor Profile List, which contains the following lists on the submenu (all of which are covered in this section):

- Sales Rep List
- Customer Type List
- Vendor Type List
- Job Type List
- Terms List
- Customer Message List
- Payment Method List
- Ship Via List
- Vehicle List

Sales Rep List

The Rep field on transaction windows is used to link a sales representative to a customer. You need this information if you pay commissions to sales reps, but even if you don't have a commission structure, it's often helpful to know who the primary contact is for a customer (usually referred to as a service rep instead of a sales rep).

When you create a sales rep, you enter the name and initials. The initials become the code for the sales rep, and those initials appear in the Rep field of sales transaction forms.

> *TIP*: *Paying commissions to sales reps can be complicated. To avoid making it more complicated than it needs to be, and to make sure you don't have errors in the setup and configuration of commissions, see the troubleshooting information on commissions in Appendix C.*

Creating this list is one of those "chicken or the egg" situations, because in order to add a sales rep, the name must already exist in the Employees, Vendors, or Other Names list.

If the sales rep's name is not already on one of those lists, you can create the entry in the Sales Rep list, and when you press Tab to move to the next field, QuickBooks displays a dialog that lets you add the new rep to your Employee, Vendor, or Other Names list.

Customer Type

Use the Customer Type list to sort your customers by a type you deem important or convenient when you create reports. For example, you may decide to signify wholesale and retail customers by type.

If you used a predefined company file to create your company file, you may find that QuickBooks has prepopulated the list with one or more entries. If the entries aren't useful, delete them and create your own.

Types don't work well unless they're similar in category. If you want to use types such as "retail" and "wholesale" to categorize customers, then you can't use "yellow pages" or "local newspaper ad". If you mix categories, you won't be able to sort or filter reports properly to gain useful information. If you really need more than one category of customer type, use custom fields for some of the categories (see "Creating Custom Fields", later in this chapter).

Vendor Type

Use this list to classify your vendors by type, so you can create reports sorted by the criteria you establish when you invent your vendor type entries. If you used a predefined company file to create your own company file, you may find that QuickBooks has prepopulated the list with one or more entries in this list. If the entries aren't useful, you can delete them and create your own.

As with Customer Types, Vendor Types don't work if you mix categories. Use custom fields to track information about vendors.

Job Type

The entries you create for this list help you classify jobs (if you track jobs or projects) so you can create reports sorted by different types of jobs. For example, you may want to have job types to separate fixed fee jobs from time and material jobs. Or, you may want to classify jobs by those you do with in-house personnel and those that involve outside contractors.

If you used a predefined company file to create your own company file, you may find that QuickBooks has prepopulated the list with one or more entries that are specific to your type of business. If the entries aren't useful, you can delete them and create your own.

Terms

Terms, of course, refers to payment terms. Click the arrow to the right of the text box to see the terms that are already defined, or choose <Add New> to define a new one. If you used a predefined company file to create your own company file, you probably have terms in this list that are commonly used in your industry.

The terms you create are linked to both customers and vendors, and you may need additional terms to make sure you've covered all your customer and vendor terms. QuickBooks supports two types of terms:

- Standard terms, which have a due date following a certain amount of time after the invoice date.
- Date driven terms, which are due on a particular day of the month, regardless of the invoice date.

Create a name for the new terms, using a name that makes it easy to understand the terms when you see it on a drop-down list in a transaction window. For example, if you create standard terms of 30 days, name the entry 30Days. If you create date driven terms where the payment is due on the 15th of the month, name the entry 15thMonth.

Creating Standard Terms

Select Standard, and fill out the dialog to match the terms. Net Due is the number of days you allow for payment after the invoice date. To give customers a discount for early payment, enter the discount percentage and the number of days after the invoice date that the discount is in effect. For example, if you allow 30 days for payment but want to encourage customers to pay early, enter a discount percentage that is in effect for 10 days after the invoice date.

Creating Date Driven Terms

Select Date Driven, and enter the day of the month the invoice payment is due. Then enter the number of days before the due date that invoices are considered to be payable on the following month (for example, it's not fair to insist that invoices be paid on the 10th of the month if you mail them to customers on the 8th of the month).

To give customers a discount for early payment, enter the discount percentage and the day of the month at which the discount period ends. For example, if the standard due date is the 15th of the month, you may want to extend a discount to any customer who pays by the 8th of the month.

NOTE: *Terms that provide discounts for early payment are commonly used by manufacturers and distributors of products. It's not standard practice to provide discounts for early payment if you sell services. If you need an incentive for customers to pay their bills on time, use finance charges.*

Customer Message

This list holds the messages you can print at the bottom of customer transaction forms (invoices, sales receipts, estimates, etc.). The messages can contain up to 101 characters (including spaces and punctuation).

If you used a predefined company file to create your own company file, you may find that QuickBooks has prepopulated the list with one or more entries that are specific to your type of business. If the entries aren't useful, you can delete them and create your own.

Payment Method

This list contains specifies the various types of payments you receive from customers. Tracking the payment method for customers helps you resolve disputes because you have a detailed report of every payment you receive.

In addition, specifying the payment method lets you group deposits by the appropriate categories when you use the Make Deposits window. Your bank statement probably displays separate entries for credit card receipts, electronic transfers, and cash and checks. Depositing funds by payment method makes it easier to reconcile the bank account.

TIP: *When you receive a credit card payment from a customer, use the Memo field in the transaction window to note the Authorization ID Number and the Transaction Number.*

Ship Via

Use this list to specify the way products are shipped when you sell products to customers. The list is prepopulated with the major carriers, as well as the US Postal Service. If you have your own trucks or cars, add self-delivery to your list.

Vehicle

A vehicle list in the Customer & Vendor Profile list group? Don't ask me, I can't figure it out either.

Use this list for vehicles for which you want to track mileage. You can bill customers for mileage automatically, or just track the numbers for tax or vehicle maintenance purposes.

Information on tracking mileage is in Chapter 6 of QuickBooks 2006: The Official Guide (in your Premier Edition software package).

Customers & Jobs List

If you've used QuickBooks before, you think I've named this list incorrectly, because you're used to seeing this list with the name "Customer:Job List". Starting in QuickBooks 2006, and the introduction of the Customer Center as the only place to see a list of your customers, the name has changed. The list in the Customer Center is named Customers & Jobs.

Well, the name has changed some of the time, because when you're entering transactions, any field that requires the entry of a customer name, or a job, uses Customer:Job as the field name.

In QuickBooks, customers and jobs are handled together, because job tracking is built into QuickBooks. You can create a customer and consider anything and everything you invoice to that customer a single job, or you can have multiple jobs for the same customer.

If you don't need job costing, you can ignore the feature, and use the Customer:Job list to track each customer as a discrete entity. Jobs can't stand alone as an entity; they are linked to customers. You can link as many jobs to a single customer as you need to.

TIP: If you are going to track jobs, it's more efficient to enter all the customers first, and then create the jobs.

Customer Name Protocols

You have to develop a set of rules, or protocols, for naming your customers. Some businesses use number codes, some use a combination of letters (using the first few letters of the customer name) and numbers, and some use the actual name. What's important is to have a consistent pattern for creating customer names; otherwise, you run the risk of entering the same customer multiple times. Imagine trying to track receivables under those circumstances!

When you create a customer in QuickBooks, the first field in the New Customer dialog is Customer Name. Don't take the name of that field literally; instead, think of the data you enter in that field as a code rather than a real name. This code is a reference that's linked to all the information you enter in the customer record (company name, primary contact name, address, and so on).

The code doesn't appear on printed transactions (such as invoices or sales receipts); the Customer:Job dialog has a field for the Company Name, and that's what appears on transactions, not the Customer Name. You must invent a protocol for the customer name (the code) so you enter every customer in the same manner.

Avoiding punctuation and spaces in codes is a good protocol for codes. This avoids the risk that you'll enter any customer more than once. Consider the following customer codes I've found in client files (each of these represents a single customer entered multiple times):

- O'Neill and Oneill
- Sam's Pizza, Sams Pizza, and SamsPizza
- The Rib Pit, Rib Pit, and RibPit

Incidentally, the last listing in each entry of this list represents the best protocol. Customer names such as SamsPizza and RibPit have a capital letter in the middle of the name to make it easier to read the name. However, if you're typing the name in a list box (it's easier to select a name from a long drop-down list by typing than by scrolling), you don't have to capitalize any letters—data in drop-down lists is not case-sensitive.

If your business has most of its customers in the same industry, you may find that many customers have similar (or identical) names. I have a client who sells supplies to video rental stores, and at least seventy percent of the customer names start with the word "Video". A large number of those stores have identical names, such as Video Palace, Video Stop, Video Hut, and so on. In fact, some customers are individual stores that are owned by a chain; so all the names are identical (except for the store number). To make it possible for each customer in the system to have a unique customer name, we use telephone numbers (including the area code).

If you have multiple customers named Jack Johnson, you may want to enter them as JohnsonJack001, JohnsonJack002, and so on. You can use all of these suggestions to come up with a protocol for creating unique customer codes in your QuickBooks company file.

NOTE: *You can use up to 41 characters in the Customer Name field.*

Importing the Customer List

If you've been keeping a customer list in another software application, you can avoid one-customer-at-a-time data entry by importing the list into QuickBooks. You have two methods at your disposal for importing the list:

- Import the list directly from an Excel file or a CSV file.
- Import the list from an IIF file.

If you've been using another application, you must export the data from that application to create your import file. This is only possible if your current application is capable of exporting data to one of the following formats:

- Excel file
- CSV (comma separated value) file
- Tab-delimited text file.

All three of these file types can be opened in Excel. If you use another spreadsheet application, you can use a CSV file or a tab-delimited text file (and some spreadsheet software is capable of loading Excel files and converting them to their own document type).

If you keep your customer list on paper, or in a software application that can't export to the required file type, you can enter the customer information in a spreadsheet and then import the data. It's much faster to work in the rows of a spreadsheet document than to move from field to field, one customer dialog at a time, in QuickBooks.

A QuickBooks customer import file can contain all the information you need to fill out all the fields in the customer dialog, such as customer type, sales tax status, and so on. It's unlikely you've kept records in a manner that matches these fields, but you can import whatever information you already have, and later enter additional information by editing the customer records.

Detailed instructions for creating and importing Excel/CSV files are in Appendix A, and detailed instructions for creating and importing IIF files are in Appendix B. These instructions include all the column headings and keywords for importing customers and jobs.

Vendor List

Your vendors have to be entered into your QuickBooks system, and it's easier to do it while you're setting up your company instead of during transaction entry.

NOTE: *If you've used QuickBooks before, note that the Vendor List is now available only in the Vendor Center. The list no longer appears in the List menu or the Vendors menu.*

Importing the Vendor List

If you've been tracking vendors in Excel, or even in Word, or in another software application, you can import the vendor list into QuickBooks, which saves all that one-customer-at-a-time data entry you'd have to perform in QuickBooks. You have two methods at your disposal for importing the list:

• Import the list directly from an Excel file or a CSV file.
• Import the list from an IIF file.

If you've been using another application, you must export the data from that application to create your import file. This is only possible if your current application is capable of exporting data to one of the following formats:

• Excel file
• CSV (comma separated value) file
• Tab-delimited text file.

All three of these file types can be opened in Excel. If you use another spreadsheet application, you can use a CSV file or a tab-delimited text file (and some spreadsheet software is capable of loading Excel files and converting them to their own document type).

If you keep your vendor list on paper, or in a software application that can't export to the required file type, you can enter the vendor information in a spreadsheet and then import the data. It's much faster to work in the rows of a spreadsheet document than to move from field to field, one customer dialog at a time, in QuickBooks.

A QuickBooks vendor import file can contain all the information you need to fill out all the fields in the vendor dialog. Detailed instructions for creating and importing Excel/CSV files are in Appendix A, and detailed instructions for creating and importing IIF files are in Appendix B. These instructions include all the column headings and keywords for importing vendors.

Fixed Asset Item List

Use the Fixed Asset Item List to track information about the assets you depreciate. As you can see in Figure 4-1, the dialog for a fixed asset includes fields that allow you to keep rather detailed information. The dialog also has fields to track the sale of a depreciated asset.

Why to Skip the Fixed Asset Item List

The Fixed Asset item List is inert. It doesn't do anything, and isn't used for any type of transaction in QuickBooks. It's not any different from a list you could keep in Microsoft Word. If you design a table in Word, with a column for each category you want to track, you can sort the table to match whatever information you need to see.

QuickBooks has a tool named Depreciate Your Assets, and you can use it to determine depreciation rates in QuickBooks. The Depreciate Your Assets tool doesn't link to the Fixed Asset Item list. This means that when you use the tool you have to enter fixed asset information manually—all the same information you entered in the Fixed Asset Item List. (The Depreciate Your Assets tool is discussed in Chapter 13 of *QuickBooks 2006: The Official Guide*).

However, those are minor annoyances. The real problem with putting all your fixed assets in this list is that QuickBooks adds all the fixed assets you keep in this list to the Items list you see when you're creating a transaction. You have to scroll through all the fixed asset entries as well as your "regular" items to select an item for the transaction. If you have a lot of items and a lot of fixed assets, this is really a pain!

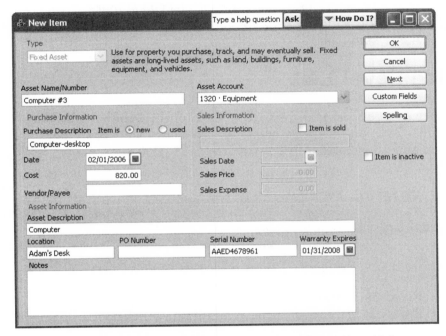

Figure 4-1: Track depreciable assets in the Fixed Asset Item List.

When the Fixed Asset Item List is Useful

QuickBooks Premier Accountant Edition includes Fixed Asset Manager, a tool that *does* use the information in the Fixed Asset Item list to generate depreciation.

Fixed Asset Manager automatically performs depreciation transactions, applying depreciation amounts to the appropriate fixed asset accounts. If your accountant uses Fixed Asset Manager, you can send your company file or an Accountant's copy file to automate the process of depreciating your assets. Since this may make your accountant's work easier and faster, it may reduce your bill for tax preparation. That trade-off may be worth the annoyances that come with the decision to use the Fixed Asset Item List.

NOTE: *See Chapter 11 of this book, and Appendix A of the copy of QuickBooks 2006: The Official Guide that's in your Premier Edition package for information about using Fixed Asset Manager.*

Price Level List

The Price Level List is a nifty, easy way to fine-tune your pricing schemes. You can use price levels to make sure your customers are happy, and your bottom line is healthy.

NOTE: *The Price Levels List only appears on the Lists menu if you enabled Price Levels in the Sales & Customers section of your Preferences dialog.*

QuickBooks Premier editions offer two types of price levels:

- Fixed percentage price levels
- Per item price levels (not available in QuickBooks Basic and Pro editions)

Fixed Percentage Price Levels

Fixed percentage price levels can be applied to a customer, a job, or an individual sales transaction. The price levels are applied against the standard price of items (as recorded in each item's record).

For example, you may want to create a price level that gives your favorite customers an excellent discount. Another common price reduction scheme is a discounted price level for all customers that are nonprofit organizations.

On the other hand, you may want to maintain your item prices for most customers, and increase them by a fixed percentage for certain customers. (You can also apply the price level to an individual sale, such as an estimate, invoice, or cash receipt.)

To create a percentage-based price level, open the Price Level List by choosing Lists → Price Level List from the QuickBooks menu bar. When the Price Level List window opens (see Figure 4-2), follow these steps:

1. Press Ctrl-N to open the New Price Level dialog.
2. Enter a name in the Price Level Name field. Use a name that reflects the algorithm you're using for this price level, such as 10Off (for a ten percent reduction).
3. In the Price Level Type field, select Fixed % from the drop-down list, if it's not already selected.
4. Specify whether the price level is a decrease or increase against an item price.
5. Enter the percentage of increase or decrease. (You don't have to enter the percent sign—QuickBooks will automatically add it.)
6. Click OK.

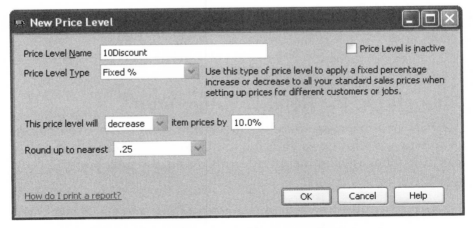

Figure 4-2: A fixed percentage price level is uncomplicated and easy to create.

Rounding Prices

When you use a percentage-based price level, the resulting price is usually not an even dollar amount (and can also result in partial cents). QuickBooks lets you set a rounding algorithm for your price levels.

To select a rounding algorithm, click the arrow to the right of the field labeled Round Up To Nearest, and select the rounding amount to apply to this price level from the drop-down list (see Figure 4-3).

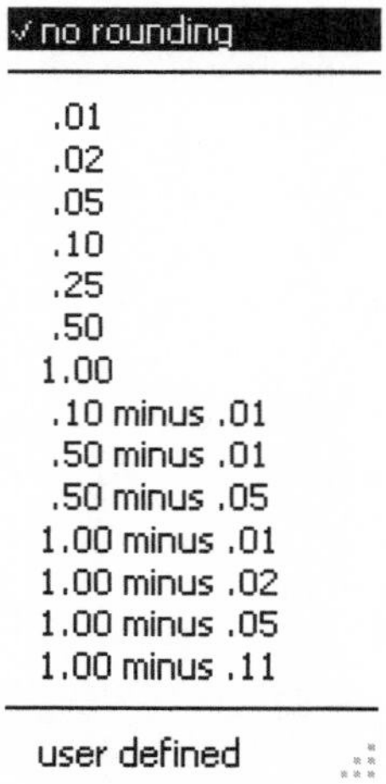

```
√ no rounding

  .01
  .02
  .05
  .10
  .25
  .50
 1.00
  .10 minus .01
  .50 minus .01
  .50 minus .05
 1.00 minus .01
 1.00 minus .02
 1.00 minus .05
 1.00 minus .11

 user defined
```

Figure 4-3: Tell QuickBooks how to round up the resulting price after this price level is applied.

Customizing the Rounding Algorithm

You can customize the rounding algorithm, which gives you more precision, and also gives you the ability to use standard, normal, rounding rules (which means you can round down when it's appropriate).

To create your own, customized, rounding scheme, select User Defined from the Rounding drop-down list (it's at the bottom of the list). The dialog adds fields to accommodate your creation of the custom rounding algorithm (see Figure 4-4).

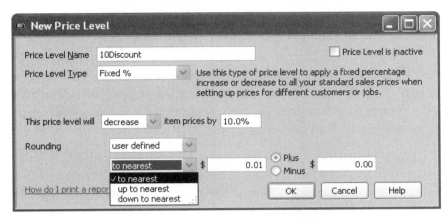

Figure 4-4: Create a rounding scheme that is precisely what you
want.

Applying the Fixed Percentage Price Level

You can link price levels to customers and jobs, or apply price levels
while you're creating sales forms (invoices, sales orders, sales receipts,
and credit memos). The method you use produces different results, as follows:

- If you link a price level to customers or jobs, the price level is
  automatically applied to all items whenever you use that customer
  or job on a sales form.
- If you apply the price level while you're creating a sales form, the
  price level is applied against the standard price for the item. If the
  item is already discounted because of a price level applied to the
  customer, that discounted price is ignored in favor of the price
  level you're applying to the sales form.

Linking a Fixed Percentage Price Level to Customers and Jobs

To link a price level to a customer or a job, you need to edit the customer
or job record to reflect the link. Open the Customers & Jobs list in the
Customer Center and take the following actions:

1. Double-click the listing for the customer or job you want to link to
   a price level, to open the Edit Customer dialog.
2. Move to the Additional Info tab.

3. Click the arrow in the Price Level field to display a drop-down list of all the price levels you've created.
4. Select the appropriate price level.
5. Click OK.

Repeat this for all the customers and jobs you want to link to a price level. Be aware of the following "rules" governing the application of price levels to customers and jobs:

- If you link a price level to a customer, it does not apply to that customer's jobs. You will only see the price level applied if you create a sales form for the customer (which is hardly ever done when you're tracking jobs).
- If you link a price level to a job, only sales forms related to that specific job reflect the price level.

These rules make it possible to apply different price levels to each of a customer's jobs, if that's your plan. Unfortunately, that's hardly ever the plan (at least it's rare in the client sites I visit, and in the accountant seminars I give or attend).

Unfortunately, QuickBooks didn't think to include a dialog that pops up when you apply a price level to a customer, and asks if you want to apply that price level to all of the jobs for that customer.

It would be even nicer if such a dialog box included the selection "apply to future jobs for this customer".

It would be absolutely terrific if the dialog listed all the current jobs, so you could select those that should be configured for this price level, along with the "Apply this to future jobs" option.

Since none of these helpful tools are available, I created a workaround. See the section "Applying Price Levels to Customers and Jobs in Batches", later in this chapter.

Applying a Fixed Percentage Price Level in a Sales Form

You can change the price of an item on a sales form by applying a price level as you create the sales form. This gives you quite a bit of flexibility for passing along discounts (or price hikes) to any customer. Use the following steps to apply a price level to a sales form:

1. Fill out the sales form in the usual way.
2. Click the arrow in the Rate column to display your price levels (see Figure 4-5).
3. Select a price level to apply to the item.

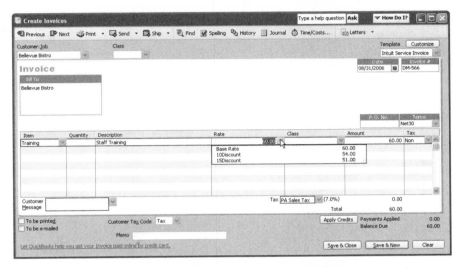

Figure 4-5: The drop-down list shows each price level, and its resulting price.

This can get complicated, because the price level you're selecting is applied to the recorded price of the item (the price you entered in the item's record when you created the item), which may not be the price displayed on the sales form.

If you linked a price level to the customer, the price on the sales form reflects the application of the price level. Applying another price level at this point may be butting into a rate that has already had a price level applied. The price level you select while working in the sales form wins—any amount calculated by a customer-linked price level is overwritten.

For example, the customer in the invoice seen in Figure 4-6 is linked to a price level that caused the item's price to be reduced automatically by 15%. If you select a 10% price level decrease from the drop-down list in the sales form, the customer pays more. While the ability to set a price level in a sales form gives you some flexibility in determining prices for a customer, you need to be careful about undoing a promised discount.

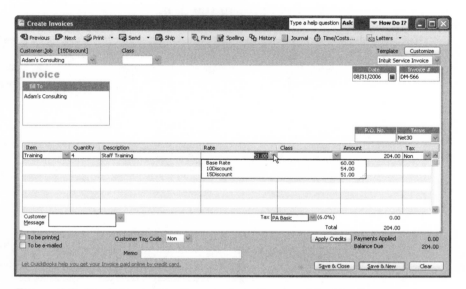

Figure 4-6: Don't inadvertently select a price level that isn't as good as the discount already linked to this customer.

Applying Price Levels to Customers in Batches

If you already had a large number of customers and jobs in your system when you created percentage-based price levels, you have to open each customer record, and each job record, move to the Additional Info tab, and assign a price level by selecting one from the drop-down list in the Price Level field.

That's a lot of work, and besides, it's so boring! And, you have to do the same thing if you create new price levels that you want to assign to customers to replace existing price levels, or assign to customers for whom you hadn't previously assigned price levels. More time consuming, boring work!

There's an easier way. Export your customer list to an IIF file, and assign the price levels in Excel, which is a snap to do! Then import the new data into your QuickBooks customer records.

The following sections offer some tricks and tips to help you do this smoothly. But first, back up your company file before doing anything else. Whenever you're going to import data, you should have a current backup to restore in case something goes wrong.

Note the Names of the Price Levels

You must use the price level names that exist in your system in your import file, so you must make sure you have the names exactly right. Punctuation, spaces, etc. must be exactly the same as the price level names in your system. I have a foolproof system for this that you can use, too.

1. Open a word processing program. I use Word, but you could just as easily use WordPad or Notepad.
2. Double-click the first price level listing to open its record in edit mode. The price level name is highlighted.
3. Press Ctrl-C to put the highlighted text on the Windows clipboard.
4. Switch to the word processor and press Ctrl-V to paste the text.
5. Open each fixed percentage price level listing and repeat the process.

Save the document, and leave it open. It provides the text you'll paste into your worksheet when you create your import file.

> *TIP*: Remember that you can only assign fixed percentage price levels to customers, so don't use per-item price levels for this task.

Eliminate Unneeded Cells

After you export the file and open Excel, select all the rows on top of the first row of real data. The first row of real data is the row that has !CUST in column 1.

To select the rows, click the row number to the left of Column A and then hold the Shift Key and click the last row above the first row of real data. When all the rows are selected (see Figure 4-7), click Edit → Delete.

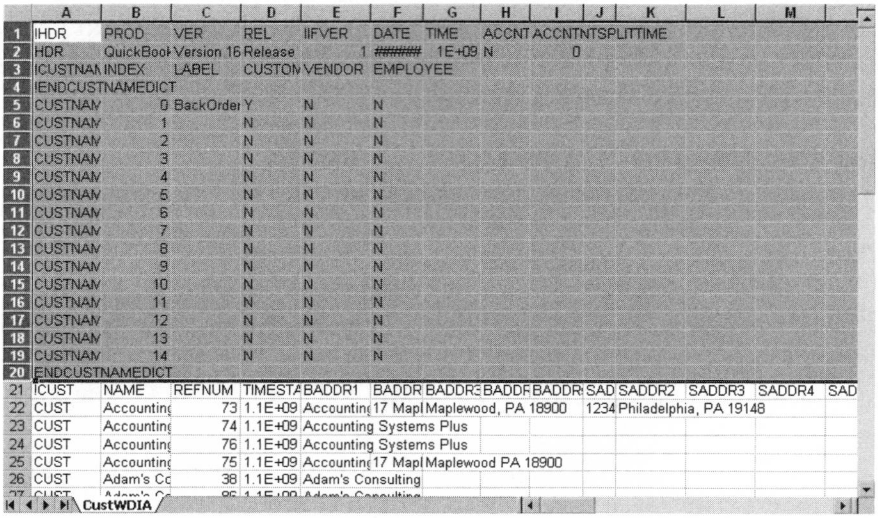

Figure 4-7: Eliminate unneeded data to make it easier to work in the spreadsheet.

Now your worksheet contains only the data about your customers, but some of the columns aren't need, so let's get rid of them. The following two columns contain information you don't need when you import the file back into QuickBooks: REFNUM and TIMESTAMP.

However, you need a blank column near the NAME column, so you can enter the price level information (the PRICELEVEL column is way way over to the right, and it's easier to move it next to the customer data so you can see your customers' names as you enter the price level data). Therefore, take the following steps:

1. Select one of the two unneeded columns (it doesn't matter which one) by clicking its column heading above Row 1.
2. Click Edit → Delete to remove the column.
3. Select the other column by clicking its column heading above Row 1.

4. Press the Del key to remove the data, but keep the column—you have a blank column.

Move the Price Level Column Next to the Name Column

It's easier to link price levels to customers when the data columns are next to each other. A QuickBooks import file doesn't have to be in any particular column order, so you can put the price level column next to the customer name column.

If you've already linked price levels to some customers, you don't want to lose that data, so use the following steps to move the data to a more convenient place in the worksheet:

1. Scroll all the way right to find the column named PRICELEVEL, and select the entire column by clicking its column heading, above Row 1.
2. Choose Edit → Cut
3. Move to the blank column you created (next to the NAME column), and click the cell in Row 1 to select it (don't select the column, just click in the top cell).
4. Choose Edit → Paste.

Your existing price level data is in Column C, next to the NAME column.

If you haven't linked any price levels to any customers, use the first two steps in the previous section to remove the PRICELEVEL column from its position at the end of the worksheet.

Then, in Row 1 of the blank column, enter the text PRICELEVEL to create a column for receiving price level data.

Entering Price Level Data

When you're working in Excel, you can take advantage of the Windows clipboard and the Excel data entry tools to enter data.

1. In your word processor, select the first price level name you want to assign to customers. Press Ctrl-C to place the text in the Windows clipboard.

2. In the PRICELEVEL column, select the cell next to the first customer to whom you want to assign this price level

3. Press Ctrl-V to paste the price level name into the cell (or right-click in the cell and choose Paste).

4. Move to the cell next to the next customer you want to assign this price level to and press Ctrl-V to paste the text there. Continue to paste until you've pasted this price level for all the customers who should have it. (Once you have text in the Windows clipboard, you can continue to paste it endlessly, as long as you don't stop pasting to perform another task.)

5. Select the next price level from the word processor, press Ctrl-C to copy it to the clipboard, then return to the worksheet and paste the text in the PRICELEVEL column next to every customer who gets this price level.

6. Keep going until you've assigned all your price levels to all the customers who get price level assignments.

You've probably noticed that I said "customer" not "customer and job" when I discussed assigning price levels.

If you want all the jobs for a customer to have the same price level as you assigned to the customer, there's an easier way to accomplish that—you don't have to paste text one cell at a time.

1. Return to the first customer with a price level assignment, and select the cell that has the price level.

2. Position your mouse pointer in the lower right corner of the cell, until the pointer changes to vertical and horizontal intersecting lines.

3. Drag the right corner down the column, through all the job listings for this customer. Excel copies the text, and the same price level is now assigned to every job.

4. Repeat for every customer that has jobs.

If there are any jobs that have a different price level than that assigned to the customer, or any customer who has a job with a price level, but the customer doesn't have a price level assignment, you can enter that data manually.

Importing the Price Level Data

You can import the data back into your QuickBooks company file with an IIF file, or with an Excel file. An Excel file import is easier and faster, so that's the method I'll discuss.

Choose File → Save As in Excel, and save the worksheet as an Excel File. Name the file appropriately (e.g. Price Levels.xls). Then close Excel.

In QuickBooks, choose File → Utilities → Import → Excel Files to open the Import a File dialog (see Figure 4-8). Complete instructions and explanations for importing Excel files into QuickBooks are in Appendix A, but I'll go over the steps here in a brief fashion.

Figure 4-8: Configure the QuickBooks Import feature to accept the data in your Excel file.

1. Click Browse and select the file containing the price level data.
2. Select a sheet from the drop-down list.
3. In the Choose A Mapping field, choose <Add New> from the drop-down list.
4. In the Mapping dialog, name the mapping (e.g. Price Levels).
5. In the Import Type field, select Customer (this is a required entry when importing to a customer file).
6. In the Import Data list box, click next to the Job or Customer Name listing, and choose NAME from the drop-down list.
7. Scroll through the list box to find the Price Level listing, click in the Import Data box to the right of that listing, and choose PRICELEVEL from the drop-down list. (The PRICELEVEL listing is near the top of the drop-down list because you moved that column next to the NAME list in your worksheet).
8. Click Save.
9. Click Import. (QuickBooks asks if you want to continue the import rather than back up your file first—click Yes to continue the import because you backed up before you started all of this).

All the data is now in your QuickBooks customer and job records. Every time you create a sales transaction, the customer will have the right price.

TIP: You can do the same thing for any data you want to add to QuickBooks records in one fell swoop instead of opening each record one at a time. For example, you may need to add or change Terms (for customers and vendors), Sales Tax Items, Types for customers and vendors, data for custom fields (for customers, vendors, and items), etc. etc.

Per Item Price Levels

Available only in QuickBooks Premier editions, per item price levels let you set different prices for each item you sell, and then apply the appropriate price level when you're creating a sales form. This paradigm gives you a great deal of flexibility as you try to enhance your business by balancing individual customer activity and competitive prices.

A per item price level can be a fixed amount (an amount different from the standard price you entered when you created the item), or a percentage (higher or lower than the standard price).

To create an item price level, choose Lists → Price Level List to open the Price Level List window. Then, follow these steps:

1. Press Ctrl-N to open the New Price Level dialog.
2. Enter a name for the price level in the Price Level Name field.
3. Select Per Item in the Price Level Type field. The dialog displays all the items in your Items list, as seen in Figure 4-9.

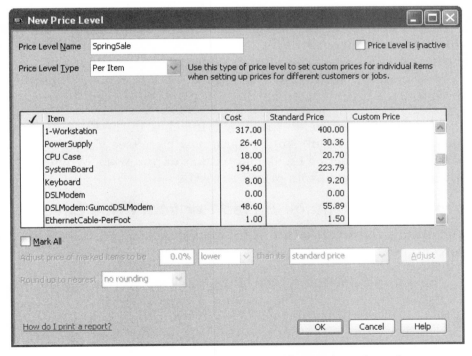

Figure 4-9: Create special price levels for specific goods and services.

Now you can create a fixed price level, or a percentage-based price level, as described in the following sections.

NOTE: *The Per Item Price Level dialog includes columns for the cost and the price of inventory items, so you can't inadvertently reduce a price to the point that you lose money. However, other item types (services, other charges, non-inventory items) have no costs associated with them. You must be aware of cost, including overhead, when you create reduced prices for these items.*

Creating Fixed Rate Per item Price Levels

You can create a specific price as the new price level, and it can be higher or lower than the standard price (depending on the way in which you plan to use price levels).

Start by naming the price level, using text that will remind you of the algorithm you're using for the price changes. For example, if you're creating special prices for a limited-time sale, use a name like SpringSpecial. If you're creating special prices that have a specific dollar discount, use a name like 10$Off.

To set a new price level for any item, click in the Custom Price column of the item's listing, and enter a new price (see Figure 4-10). You can perform this action on as many items as you wish. When you are finished entering the custom prices, click OK.

Creating Percentage-Based Per Item Price Levels

You can also create price levels for individual items that are based on a percentage of the item's standard price or cost.

Select an item, or multiple items, by clicking in the leftmost column to place a check mark in that column. You can choose the Select All option to select all the items, and if you want to exclude a few items, click the leftmost column to remove their check marks (the check mark is a toggle).

When all the items for this percentage-based price level are selected, fill in the fields at the bottom of the dialog (the section labeled Adjust Price Of Marked Items To Be).

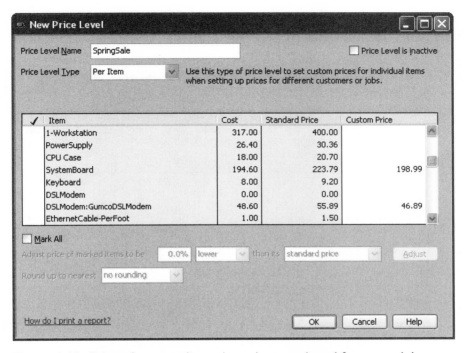

Figure 4-10: Prices for some items have been reduced for a special sale.

Enter the percentage for this price level. You aren't restricted to whole numbers; you can enter 8.5 or 7.25 if you wish. You only have to enter the number—QuickBooks automatically adds the percent sign.

In the next field, select Lower or Higher from the drop-down list. Then select one of the following options from the drop-down list in the next field:

- Standard Price, which applies the percentage to the item's price as established in the item's record. Usually this would be applied to a price level for which you selected Lower in the previous field.
- Cost, which applies the percentage to the item's cost as established in the item's record. Usually this would be applied to a price level for which you selected Higher in the previous field.
- Custom Price, which applies the percentage to a custom price you created for the item (covered next).

Select a rounding algorithm, and then click the Adjust button to have QuickBooks calculate the prices (see Figure 4-11)

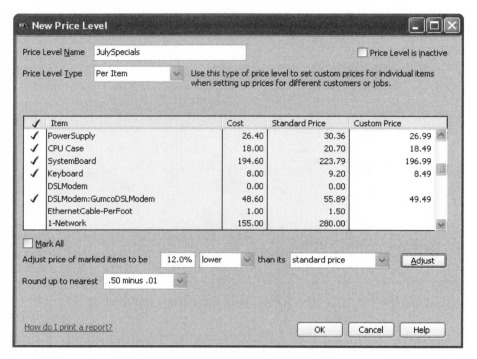

Figure 4-11: You can design a percentage-based price level based on the price or cost of selected items.

Creating Percentage Changes for Custom Prices

If you've created a per-item price level that's a fixed amount (instead of a percentage change), you can apply a percentage-based price level against that custom price. This is useful for raising or lowering custom prices for a specific reason, commonly for a sale that lasts a specific amount of time.

To accomplish this, create a price level for per-item fixed custom prices, changing the prices of selected items. Select the items that have custom prices that you want to include in this price level scheme. Then use the fields at the bottom of the dialog to enter a percentage amount, select Lower (unless you're raising prices, in which case select Higher), and in the last field choose Current Custom Price.

When you click Adjust, QuickBooks applies your percentage change against the custom price of the items you selected.

Printing Price Level Reports

QuickBooks provides printable reports on price levels, but they're not well thought out, and not well designed, so you have to modify the reports to make them useful. You can create and print a report on a specific price level, or on all the price levels in your system.

Printing a Specific Price Level Scheme

To create a report on a specific price level, right-click the price level's listing in the Price Level List window and choose Price Level Report from the shortcut menu.

The report that opens isn't suitable for printing and sending to customers, nor for your own use if you want to discuss special pricing with a customer. By default the report displays four columns: Item, Description, Preferred Vendor, and the prices for each item in this price level scheme.

You need to modify the report so it displays the standard price of each item, in addition to the price for this price level (so you can see the difference). Also, there's no need to include the preferred vendor. Follow these steps to modify the report:

1. Click Modify Report to open the Modify Report dialog with the Display tab in the foreground.
2. In the Columns list, deselect the Preferred Vendor.
3. In the Columns list, select Price.
4. Click OK.

If the report displays items that have no prices (the price is set at zero), use the Filters tab in the Modify Report dialog to remove them from the report. Select Price in the Filter list, and filter the criteria so only prices greater than .01 are displayed (see Figure 4-12).

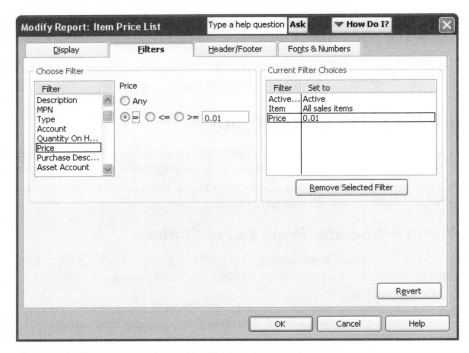

Figure 4-12: Remove items that lack prices.

If this price level scheme only applied price levels to one type of items (e.g., inventory items), you can remove the other item types from the report, which usually makes the report much shorter and easier to read.

To restrict the report to the single item type involved in this price level, go to the Filters tab and select Type in the Filter list. In the Type field, select the appropriate item type from the drop-down list.

Unfortunately, there's no way to have the report list only those items with prices that differ in this price level scheme, and eliminate the items that aren't affected.

If you want to send a printed copy of this report to customers, you can hope they'll notice which items are affected, or you can export the report to Excel, tweak it, and then print it from Excel.

To tweak the report in Excel, you can remove all the items that aren't affected by this price level, and enter formulas that show and "sell" the difference in price, as seen in Figure 4-13.

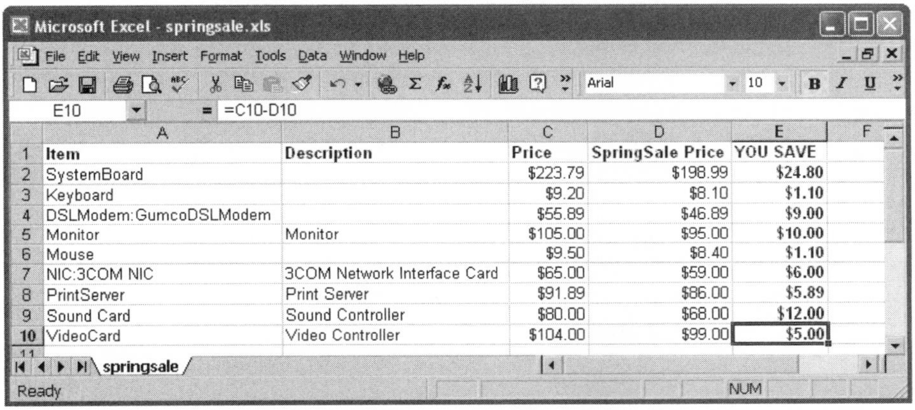

	Item	Description	Price	SpringSale Price	YOU SAVE
2	SystemBoard		$223.79	$198.99	$24.80
3	Keyboard		$9.20	$8.10	$1.10
4	DSLModem:GumcoDSLModem		$55.89	$46.89	$9.00
5	Monitor	Monitor	$105.00	$95.00	$10.00
6	Mouse		$9.50	$8.40	$1.10
7	NIC:3COM NIC	3COM Network Interface Card	$65.00	$59.00	$6.00
8	PrintServer	Print Server	$91.89	$86.00	$5.89
9	Sound Card	Sound Controller	$80.00	$68.00	$12.00
10	VideoCard	Video Controller	$104.00	$99.00	$5.00

Figure 4-13: Use the features in Excel to show customers how this price level saves them money.

Printing a Report on All Price Levels

It's a good idea to have a list of all price levels in the office, so your sales calls can quote accurate current prices. QuickBooks doesn't offer such a report, but it's rather easy to build one, using the following steps:

1. Choose Reports → List → Item Price List. All of your items appear, along with their recorded standard prices.
2. Click Modify Report.
3. In the Display tab, deselect the Preferred Vendor listing (I also remove the Description listing to make the report less crowded).
4. In the Display tab, scroll through the Columns list and select your price levels by name (the listings are at the bottom of the Columns list).
5. In the Filters tab, remove zero prices, and, if applicable, select the Type that your price level schemes affect.
6. Click OK to return to the report window, which now displays columns for all your price levels (see Figure 4-14).

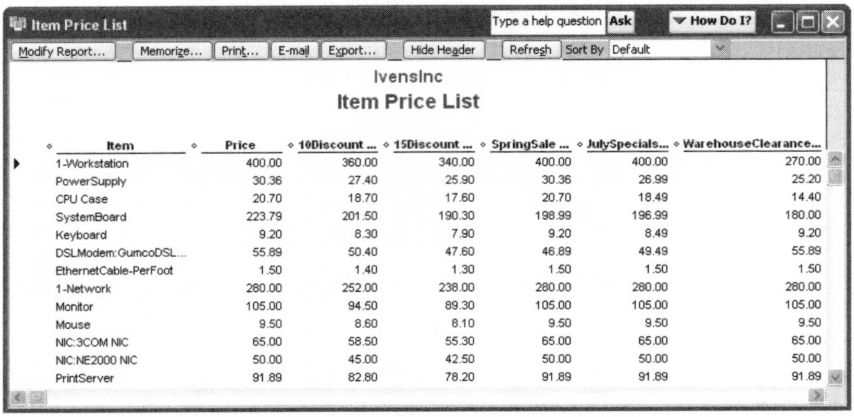

IvensInc

Item Price List

Item	Price	10Discount ...	15Discount ...	SpringSale ...	JulySpecials...	WarehouseClearance...
1-Workstation	400.00	360.00	340.00	400.00	400.00	270.00
PowerSupply	30.36	27.40	25.90	30.36	26.99	25.20
CPU Case	20.70	18.70	17.60	20.70	18.49	14.40
SystemBoard	223.79	201.50	190.30	198.99	196.99	180.00
Keyboard	9.20	8.30	7.90	9.20	8.49	9.20
DSLModem:GumcoDSL...	55.89	50.40	47.60	46.89	49.49	55.89
EthernetCable-PerFoot	1.50	1.40	1.30	1.50	1.50	1.50
1-Network	280.00	252.00	238.00	280.00	280.00	280.00
Monitor	105.00	94.50	89.30	105.00	105.00	105.00
Mouse	9.50	8.60	8.10	9.50	9.50	9.50
NIC:3COM NIC	65.00	58.50	55.30	65.00	65.00	65.00
NIC:NE2000 NIC	50.00	45.00	42.50	50.00	50.00	50.00
PrintServer	91.89	82.80	78.20	91.89	91.89	91.89

Figure 4-14: Keep all your price level data in front of you by printing this customized report.

***TIP**: Memorize this report so you don't have to go through all this customization again.*

Using Per Item Price Levels in Sales Forms

Because per item price levels can't be linked to customers, you can only apply the price level when you're creating a sales form. Enter the item in the sales transaction, click the arrow in the Rate column to display your price levels, and select the appropriate price level.

But wait! It's not as easy and straightforward as the previous paragraph implies. Assigning a per-item price level is dandy, if the price in the Rate column is the standard, recorded price that appears in the item's record. However, if the price displayed in the Rate column is the result of an assigned price level, be careful about assigning a per-item price level that conflicts with customer expectations.

Billing Rate Level List

The Billing Rate Level list lets you assign a billing rate to a person performing a specific service (the *service provider*). This list is only available in the following Premier Editions:

- Accountant Edition
- Contractor Edition
- Professional Services Edition

After you create billing rate levels, and associate them with service providers, invoicing for services becomes automatic. Every time you create an invoice with billable time, QuickBooks automatically fills in the correct rate for the service, based on the person who performed the work.

To track services for each service provider and associated billing rate level, the service providers must use the QuickBooks Timesheet feature. You can learn how to set up and use timesheets in Chapter 18 of *QuickBooks 2006: The Official Guide.*

Creating Billing Rate Levels

To create a billing rate level, choose Lists → Billing Rate Level List. When the list window opens, press Ctrl-N to open the New Billing Rate Level dialog. You can choose either of the following types of billing rate levels:

- A Fixed Hourly Rate, which is a specific hourly rate assigned to certain service providers.
- Custom Hourly Rate per Service Item, which is a rate tied to a service, but it differs depending on the rate assigned to the service provider.

Creating a Fixed Hourly Billing Rate

To create a fixed billing rate that you can assign to a service provider, select Fixed Hourly Rate as the rate type. Then, enter a name for this billing rate level, and enter its hourly rate (see Figure 4-15).

After you link this billing rate to service providers, you can automatically invoice customers at this rate for any service performed by those people. Create all the fixed hourly rates you need.

Creating a Custom Hourly Billing Rate

To create a custom hourly rate, enter a name for the rate, and then select Custom Hourly Rate Per Service Item. The dialog changes to display all your service items (see Figure 4-16). Enter the hourly rate for each service that is performed by a person linked to this billing rate.

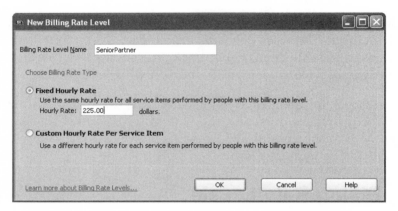

Figure 4-15: Establish an hourly billing rate you can link to specific service providers.

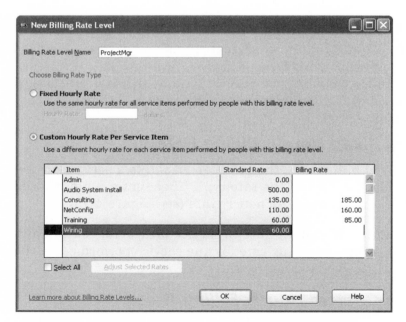

Figure 4-16: Select the services linked to this billing rate, and enter the hourly rates.

Creating a Percentage-Based Custom Rate

You can also create a custom rate by applying a percentage against the standard rate for a service. For example, you might want to set a rate of 10% more than the standard rate for service providers linked to the rate.

To accomplish this, follow the instructions for creating a custom hourly billing rate in the previous paragraph. Select the services you want to include, and then click Adjust Selected Rates (see Figure 4-17). Configure the adjusted rate as follows:

- Indicate a percentage by which you want to raise or lower the rate based on the standard rate for the selected services.
- Indicate a percentage by which you want to raise or lower the rate based on the current billing rate level (one that you entered in the dialog before beginning the adjustment).

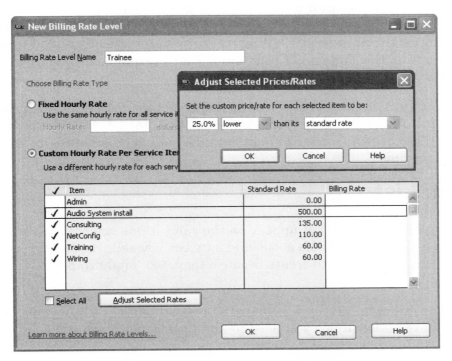

Figure 4-17: Automatically adjust a billing level by a percentage to create a custom rate.

QuickBooks multiplies the amount by the percentage, and automatically fills in the rate.

Assigning Billing Rate Levels to Service Providers

After you've created billing rate levels, you must assign a level to each service provider. To do this, open the appropriate names list (Vendor, Employee, or Other Names) and select a service provider. Edit the record by selecting a rate from the Billing Rate Level drop-down list. (In the Vendor and Employee lists, you must go to the Additional Info tab to find the Billing Rate Level field.)

Invoicing for Billing Rate Levels

To prepare invoices that use billing rate levels, you must use the timesheets that each service provider hands in. When you invoice your customers, the appropriate billing rates are automatically added to the invoice from the Time and Costs dialog that's available on the Invoice window.

You can also apply any customer's percentage price level (usually a discount) to the billing rate invoice items. Chapter 18 of *QuickBooks 2006: The Official Guide* has detailed information on creating invoices based on time.

Item List

Items are the things that appear on the sales forms you create, so your Items list contains all the goods and services you sell. However, there are other items you need to create because they, too, might appear on a sales form.

For example, sales tax is an item, as is shipping. Less obvious are some of the other items you need to add to sales forms as you sell your goods and services to customers, such as prepayments received, discounts applied, subtotals, and so on.

Understanding Item Types

Before you create the items you need to run your business, you should understand the item types that QuickBooks offers. Following are the names (and explanations) of the item types available when you create items:

Service

A service you sell to a customer. You can create services that are charged by the job or by the hour.

Inventory Part

A product you buy for reselling. This item type isn't available if you haven't enabled inventory tracking in the Purchases & Vendors category of the Preferences dialog.

Inventory Assembly

An item you build, usually from inventory parts. This item type is only available in QuickBooks Premier and Enterprise Editions. (See Chapter 6 to learn about using inventory assemblies.)

Non-Inventory Part

Use this item type for products that you don't track as inventory. This could be products you sell (without tracking inventory), or, if you *do* track inventory, the supplies you use for boxing and shipping inventory parts (e.g. tape, labels, and so on).

Other Charge

Use this item type for things like shipping charges, or other line items that appear on your invoices. In fact, some people create a separate Other Charge item for each method of shipping.

Subtotal

This item type adds up everything that comes before it on a sales form. You can use it to calculate a subtotal before you subtract any discounts or prepayments.

Group

You can use this item type to enter a group of items (all of which must already exist in your Item list) all at once. For example, if you frequently have a shipping charge and sales tax on the same invoice, you can create a group item that includes those two items.

Discount

Use this item type to give a discount as a line item. When you enter an item of the Discount Type, you can indicate a percentage as the rate.

Payment

Use this item type to add a customer's prepayment to an invoice. QuickBooks automatically calculates the total appropriately

Sales Tax Item and Sales Tax Group

Use these item types to add sales tax to an invoice. Sales tax gets complicated in some states, and you have to be extremely careful about the way you set up sales tax items. Chapter 3 explains how to set up sales tax items and groups.s

TIP: *I've described all of the item types in terms of their use on your invoices, but some are used on purchase orders, too.*

Creating Items

To create an item, open the Items List by clicking the Items & Services icon on the Home page, or by choosing Lists → Item List from the menu bar. Then press Ctrl-N to open the New Item dialog.

Select the item type from the Type drop-down list. The item type you select determines the appearance of the New Item dialog, because different item types have different fields.

NOTE: *Chapter 2 of QuickBooks 2006: The Official Guide has complete instructions for creating items.*

Creating Subitems

After you've created an item, you can create subitems. For example, for a particular product you can create subitems for different manufacturers. Or, you can create subitems for product sizes, types, colors, or other variations in the product. Not all item types support subitems—look for the Subitem Of field on the New Item dialog.

To create a subitem, use the same steps required to create an item, and then click the Subitem Of option, and select the appropriate parent item from the drop-down list.

Importing the Item List

If you've been keeping your list of items in another software application, or on paper, you can avoid one-item-at-a-time data entry by importing the list into QuickBooks. You have two methods at your disposal for importing the list:

- Import the list directly from an Excel file or a CSV file.
- Import the list from an IIF file.

If you've been using another application, you must export the data from that application to create your import file. This is only possible if your current application is capable of exporting data to one of the following formats:

- Excel file
- CSV (comma separated value) file
- Tab-delimited text file.

All three of these file types can be opened in Excel. If you use another spreadsheet application, you can use a CSV file or a tab-delimited text file (and some spreadsheet software is capable of loading Excel files and converting them to their own document type).

If you keep your item list on paper, or in a software application that can't export to the required file type, you can enter the information in a spreadsheet and then import the data into QuickBooks. It's usually faster to work in the rows of a spreadsheet document than to move from field to field, one item dialog at a time, in QuickBooks.

A QuickBooks item import file can contain all the information you need to fill out all the fields in the item dialog, but it's unlikely you've kept records in a manner that matches these fields. You can import whatever information you already have, and later enter additional information by editing the item records.

Detailed instructions for creating and importing Excel/CSV files are in Appendix A, and detailed instructions for creating and importing IIF files are in Appendix B. These instructions include all the column headings and keywords you need to import items into your QuickBooks company file.

Manipulating List Data

You can perform the following actions on records in your lists:

- Edit the fields in the record (see the Note below for exceptions).
- Delete the record, providing no transactions are attached to the record.
- Hide the record by making it inactive.
- Merge two records to combine their histories.

NOTE: *For an item record, you cannot edit the item's type unless the item is a Non-inventory Part or an Other Charge. All other item types are permanently assigned when you create the item.*

Using a Hidden Record in Transactions

Hiding a record means making it inactive, which you can do by right-clicking the listing and choosing Make Inactive. To see all the entries in a list, including inactive entries, take the following action:

- For the Customers & Jobs, Vendors, and Employees Lists, select All *<List Name>* from the drop-down list at the top of the tab.

- For all other lists, select the Include Inactive option at the bottom of the list window.

When you view all entries, the inactive entries have a large X in the leftmost column.

When a record is hidden, it doesn't appear in drop-down lists in transaction windows. Usually, you make a record inactive because you don't want anyone to use it, and you can't delete it (because it has been involved in transactions).

However, you may have other reasons to hide entries from users who create transactions. Perhaps a customer has a large overdue balance, and you don't want anyone to sell that customer more products or services. You can hide an item that is seasonal, or will be out of stock for a long time, and then re-activate it when it can be sold again. You might want to hide a vendor with whom you're having a dispute to prevent anyone from purchasing goods from that vendor.

You can hide a record and still use it, which is a feature often used by business owners and bookkeepers who don't want other users to involve certain records in transactions (so don't tell other users about this feature).

When you're entering data in a transaction window, don't use the drop-down list in the appropriate field (e.g. Vendor) because of course, the record won't appear in the list. Instead, enter the record name manually.

QuickBooks displays a message asking if you want to use the account just once, or reactivate the account. Click the option to use the account just once. (You can use the account "just once" as many times as you want to.)

Creating Custom Fields In Lists

Custom fields are useful if there's information you want to track, but QuickBooks doesn't provide a field for it. You can add custom fields to the customer, vendor, employee, and item lists.

After you create a custom field, you must populate the field with data in each record that uses the custom field. In addition, you can add the custom field to transaction templates, so you can see the data you entered while you're creating a transaction.

> **TIP**: Most QuickBooks reports let you customize the contents to include the data in custom fields.

Custom Fields for Names Lists

You can add a custom field to any names list except Other Names, which means you can add it to the customer, vendor, and employee lists.

After you create a custom field, you can assign it to multiple names list. I had a client whose business participated in a softball league, and he added a custom field labeled Team Name to his employee, vendor, and customer lists (it was a league for businesses in his industry, and many employees of his local customers and vendors participated).

You can create up to fifteen custom fields, but you can only add seven fields to an individual list. A custom field that overlaps lists count as one field on each list. For example, if you add the same field to all three lists, you can still add six other fields to each list.

To add a custom field to your QuickBooks file that you can apply to a names list, open any employee, vendor, or customer record. It doesn't matter which list you use to create the custom field; after the new field exists you assign it to the names list (or multiple names lists) for which it's intended.

In the record you open, move to the Additional Info tab and click Define Fields. Enter a name for the custom field and select the list(s) to which you want to add this field (see Figure 4-18).

Custom Fields for Items

You can add up to five custom fields for items. However, your custom field won't be available for the following item types:

- Subtotals
- Sales tax items
- Sales tax groups

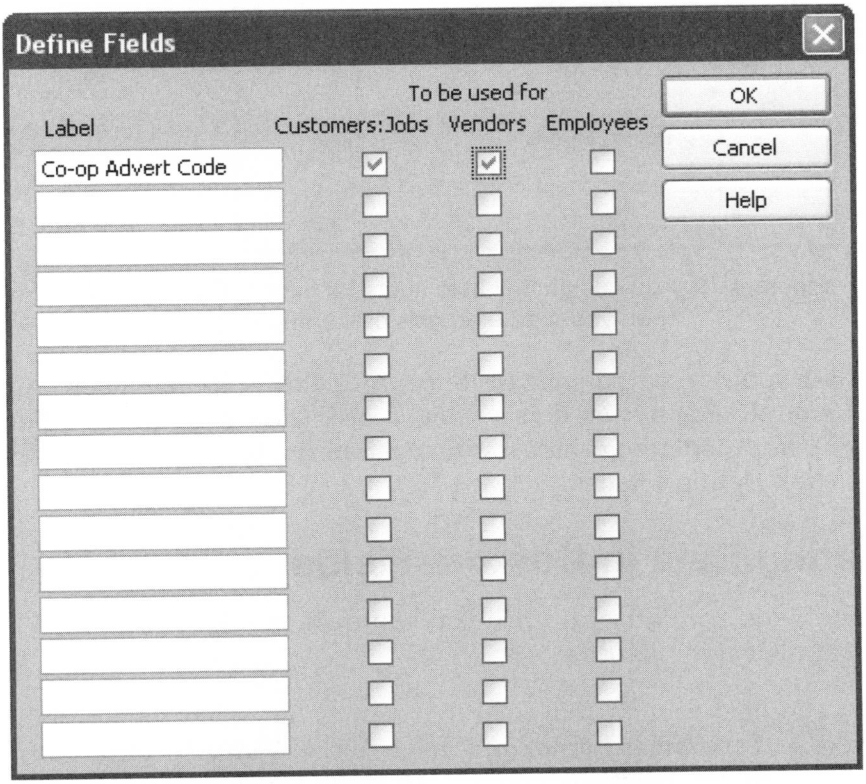

Figure 4-18: Create a custom field and assign it to as many names lists as necessary.

To create a custom field, open any item record, click Custom Fields, and then click Define fields. If this is the first custom field you're creating for items, QuickBooks displays a message saying that no custom fields currently exist, and telling you to click the Define Fields button to create a custom field.

In the Define Custom Fields for Items dialog, enter the custom field name, and select Use to place the field on item records (see Figure 4-19).

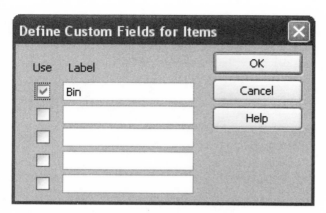

Figure 4-19: Add custom fields to items for information you need
when you create reports or transactions.

After you've created your first custom field for items, when you click
the Custom Fields button on an item record, the Custom Fields For Items
dialog opens, displaying the existing custom fields. To create additional
fields, click Define Fields.

Entering Data in Custom Fields

Custom fields aren't useful until you populate the fields with data in the
names and/or item records.

To add data to a custom field in a names list, open the appropriate
record (e.g. a customer name) and move to the Additional Info tab.
Enter data that's specific to this record, and continue to enter data in
every record that requires information in the custom fields (see Figure 4-
20).

To add data to a custom field in the items list, open the appropriate
item and click Custom Fields. Then add data for this item in the custom
fields (see Figure 4-21).

The data you enter in custom fields should be consistent from record
to record. For example, let's say you're tracking vendor information or
item information in a custom field named Co-op Adv (to display the formula for co-op advertising revenue).

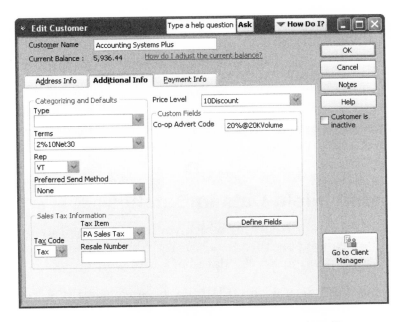

Figure 4-20: Each record in a names list requires its own specific data.

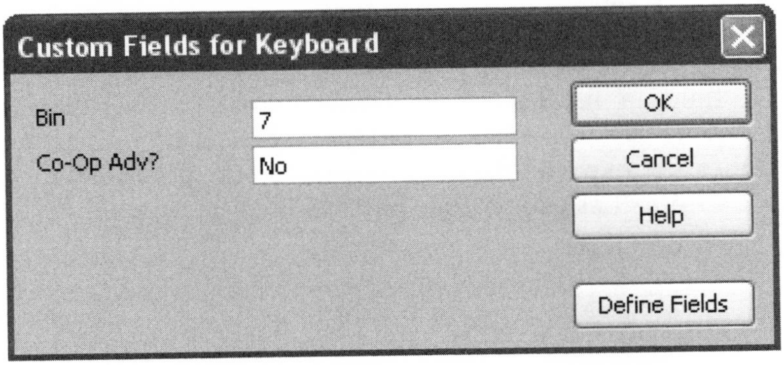

Figure 4-21: Track specific information about each item with the data you enter into custom fields.

If the formula is a percentage of co-op refunds for a minimum purchase, decide on the format of the text to use for every record. For example, you could enter 10%-20K if the co-op formula is 10% for a minimum purchase of $20,000.00. Don't enter the same type of data in different ways, such as:

- 10-20$
- 10%-20K
- 10-$20K

If your data is inconsistent, it's difficult (if not impossible) to produce reports that provide the information you need about the data in custom fields.

Adding Custom Field Data in Batches

If you have a lot of names or items for which you need to populate custom fields with data, you can export the list as an IIF file, add the data in an Excel worksheet, and then import the data back into QuickBooks.

You must import the data with an IIF file, because the Excel import feature in QuickBooks doesn't recognize custom fields. Appendix B has directions for working with IIF files, but here are some guidelines for adding custom field data:

- An IIF file in Excel is a single worksheet file. You cannot have multiple worksheets, so export, and work on, one list at a time.
- Custom field names are not exported; instead, data is held in columns with the keyword names CUSTFLD1, CUSTFLD2, and so on. Names list exported files contain 15 columns named CUSTFLD, the items list export file contains 5 columns named CUSTFLD.
- The CUSTFLD column numbers are linked to the order of the custom fields you created. Before you can enter data, view your custom fields, and note the custom field names in top-to-bottom order. (You cannot change the column title to match the name; this is for your convenience when you enter data.
- Add custom field data to the first record in each list, to have sample data in the export file.
- In Excel, remove unneeded rows at the top of the file to make it easier to work. The first required row contains the list keyword

preceded by an exclamation point in the first column, such as !INVITEM, !CUST, and so on. (IIF file keywords are in Appendix B.)

Adding Custom Fields to Transaction Templates

Some custom fields should appear in transaction templates, because the data in the field helps you create the transaction more efficiently.

For example, QuickBooks doesn't provide a field in customer records to indicate how the customer wants you to deal with backorders. There's no point in tracking backorders for a customer who indicates they want you to ship what's available, and forget the rest of the order, or for a customer who wants you to hold shipment until backordered items are available.

Create a custom field named Backorders, and enter data for each customer to indicate how backorders should be handled. Then, customize sales transaction templates to include the customer's backorder data on the screen when you're creating the transaction.

NOTE: Chapter 3 has directions for customizing templates.

You should be aware of the "rules" that govern the way custom fields are added to transaction windows. (According to the e-mail queries I receive, this rule isn't well known.):

- Custom fields in the names lists are added to the transaction template as fields in the heading section.
- Custom fields in the items list are added to the transaction template as columns in the line item section.

List Limits

QuickBooks limits the number of entries you can have in a list. Table 4-1 specifies the number of entries for each list. The entry labeled Names includes the following lists:

- Customers & Jobs
- Vendors
- Other Names
- Employees

List	Maximum
Names (each list)	10000
Chart of accounts	10000
Items (excluding payroll items)	14500
Job types	10000
Vendor types	10000
Customer types	10000
Purchase orders	10000
Payroll items	10000
Price Levels	100
Classes	10000
Terms (combined A/R and A/P)	10000
Payment methods	10000
Shipping methods	10000
Customer messages	10000
Memorized reports	14500
Memorized transactions	14500
To Do notes	10000

Table 4-1: Maximum number of entries in lists.

However, the limits are a bit more complicated, and more stringent, than the table indicates. It's important to realize the following:

- The combined total of names for all the names lists cannot exceed 14,500.
- Once you have reached 10,000 names in a single name list, you cannot create any new objects for that list.
- Once you have reached 14,500 names in your combined name lists, you can no longer create any new names in any names list.

When you reach a list maximum, QuickBooks locks the list(s), and when a list is locked, that's a permanent decision. Deleting objects doesn't free up space for new entries. It's too late.

TIP: To view your current numbers press F2 to open the QuickBooks Product Information Window. The List Information box displays the list totals.

QuickBooks also imposes a maximum on the number of transactions in a file, but since that number is 2,000,000,000 (yes, two billion), it's unlikely that a small business would exceed that number.

Each individual action you perform is a transaction. Filling out a transaction window is an obvious transaction, but when you edit, delete, or void a transaction, that counts too. If you reach the maximum number of transactions, your company file is locked and you can't work in that file. You can condense and archive older transactions to make your company file smaller and more efficient.

Classes

Classes let you group transactions to match the way you want to track and report your business activities. In effect, you can use classes to "classify" your business by some pattern, such as divisions, branches, or type of activity.

The ability to classify your business means you can produce P & L reports by class, so you can see how each department, division, or location is doing.

TIP: Plan your classes for a single purpose, or the feature won't work properly. For example, you can use classes to separate your business into locations or by type of business, but don't try to do both.

To use classes, you must enable the feature, which is listed in the Accounting category of the Preferences dialog. Once classes are enabled, QuickBooks adds a Class field to your transaction windows. For each transaction, you can assign one of the classes you create.

Classes only work well if you use them consistently, but it's common for users to skip the Class field in transactions. QuickBooks offers a feature to help everyone remember to assign a class to a transaction. You can enable that feature by selecting the option Prompt To Assign Classes, which is available in the same Preferences dialog you use to enable classes (the Company Preferences tab of the Accounting category).

When you enable this feature, any time a user tries to save or close a transaction without assigning classes, QuickBooks displays a reminder message about assigning a class. However, the message is merely a reminder, and QuickBooks will let the user continue to save the transaction without class assignments. You must train users about the importance of assigning classes, or you won't get the reports you want.

When you create your classes, include the following two classes in addition to the classes you create for departments, division, locations, etc.:

• Other, which users can select if they're not sure which class a transaction belongs to. Later, you can create a report on transactions linked to the Other class, and drill down through each transaction to apply the appropriate class.
• Administration (or Overhead), which you can use for posting expenses that aren't specifically applicable to a "regular" class. You can use the totals in this class to apply percentages of overhead to class expenses (via a journal entry).

Chapter 5

Premier-Only Accounting Functions

Advanced functions for journal entries

Advanced bank reconciliation features

The QuickBooks Premier Editions include features that add efficiency, power, and added value to your accounting tasks. These features, which are unique to the Premier editions, are the subject of this chapter.

Some of the Premier accounting tools are only available in certain Premier editions, and I'll note those restrictions when I discuss those features.

Journal Entries

Journal entries provide a quick and efficient way to create transactions directly into the general ledger (such as depreciation entries), and to fine tune existing account balances (for job costing or class assignments).

For example, if you're tracking classes, you can use a journal entry to correct transactions that weren't posted to a class. All you have to do is journalize the original transaction (in and out of the original accounts), and add the class information. Similarly, journal entries provide a way to add job costs to existing account totals; merely create a GJE that applies jobs against existing postings.

Entering a single transaction to include class or job information to multiple previous postings is faster than editing each original transaction to add the class or job.

However, I frequently hear from business owners and accountants about JEs created for job costing that don't seem to work. The job costing reports don't reflect the information that was entered in the JE.

Fine tuning your account balances with JEs can be a trip down the rabbit hole if you don't understand the way QuickBooks stores information contained in JEs. For information about the QuickBooks JE paradigm, see the section "Troubleshooting Journal Entries" in Appendix C.

I use the term journal entry, and abbreviate it JE, out of habit. QuickBooks call this transaction type a *General Journal Entry,* and uses the abbreviation *GJE.*

If you use journal entries frequently, add an icon to the toolbar, using the following steps:

1. Choose Company → Make General Journal Entries to open a blank GJE window.
2. Choose View → Add "Make General Journal Entries" to the toolbar.
3. In the Add Window To Icon Bar dialog (see Figure 5-1), you can change the default Label or Description text, and also change the default graphic for the icon.
4. Click OK to place the icon on your toolbar.

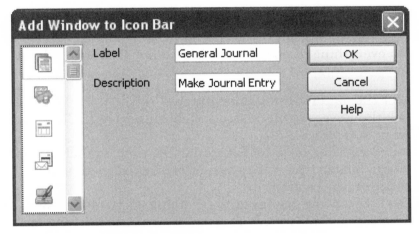

Figure 5-1: Design a toolbar icon for GJEs.

The text in the Label field represents the text that displays under the icon on the toolbar. The text in the Description field is the text you see when you hover your mouse over the icon (also called a *tooltip*). See Chapter 1 for more information about customizing the toolbar.

Advanced Options for Journal Entries

The Premier editions offer some nifty features that add convenient (and powerful) options when you're creating journal entries.

Auto Reversing Journal Entries

Usually found in high-end, more expensive, accounting software packages, automatic reversing journal entries are available in the QuickBooks Premier editions. To create an auto reversing journal entry, open the Make General Journal Entries window by choosing Banking → Make General Journal Entries.

The Help files in QuickBooks Premier Editions tell you to create a journal entry, save it, then redisplay it, and click the Reverse icon on the GJE window. (To redisplay an entry, open the GJE window if it isn't already open, and click Previous to locate the entry you want to auto-reverse).

However, I'm pathologically lazy, and I find it's much quicker and easier to do everything at once, which is accomplished using the following steps:

1. Enter the data for the journal entry.
2. Click the Reverse icon (instead of clicking Save & Close, or Save & New).
3. QuickBooks displays the Recording Transaction dialog to tell you that you haven't recorded your entry, and offers to save it. Click Yes to record the entry.
4. The GJE window displays the reversing entry (don't worry, the original entry was saved, click Previous to see it if you don't believe me).
5. Click Save & Close if you're finished with the GJE window; click Save & New to enter another journal entry.

The Reversing Entry is automatically dated the first day of the following month, but you can change the date. If you're using automatic numbering for GJE transactions, the reversing entry number has the format *xxx*R, where *xxx* is the number of the original journal entry.

AutoFill Memos in Journal Entries

In QuickBooks Pro, the text you enter in the memo field of any line in a journal entry stays with that entry line. This means you see your comments when you open the register for the account that entry line posted to.

For example, if you are entering a journal entry for a correction your accountant told you to make, you could enter the comment "Bob's Memo-9/4/05" (assuming your accountant's name is Bob).

Most people enter memo text only in the first line of the journal entry. Later, if they view the register of the account (or multiple accounts) to which the ensuing line(s) of the JE posted, there's no text in the memo field. You don't see any explanation for the transaction unless you open the original transaction. To avoid that problem, some users enter (or Copy and Paste) the text in the memo field manually, on each line of the General Journal Entry. That's extra work!

QuickBooks Premier editions offer a clever feature called AutoFill Memos in Journal Entries. This means that the text you enter in the Memo field on the first line of the transaction is automatically entered on all lines of the transaction. When you view the registers of any accounts involved in the journal entry, the memo text is available to help you remember or understand the reason for the transaction.

This feature is enabled by default in the Preferences dialog, in the My Preferences tab of the Accounting section. If your memo text isn't repeated on the second line of your GJE, somebody disabled the feature. Choose Edit → Preferences, go to the Accounting section of the Preferences dialog, and enable it.

TIP FOR ACCOUNTANTS: For your clients who aren't using one of the QuickBooks Premier Editions, you might want to pass along the suggestion to Copy and Paste memo text to every line of a JE. This means you'll know the reason for the JE when you see it in an account register. Without the memo, you have to open the original transaction to see the memo that appeared only on the first line.

Premier Accountant Edition has two additional features for JEs (covered in Chapter 11):

- Adjusting Entries
- The ability to display previous JEs in the transaction window.

Viewing Previous Bank Reconciliation Reports

The Premier editions automatically save bank reconciliation reports, even if you don't print or display the reports when you finish reconciling your bank account. Without this feature, the only way to see previous bank reconciliation reports is to remember to print a report every time you reconcile a bank account. When you need a previous report, go to your filing cabinet. That's what users of QuickBooks Pro have to do, because they only have access to the last reconciliation report. Luckily for you, QuickBooks Premier editions store multiple reconciliation reports.

You may want to see a previous reconciliation report before you begin the next reconciliation process, or you might find you need to look at a previous report when you're in the middle of reconciling the current month, and you run into a problem.

In addition, at the end of your fiscal year, most accountants want to see the reconciliation report for the last fiscal month. If you don't meet with your accountant until several months after your fiscal year end, the ability to print the right reconciliation report is very handy.

Choose Reports → Banking → Previous Reconciliation to open the Previous Reconciliation dialog seen in Figure 5-2. If you have more than one bank account, select the appropriate account from the drop-down list in the Account field. Then select the report you want to see by choosing its statement ending date.

TIP: *You can also access the Previous Reconciliation dialog from the Begin Reconciliation dialog, which is (the opening window for bank reconciliation that appears when you choose Banking g Reconcile. Click the button labeled Locate Discrepancies, and then click Previous Reports.*

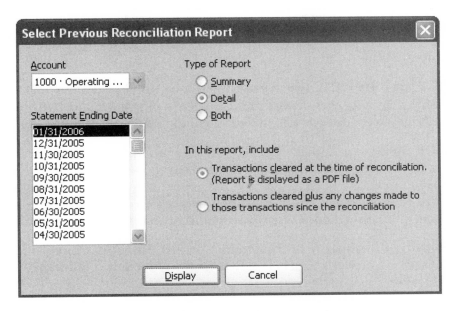

Figure 5-2: Select the reconciliation report you need.

Choosing the Type of Reconciliation Report

You have a variety of choices for the type and format of the reconciliation report for the statement period you select. The Type Of Report section at the top of the dialog has three options: Summary, Detail, and Both.

- Select Summary to see the totals for transactions that were cleared and uncleared at the time of the reconciliation. The report also lists the totals for new transactions (transactions entered after the reconciliation). Totals are by type, so there is one total for inflow (deposits and credits), and another total for outflow (checks and payments).
- Select Detail to see each transaction that was cleared or not cleared in a previous reconciliation, and see each new transaction.
- Select Both to open both reports (not one report with both sets of listings).

After you select the type of report, select the type of content you want in the report.

Selecting the option Transactions Cleared At The Time Of Reconciliation (Report Is Displayed As A PDF File), results in a Portable Document Format (PDF) file.

To view a PDF file, you must have Adobe Acrobat Reader installed. If you don't, selecting this report in QuickBooks opens a dialog with a link to the Adobe website, where you can download Acrobat Reader (it's free!).

PDF files are graphical and let you view and print information. You cannot drill down to see details, because this report is not directly linked to your QuickBooks data. However, the report gives you an accurate report of the last reconciliation. (If you printed a reconciliation report the last time you reconciled the account, the PDF file matches your printout.)

Selecting the option Transactions Cleared Plus Any Changes Made To Those Transactions Since The Reconciliation opens a standard QuickBooks report window.

Unfortunately, this report is neither useful nor accurate if you need to see a report on the reconciliation for the date you selected. This is not really a reconciliation report. It's merely a report on the current state of the account register, sorted to display the account's transactions according to cleared/uncleared/new categories.

If you, or someone else, changed a cleared transaction, the new information appears in this report, not the information that was extant at the time you reconciled the account. If you're viewing the previous reconciliation to try to determine whether any changes were made to cleared transactions, this report fools you—it's dangerous to rely on its contents.

If you need to see an accurate, trustworthy, previous reconciliation report in order to track down discrepancies, either use the PDF file or make sure you print and file a detailed reconciliation report every time you reconcile a bank account.

Resolving Reconciliation Problems

The common reason for opening a previous reconciliation report is to investigate the reason for problems in the current reconciliation. Usually, this means the Begin Reconciliation dialog displays a beginning balance that differs from the opening balance shown on your bank statement.

Click the Locate Discrepancies button on the Begin Reconciliation dialog to open the Locate Discrepancies dialog (see Figure 5-3). You have access to your previous reconciliation reports in this dialog, as well as a discrepancy report that may help you locate the reason for the difference between the beginning balances.

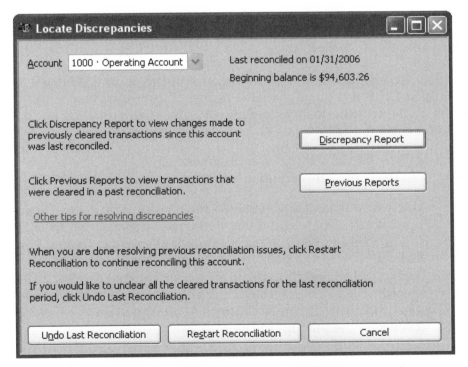

Figure 5-3: Use the tools available in the Locate Discrepancies dialog to troubleshoot reconciliation problems.

If the previous reconciliation reports don't provide the answer to your problem, choose Discrepancy Report. As you can see in Figure 5-4, this report displays information about transactions that were changed after they were cleared during reconciliation.

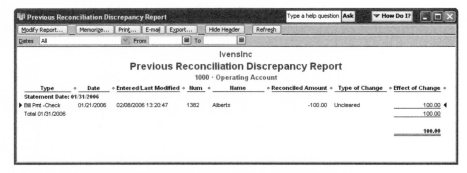

Figure 5-4: This report should be empty—if it displays any transactions, somebody manipulated a cleared transaction—
that's a no no.

The reconciled amount is the amount of the transaction as it was
when you cleared it during reconciliation. If that amount is a positive
number, the transaction was a deposit; a negative number indicates a
disbursement (usually a check).

The Type Of Change column provides a clue about the action you
must take to correct the unmatched beginning balances:

- Uncleared means you removed the check mark in the Cleared column of the register (and you persisted in this action even though
  QuickBooks issued a stern warning about the dangers).
- Deleted means you deleted the transaction.
- Amount is the original amount, which means you changed the
  amount of the transaction. Check the Reconciled amount and the
  amount in the Effect Of Change amount, and do the math; the difference is the amount of the change.

Unfortunately, QuickBooks doesn't offer a Type Of Change named
"Void," so a voided transaction is merely marked as changed. A transaction with a changed amount equal and opposite of the original amount is
usually a check that was voided after it was cleared.

To resolve the problem, open the bank account register and restore
the affected transaction to its original state. This is safe because you
can't justify changing a transaction after it was cleared—a transaction

that cleared was not supposed to be changed, voided, deleted, or uncleared; once cleared, it must remain what it was forever.

If you don't see the problem immediately, trying comparing previous reconciliation reports to the account register. Any transaction that is listed in a reconciliation report should also be in the register, with the same amount.

- If a transaction is there, but marked VOID, re-enter it, using the data in the reconciliation report. That transaction wasn't void when you performed the last reconciliation, it had cleared. Therefore, it can't possibly meet any of the criteria for voiding a transaction.
- If a transaction appears in the reconciliation report, but is not in the register, it was deleted. Re-enter it, using the data in the reconciliation report.
- Check the amounts on the printed check reconciliation report against the data in the register to see if any amount was changed after the account was reconciled. If so, restore the original amount.

WARNING: If you merge bank accounts, you lose the previous reconciliation reports for both accounts involved in the merge procedure.

Incidentally, a number of people have written to ask me about the location of the PDF reconciliation files. They wanted to open the files directly in Acrobat, when QuickBooks was not open. Sorry, these files are not discrete documents; they're stored within the company data file. The only way to open them is from within QuickBooks.

Chapter 6

Enhanced Sales Features

Sales orders

Back orders

Creating transactions automatically

Inventory assemblies

The QuickBooks Premier editions have features that enhance the functions available to you for sales transactions. These features aren't available in QuickBooks Pro, and in this chapter, I'll discuss the additional power you get in your Premier edition.

Sales Orders

The QuickBooks Premier Editions include support for sales orders, and that makes life a lot easier for you if you sell products. Inherent in sales orders is the ability to track back orders—a sales order that has items waiting to be shipped and invoiced is, in effect, a back order.

Without the additional features in QuickBooks Premier editions, you have to use complicated workarounds to track these functions. (For accountants who support clients who don't have Premier Edition, *QuickBooks 2006: The Official Guide* offers detailed instructions on creating and using workarounds to track back orders in QuickBooks YPro.

> **NOTE**: *If you sell both services and products, don't use a sales order for services. Sales orders are only useful for inventory items.*

Enabling Sales Orders

To use sales orders, you must enable their use by choosing Edit → Preferences and selecting the Sales & Customers category. In the Company Preferences tab, make sure the option Enable Sales Orders is selected. You can also enable the following additional sales order options:

- **Warn about duplicate sales order numbers**. Sales orders have their own self-incrementing number system (unconnected to invoice numbering). It's a good idea to select this option to keep your sales order records accurate.
- **Don't print items with zero amounts**. Selecting this option removes any line item that has a zero amount in the Ordered column or in the Rate column from the printed version of the sales

order (or the invoice created from the sales order). The onscreen copy of the sales order still shows all the lines.

Enabling Warnings about Inventory Stock Status

All editions of QuickBooks offer the option to warn you that the Quantity On Hand (QOH) is insufficient to ship the product you're selling, when you're creating an invoice.

In Premier Editions, you can enable warnings that are more precise. You can enable a function that tells QuickBooks to examine additional data when determining whether you have sufficient inventory to turn a sales order into an invoice.

All of the options for enabling warnings about inventory stock status are in the Company Preferences tab of the Purchases & Vendors Preferences dialog (see Figure 6-1), which you open by choosing Edit → Preferences.

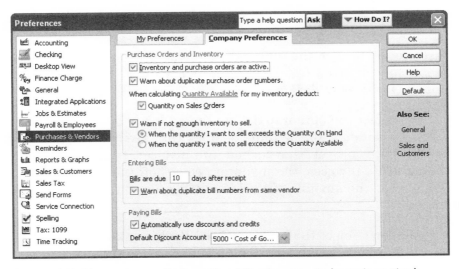

Figure 6-1: You can specify how QuickBooks reports inventory stock status when you create a sales order.

In some QuickBooks Premier editions this dialog has additional choices, because there are additional features. The following Premier editions have advanced features for tracking inventory stock status while creating sales transactions:

- Manufacturing & Wholesale Edition (see Chapter 13)
- Retail Edition (see Chapter 16)
- Accountant Edition (see Chapter 11)

These advanced features are discussed in the chapters specific to each of those editions.

Quantity on Hand vs. Quantity Available

The options referring to calculating and reporting quantities while you're creating sales transactions are actually giving you a choice between tracking Quantity on Hand or Quantity Available.

- Quantity on Hand (QOH) is the number of units in the warehouse (or the garage, or wherever you store your inventory). It's a "shelf count".
- Quantity Available is a more precise figure; it's the number of those units on the shelves that you can actually sell at the moment you're creating a sale.

Notice the text on the dialog that reads, " When calculating quantity available for my inventory, deduct:" under which is the option labeled Quantity On Sales Orders.

If you select the option to deduct the quantity on sales orders, QuickBooks deducts all the units of stock that are currently on sales orders that haven't yet been turned into invoices. (When sales orders are turned into invoices, the inventory comes off the shelves.) The resulting number is the amount of stock available for you to enter in a sales order.

If you don't select that option, QuickBooks makes no deductions in stock status numbers, and you'll think that the quantity available is the number of units on the shelves.

If anyone else converts a sales order with the same product into an invoice before you do, and packs and ships the stock, you'll be surprised, because the 10 units of widgets you thought you could sell a customer are not available. That's because you didn't know about those sales orders that were entered before you created your sales order.

Having selected the options that define the QOH and the Quantity Available, the next set of options lets you decide when you want QuickBooks to warn you about insufficient stock levels when you want to sell items.

Don't get too excited about this feature—unfortunately the warning doesn't appear when you're entering a sales order (which is, of course, when you need to know these things). The warning appears when you convert the sales order to an invoice.

If you're using one of the three Premier editions with advanced features mentioned earlier in this chapter, the insufficient stock level warning is displayed while you're creating the sales order.

Sales Order Postings

When you create and save sales orders, no financial accounts are affected. The transaction itself is posted to the Sales Order account in your chart of accounts, which is a non-posting account. You can open the account register (non-posting accounts are listed at the bottom of the chart of accounts) to view or manipulate the sales orders you've created.

The inventory items included in a sales order are marked to indicate the fact that they're reserved on a sales order, and the appropriate calculations are made to Quantity Available reports. However, no financial postings are made to income, COG, or the inventory asset accounts.

Creating Sales Orders

After you enable sales orders in the Preferences dialog, a Sales Order icon appears on the Home page, and the Create Sales Orders command appears on the Customer menu. Perform either action to open a blank Create Sales Orders window, which looks very much like an invoice window (see Figure 6-2). Fill in the heading and line item sections, and save the sales order.

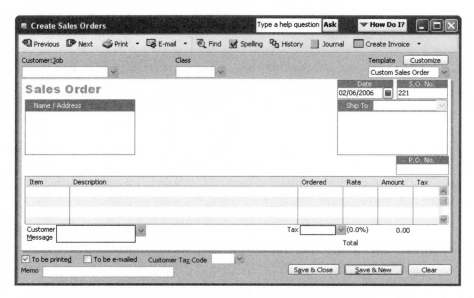

Figure 6-2: The Sales Order transaction form is similar to an invoice.

Sales Order Templates

The first time you open the sales order transaction window, the ustom Sales Order template is selected by default. QuickBooks provides several templates for sales orders, and you can select the template you prefer from the drop-down list in the Templates field.

Sales Order With Rep adds the Rep field to the Custom Sales Order template. The sales rep for the customer is automatically filled in. If the person creating the sales order isn't the sales rep linked to the customer, you can select a different sales rep from the drop-down list. When you save the sales order, QuickBooks displays a dialog that asks if you want to change the sales rep on the customer's record to match the new selection. Select Yes or No, depending on the circumstances and your policies about sales reps and commissions.

Work Order is the same as the Custom Sales Order, but the transaction title (above the customer's name box) is Work Order instead of

Sales Order. Use this template when you're creating a custom-built product or an assembly.

Standard Work Order adds the following fields to the Work Order template: Terms, Rep, and Ship Date.

NOTE: QuickBooks also offers a Sales Order Pick List and a Sales Order Packing Slip in the Template drop-down list.

Turning Sales Orders into Invoices

Businesses have a variety of standards and protocols upon which they base the decision to turn a sales order into an invoice. Some require a sales person to obtain a manager's approval to verify the customer's credit status, or to approve a price change (usually a discount). Others merely wait until the items on an order are picked and packed.

Regardless of the protocols you use, eventually you turn a sales order into an invoice, and you have two methods for accomplishing this task:

- Open a blank Create Invoices window, and load the sales order into the form.
- Open the original sales order, and convert it to an invoice with a click of the mouse.

Using the Create Invoices Window

To create an invoice from an existing sales order, click the Invoices icon on the Home page, or press Ctrl-I. Either action opens a blank Create Invoices window.

When you select the customer or job, QuickBooks opens the Available Sales Orders dialog seen in Figure 6-3, which lists all the current open sales orders. (If no sales orders exist for the selected customer or job, the dialog doesn't appear.)

Select the appropriate sales order, and click OK. See "Creating the Invoice", later in this section to learn how to move through the rest of the procedures.

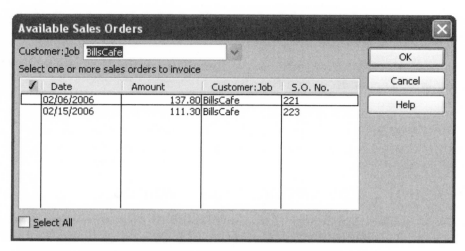

Figure 6-3: QuickBooks automatically displays all the open sales
orders for the selected customer or job.

Converting the Original Sales Order

To open the original sales order to create the invoice for this order,
choose Customers → Create Sales Orders to open a blank Create
Sales Orders transaction window. Then click the Previous button to
move backwards through your sales orders to reach the appropriate
one.

However, if you have many sales orders, this is terribly inefficient.
Luckily, QuickBooks provides a Find feature, which is much more effi-
cient. Click the Find icon on the transaction window's toolbar to open the
Find Sales Orders dialog seen in Figure 6-4.

Enter the customer or job name, and click Find. If you know there
are many sales orders for this customer, use the fields in the Find Sales
Orders dialog to narrow the search. For example, if you know the approximate date of the sales order you need, enter beginning and starting
dates in the their respective date fields.

The Find dialog expands, and after searching through all the sales
orders, the bottom of the window displays a list of all the sales orders
that match your criteria (see Figure 6-5).

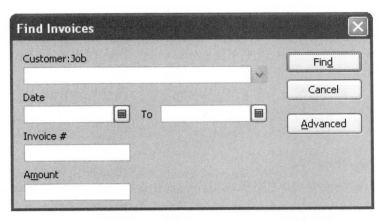

Figure 6-4: The Find dialog makes quick work of locating a specific sales order.

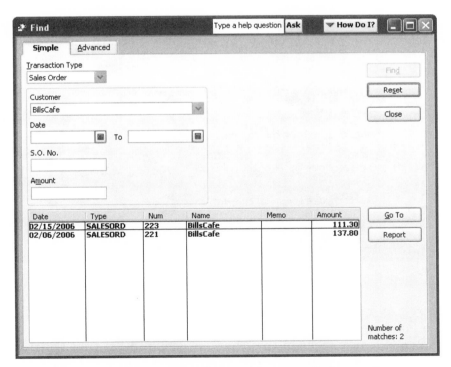

Figure 6-5: All the sales orders that match your criteria are displayed.

Double-click the listing for the sales order you need. If you're not sure which sales order to choose, double-click each in turn, and if the sales order that opens isn't the correct one, close it to return to the Find dialog and select another sales order.

When the correct sales order opens, click the Create Invoice button on the Sales Order window's toolbar to begin the process of creating an invoice (covered next).

Creating the Invoice

Whether you start from the Sales Order window or the Create Invoices window, creating an invoice from a sales order works the same way.

QuickBooks displays the Create Invoice Based on Sales Order dialog (see Figure 6-6), so you can decide whether to create an invoice for the entire sales order, or create an invoice for only specific items on the sales order. The latter option is available in case some items aren't available (in which case they stay open on the sales order, creating a virtual back order).

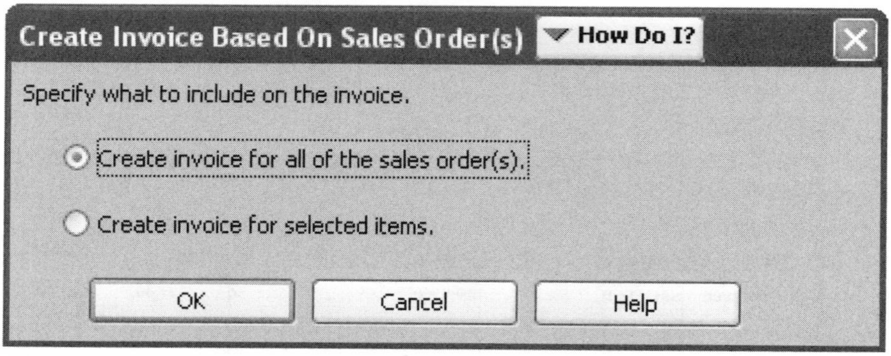

Figure 6-6: Select the appropriate option for filling the order.

Here's an important tip (or trick)—it's usually better to select Create Invoice For Selected Items, even if you want to invoice the entire sales order. Remember, earlier in this chapter I pointed out that QuickBooks does not inform you of insufficient quantities when you create a sales order—you only learn about stock problems when you create an invoice.

(This does not occur if you're running one of the Premier editions mentioned earlier in this chapter that have advanced sales order options).

If there's not enough stock to fill this sales order, after you select the option to create an invoice for the entire sales order, you encounter some problems.

However, I'll go over both scenarios, and I'll show you what happens if you opt to fill the entire sales order and find out you don't have enough stock.

Invoicing the Entire Sales Order

If you selected the option to invoice the entire sales order, and you have enough stock to fill the order, the Create Invoices window opens with everything filled in from the sales order. QuickBooks automatically uses the Custom S.O. Invoice template, because it is configured to display columns that can hold the information from the sales order.

Add the shipping costs, if you charge customers for shipping. Add other items to the invoice, such as service items, or any additional products the customer has ordered. Then, print and send the invoice as you usually do.

Managing Insufficient Quantities

If any items on the sales order don't have a sufficient QOH, the warning message seen in Figure 6-7 appears. Unfortunately, the warning message doesn't tell you which item is in short supply.

Figure 6-7: Uh oh

Click OK to clear the message and the invoice appears, automatically filled in with all the items that were on the sales order. However, you still have no indication about which item lacked sufficient QOH to ship this order. There are several methods for solving this mystery:

- If you think the inventory records are wrong, or you know you have sufficient quantity to ship because the order has been picked, you can safely ignore the message.
- If you don't use pick slips, or you don't pick and pack an order until it's invoiced, you can walk into the warehouse and count the QOH for each item on the invoice. For short counts, come back and change the quantity in the Invoiced column.
- Choose Lists → Item List on the QuickBooks menu bar, select the listing for the first item in the invoice, and press Ctrl-Q to see a status report on the QOH. Then, if necessary, adjust the quantity in the Invoiced column. Repeat for each item in the invoice.

When you change the number in the Invoiced column, QuickBooks automatically enters the difference between the Ordered and Invoiced columns in the Backordered column (see Figure 6-8).

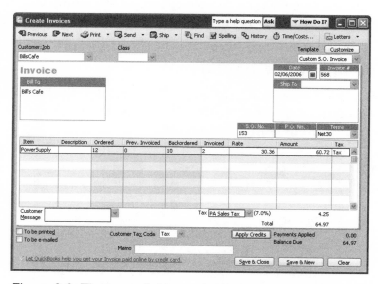

Figure 6-8: The unavailable products are automatically treated as a back order.

If the customer doesn't accept back orders, enter a zero in the Backordered column. Otherwise, the sales order remains alive, and when you receive the products you can invoice the remainder of the order.

Invoicing Selected Items

If you chose the option Create Invoice For Selected Items, when you click OK the Specify Invoice Quantities For Items On Sales Order dialog appears (see Figure 6-9).

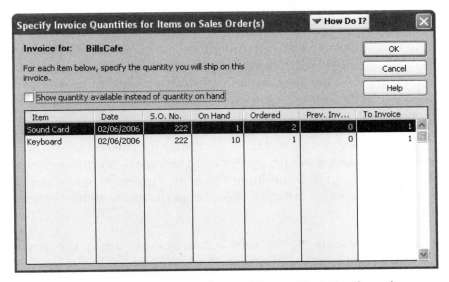

Figure 6-9: There's a shortage of one of the products on the sales order.

The QOH for each item is displayed, and if there aren't any shortages, just invoice the total number of items in the sales order. In effect, you've created an invoice for the entire sales order as if you'd selected that option originally—except you know whether there are any shortages, and for which items. This is so much better than risking a shortage you can't discern by selecting the option to create an invoice for the entire sales order.

However, you cannot trust the numbers on this dialog unless you select the option to show the quantity available instead of the quantity on hand. The QOH does not take other sales orders into consideration. It might be that selecting the option Show Quantity Available Instead Of Quantity On Hand, reveals the fact that the items on hand are already linked to one or more sales orders.

Earlier in this chapter, I told you how to set your preferences to warn about the available quantity instead of the QOH, but that preference only kicks in when you're creating an invoice. The Specify Invoice Quantities For Items On Sales Order dialog obviously doesn't check that preference. Therefore, you have to select the option Show Quantity Available Instead Of Quantity On Hand manually.

When the quantity that's available is less than the QOH, it means the item is on a sales order (including the sales order you're currently converting to an invoice), or on multiple sales orders In most companies, this kicks off any of several amusing scenarios involving sprint races and arguments.

If the other sales orders aren't yet ready for invoicing, you win. But before you can claim your prize (the right to create an invoice), you have to prevent other people from doing the same thing. Someone may be ready to invoice a sales order that contains the same item. Here's how to win for real:

1. Run, don't walk, to the warehouse, and gather up the quantity you need of the items that are in short supply.
2. Take the items to the shipping desk and mark them with the invoice number you're preparing. (It doesn't hurt to add a threatening note about the consequences to anybody who thinks about appropriating these items to create an invoice from one of the other sales orders.)
3. If you think Step 2 won't work, bring the items back to your desk and hide them until you finish your invoice. Then take them to the shipping desk and stay there to supervise the packing process.

If multiple users are working on multiple computers on the network, turning sales orders into invoices, it's more difficult to declare yourself the winner. Somebody else may have already confiscated the items, or several of you may arrive in the warehouse at the same time.

Instead of a tug-of-war, you need to set shipping priorities. I've seen these discussions turn into real arguments, although there's usually an executive who declares the winner. Here's the priority list many companies use:

- The first priority is a customer who doesn't accept back orders, and wants you to ship and invoice only what's in stock.
- The second priority is a "best customer"—a customer it's important to keep happy (of course, a "best customer" is usually defined by the amount of money the customer spends with your company).
- The third priority is whatever argument the best debater in the group presents. This usually involves listening to phrases such as "this is the first order from a new customer", or "we've done this to this customer three times already".

When you can't ship all the items, you have to change the numbers in the Specify Invoice Quantities For Items On Sales Order dialog. In the To Invoice column, enter the quantity you want to invoice, and click OK.

If any item isn't available, and you entered zero for the amount to invoice, QuickBooks issues a warning message about handling zero amount items (see Figure 6-10).

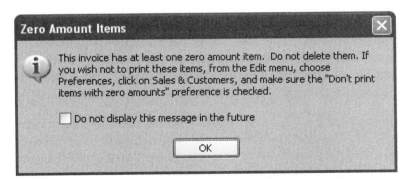

Figure 6-10: QuickBooks warns you not to delete items from the invoice.

The warning is important, because if you delete the zero amount line items, you won't be able to track back orders. Setting a preference to avoid printing zero items is discussed earlier in this chapter, and you should enable it if you don't want your customer to see the zero amount line on the printed invoice.

I'm not sure I agree that it's harmful to print zero amount line items. After all, the customer certainly remembers the original order, and you're showing the customer that you, too, remember the items in the original order. However, if you choose not to print the zero-based lines, they remain on the on-screen version so you can track the items for back orders. If you're shipping and invoicing less than the number of items in the sales order (but not zero), that also qualifies as a back order.

TIP: *If you know this customer won't accept back orders, and has issued instructions to ship whatever is available, it's OK to delete the zero-based lines. You won't be tracking back orders for this customer.*

Save the invoice, print it, and ship the goods that are in stock. If the invoice matches the sales order (meaning everything on the sales order was shipped), the original sales order is marked Invoiced In Full when you open it to view it. All you have to do is wait for the customer's check to arrive.

If the invoice didn't match the sales order, the unshipped goods remain on the sales order, and the Backordered column displays the number of units remaining to fill this order. When the products arrive, open the sales order, click the Create Invoice button, and start the process again.

When you save the invoice, only the amounts on the invoice are posted to the Accounts Receivable, Income, Inventory, and Cost of Goods accounts. The amounts for back ordered items are not posted to the general ledger.

Managing Back Orders

When you aren't able to ship and invoice all the items in a sales order, the sales order becomes a back order, because it maintains information about uninvoiced items.

For example, in Figure 6-11, the full quantity of the item in the second line is invoiced, and the line item is marked "closed" (which is what the check mark in the column labeled Clsd means). The first line item has a quantity of zero in the Invoiced column, and the check mark is missing. This item is on back order.

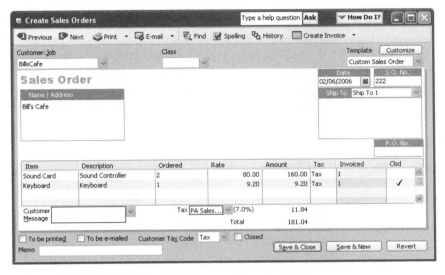

Figure 6-11: This sales order is now a back order.

Tracking Receipt of Goods

Unfortunately, as new products arrive in your warehouse, QuickBooks does not assign the products to existing unfilled sales order (back orders) automatically. Instead, you must manually track incoming goods against the back orders in your system.

You can track incoming goods within QuickBooks, or outside of QuickBooks. In this section, I'll go over some of the techniques that are working well for my clients.

Using Stock Status Reports

You can track the status of items by viewing a stock status report, and comparing the contents to the back orders you're tracking. Get into the habit of printing your back orders, by calling up a sales order after its linked invoice has been created, and clicking the Print button.

To see a stock status report, choose Reports → Inventory → Inventory Stock Status By Item. The report that opens lists every item in inventory, along with its current status (on hand, on purchase order, on sales order).

The usefulness of this report varies, depending on the number of items you stock, and the number of back orders you're tracking. If your company has a limited number of items, it's not terribly difficult to go through the report to find the items you're looking for in order to fill your back orders. However, if you have a lot of items, or many back orders (or both), it's more efficient to design reports that give you what you need quickly.

Creating Customized Stock Status Reports

If you create customized stock status reports for back orders, you can check each customer's back order quickly, which is handy if the customer calls and asks when you expect to ship the remaining products.

To do this, you need to customize the report on a per-customer basis, or on a per-back order basis. Either way, start by choosing Reports → Inventory → Inventory Stock Status By Item.

Customizing the Display

When the report opens, make it easier to read by eliminating columns that don't provide information you need. You cannot use the Modify Report feature to remove columns on this particular report, but you can close up the columns so you don't have to scroll through the report.

Use the diamond-shaped marker to the right of any column you don't need, dragging it to the left until the column disappears. The following columns can safely disappear for the purpose of tracking back orders:

- Pref Vendor
- Reorder Pt
- Order
- Sales/Wk

Customizing the Content

To customize the report for customers or back orders, click Modify Report, and make the following customizations:

1. In the Filters tab, select Item from the Choose Filters list.
2. In the Item field, click the arrow and scroll to the top of the list, and choose Selected Items to open the Select Items dialog.
3. Select Manual, and then select the appropriate items:
   - For a customer report, select all the items a single customer is waiting for (all the customer's back orders).
   - For a back order report, select all the item(s) attached to a particular back order.
4. Click OK to return to the Filters tab, then click OK again to return to report window.

The report displays only those items you selected, and you can use it to compare stock status against existing back orders.

Checking Receipt of Goods Manually

It's always a good idea to keep an eye on the items you're waiting for by tracking what comes in. This works well if you enlist the help of the warehouse personnel who receive goods. In fact, it's a good idea to establish a policy that receiving personnel must check back order lists.

Print a list of the products you're awaiting to fill back orders by choosing Reports → Sales → Open Sales Orders By Item. The report displays each item on a back order, along with the customer's name, the sales order number, the quantity on the back order, and the quantity already invoiced (see Figure 6-12). The quantity you need is the difference between the quantity ordered and the quantity invoiced.

Hang the list in the receiving area, and write your name and telephone extension on the document so you can receive a call when the goods arrive.

If you need to order goods from vendors to fill back orders, have the order delivered directly to the person who's tracking the back orders for these items (maybe that's you). If you use purchase orders, make sure the shipping address has your name on it. If you order by telephone, or over the Internet, be sure to indicate the shipment is to be directed to the person who's tracking the back orders for these items.

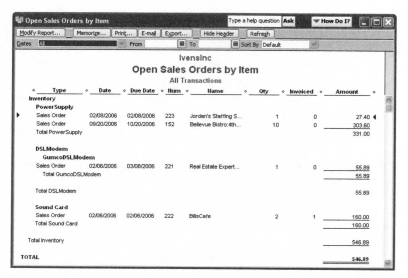

Figure 6-12: Let warehouse personnel know what you need when incoming orders arrive.

Even if you have shipments sent to your attention, or to the attention of the person who's tracking back orders, you cannot immediately fill the back orders. You must first use the Receive Items procedures to record the fact that the items came in. Then you can create invoices from the back orders to ship the items to customers. No shortcuts, please, it really messes up the accounting records.

> **NOTE**: See Chapter 6 of QuickBooks 2006: The Official Guide to learn how to use the Receive Items features.

Creating Transactions Automatically

In QuickBooks Premier editions, you can automatically create transactions from transactions, which is rather nifty. I've already explained how to create an invoice automatically from a Sales Order.

You can perform the same one-click transformation for other transactions by clicking the arrow to the right of the Create Invoice button on the transaction window and selecting the appropriate transaction type.

- Create a Purchase Order from a Sales Order
- Create a Sales Order from an Estimate
- Create an Invoice from an Estimate
- Create a Purchase Order from an Estimate
- Create a Sales Order from a Quote
- Create an Invoice from a Quote
- Create a Purchase order from a Quote
- Create an Invoice from a Proposal
- Create a Sales Order from a Proposal
- Create a Purchase Order from a Proposal
- Create an Invoice from a Work Order
- Create a Purchase order from a Work Order

NOTE: Quotes, Proposals, and Work Orders are transaction templates that are built into some of the industry-specific versions of QuickBooks. All of them are customized versions of estimates or sales orders.

Automatic Purchase Orders

The most useful (or, at least the most commonly used) automated transaction type is the ability to turn a sales order into a purchase order automatically. When you're creating a sales order that includes an item you know you're out of, a mouse click creates a purchase order.

TIP: This is also a useful feature for items you don't keep in stock, and purchase only when a customer places an order.

Fill in the sales order, and then click the arrow to the right of the Create Invoice button. Select Purchase Order from the drop-down list. QuickBooks displays the Create Purchase Order Based On The Sales

Transaction dialog, seen in Figure 6-13. (The word "allowed" appears in the dialog because items that are percentage based won't be automatically transferred to a purchase order.)

The option to create a purchase order for all allowed items only works if all the items on the sales order are purchased from the same vendor (or if the sales order contains only one item).

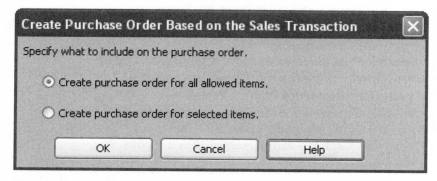

Figure 6-13: Select the appropriate option for purchasing the item(s) on this sales order.

Selecting this option opens a Create Purchase Orders window with the line items pre-filled with all the items on the sales order. If the items have a Preferred Vendor entry in the item record, the vendor's name is also filled in automatically.

Most of the time, the option to create a purchase order for selected items works best. Selecting that option opens the dialog seen in Figure 6-14, where you can select the item(s) you want to purchase.

Select each item you need to purchase by clicking in the leftmost column to place a checkmark in the column. QuickBooks displays the current QOH, and automatically fills in the quantity to order, using the quantity entered in the sales order. You can change the value of the Qty column if you want to order more than needed for this sales order.

Click OK to open a Create Purchase Orders window with the product information filled in (see Figure 6-15).

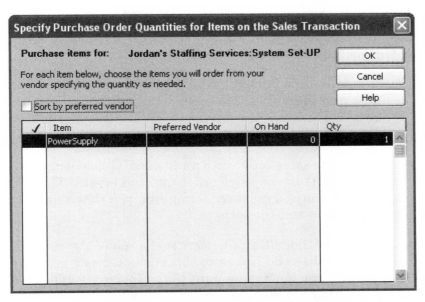

Figure 6-14: Select the items you need to purchase to fill this order.

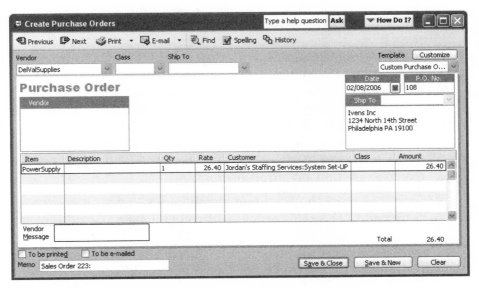

Figure 6-15: The customer's missing merchandise is automatically
ordered, and linked to the customer.

Delete the customer or job name from the Customer column. The fact that the customer name (or job) is automatically inserted in the line item makes the transactions involved in the future very complicated.

If the customer or job is linked to the purchase order, when you receive the goods, and the bill for the goods, the fact that a customer or job name is on the transaction automatically makes this a reimbursable expense.

When you turn the sales order into an invoice, QuickBooks automatically enters the products in the sales order into the invoice. QuickBooks also automatically displays a message reminding you that this customer has outstanding billable time or costs.

When you click the Time/Costs button at the top of the invoice window, you see the purchase you linked to this customer as a reimbursable expense. If you don't transfer the amount to the invoice, you'll see the message about outstanding billable time or costs every time you create an invoice for this customer or job.

Using both the automatic conversion of a sales order to an invoice and the reimbursable costs creates two item lines.

- If you delete the item line that's connected to the reimbursable costs, the costs go back to their "uncollected" status and you will see a reminder to include them in invoices forever.
- If you delete the item line that was transferred from the sales order (and correct the amounts for the reimbursable expense line that remains on the invoice), the inventory isn't decremented and no postings are made to the COG account. The reimbursable expense isn't an inventory item.

After you remove the customer or job name, save the purchase order. You're returned to the sales order, and you can save the sales order.

NOTE: *QuickBooks enters the sales order number in the memo field of the purchase order to indicate it was created automatically.*

Creating Automatic Sales Orders

If you create an estimate (or a proposal or quote) for a customer, after the customer approves your estimate you can create a sales order automatically. Then, from the sales order, you can automatically create purchase orders and invoices.

Click the arrow to the right of the Create Invoice button on the transaction window, and choose Sales Order. When the sales order opens, you can add items, change the shipping address, and make any other needed changes. Save the sales order, automatically create a purchase order for any needed items, and when you're ready to invoice the customer, that's automatic, too.

TIP: You can also create a purchase order automatically from the estimate.

Inventory Assemblies

Assemblies are products you create using existing inventory parts. Only QuickBooks Premier and Enterprise Editions offer the software features for assemblies (which are sometimes called *pre-builds*). In the following sections I'll go over the tasks involved in creating and managing assemblies.

TIP: This feature works slightly differently in the Accounting, Manufacturing & Distribution, and Retail Premier editions, because those products have additional features for creating and managing assemblies. See the respective chapters for those Premier editions for details.

Creating the Assembly Item

An assembly is an item, and you start by adding it to your Items list. Choose Lists → Item List to open the Item List window, and then press Ctrl-N to open the New Item dialog.

Select Inventory Assembly as the type of item, and the New Item dialog displays all the fields you need to create an assembly (see Figure 6-16).

Most of the fields are self-explanatory, but a few of them merit discussion, so I'll present some guidelines.

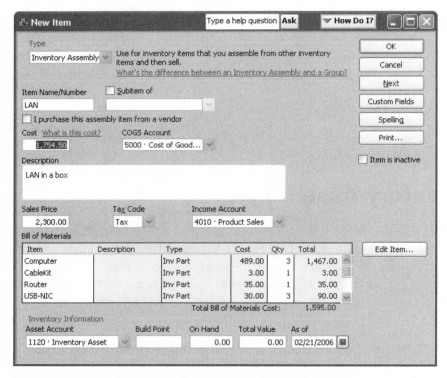

Figure 6-16: The New Item dialog holds all the information you need for assemblies.

In the Bill of Materials section, select the inventory parts required to build this item, and the quantity of each component. (You can use items other than inventory parts—see the section "Using Non-Inventory Parts in an Assembly", later in this chapter.)

The Cost field at the top of the dialog (highlighted in Figure 6-16) is optional. You can use it to create a marked-up cost for the assembly.

Then you can use that marked-up cost to do cost-plus pricing (choose Customers → Change Item Prices to calculate and save cost-plus pricing). The data you enter in this field does not affect the postings to your COG account, which continues to post the real cost (the total cost of the items in the Bill of Materials list).

The Sales Price field must be filled in manually. If you configured QuickBooks for automatic markups (in the Sales & Customers Preferences dialog), that feature doesn't apply to assemblies. (When you create inventory items, after you enter the cost, QuickBooks automatically enters the price based on the markup percentage you configured.)

The dialog has a field for entering a vendor from whom you purchase this assembly, which you probably won't use. If you subcontract the work to a vendor, you purchase the completed item the way you'd purchase any other item. That makes this an item, not an assembly.

Using Non-Inventory Items in an Assembly

By default, QuickBooks won't let you add any item that isn't an inventory part to the Bill of Materials for an assembly. That's because the items in the Bill of Materials each carry a cost, and the total cost becomes the posting to Cost of Goods when you sell the assembly.

You can edit the records of non-inventory items that you want to add to the assembly so that those items have a cost attached (or create new non-inventory items specifically for this purpose). The following item types can be used in assemblies if they're properly configured:

- **Service**. Useful for adding the cost of labor. Create a service item that's suitable for this if your Items list doesn't already contain one.
- **Non-inventory part**. Useful for adding the cost of parts that you don't track as inventory items. This could include boxes, tape, consumable goods (nails, screws, etc.).
- **Other Charge**. Useful for adding the cost of almost anything, but I usually use it for overhead (I calculate the approximate cost per hour to run the room in which assemblies are built).

To create or edit a non-inventory item so it can be used in an assembly, select the option with a label that begins "This item is used in assemblies..." (the remainder of the label text changes depending on the item type).

When you select that option, the item's dialog changes to include information about cost (see Figure 6-17).

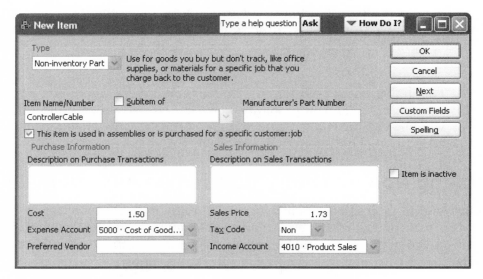

Figure 6-17: Configure a non-inventory item so it can be used in an assembly.

Editing Assemblies

You can edit an assembly in much the same way you can edit any other item. Double-click the assembly's listing in the Item list and make the required changes.

For example, you may decide to configure other item types for inclusion in assemblies, as discussed in the previous section. In the assembly's dialog, move to the next available line in the Bill of Materials section, and add the item(s). The cost of the assembly changes to reflect the new material.

Building an Assembly

After your assembly item is in your Item list, you can build it.
During this process, the component inventory items are removed
from inventory, and the finished assembly item is received into inventory.

Click the Build Assemblies icon on the Home page, or choose Vendors
→ Inventory Activities → Build Assemblies to open the Build Assemblies
dialog. Select the assembly item (only assembly items appear in the drop-
down list).

QuickBooks automatically fills in the components required for the
assembly item, along with the QOH for each inventory component (see
Figure 6-18).

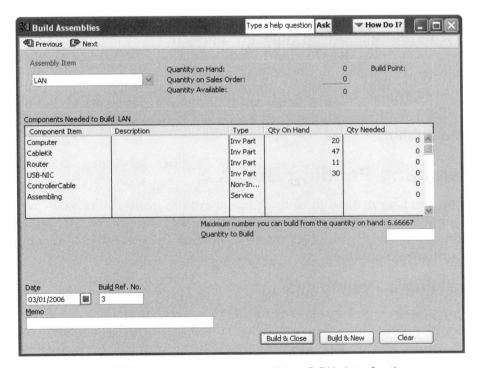

Figure 6-18: QuickBooks automatically provides QOH data for the
assembly and for the inventory component parts.

> *TIP*: *Non-inventory components aren't tracked for QOH, so if they're not service items, you must make sure you have sufficient supplies.*

The Qty Needed column remains at zero for each component until you indicate the number of builds you're creating. The dialog displays the maximum number of builds you can create with the current QOH of inventory parts (frequently a number with a lot of numbers to the right of the decimal point).

> *NOTE*: *You can build more than the maximum number you have component parts for, but builds that are missing parts are recorded as pending builds (see the section "Managing Pending Builds").*

Enter the quantity to build, and press Tab. The component quantities are adjusted: Qty On Hand is reduced, and Qty Needed is increased to match the number of builds you indicated, as seen in Figure 6-19.

Click Build & New if you want to build another assembly, or click Build & Close if you're finished. The build is moved into inventory and you can sell it.

Managing Pending Builds

If you don't have enough of the components to build the number of assemblies you need, you can continue with the build process, but the build is marked Pending. Pending builds are finalized when all the components are available.

Creating a Pending Build

When you specify a number of builds that exceeds the available quantity of components, QuickBooks displays a dialog to warn you that you don't have enough components (see Figure 6-20).

- Click Cancel to return to the Build Assemblies window, and reduce the number of builds to match your available components.

- Click Make Pending if you want to leave the number of builds as is. The build is marked pending, and you can finalize the build when the missing components arrive.

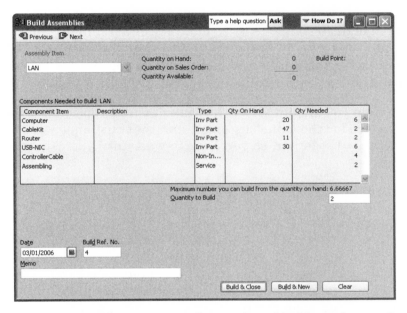

Figure 6-19: When you enter the number of builds you're creating, QuickBooks fills in the Qty Needed column.

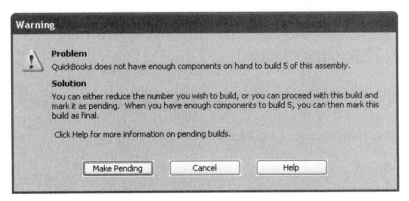

Figure 6-20: You can either make this a pending build, or cancel the build.

The entire build is marked pending. No assemblies are brought into inventory, and no components are decremented from inventory. This is true even if sufficient quantities of some of the components exist to complete the builds.

If you have enough components to build fewer assemblies than you'd specified in the Build Assemblies window, you should click Cancel. Then start again, reducing the number of assemblies so you can get the build into inventory and generate income.

The only time you should select the Make Pending option is when all the assemblies are for the same customer, and that customer wants everything delivered together, so you have to wait until you can build all the assemblies.

If you create another build for the same assembly before additional components arrive, the Build Assemblies window displays the same QOH for the components as existed when you created the previous, pending, build.

For example, when you created the pending build for two assemblies, you may have had enough components to build one assembly, but not two. The next time you open the Build Assemblies window for this assembly product, you still have enough components to build one assembly. If you build the new assembly you use up components, and the pending build has more missing components than it did when you originally saved it.

Tracking Pending Builds

Check the pending builds frequently, so you can purchase components as you need them. To see a report on the current pending bills, choose Reports → Inventory → Pending Builds. When the report opens (see Figure 6-21), it lists all pending builds.

Unfortunately, QuickBooks doesn't provide a report called "components needed for pending builds". Nor is there any way to produce a stock status report that shows items that are listed on pending bills.

Lacking those useful functions, you have to double-click each listing in the Pending Bills report to see the current stock status for components. Make notes, and then buy the components you need.

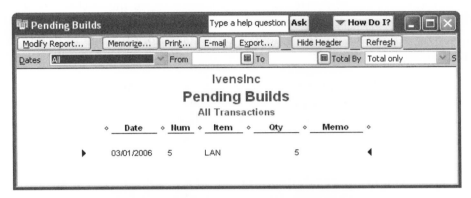

Figure 6-21: Keep an eye on pending bills to make sure you keep up with purchases.

Finalizing a Pending Build

When you receive the components that are missing in a pending build, you can finalize the build and put the assembly item into your inventory. Open the pending build by opening the Pending Builds report, and double-clicking the listing for the build you're ready to finalize.

When the window opens, the current QOH of components is displayed, and the maximum number you can build is updated to match the component availability.

If you now have sufficient quantities of components to build the assemblies, the Remove Pending Status button at the bottom of the window is activated. (The button is grayed out and inaccessible if the components aren't available).

Click Remove Pending Status to finalize the build, and close the window. QuickBooks asks you to confirm that you want to save your changes. Click Yes. The assembly item is moved into your inventory, and the inventory item components are removed from inventory.

Disassembling an Assembly

You can disassemble a built assembly item, which automatically returns the inventory components to inventory.

While you could manually adjust inventory to move the components back into inventory, and remove an assembly from inventory, that's onerous. The quickest way to remove a built assembly item is to delete the transaction that built it.

Deleting the build's transaction only works if the number of builds in that transaction matches the number of built assembly items you want to disassemble. For example, if the transaction was for three builds, and you only want to remove one, you can't use this method, you must manually adjust your inventory numbers.

Open the original build window, and choose Edit → Delete Build from the QuickBooks menu bar. If the build is finalized, QuickBooks readjusts your inventory appropriately. If the build is pending, no adjustments need to be made.

Chapter 7

Advanced Reporting Tools

Exporting report templates

Importing report templates

Closing date exception report

The QuickBooks Premier editions contain features for managing reports that aren't available in QuickBooks Pro or QuickBooks Basic. In this chapter, I'll go over some of the advanced reporting capabilities you have available in your Premier edition.

Exporting Reports as Templates

The ability to customize reports is one of the most popular features in QuickBooks. You can customize the layout, filter the content, and modify the sort order of reports. This means you can get exactly the information you want, omitting the need to wade through information you don't care about.

Adding to the power inherent in report customization is the ability to memorize a customized report. The memorization is intelligent, ignoring the actual data, and retaining only the customized settings for layout, filters, and sorted order. When a previously memorized report is opened, the data that appears is fetched from transactions, and is therefore current and correct.

QuickBooks Premier editions add a third layer of power to reports, by providing the ability to export templates of customized, memorized, reports. Here's how it works:

- Only QuickBooks Premier editions can export templates.
- All QuickBooks editions can import templates.

You can export a template when you want to move a customized report to another company file, or even to another edition of QuickBooks. If you're an accountant, you can export report templates to your clients to make sure you get exactly the reports you need.

Customizing Reports for Templates

A template is an exported copy of a memorized report, and it's assumed the report has been customized. However, the type and scope of the customizations you can apply are limited, because the report must be able to work with any company file.

When you click the Modify Report button in a report window, the tabs in the Modify Report dialog offer a wide range of customization options. The following section describes the modifications you must avoid.

Selecting Display Options

When you modify a report, the Display tab of some reports has a Columns list. You can display or remove any of those columns. Generally, summary reports don't offer this list, but detail reports do.

You can customize the report by adding or removing columns, but you must be careful to avoid using any custom fields you created for your names lists or items list (see Figure 7-1).

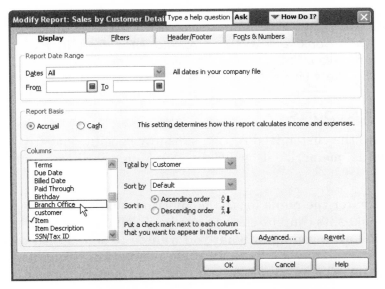

Figure 7-1: Deselect the columns for custom fields you created.

TIP: *I frequently deselect the column labeled "left margin" (which is automatically selected), because removing that column makes it easier to fit more information on a printed page, and lessens the amount of scrolling required when you display reports on the screen.*

Selecting Filters

You cannot include filters that are unique to the company file that's open when you customize the report. Instead, as you choose the filters, you must be careful to select filters that work anywhere, anytime, for any QuickBooks data file. For example, if you're filtering for accounts, you cannot select specific accounts. Instead, you must select an account type.

Most of the filters offer universal choices that allow you to customize the report to obtain the data you need. Some filters don't have lists; instead, they have simple options such as Open or Closed. You can't get into trouble with those filters, because they offer no opportunity to use data from the company file.

NOTE: *QuickBooks displays an error message if you try to export a template that contains anything specific to your own files in the filters you set.*

Memorizing Reports

After you create the customized report, sans any specific data from your own company file, memorize it by clicking the Memorize button on the report window.

When you enter the name for the memorized report, be sure to create a name that makes its content clear to everyone. Names that are meaningful to you (because you knew what you wanted to accomplish with your customizations) may not work for other people. For example, the name "OpBillNoAge" may signify to you that the Open Bill report lacks the aging days because you removed the Age column. However, if you're planning to export the report, a name such as OpenBills-DateOnly" might be a better report title.

Exporting a Template

QuickBooks creates templates for export by saving the report in its own proprietary format, which has a file extension .qbr. To export a memorized report as a template than can be imported into QuickBooks, use the following steps:

1. Choose Reports → Memorized Reports → Memorized Report List to open the Memorized Report List.
2. Select the report you want to export.
3. Click the Memorized Report button at the bottom of the window to display the command list.
4. Select Export Template to open the Specify Filename For Export dialog (which looks like a Save dialog).
5. Accept the default name for the template (which is the name of the report), or enter a different name.
6. Click Save.

Only the settings are saved in the template, not the data that appeared in the customized report. The data, of course, was specific to the QuickBooks company file that was open when you created the report.

By default, QuickBooks saves the template in the QuickBooks software folder. It's a good idea to create a folder for your templates so you can find them easily (the QuickBooks folder is crowded).

Sending a Template

Report templates (files with the extension .qbr) use very few bytes, so the easiest way to send them is as an attachment to an e-mail message. You could also use a floppy disk (multiple templates easily fit on a floppy disk), or burn a CD, and mail it.

If you're an accountant, don't forget to send your client instructions for importing the template (see the section, "Importing a Report Template", later in this chapter).

Of course, you can deliver the disk in person, or send your QuickBooks service person. If you do, you can perform the import yourself, instead of sending instructions with the file.

Using Memorized Report Groups

It's a good idea to create memorized report groups, so you can quickly find the right report when you need to export its template. Create your groups to match the type of memorized reports you amass.

For example, an accountant may export templates for reports needed to create taxes, so your report groups may be named BalSheet and P&L. If you create templates for other types of reports, you may have groups for A/R and A/P. Here's how to create a memorized report group:

1. Choose Reports → Memorized Reports → Memorized Report List, to open the Memorized Report List.
2. Click the Memorized Report button at the bottom of the window, and select New Group.
3. In the New Memorized Report Group dialog, enter a name for the group, and click OK.

If you already have some memorized reports that you plan to export as templates, you can move them into the new group, using the following steps:

1. In the Memorized Report List window, select the report you want to move into a group.
2. Press Ctrl-E to edit the report listing.
3. Select the Save In Memorized Report Group check box.
4. Select the appropriate group from the drop-down list.
5. Click OK.

Exporting a Group of Memorized Reports

If you've created report groups, you can export an entire group of memorized reports in one fell swoop. Use the following steps to accomplish

1. Choose Reports → Memorized Reports → Memorized Report List
2. In the Memorized Report List window, select the group to export.
3. Click the Memorized Report button, and choose Export Template from the menu.
4. In the Specify Filename For Export dialog, create a name for the file, or accept the default name that QuickBooks inserts.

(QuickBooks uses the name of the group, followed by the word "Group".)

5. Click Save to create the file.

The recipient can import the group, adding this group to his or her Memorized Report List (see the section "Importing a Group of Memorized Reports").

Importing a Report Template

Importing a report template actually does nothing more than convert the template file into a memorized report. The report is added to the Memorized Report list of the company file that's open during the import process. To import a template, use the following steps:

1. Choose Reports → Memorized Reports → Memorized Report List.
2. Click the Memorized Report button at the bottom of the window, and select Import Template.
3. Navigate to the drive or folder that contains the template file, and double-click its listing.
4. In the Memorize Report dialog, enter a name for the report, or accept the displayed name (which is the name used by the person who exported the template).

The report is now available in the Memorized Reports list.

Importing a Group of Memorized Reports

For the recipient, importing a report template file that is a group of memorized reports is the same as importing a single report template. When the template is imported, the recipient gains the new group, along with its contents (multiple memorized reports). The group name appears in the Memorized Report List window, and the individual reports are listed.

Closing Date Exception Report

The Closing Date Exception report, available only in QuickBooks Premier editions, tells you whether closed transactions were modified or created.

To understand the importance of the Closing Date Exception report, you have to understand what closing the books means in QuickBooks.

QuickBooks doesn't "close" the books the way most other accounting software applications do. For businesses that use most other accounting software, closing a period is a definitive action, and can't be undone. Once closed, a period is locked, and no transactions in that period can be added or changed.

Those "real" closings have some important advantages. The biggest benefit to a closing process that's a true lock-down is that all the reports that were produced about the locked period remain accurate and valid forever. There is no chance that anything can change.

Another benefit is the fact that someone bent on illegal activities (such as embezzling) cannot get into a prior period to hide an illegal transaction. This is a temptation that is based on the assumption that business owners (and even accountants) rarely look closely at prior period transactions. Unfortunately, this assumption is usually accurate.

On the other hand, a real closing procedure can be a frazzling experience, because you can't close the books until you're sure you've recorded everything that needs to be entered. I have many clients with accounting departments that fall behind on the day-to-day work for a few days each month, because they're closing the previous month.

The same thing happens, with even more intensity, every January or February, when it's time to close the year. Even with all that effort and pressure, it's not unusual to hear "uh oh" after the books are closed. The bookkeeper, controller, or accountant has found a transaction that should have been recorded in the prior year (usually a journal entry).

QuickBooks Closing Date Procedures

QuickBooks only has a closing procedure for the end of the fiscal year; monthly closings don't exist. When you close a year in QuickBooks, the lock you put into place isn't impenetrable. It's a combination lock (remember the lock on your high school locker?) and anyone can enter who knows, or can guess, the combination.

In QuickBooks, you close a year by setting a closing date. Once the date is entered, users shouldn't change or add transactions that have a date before, or on, that closing date. You perform this action by entering a closing date in the Accounting category of the Preferences dialog (see Figure 7-2).

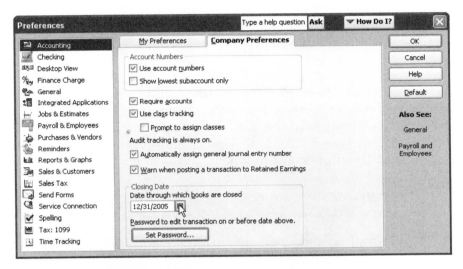

Figure 7-2: Enter your closing date.

In addition to entering the date, you can specify a password to allow users (including yourself) to add or modify transactions on or before the closing date. The password is not required, and if it's omitted, any user can continue to record, edit, void, or delete transactions in the previous year.

When a user creates, modifies or deletes a transaction that carries a date falling in the closed year, QuickBooks issues the warning seen in Figure 7-3.

If you specify a password when you set your closing date, QuickBooks asks for the password before displaying the warning about affecting transactions in the closed period. If the user has the password, QuickBooks permits transactions to occur in the prior year, changing prior year balances.

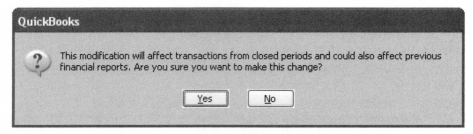

Figure 7-3: Just click Yes to add or change a transaction in a closed
           period.

If a user attempts to void a transaction in the closed period, QuickBooks displays a message offering to create an automatic reversing JE to cover the changes in the closing and opening balances of the past and current year (see Figure 7-4). Unfortunately, the dialog includes an option to omit this important balancing transaction.

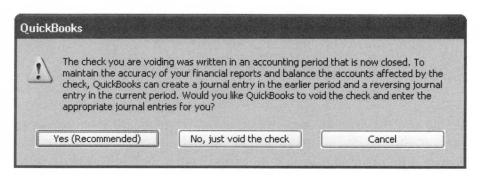

Figure 7-4: It's easy to make changes that disturb the closing bal-
           ance

Wait, it gets more interesting. You can re-open your books after you've closed them. Just delete the Closing Date and click OK. Period. That's it. Sigh!

If anyone re-opens your books, users have access to the previous year and can enter, modify, or remove transactions. If you previously printed your year-end reports, or, even worse, prepared your tax forms, you have a potential disaster on your hands.

Dangers of Changes to Previous Year Transactions

If a password is linked to the closing date, only users who know the password can work in the previous year. I've seen this paradigm fail many times, as I've worked with clients to uncover problems that turned out to be embezzlement activities.

I've encountered situations where a business owner trusted a user enough to give that person the password, and the trust was misplaced. Sadly, in a number of those cases, the nefarious user was a family member. (Business owners tend to entrust passwords to members of their family who work in the business.)

I've also had clients who discovered illegal activities in a closed period that were eventually traced to employees who hadn't been given the password. In every case, the closing date password was easily available—a note in an unlocked drawer, an easy-to-guess password (the owner's birth date, nickname, dog's name, or other easy deduction), and even notes affixed to monitors.

I've found orders that were shipped with a date previous to the closing date, and the neer-do-well employee happily enjoyed the ill-gotten goods. The shipment was often sent to an accomplice who was the customer on the transaction. The shipment didn't appear on reports that were generated as a matter of course, because the transactions didn't fall in the date range of the report (which is almost always a date range in the current fiscal year). Eventually, the accountant, or a sharp bookkeeper, may notice the problem, and the hunt for a solution sometimes (but not always) uncovers the crime.

Other problems I've encountered were inventory adjustments (to cover pilfering), and even the deletion of a check made out to cash that somehow made it through the reconciliation process without raising questions. However, to ensure long-term secrecy, the check was deleted after the books were closed. Because the changed balances don't show up on current reports, they frequently escape notice. If they *are* noticed, they're often difficult to track.

Sometimes, discovery occurs because of a disparity between the closing balances of the year-end reports, and the opening balances of current reports. Another clue is an out-of-sequence number, or a missing number. For example, if the first invoice in the current year is number 501, and you find that Invoice 506 is missing, or is dated in the prior year, be suspicious.

If the transaction has been deleted (a missing transaction number), detection can be quite difficult. If the transaction wasn't deleted, it's easy to find the problem if the customer name attached to the transaction isn't familiar. However, a smart embezzler merges that customer into an existing customer, making the investigation more difficult.

Lest you think I dwell only on the darkest side of the world, let me hasten to tell you that the majority of incidents that involve messing around with transactions in the closed period aren't nefarious.

Innocent changes to transactions are frequently made by users who are honestly trying to correct a problem. These users think it's faster and more efficient to change a transaction that was entered erroneously last December than it is to create a journal entry in January to correct balances. For perfectly harmless reasons, users delete or void transactions in the previous year, or add transactions by dating them in the previous year.

Changes to previous periods drive accountants crazy, because the notion that a closing balance must equal the next opening balance is a basic rule of accounting. Incorrect opening balances can also affect your tax returns. And, of course, unexplained changes in opening balances can present difficult challenges if you're undergoing an audit.

Generating the Closing Date Exception Report

To view the Closing Date Exception Report, choose Reports → Accountant & Taxes → Closing Date Exception Report. As you can see in Figure 7-5, the report lists all transactions that were added or changed after the closing date was set.

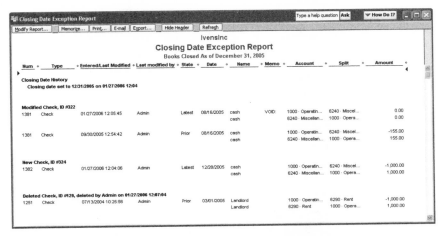

Figure 7-5: Checks payable to cash were modified, and another was created, after the books were closed. Hmmm.

Interpreting the Closing Date Exception Report

I think it's important to understand how to read and interpret the Closing Date Exception Report, which can be confusing.

The top of the report is the history of your use of the closing date feature. Normally, it displays the following information:

- The fact that a closing date was set
- The closing date (the last day of the previous year)
- The date on which this closing action took place

If the closing date was set, then removed (the books were re-opened), and then the closing date was set again, the report shows that fact (see Figure 7-6).

The section below the closing date information displays the details of each exception (change). A description of the type of change (modified, new, deleted, etc.) appears above each entry, along with an internal QuickBooks ID number. Incidentally, modified means any type of change, which could range from changing the amount, the customer, vendor, or employee name, or voiding the transaction.

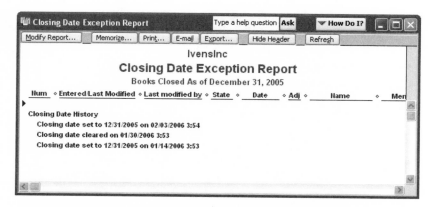

Figure 7-6: The report shows all closings and openings in reverse
chronological order.

The columns display additional information about each transaction,
and the important data is the following:

- The Type column displays the type of transaction (see the next
  section "Transaction Types").
- The Entered/Last Modified Date column displays the date on
  which the transaction was changed (or entered, if the transaction
  is new). This date is after the closing date, or the entry wouldn't
  exist in this report.
- The Date column displays the date on which the original transaction occurred.
- The columns on the right display the financial information (posting accounts, amount)

If you configured your company file to use logins, the Last Modified
By column displays the name of the user who modified the transaction. If
you're not using logins, you still know what was changed (which is the
important financial information) but you won't know who did it.

---

*TIP: User logins don't work unless you enforce security rules.
To make sure users bent on nefarious actions can't gain entry
via another user's login and password, insist that all users
close the company file when they leave their desks.*

QuickBooks Transaction Types

Most of the codes for transaction types (the column labeled Type) are self explanatory, but some are not. To help you translate, Table 7-1 explains the QuickBooks transaction types.

Transaction Code	Meaning
BILL	Bills from vendors created in the Enter Bills window, or added directly to the A/P register.
BILLCRED	Credits from vendors created in the Enter Bills window.
BILLPMT	Payments to vendors created in the Pay Bills window.
CREDMEM	Credit memos to customers created in the Create Credit Memos/Refunds window.
CC	Credit card charges created in the Enter Credit Card Charges window, or in a credit card account register.
CC CRED	Credit card credits created in the Enter Credit Card Charges window, or in a credit card account register.
CHK	Checks created in the Write Checks window, or in a bank account register.
DEP	Bank deposits created in the Make Deposits window or in a bank account register.
DISC	Discounts automatically calculated based on payment terms for a customer or vendor.
GENJRNL	General journal entries created in the General Journal Entry window, or in the account register of an asset, liability, or equity account.
INV	Invoices created in the Create Invoices window.
ITEM RCPT	Item receipts created in the Create Item Receipts window.
LIAB CHK	Checks for payroll taxes and other payroll liabilities created in the Liability Check window.
PAY CHK	Paychecks to employees created in the Select Employees to Pay and Preview Paychecks windows.
PMT	Payments from customers created in the Receive Payments window.
STMTCHG	Statement charges billed to customers, created in a customer's register or in the A/R register.
RCPT	Sales receipts created in the Enter Sales Receipts window.
TAXPMT	Sales tax payments created in the Pay Sales Tax window.
TRANSFR	Transferred funds created in the Transfer Funds Between Accounts window, or between any two balance sheet accounts registers.

Table 7-1: QuickBooks transaction codes and their meanings.

Some types of transactions have no codes, because they don't post amounts to your general ledger (they have their own account registers that do not affect your financial totals). The following transaction types have no codes:

- Estimates
- Pending assembly builds
- Pending invoices
- Purchase orders
- Sales orders

The transaction codes are displayed in account registers as well as in reports such as the Closing Date Exception Report.

Chapter 8

Planning and Forecasting

Using Business Planner

Creating a Forecast

Q uickBooks Premier editions include tools you can use to plan and predict your growth: Business Planner, and the Forecasting tool.

The Business Planner is a powerful software application that lets you project your business finances for the next three years. The business plan it produces is detailed and professional.

NOTE: *The business plan you produce is based on the format recommended by the U.S. Small Business Administration for loan applications or a bank line of credit.*

The forecasting tool lets you predict revenue and cash flow for a year. You can modify the data in your forecast to create "what if" scenarios to help you make decisions about the direction and speed of your growth.

Business Planner

B usiness Planner is a robust application that walks you through the process of creating a comprehensive business plan, which is a detailed prediction of your company's future. The tool's user interface is wizard-like, and it works very much like the EasyStep Interview you use to set up a QuickBooks company file. A series of sections, each of which has multiple windows to go through, cover the categories involved in building a plan.

Creating a comprehensive business plan isn't a cakewalk, and you should plan on devoting quite a bit of time to complete yours, if you want a truly comprehensive plan. You can create a business plan for your own business, or, if you're an accounting professional, for a client's business.

WARNING: *You must have a copy of Adobe Reader to use Business Planner. If you don't have Adobe Reader (or you have a very old copy of the software), QuickBooks issues a message with a link to the Adobe download page. After you install Adobe Reader, launch the Business Planner again.*

Launch the Business Planner by choosing Company → Planning & Budgeting → Use Business Plan Tool. The program opens with the user license agreement, which you must agree to. Then the Welcome screen appears, which explains the processes involved in creating the business plan (see Figure 8-1). Click Next to move through the windows and the sections that follow.

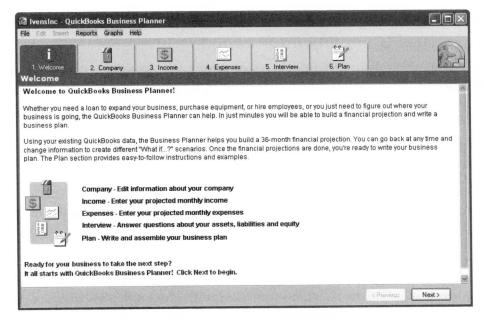

Figure 8-1: The Business Planner window has tabs for each section of the process.

NOTE: *Each time you open the Business Planner, the information you've already entered remains, and you're taken to the last window you were using. To make changes to any information you entered earlier, click Previous to back up. You can take your time creating your plan without worrying about starting from scratch every time you open the software.*

Entering Company Information

The first set of wizard windows consists of the Company section, where you enter basic information about your business. Depending on the information you enter in each window, the questions in the ensuing windows differ. The following sections offer some guidelines to help you understand the questions you may see, and the information you're asked to enter.

General Company Information

The general company information section has several windows. Click Next to move through the section. Your responses appear on the cover of your printed plan, so enter information in the windows with that in mind.

For the company name, enter the name you do business as (if your business has both a legal name and a DBA name). Then enter your contact information.

For the company contact information, enter the name, title, and telephone number of the person who will be the contact for the recipient of your plan. For example, if you're planning to give the business plan to a bank, use the name of the person who has the answers to any questions the bank's officers may ask. On the other hand, you may want to list the person who has the best relationship with the bank's officers.

Income Tax Information

Enter the income tax form you use. Only C Corporations (and some LLCs) pay taxes (using Form 1120), so if your business is organized as any other type of entity, no company tax information is calculated. Businesses other than C Corps (and LLCs that report as corporations) pay no income taxes (profits or losses are transferred to your personal tax return).

If your company is a C corp or LLC filing a corporate tax return, the business planner calculates your estimated tax payments. After you select Tax Form 1120, and click Next, you're asked to estimate your corporate tax rate. Remember that you probably have a combined tax rate, because you have to consider both federal and state corporate taxes. For your convenience, the wizard displays a federal tax table you can consult (see Figure 8-2).

TIP: I've found that many small business owners have a problem finding the appropriate tax form if they're operating as a proprietorship. They look for Schedule C, which isn't listed in the drop-down list of tax forms. Instead, select Tax Form 1040, which is where proprietors file their business income. Schedule C is merely an attachment to that form.

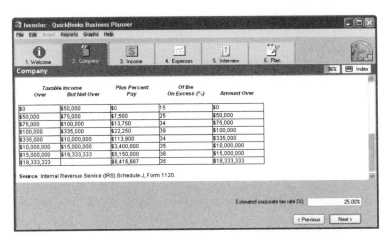

Figure 8-2: The corporate tax table from Schedule J is available to help you estimate your corporate tax percentage.

Incidentally, even though you remit your estimated corporate taxes quarterly, the business planner calculates the payments on a monthly basis, using the profits for that month. If a month shows a loss, the planner carries over the loss to the next month in order to calculate income taxes.

If your business does not file Form 1120, the software doesn't factor in business income tax expenses. In that case, fill in the estimated monthly amount for owner distributions (you don't have to enter the dollar sign).

> *TIP: If your company is an S Corporation, owner distributions don't include salaries paid to the owners (those amounts are expensed).*

Customer Credit Information

In the next window, enter the approximate percentage of your sales that are credit-based. If you don't extend credit to your customers, enter zero, and you won't see the ensuing windows that deal with receivables.

Except for over-the-counter retail sales businesses, most businesses provide credit to their customers. Using agreed upon terms of credit, you send invoices, which means you probably have current (and probably overdue) receivables.

> *NOTE: Credit card sales are cash sales, and accepting credit cards from customers is not the same as extending credit.*

If you entered any figure except zero for the question about the percentage of sales that involve credit, the next window asks about terms. Select the payment terms you offer customers from the drop-down list. If you offer multiple terms, enter the terms you apply most frequently.

The drop-down list doesn't offer any terms that imply discounts for timely payment (e.g. 2%10 Net 30), because the business planner doesn't factor in those discounts. The terms drop-down list includes the common terms: Less than 30, Net 30, Net 60, Net 90, Net 120.

In the next window, enter the percentage of your credit sales that you think could qualify as bad debt. Bad debt means money you know you'll never collect.

Business Plan Start Date

Enter the start date for the business plan, which doesn't necessarily have to coincide with the start date of your fiscal year. By default, the selection is the first month of your next fiscal year.

Enter a start date that seems appropriate for the purpose of your business plan, and for the recipient of your business plan documentation.

For example, you may have a specific project in mind (physical office expansion, product line expansion, and so on), for which you're presenting the business plan to banks or investors. Use a business plan start date that matches, or comes close to, the date on which you plan to begin this new financial project.

Income Projection

In the Income section, you face several chores. You must set up income categories (you can have up to twenty), and project the income for each category for the next three years.

The first time you visit the first window in the Income section, a Projection Wizard appears to ask if you'd like to set the figures by pulling information from your QuickBooks company file.

The Projection Wizard saves you a lot of work, and you can always change any of the figures that are automatically entered if you want to create "what if" scenarios.

However, if you've just started using QuickBooks, you won't have sufficient data in your company file to extract anything meaningful, so you must enter the information manually.

Even if you have sufficient data in your QuickBooks company file, you may prefer to enter the income information manually, especially if you're about to embark on a new product or service, or you've just started to reach a new customer base. In that case, you probably want to project income that reflects your new, expanded, business expectations.

If you're an accounting professional who is creating the business plan and projections for a client, you can dismiss the wizard and manually enter the figures you obtained from your client. Or, you can ask the client for a copy of the company file, load it in QuickBooks, and launch the business plan software. Then you can let the wizard fetch data from the file.

If you cancel the Projection Wizard, or leave the Business Planner software at this point, the next time you get to this window, the Projection Wizard doesn't appear automatically. Click the Projection Wizard toolbar icon to open the wizard. Incidentally, the toolbar isn't at the top of the Business Planner window, it's atop the income category table (see Figure 8-3).

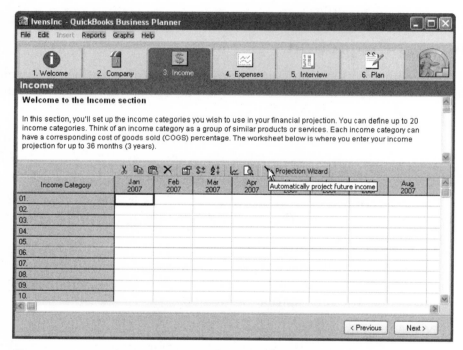

Figure 8-3: You can launch the Projection Wizard whenever you wish.

In the following sections, I'll cover both scenarios, starting with the Projection Wizard, and then explaining how to enter projections manually.

Using the Projection Wizard

The Projection Wizard opens with an introductory window. Click Next to begin the real work. Enter the beginning date for your business plan. By default, the wizard enters the month and year you earlier specified as the beginning of your business plan, but you can change that date.

Choosing the Projection Basis

When you click Next, the wizard examines the company data, and then asks how to proceed (see Figure 8-4).

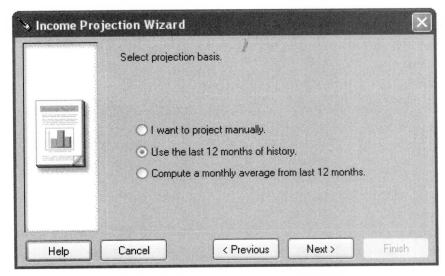

Figure 8-4: Select the method you want to use to project future income.

The method you choose depends on the amount of data in your QuickBooks company file, and the financial differences among the months of data. The Business Planner uses monthly data to project a percentage of increase (or decrease).

If you select the option Use The Last 12 Months Of History, the algorithm is rather complicated, and is adjusted to take into consideration the current month, and the interval between your first month and the current month. The algorithm also attaches more weight to recent months than it does to earlier months. If your monthly figures are fairly consistent, you can select the option to use the last twelve months of history.

If your recent months have shown a substantial upturn or downturn in performance, and the cause of that inconsistency isn't permanent, those monthly figures might influence the projections, and make them less reliable. In that case, tell the wizard to compute a monthly average.

Applying a Growth Factor

When you click Next, you're offered the opportunity to apply a yearly growth factor (see Figure 8-5). Select a number from the drop-down list, or enter a number directly into the field. The number is interpreted as a percentage.

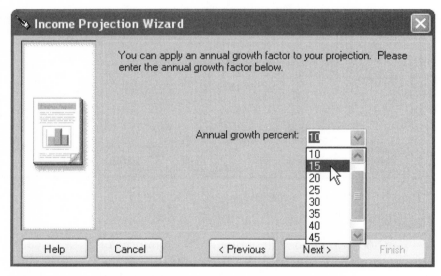

Figure 8-5: Project the yearly growth of your company.

Selecting the Type of Income to Project

Click Next to see a list of the income accounts the wizard found in your chart of accounts. Each account is pre-selected for inclusion in the wizard's calculations (see Figure 8-6).

You can deselect any income account you don't want to use by clicking the check box to remove the check mark. For example, it's common to exclude an interest income account, or a miscellaneous income account that doesn't reflect ongoing revenue. Click Finish to start the calculations.

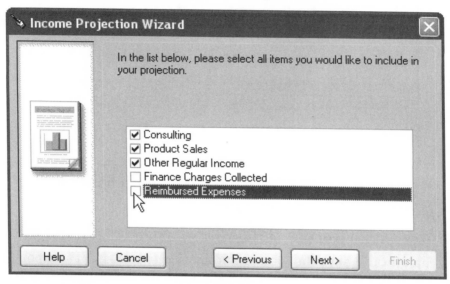

Figure 8-6: Deselect the type of income that doesn't belong in your projection.

NOTE: If you're using subaccounts for income tracking, note that the wizard only uses parent accounts.

Viewing the Results

The wizard performs its calculations and fills in the monthly figures, as seen in Figure 8-7. You may see an informational message first, telling you that the wizard used a percentage of gross revenue to calculate cost of goods. The message also explains that you can change the wizard's mathematical assumptions by editing the properties of any income category (see the section "Editing the Properties Behind the Data", later in this chapter).

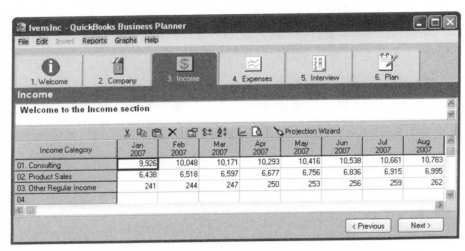

Figure 8-7: The wizard enters monthly figures for a 36-month projection.

Editing the Wizard's Data

You can edit the data the wizard automatically inserts. It's important to note that the wizard automatically adjusts income figures by subtracting a percentage of the gross to cover cost of goods. You should clean up those numbers, either because the wizard's percentage for cost of goods is radically different from your real costs, or because you don't have any cost of goods deductions since you only sell services.

To change the contents of a cell, select it. Then enter a number to replace the existing number. If you want to change the number by a specific percentage, after you select the cell, press Ctrl-F (or click the Function icon on the toolbar) to open the Functions dialog for the cell, seen in Figure 8-8. Then specify the percentage by which you want to raise or lower the figure.

You can also edit the calculation basis for an entire row by clicking the row heading (the title on the left edge of the row) to select the entire row. Then press Ctrl-F (or click the Function icon on the toolbar). The same Functions dialog appears, so you can change the algorithm used on the row.

Here are the guidelines for using the Functions dialog for a row:

- Select Annual Growth, and then enter a percentage figure, to change the projection for any selected row. This is a good way to project your company's future income by revenue type, instead of using a single percentage for the entire business.
- Select Raise or Lower, and then enter a percentage, to change all the figures in the row by that percentage.
- Select Repeat to copy the contents of the first cell in the row to all the other cells in the row.

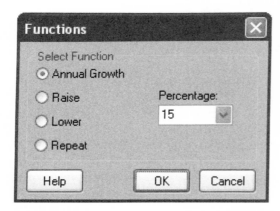

Figure 8-8: Use the Functions dialog to change the value of a cell by a percentage.

Editing the Properties Behind the Data

You can change the basic properties of a row (an income account), including its title, and the way Business Planner calculates Cost of Sales. Double-click a row heading to open its Properties dialog, seen in Figure 8-9.

If the selected income category has labor or other costs in addition to, or instead of, standard cost of goods, adjust the data in the dialog to gain a more realistic projection. If no costs of good are involved for this type of income, change all the fields to zero.

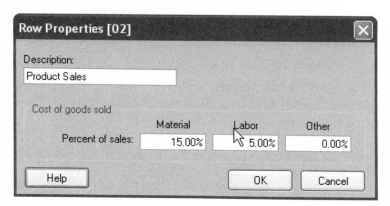

Figure 8-9: Changing the properties for an income category changes
the way the data is calculated.

Entering Income Data Manually

If you opt to skip the wizard, or if the wizard tells you there isn't enough
data in your company file to proceed, you can enter the numbers for your
income manually. Click Next, and then click Finish in the next wizard
window to close the wizard. The bottom of the program window resem-
bles a blank spreadsheet, with rows for categories and columns for
months.

Double-click the row header for the first category to open its
Properties dialog (refer back to Figure 8-9), and enter the title (an income
category). If the category involves a product, also enter the information
for costs of goods (in percentages). If the category is a service, you can
omit the cost of goods figures.

After you set up all your categories, you can begin entering figures.
Move horizontally through the months by pressing the Tab key. If you
want to fine tune your figures by raising or lowering amounts by a percentage, click the Functions icon to perform the task.

Expenses Projection

Entering data for expenses is similar to entering data for income. The
Projection Wizard is available for finding expense account names and

amounts in your QuickBooks company file, or you can choose to design the expenses section manually.

Using the Wizard for Expenses

You can click the Projection Wizard icon to automate your expenses projections, which involves almost exactly the same steps involved in using the wizard for projecting income. Click Next to move through the windows.

As with income projections, you can apply an annual growth percentage to the expense data in your business plan. The Projection Wizard selects and displays the expense accounts that are used for the projection (see Figure 8-10).

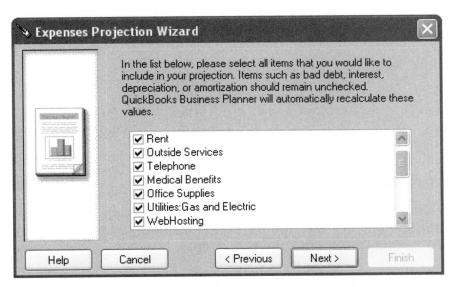

Figure 8-10: Deselect any expense accounts that shouldn't be used in your projections.

Expense accounts that are selected include both parent accounts and subaccounts. The Projection Wizard skips the following expenses:

- Interest
- Depreciation

- Amortization
- Bad debt expenses

NOTE: *Business Planner automatically enters the appropriate amounts for the expense types it skips, using information from answers you provide as you go through the interview.*

You can manipulate the data the Projection Wizard enters. Use the instructions in the previous section on Income Projections to define expense categories, enter financial data, and set the calculation methods.

Entering Expenses Manually

As with the income section, you can enter the numbers for your expenses manually, and use that data for your projections.

Double-click the row header for the first category to open its Properties dialog and enter the title (an expense category). After you set up all your categories, you can begin entering figures. Move horizontally through the months by pressing the Tab key. If you want to fine tune your figures by raising or lowering amounts by a percentage, click the Functions icon to use the utilities it offers.

Interview Section

The next part of the Business Planner is the Interview section. Most of the information you enter in this section is connected to your balance sheet accounts (assets, liabilities, and equity).

Assets

The wizard displays the current balances in your asset accounts, including cash, fixed assets, accumulated depreciation for fixed assets, accounts receivable, and any other asset accounts (see Figure 8-11). These figures are taken from your company file.

The current balances are considered opening balances for the business plan. If you expect significant changes in any of these accounts before the first day of your business plan, make an adjustment to the appropriate account(s) in the Balance column.

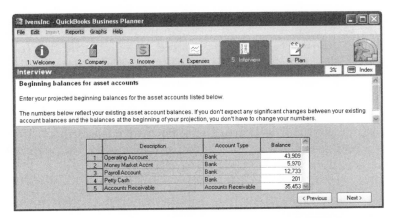

Figure 8-11: The Business Planner transfers data from your general ledger.

Minimum Bank Balances

The next window asks for the minimum bank balance your company must have available at all times. (The window also displays the current balance in each of your bank accounts.) Enter an amount that represents the total cash on hand you believe to be a minimum for sustaining your business.

To define the minimum balance, you must consider your monthly expenses, the number of times you have unexpected expenses (and their average amounts), and any other bank balance considerations you must meet. There are no rules or percentages for you to follow, this is a figure that is closely related to your type of business, and the way you do business. Ask your accountant for advice if you're having difficulty ascertaining a number.

Inventory

The next window asks if you maintain inventory, and if you answer affirmatively, the ensuing windows ask for information related to inventory issues, including the following:

- Inventory related accounts (assets and expenses).
- Terms you have with vendors that supply inventory items. Only net terms are offered in the drop-down list, the Business Planner ignores discounts for timely payment.
- Inventory levels. Specify fixed or variable. Companies with fixed levels usually have regular, predictable, sales of products (especially common with retail businesses). Companies with variable levels usually have irregular sales, and commonly respond to special orders, seasonal sales, or other variable patterns.
- Inventory values. If you select a fixed inventory level, you need to specify the amount of inventory you maintain, in dollars. If you select a variable inventory level, you must specify the number of days of inventory you like to keep on hand.

New Asset Purchases

The Business Planner needs to know whether you plan to purchase additional assets at the beginning of the business plan projection. The assets can be anything except inventory, such as the following:

- Land
- Buildings
- Building improvements
- Equipment (business, manufacturing, vehicles, furniture, fixtures, etc.)
- Deposits

If you select No, the Business Planner moves on to the next category (Liabilities). If you select Yes, you have additional information to enter. Start by providing information about the category and cost of your upcoming asset purchase, as seen in Figure 8-12.

The Business Planner asks if you'll be financing any of the asset purchases. If you respond in the affirmative, enter the loan information. Specify whether the loan is a standard loan (fixed monthly payments covering interest and principal), or a one-pay loan (interest only, with a single payment for principal at the end of the loan). The Business Planner can calculate the monthly payment, term, interest rate, or total amount of the loan, as long as you enter data in three of those four categories.

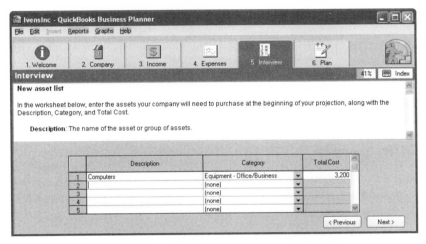

Figure 8-12: Business Planner uses the category to determine the
type of depreciation to apply.

Liabilities

The next part of the Interview section is about your company's liabilities. The Business Planner displays the liability accounts it finds in your chart of accounts, along with the current balance for each of those accounts.

Set Beginning Balances for Liability Accounts

The Business Planner needs to establish beginning balances for the three years of the projection. You can change the amount of any displayed balance to reflect a more accurate amount for projecting your company's financial position.

Enter Line of Credit Information

All of the accounts of the type Credit Card are displayed, along with their current balances. In addition, the Business Planner displays the names of your accounts of the type Current Liability, and asks if any of these accounts are line of credit accounts.

The current balances of the accounts you select as line of credit accounts are added to the total balances of your credit cards, and the grand total is treated as your current line of credit obligation.

In the next window, enter the total credit limit for the aggregate line of credit accounts. If you don't know the limit for any credit card, try to find a copy of a bill—the limit is displayed on every statement you get.

In the following window, enter the average interest rate for all your line of credit accounts.

Long Term Loans

In the Long Term Loans section, the Business Planner displays the name and current balance of all the accounts in your chart of accounts that are of the type Long Term Liabilities.

Enter the description, type of loan, APR, interest rate, and other financial information for each long-term loan.

Investing in Your Business

As you entered data in each of the Business Planner windows, the software performed calculations in the background. The calculations took into consideration your income, the status of your receivables, your debt, and other financial factors. The results of the calculations are displayed in the next window.

If no additional capital is deemed to be required to meet your financial goals and obligations, you're asked if you'd like to invest capital anyway. If you're planning to infuse your business with capital, enter the amount; otherwise leave the amount at zero, and click Next.

However, as a result of the calculations, you may be advised to provide additional capital to meet your monthly expenses over the course of the three years of the projection. For example, if you'd indicated you were planning to purchase an automobile, and didn't indicate an auto loan, you're probably going to be short of cash. Or, perhaps you entered a figure for a minimum bank balance that is larger than your current capital can handle.

The Business Planner displays the amount you need to invest to cover the shortage. Enter the amount you're planning to put towards the shortage, and click Next. If you didn't enter an amount sufficient to cover the shortage, the next window asks about the loans you're planning to cover your shortage.

The next two windows ask about financial transactions you may be considering during the three years of the projection. Enter the amounts for any additional assets you think you may purchase, and the amounts of any loans you think you may incur.

Writing Your Business Plan

Now that all the information about your company's finances has been recorded in the Business Planner, you can begin writing your business plan.

Business plans include detailed written sections that cover a wide range of topics. You must explain the figures, your plans for growth, your marketing goals, and so on. The terminology you use should be chosen with the reader in mind (a bank, a venture capitalist, a potential partner, etc.).

As seen in Figure 8-13, the Business Planner provides assistance by displaying the components of the written plan in the left pane. Expand each section by clicking the plus sign, which reveals the subsections. Move through the components by clicking Next.

> *TIP*: Click the Example tab to see sample text for each component.

The writing area offers standard formatting tools so you can make the written plan look more professional. In addition, the toolbar has icons for inserting data and graphs (linked to the data) from the Income and Expenses sections you completed in the Business Planner.

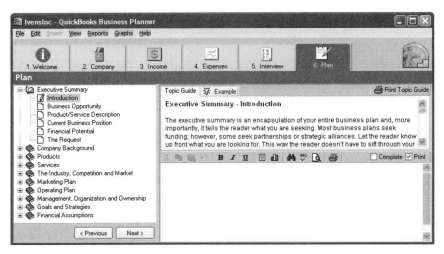

Figure 8-13: Step through each section in the left pane to complete the written plan

---

TIP: Click the Print Topic Guide button above the writing area to print helpful guidelines about the current topic, or about all topics. You can opt to include the sample text in your printout.

You may find that some of the subsections in the left pane are irrelevant to your business, and if so, just skip them. You can rename the section titles you're using in your plan, except for "Introduction".

There's no hard and fast rule that you have to write your plan using the order in which the categories are presented in the left pane. You're perfectly free to organize your writing in a way that makes sense for your company.

Previewing Your Business Plan

To examine your plan, choose File → Preview Business Plan from the Business Planner menu bar. The Preview Business Plan window displays a summary of your plan's contents (see Figure 8-14). Notice that the financial projections have been placed in the appendixes for the reader's reference.

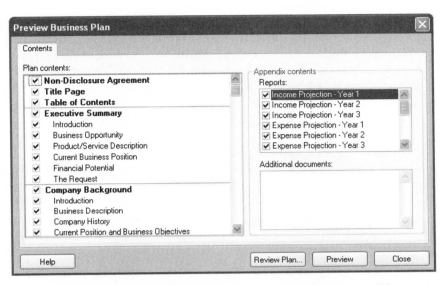

Figure 8-14: Check the Table of Contents to make sure everything
you wanted to cover is there.

Click the Preview button to view the document. (The document is a
PDF file, so you must have Adobe Reader installed to view it.) If everything looks fine, use any of the buttons on the document window to proceed (covered next).

Save the Business Plan as a PDF File

Click Save As PDF to save a copy of the PDF document on your hard
drive. In the Save As PDF dialog, name the document, and save it in any
folder you choose. By default, the Save As PDF dialog selects the folder
in which your company files are stored, but you can change the folder.

Export the Business Plan

Click Export to send the file to your word processor. If you have Microsoft
Excel installed on your computer, the Export dialog includes an option to
export the financial projections (your appendixes) to a Microsoft Excel
spreadsheet.

If you select the option to export the financial projections to Excel, a
message appears telling you that the QuickBooks Business Planner will

launch Microsoft Excel and your default word processor. I assume anyone running Excel is also running Microsoft Word, which the Business Planner would probably select as the default word processor. However, I know of no Windows setting that specifies a "default" word processor, so I can't explain what would happen if you had two word processors loaded in your system. (If you don't have a word processor installed on your computer, the Business Planner loads the file in WordPad.)

The text part of your business plan is loaded in your word processor, and you can format, edit, and otherwise manipulate the document as you wish. Your projections are loaded in Excel, with a separate worksheet for each year's income and expense projection (see Figure 8-15). You can save either (or both) documents using the File → Save As command.

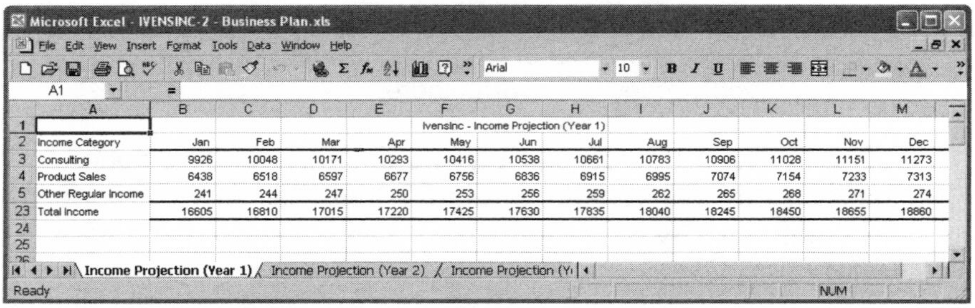

Figure 8-15: Your projection figures are automatically exported to Excel.

TIP: If you export the business plan and manipulate its contents, you must generate the Table of Contents again to make sure the pagination is correct. Use the Table of Contents feature in your word processor to accomplish this task

---

Print the Business Plan

To print your business plan from the Business Planner software window, choose File → Print Business Plan on the Business Plan menu bar. In the Print Business Plan dialog (see Figure 8-16), select the components you want to include in this printing.

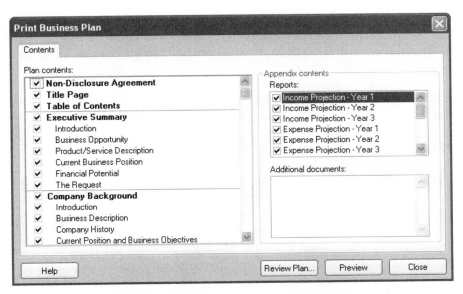

Figure 8-16: Select the components to include in this printing of your business plan.

Click Preview to load the document, and in the Preview window, click the Print button at the top of the window. Choose the options you need in the Print dialog, and print the document.

Forecasting

You can create a forecast to help you predict your future revenue and cash flow, and then use the data in the forecast to create "what if" scenarios that help you plan and control the growth of your business.

TIP: A forecast is sometimes called a Cash Flow Budget.

A good forecast doesn't have to be terribly complicated; it just has to provide the information you need to plan for survival, or for expansion (depending on the current state of your business and your reason for creating the forecast).

The forecasting tool in QuickBooks works on a one-year basis, which is the common duration for a forecast. The forecast is based on income and expense accounts, although you can further narrow it by focusing on a customer or a class.

When you create a forecast, you're bound to notice that the user interface, as well as the processes, is very similar to the QuickBooks budget feature. In fact, everything about a forecast smells a lot like a budget.

I couldn't find an official set of definitions that spelled out the differences between a forecast and a budget, but most accountants think of these two documents as entirely different from each other. Of course, if you ask an accountant, "What's the difference?" you get a rather vague, broad answer. My own accountant tells me that in his mind, a forecast is a set of projections you make based on both history and any logical assumptions you care to make about the future, while a budget is based on the "knowns", and excludes assumptions.

Creating a Forecast

To create a forecast, choose Company → Planning & Budgeting → Set Up Forecast. If this is the first forecast you're creating, you see the Create New Forecast window. If this is not the first forecast you're creating, the last forecast you created opens. Click Create New Forecast to create a new forecast.

Enter the year for this forecast, and click Next. By default, QuickBooks fills in the forecast year field with next year, but if it's early in the current year, you may prefer to create a forecast for this year.

Setting the Criteria for a Forecast

In the next window, you can select the criteria for this forecast. The criteria for accounts are set in stone; you must use Profit & Loss accounts for your forecast. However, you can set additional criteria, such as basing the forecast on a customer, a job, or a class.

In this discussion, I'm going to assume you aren't setting additional criteria, and QuickBooks also assumes you aren't setting additional criteria, because the No Additional Criteria option is selected by default. Click Next to move on.

Choosing the Method for Obtaining Data

In the next window, specify whether you want to create your forecast with data you enter manually, or with data from your QuickBooks company file. Then click Finish.

Of course, if you just started using QuickBooks, you have no data for last year, so you'll enter the data manually. If you opt to use existing QuickBooks data, monthly data from the year is transferred to the forecast window (see Figure 8-17). If you chose manual data entry, the forecast window has no data.

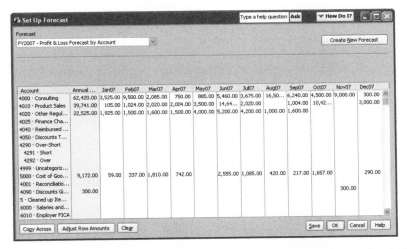

Figure 8-17: For this forecast, last year's monthly totals are loaded to serve as a base.

Entering Data Manually

If you want to enter the data manually, you can run a Profit & Loss report to get an idea of the actual numbers. If you're creating a forecast because you're expecting to change the way you do business, the existing numbers may not be the figures you want to insert in your forecast.

Use the numbers in the Profit & Loss report (choose Reports → Company & Financial → Profit & Loss Standard) as a base, enlarging or reducing totals to match what you think your plan for the next year will produce.

Data Entry Shortcuts

To save you time (and extraordinary levels of boredom), QuickBooks provides some shortcuts for entering forecast figures. You can use these tools if you're entering your data manually, or if you're changing existing data to create a new scenario.

Copy a Number across the Months

To copy a monthly figure from the current month (the month where your cursor is) to all the following months, enter the figure and click Copy Across. The numbers are copied to all months to the right.

This is handier than it seems. It's obvious that if you enter your rent in the first month, and choose Copy Across, you've saved a lot of manual data entry. However, if your rent is raised in June, you can increase the rent figure from June to December by selecting June, entering the new figure, and clicking Copy Across.

The Copy Across button is also the quick way to clear a row. Delete the data in the first month and click Copy Across to make the entire row blank.

Automatically Increase or Decrease Monthly Figures

You may want to raise an income account by an amount or a percentage starting in a certain month, because you expect to offer new products and services, or increase your customer base.

On the other hand, you may want to raise an expense account because you're expecting to spend more on supplies, personnel, or other costs as the year proceeds.

Select the first month that needs the adjustment and click Adjust Row Amounts to open the Adjust Row Amounts dialog seen in Figure 8-18.

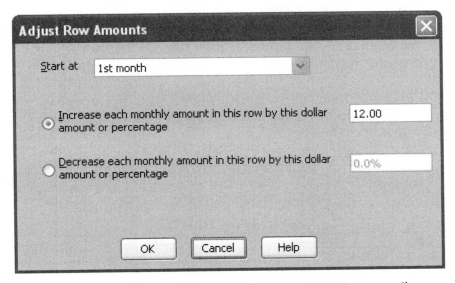

Figure 8-18: Automatically increase or decrease amounts across the months.

Choose 1st Month or Currently Selected Month as the starting point for the calculations. You can choose 1st Month no matter where your cursor is on the account's row. You must click in the column for the appropriate month if you want to choose Currently Selected Month.

- To increase or decrease the selected month, and all the months following, by a specific amount, enter the amount.
- To increase or decrease the selected month and all the months following, by a percentage, enter the percentage rate and the percentage sign.

Compounding Automatic Changes

If you select Currently Selected Month, the Adjust Row Amounts dialog adds an additional option named Enable Compounding. When you enable compounding, the calculations for each month are increased or decreased based on a formula starting with the currently selected month and taking into consideration the resulting change in the previous month.

TIP: Although the Enable Compounding option appears only when you select Currently Selected Month, if your cursor is in the first month and you select the Currently Selected Month option, you can use compounding for the entire year.

For example, if you entered $1000.00 in the current month and indicated a $100.00 increase, the results differ from amounts that are not being compounded, as seen in Table 8-1.

Compounding Enabled?	Current Month Original Figure	Current Month New Figure	Next Month	Next Month	Next Month
Yes	1000.00	1000.00	1100.00	1200.00	1300.00
No	1000.00	1100.00	1100.00	1100.00	1100.00

Table 8-1: Compounded Vs. non-compounded changes.

Forecast Window Buttons

The Set Up Forecast window has the following buttons:

- **Clear** deletes all figures in the forecast window—you cannot use this button to clear a row or column.
- **Save** saves the current figures and leaves the window open so you can continue to work.
- **OK** saves the current figures and closes the window.
- **Cancel** closes the window without any offer to record the figures.
- **Create New Forecast** starts the whole process again. If you've entered any data, QuickBooks asks if you want to record your data before closing the window. If you record your data (or have previously recorded your data with the Save button), when you start again, the forecast window opens with the saved data. You have to clear all the figures to create a new forecast.

No Delete button exists in the forecast window. To delete a forecast, load it in the forecast window, and choose Edit → Delete Forecast.

Editing the Forecast

After you save the forecast, you can modify it as needed. To make changes, choose Company → Planning & Budgeting → Set Up Forecast.

If you only created one forecast, it opens in the Set Up Forecast window. If you've created multiple forecasts (for customers, jobs, or classes), select the forecast you want to modify from the drop-down list in the Forecast field (at the top of the window). Use the instructions in the previous section to change the data, and then save the forecast.

Creating Reports on Forecasts

You can view your forecast, or compare its data to real figures, by choosing Reports → Budgets & Forecasts, and then selecting either Forecast Overview or Forecast vs. Actual. Selecting either report launches the Forecast Report wizard.

Forecast Overview Report

To view the forecast, select it from the drop-down list in the first wizard window, and click Next. (If you only created one forecast, you don't have any choices, of course.)

In the next wizard window, select the layout for the report. If the forecast you're viewing is a Profit & Loss Accounts forecast, your only choice is Account By Month, which is the spreadsheet-type layout you used when you created the forecast.

If the forecast you're viewing is a Customer:Job or Class forecast, choose Account By Customer:Job, or Customer:Job By Month (substitute Class for Customer:Job if you created class forecasts).

The name of the layout choice holds the description: the first word in the choice represents the rows, and the word after the word "by" represents the columns.

For example, the Account By Customer:Job report, seen in Figure 8-19, displays accounts in rows. Each job and the job totals for each customer are displayed in their own columns.

Ivensinc
Profit & Loss Forecast Overview

Accrual Basis

	4th Street... (Bellevue... Jan - Dec 07	Kelly Drive (Bellevue... Jan - Dec 07	Main Street (Bellevue... Jan - Dec 07	Total Belle... Jan - Dec 07	BillsCafe Jan - Dec 07	On-Site W... (Gotham) Jan - Dec 07	Total Goth... Jan - Dec 07	Employee... (Jordan's... Jan - Dec 07	Software (Jordan's... Jan - Dec 07
4010 · Product Sales		105.00	500.00	605.00	524.00	2,020.00	2,020.00		1,600.00
4020 · Other Regular Income		425.00	1,500.00	1,925.00				1,000.00	
Total Income	1,785.00	1,970.00	3,290.00	7,045.00	524.00	2,320.00	2,320.00	1,600.00	1,600.00
Cost of Goods Sold									
5000 · Cost of Goods Sold		59.00		59.00	217.00	1,085.00	1,085.00		
Total COGS		59.00		59.00	217.00	1,085.00	1,085.00		
Gross Profit	1,785.00	1,911.00	3,290.00	6,986.00	307.00	1,235.00	1,235.00	1,600.00	1,600.00
Net Ordinary Income	1,785.00	1,911.00	3,290.00	6,986.00	307.00	1,235.00	1,235.00	1,600.00	1,600.00
Net Income	1,785.00	1,911.00	3,290.00	6,986.00	307.00	1,235.00	1,235.00	1,600.00	1,600.00

Figure 8-19: See the forecast totals for each job in your system.

Forecast vs. Actual

This report lets you see how the forecast matches up against actual figures. The wizard offers the same display options as described for the Overview Report. The report displays the forecast, the actuals, the difference between them in dollars and the difference in percentage.

Chapter 9

Expert Analysis

Configuring Expert Analysis

Entering Data

Generating a report

Expert Analysis benchmarks your company's financial performance against other companies in the same industry, and against your company's own past performance. The reports are extremely comprehensive, plainly written, and quite easy to understand—making them a powerful resource for planning and analysis.

Accountants can use Expert Analysis to examine and report on the performance of client companies, providing an opportunity for accountants to offer their clients another professional service.

Expert Analysis is a product of Sageworks, Inc. The company offers several products, and its popular product ProfitCents is the basis of the Expert Analysis product that's offered to Premier editions users. Learn more at www.profitcents.com.

Creating an Expert Analysis Report

To create an Expert Analysis report on your company's financial condition, choose Company → Planning & Budgeting → Use Expert Analysis Tool.

NOTE: *If you're using logins and permission levels, only a user with permission to access sensitive reports can use Expert Analysis.*

A welcoming window appears, inviting you to examine Expert Analysis Professional, a more powerful tool (discussed later in this chapter).

TIP: *The window has a check box labeled Hide This Screen During Startup. Click it to skip the welcoming window in the future.*

Click Continue to begin creating a report. (The first time you use Expert Analysis, the End User License Agreement appears. You must agree to the terms of the license in order to use the product).

The Expert Analysis window opens, as seen in Figure 9-1, looking very much like a wizard (and also like the EasyStep Interview you used when you first created your company file).

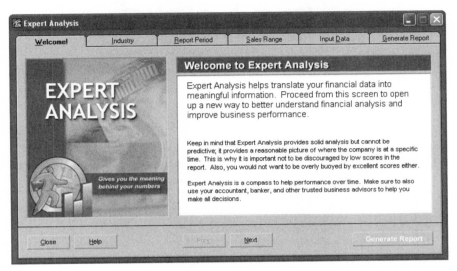

Figure 9-1: The tabs represent the categories of information you provide as you move through the program.

Select an Industry

Click Next to move to the Industry tab (see Figure 9-2), where you can select a business category that describes your company. The window offers several levels of descriptive phrases, so you can get as close a match as possible.

Fill in the Company Name field at the top of the window if you want your company name to appear on the report. If you're analyzing your own company, it's not necessary to enter the name, unless you're planning to print the report and deliver it to your bank or another entity that's asking for a report. If you're an accountant, and you're preparing this report for a client, enter the client's company name.

Filling out the information in the Industry tab lets Expert Analysis compare your company's performance to other similar companies. If you're not interested in an industry comparison, merely select None Of The Above from the list in the right pane (it's the last listing).

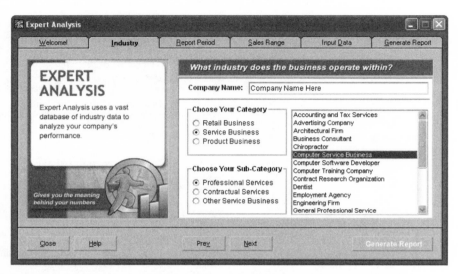

Figure 9-2: Choose a category, a sub-category, and a service or product that best describes your company.

Lacking industry information from you, Expert Analysis produces a report that analyzes your company within the scope of general private company benchmarks. This is usually not as useful as benchmarking your company against other companies in the same industry.

The Choose Your Category pane offers three choices of business categories: Retail, Service or Product. If you select Service Business or Product Business, a Sub-Category pane appears to help you narrow your description. The right pane lists specific business types. Click Next when you have finished making your selections.

Choose the Report Periods

In the Report Period tab (see Figure 9-3), select the periods you want to compare to analyze your company's performance. Expert Analysis performs a period comparison, so you must select a period, and then select the way you want to compare that period.

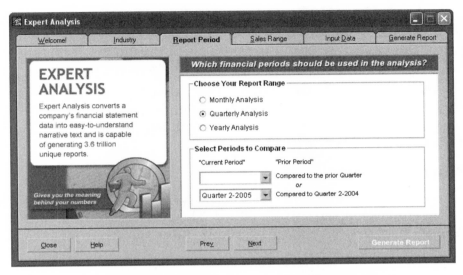

Figure 9-3: Choose a range and the way you want to compare the range.

Monthly Analysis

If you want to compare months, select Monthly Analysis and then fill in the Select Periods To Compare section of the window, using the following guidelines:

- To compare a month to the previous month, select a month from the drop-down list in the upper box.
- To compare a month to the same month in the previous year, select a month from the drop-down list in the lower box.

The month you select becomes the "current period" referred to in the analysis report. References to "prior period" in the report mean either the previous month or the same month in the previous year (depending on your selection in this window).

Quarterly Analysis

To analyze two quarters, select Quarterly Analysis, and then fill in the Select Periods To Compare section of the window, as follows:

- To compare a quarter to the previous quarter, select a quarter from the drop-down list in the upper box.
- To compare a quarter to the same quarter in the previous year, select a quarter from the drop-down list in the lower box.

The quarter you select becomes the "current period" referred to in the final report. References to "prior period" in the report mean either the previous quarter or the same quarter in the previous year (depending on your selection in this window).

Yearly Analysis

To compare two years, select Yearly Analysis, and then select the year you want to use as the current period. The previous year automatically becomes the "prior period" in the report. After you've selected the reporting periods, click Next.

Sales Range

The information you enter in the Sales Range tab (see Figure 9-4) doesn't have to be exact, because the information in this tab is used rather generally when Expert Analysis calculates your company's financial data.

Select the sales range that matches your company's revenue from sales. Don't include income that's unrelated to your sales of products or services. For example, if your company holds investments, don't include the gain or loss of equity, nor the gain or loss you received when you sold an investment.

Enter the number of full time employees and contractors for the current period, and the prior period. If you have part time employees or contractors, add those numbers to get to a number for full time employees and/or contractors.

It doesn't matter how you define "employee" or "contractor", because the reason for this entry isn't strictly mathematical (which is obvious, I guess, because you're not being asked to supply amounts). One of the benchmarks used for an in-depth analysis of a company's condition is a measurement that I loosely term "revenue per worker", or "profits per worker".

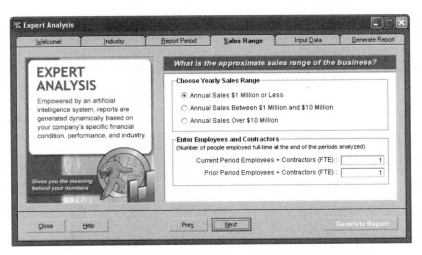

Figure 9-4: Enter information about your sales income, and your personnel expenses.

For instance, if you have revenue or profits of $150,000.00 with ten employees, and another company in a similar industry also has revenue or profits of $150,000.00, with seven employees, there's usually a conclusion that can be drawn.

Even though the data you enter in this window isn't used as the underlying basis of the financial analysis, it's important to an overall fine-tuned report.

Input Data

When you click Next to move to the Input Data window, Expert Analysis displays a message asking you if you want to take data from the QuickBooks company file that's currently open.

If you are creating an Expert Analysis report for the company that's currently open, click Yes. There's a short delay while the program retrieves data from your Profit & Loss accounts, and your Balance Sheet accounts.

If you are creating a report for another company (which probably means you're an accountant and you're doing this for a client), click No, and then read the section "Entering Data Manually", later in this chapter.

Before you can view the contents of the Input Data window, the message seen in Figure 9-5 appears, suggesting you add back salaries of owners that you may have posted as expenses.

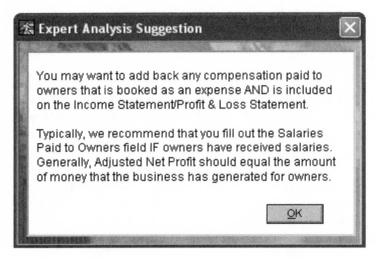

Figure 9-5: Expert Analysis is advising that you correct an expense that should have been posted as a draw.

NOTE: *This message always appears, even if you told Expert Analysis to fetch information from your company file, and your company information indicates you file a corporate tax return.*

It's easier to explain that message when I discuss the figures you see in the Input Data window, so if you're following along, click OK to clear the message and see the data.

Figure 9-6 shows the data that appeared as a result of the configuration options I specified as I went through this example. If you didn't select the option to retrieve data from the files of the currently opened company, all the figures would be zero. See the section "Entering Data Manually", later in this chapter, for instructions about filling in amounts.

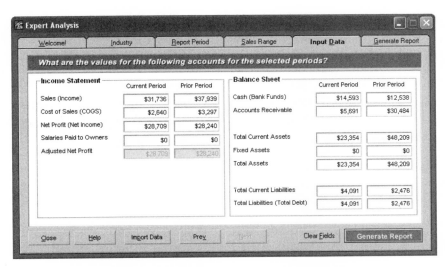

Figure 9-6: Figures from the relevant accounts are loaded in the
Input Data window

The current date has an impact on the figures. For example, if you're creating a report that looks at both the current quarter and the last quarter, and today's date falls early in the current quarter, your numbers won't be the same as they will at the end of the current quarter.

For a straightforward report, don't change the figures, with the possible exception of the Salaries Paid To Owners figure, which bears some discussion (and is related to the message that appeared about adding back the salaries of owners).

For the Salaries Paid To Owners figure, first of all, don't take the name of the field literally—especially the word "Owners". If your business is a proprietorship, you probably didn't post the money you withdrew as an expense. The same statement can be made about many partnerships. Owners and partners take draws, which are not posted as an expense. Draw is removal of equity, and the Draw account is in the equity section of your chart of accounts.

If your business is a partnership and you've established a "guaranteed payment" agreement, the withdrawals you make are posted to an expense account, and are reported on Line 10 on Page 1 of the 1065 partnership tax return. However, for all intents and purposes (speaking philosophically) this should be thought of as a draw, because it's the owners' removal of profits.

This field is a great equalizer. Any figure you enter in this field, regardless of its origin (that is, it really doesn't have to be an amount connected to payroll), adjusts the net profit/loss figure that is used in the Expert Analysis report.

If you enter a positive amount, it increases your net profit by a process called *adding back*. Adding back means removing amounts from expenses, causing them to be automatically added back to the profit.

If you enter a negative amount, it decreases your profit by removing that amount from the gross profit and treating it as an expense. It's a *takeback*.

Adding Back to Your Bottom Line

You can use the Salaries Paid to Owners field to adjust figures to provide a "reality check". It's a general adjustment field that helps you avoid the pitfall of understating profits. Regardless of the name of the field, you aren't restricted to entering figures related to salary or draw.

For example, you should enter a positive number in the field to include amounts that fall under the following categories:

- Expenses you posted that are really draws.
- Guaranteed payments for partnerships you posted to an expense account (because you really should treat them as equity when you analyze your business).
- Non-business tax payments you posted to an expense account. These include estimated personal income taxes paid to the IRS, and state and local income taxes (all of which are personal expenses, and should be posted to the Draw account in the equities section of your chart of accounts).
- Any other personal expenses you posted to an expense account.

All of the scenarios in this list are adjusted by your accountant when he or she prepares your taxes. For some reason, many accountants don't explain those adjustments, they just make them. As a result, business owners continue to post expenses that are really draws. Have your accountant explain adjustments so you can avoid incorrect posting in the future.

You can also use a positive number in the field to adjust other types of figures. In effect, you're asking Expert Analysis to make certain assumptions that aren't evident in your accounts. These assumptions help you avoid an analysis based on understated profits. Following are some examples I've encountered at client sites, and you can probably think of others:

- Automobile expenses (fuel, repairs, and maintenance) that are partially business and partially personal expenses. While you probably make a percentage-based adjustment at tax time, make the adjustment here to get a more realistic analysis. Enter the figure that represents the total amount for personal use.
- Travel expenses that you post to a business expense, but may include personal expenses. Enter the figure that represents the total personal expense.
- Certain one-time-only expenses—an equipment purchase that you didn't post to a fixed asset account, a large depreciation expense posted against a fixed asset that you don't have to replace every few years, expenses connected to startup such as a contractor you hired to help you build the office space (shelving, cubby hole walls, etc) or a large neon sign.

The important thing to remember is that this is truly a reality check for you. You're attempting to analyze your business. Be honest and realistic about adding back amounts you've posted to business expenses that are really personal expenses. You're not filling out a tax return, no IRS agent is watching what you do, and you're almost certainly not planning to send this report to a tax authority.

Taking Back From Your Bottom Line

To get a realistic appraisal of your business from Expert Analysis, you can also adjust your net profit in the opposite direction, if the circumstances warrant this action. In this case, you'd enter a negative amount in the Salaries Paid to Owners field.

For example, if you're donating something to the business, you must assume that at some time in the near future the business will have to pay for the service that's currently free. Or, even if you plan to donate the service for a long time, you may want to see how your business measures in the absence of such freebies. Some types of "donations" I've run into include (but are certainly not limited to), the following:

- Rent.
- Salaries, wages, and outside contractor fees (a family member spends time performing a necessary service without being paid).
- Miscellaneous supplies you donate; perhaps you bring postage stamps from your home to your office, and you don't have a postage expense.
- Equipment or furniture you brought to your office, but plan to take back.

Enter the fair market value for your freebies, preceded by a minus sign. This negative entry is interpreted by Expert Analysis as a "take back", which means the amount is added to your total expenses, thus reducing your net profit (and also creating a more realistic analysis of your business).

Entering Data Manually

If you're an accounting professional, you can enter your clients' numbers into the Data Input screen manually. Then you can customize the analysis report, and send it to the customer (for whatever fee you normally charge for in-depth analysis of a business).

This is also an added service you can sell your clients when they need to arrange credit lines. The depth and breadth of the Expert Analysis report, which can compare your "credit worthy" clients to other businesses in the same industry, could make a real difference in a bank's attitude.

Of course, you must have the numbers, and you can ask your client to send you the numbers in any manner that's convenient to both of you.

- If you use Remote Access, you can connect to your client's QuickBooks files to get the figures. (See Chapter 10 to learn about Remote Access.)
- You can obtain the figures from a QuickBooks Accountant's Review copy that your client sends.
- You can ask the client to produce the requisite reports, print them, and fax the output to you.
- You can ask the client to produce the reports and export them to Excel (an easy task if your client is using QuickBooks, and most accounting software applications have an equally facile feature for exporting reports to Excel). Have the client e-mail the Excel worksheets to you.

TIP: Expert Analysis Professional automatically imports data from Excel spreadsheets. See the section "Expert Analysis Professional", later in this chapter.

The reports required for Expert Analysis differ, depending on the periods you want to compare. For yearly reports, clients using QuickBooks can select the P&L Previous Year Comparison, and the Balance Sheet Previous Year Comparison reports. Both of those reports can be adjusted for monthly periods (month compared to same month in previous year), and quarterly periods (quarter compared to same quarter in previous year). To make the adjustments in QuickBooks, change the dates in the Date Range boxes on the report window. Other accounting software applications have similar reports.

Your client can also create a comparison report that shows month vs. prior month or quarter vs. prior quarter within the same year. To do this in QuickBooks, select the P&L and Balance Sheet Previous Year Comparison reports. For each report, click the Modify Report button on the reports. Under Report Date Range, enter the current period date in the "From" and "To" fields. Under Columns, deselect the Previous Year check box and select the Previous Period check box. Clients using different accounting software should be able to produce the same reports.

To provide complete instructions to your clients, you can buy the Premier 2006 Client Kit CD. This comprehensive CD has letters, forms, and step-by-step instruction manuals for the client tasks involved in sending you these reports (as well as instructions for other procedures, including using Remote Access). All of the documents and materials can be personalized for your own practice. Information about the Premier 2006 Client Kit CD is available at the CPA911 Publishing website (www.cpa911publishing.com).

Generating the Report

Click Generate Report and wait a few seconds for the report to appear. As you can see in Figure 9-7, the report displays information by category, with detailed explanations about the company's performance, or lack of performance, for each category.

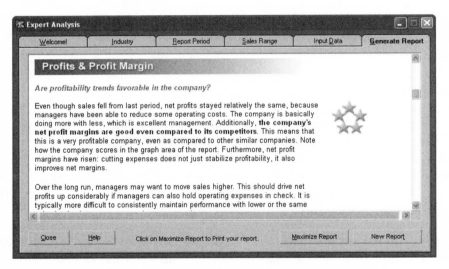

Figure 9-7: This company earned five stars in several categories, and the details in the text explain why.

Check the number of stars displayed for each category—they're a quick indicator of the company's fortunes. Scroll through the document to view the detailed report for each category Expert Analysis examines. You'll be impressed by the level of detail, the recommendations and suggestions, and other helpful information. The following indicators are addressed in detail in the report:

- Liquidity
- Profits and Profit Margin
- Sales
- Borrowing
- Fixed Assets
- Employees

The bottom of the report contains graphs, which are a good way to get at-a-glance information.

Printing the Report

To print the report, click the Maximize Report button to open a new, full-screen, window with the report loaded in it. Click the Print button at the top of the window to open the Windows Print dialog.

Choose a printer (if you have multiple printers), and specify the number of copies you want to print. Then click Print to send the document to the printer, and return to the Expert Analysis window.

Click the Close Window button to return to the Expert Analysis wizard (where your report is still displayed). You can click the Close button to close the wizard, or select a tab to change some of the data in order to produce another report.

Click the New Report button to launch a new Expert Analysis wizard and start anew.

Saving the Report

You cannot save this report to a file. The Expert Analysis program that's built into your copy of QuickBooks Premier Edition doesn't provide a way to save the report. This is quite a hindrance to accountants who are preparing reports for clients, and need to edit and customize the contents.

(Expert Analysis Professional includes the ability to save the report to Microsoft Word. See the next section, "Expert Analysis Professional" for more information.)

Until you upgrade, however, here's a quick workaround for saving the text (but not the formatting, nor the charts). Create a text printer that prints to a disk file.

Open the Printers folder (or the Printers and Faxes folder, depending on your version of Windows), and double-click the Add New Printer icon to launch the Add New Printer Wizard. Use the following specifications to create the printer:

- The printer is local
- The Port is File (not a printer port)
- The Manufacturer Name is Generic
- The model is Text Printer

When you click the Print button on the maximized report window, select that printer. Windows will ask you for a filename—enter a filename that's related to the report.

Open the resulting file, which you can find by searching Windows Explorer or My Computer, in a word processor. The file is plain text. Even worse, each line ends with a paragraph mark (as if you'd pressed the Enter key instead of letting the text wrap the way it does when you're working in software). You have to remove those paragraph marks, format the text, and generally make the report clean and slick for your client. It makes more sense to upgrade to Expert Analysis Professional.

Expert Analysis Professional

Upgrading to Expert Analysis Professional brings a wide range of additional features and power. If you're an accounting professional, the strength of this application provides an enormous assortment of expertise you can sell to your clients. Here are some of the additional indicators that are discussed and analyzed in detail in the Expert Analysis Professional reports:

- Accounts Payable Days
- Accounts Receivable Days
- Asset Composition
- Cash Flow Coverage

- Cash Flow Leverage
- Debt-to-Equity Ratio
- Fixed Asset Turnover
- Inventory Days
- Labor Cost Ratio
- Operating Cash Flow
- Operating Cash Flow Margin
- Operating Cycle
- Profit per Employee
- Return on Assets
- Return on Equity (ROE)
- Return on Labor
- Sales Per Employee
- Working Capital

Remember that Expert Analysis not only computes and analyzes the numbers in these categories, it also compares the results to standard results for your industry. Benchmarks such as these can provide important information to business owners.

In addition, you can save the report to Microsoft Word, where you can tweak, format, and customize the contents. Imagine sending your client a booklet containing the analysis and detailed discussions that Expert Analysis provides. Add your own comments and recommendations. Meet with your client to help implement the suggestions. This is a terrific added value service you can sell your clients.

Chapter 10

Remote Access

Remote Access

Accountant Edition Remote Access

QuickBooks offers a free one-year subscription to Remote Access for Premier editions, although the Remote Access program that's offered for Premier Accountant Edition is not the same program offered in the other Premier editions.

The Premier Remote Access feature lets you work on your QuickBooks files from any remote location. The Premier Accountant Remote Access feature lets accountants work on client files across the Internet. Both Remote Access programs are covered in this chapter.

Remote Access

For all Premier editions except Accountant Edition, Remote Access lets you work on your QuickBooks files from a remote computer. The remote computer could be in a different part of town, or in a different part of the world.

This means if you're traveling, taking a day off, or visiting a customer's site, you can get to your QuickBooks files as long as you can get your hands on a computer that has access to the Internet. The remote computer doesn't have to be running QuickBooks.

Remote Access also provides a way for your bookkeeper to work on your books without coming into your office. If you have a part time bookkeeper, this means nobody in the office has to stop working to provide a computer for the bookkeeper. Telecommuting is advantageous on many levels, and installing Remote Access is a quick and easy way to take advantage of this popular approach to office staffing.

Understanding the Remote Connection

When you use Remote Access to connect to the computer that holds your QuickBooks files from a remote computer, the two computers don't actually connect to each other. Instead, WebEx, which is a third-party company, brings the computers together via an Internet connection. Both computers enter the same Internet site (a WebEx site), and that site provides all the tools, services, and security required for communication.

As illustrated in Figure 10-1, the computer that holds your QuickBooks files is referred to as the *server*, and the computer you're using to get to the server computer over the Internet is referred to as the *client*.

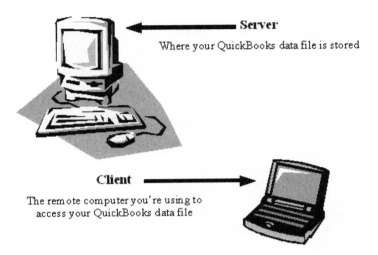

Server
Where your QuickBooks data file is stored

Client
The remote computer you're using to access your QuickBooks data file

Figure 10-1: It's easier to understand the tasks involved if you know the jargon and the concepts.

Server Requirements for Remote Access

The server (the computer that holds your QuickBooks files) must have an always-on, dedicated broadband Internet connection, such as a DSL modem, a cable modem, or a T1 connection.

The reason the server requires a broadband connection isn't that you need the speed (although speed is desirable), it's because you need the "always on" status. That way, when you're away from the office and want to work on your QuickBooks files, you don't have to worry that the computer is not connected to the Internet.

Remote Computer Requirements for Remote Access

The client (the computer you use at a remote location to connect to your QuickBooks files on your server) can have either a modem or a broadband connection.

The client (remote) computer does not need to have QuickBooks installed (and if QuickBooks happens to be installed, you won't be using it). It needs only an Internet connection and a browser.

Setting Up Remote Access

To access your QuickBooks Premier data files from a remote location, you have to obtain a Remote Access account. You must also install and configure the software that enables this feature. I'll go over these tasks in the following sections.

Signing Up for a Remote Access Account

To access your QuickBooks Premier data files from a remote location, you must have a Remote Access account, and you must install and configure the software that enables this feature.

As a QuickBooks Premier user, you have a free year of the Remote Access service, after which you must agree to pay a monthly fee to continue using the service.

All of the procedures involved in signing up for an account must be performed at the computer you've designated as the server (the computer that contains your QuickBooks company file).

To sign up, open QuickBooks, and choose File → Utilities → Remote Access. In the Remote Access window, click Register Now. QuickBooks travels to the Internet and opens the Sign Up window on the WebEx Remote Access site (see Figure 10-2).

After you fill out the information, click the Sign Up Now button at the bottom of the window. The data you entered in the form is sent to the WebEx database, and the QuickBooks Remote Access window displays a message telling you that you've successfully signed up for the service. The success message displays the following information:

- Your login ID (your e-mail address)
- Your password
- The expiration date for your free trial

- The URL to use for the Remote Access service
- Instructions for setting up your computer (which I'll discuss in this section)

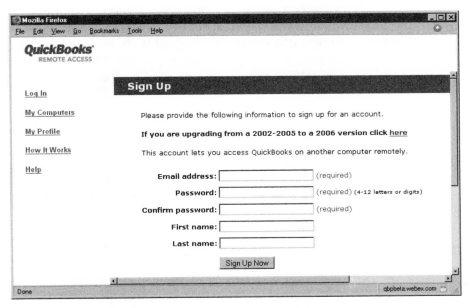

Figure 10-2: The first step is to sign up for an account.

Be careful! The message shows your password in plain text, so anyone who can view your monitor can get your password. The message also includes a directive to print the page, and if you do, remember that the printed document has your password in readable text. Don't print the document if you use a shared printer that is in a hallway or another office, unless you want to share your password with anyone who happens to be near the printer (giving away a password is never a good idea).

You don't have to print the window, because you'll be sent a confirmation of your registration via e-mail in a matter of minutes. The e-mail message includes your login ID (which is the e-mail address you entered in the Sign Up form), your password, and a link to the URL for the Remote Access service. Put the information in a safe place.

> **WARNING**: *If the expiration date that appears on the window after you sign up is earlier than the current date, it means you had the QuickBooks sample company loaded when you signed up for Remote Access. You can't re-apply. You must contact technical support to correct this problem. Send e-mail to Intuitsupport@webex.com. In the message, include your first and last name, the e-mail address you used when you signed up, and a brief explanation of what happened.*

You won't be asked for a credit card number nor for any other payment information at this point, because you have a free account (one of the perks of purchasing QuickBooks Premier Edition) for a limited time. When the free account service ends, you'll have to pay a monthly fee, and at that time, you'll be asked to provide credit card information. In the meantime, this period of free access lets you decide whether the service is useful enough to buy it later.

Installing and Configuring Remote Access

The software that manages Remote Access sessions is called the Access Anywhere Agent. This software application is downloaded from the WebEx website as part of the process of setting up your server computer. After you download the software package, you must install it, and then you must configure its settings.

You can start setting up your server immediately, if the WebEx Signup Successful page is still open in QuickBooks, or you can defer the task until later. In this discussion, I'm assuming you closed the WebEx window after you signed up, and I'll explain all the steps involved in setting up your computer and installing the software.

QuickBooks does not have to be open to set up your computer, or to download and install the software. However, you do have to perform the tasks on the computer that holds your QuickBooks file (the server). Merely open Internet Explorer and enter the URL you were given for Remote Access. In fact, you can open the e-mail message you received and click on the link to the URL. The Log In window, seen in Figure 10-

3, opens in Internet Explorer. Enter your e-mail address and password, and then click the Log In button.

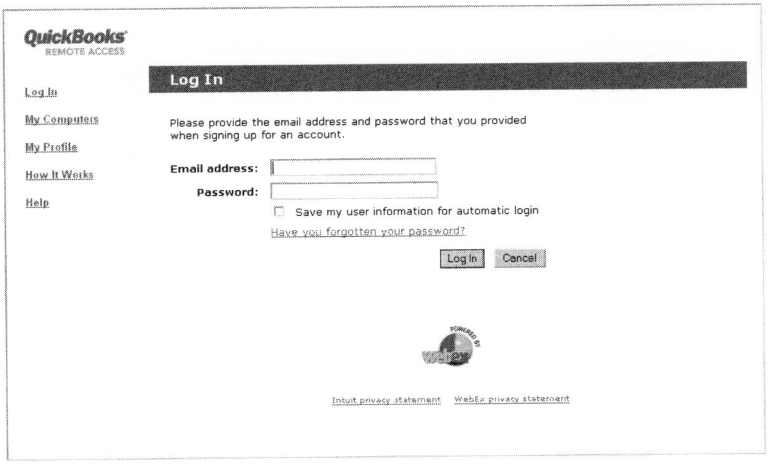

Figure 10-3: Log in to the Access Anywhere website.

TIP: *Save the URL in your Favorites list.*

To avoid filling out your login name (your e-mail address) and your password each time you use Remote Access, you can click the check box next to Save My User Information For Automatic Login, to place a check mark in the box.

Automatic login means that every time you go to the WebEx website, your login information is filled in automatically. In order to automate the login process, you must have Internet Explorer configured to accept cookies (which is the default setting for Internet Explorer). If you've turned off cookies, you must log in manually whenever you want to use Access Anywhere.

WARNING: *If you opt for automatic login, it means any user who uses this computer can automatically log in without knowing the password.*

If you can't remember your password, click Have You Forgotten Your Password? to send a message to support technicians, who will send your password to the e-mail address you specified when you signed up for the service.

Setting Up the Server

The first task you face is setting up this computer, so its QuickBooks files are available from a remote site. After you log in, you see the My Computers window. Scroll through the window to find the section that lists the computers you set up (none are listed yet), and click the button labeled Set Up Computer.

> **NOTE:** The WebEx window includes a link you can click to sign up for Gold Services. This expands your ability to use software on this computer from a remote computer—you can use any software that's installed on the computer, not just QuickBooks.

Downloading the Remote Access Software

Clicking Set Up Computer kicks off a two-step process: the files are downloaded, and then the installation of those files begins automatically (with the help of a wizard).

> **NOTE:** The web page offers an option to download and install the software manually. This is only necessary if you're performing this task from a different computer—not the server that holds your QuickBooks files. After you download the file, you must transfer it to the server and install the software. This is definitely a more difficult and time-consuming way to set up your computer, so I suggest you perform these tasks from the server.

Internet Explorer displays a Security Warning message that asks if you're sure you want to install software from this website. WebEx provides the security features that Internet Explorer and Microsoft Windows requires, so it's okay to click Yes. In fact, it's okay to put a check mark into the check box that says Internet Explorer can always trust content from WebEx.

The software download begins, and you can see a progress bar as the files are transferred to your computer.

Installing and Configuring the Remote Access Software

When all the files are transferred, the Access Anywhere Setup Wizard appears. Click Next to begin installing and configuring the software.

Enter a name for this computer, enter your password, and click Next. (If your login information, including the URL, isn't displayed, you must fill it in).

The computer name you enter appears in the Computer List when you log in to WebEx from a remote site. If you're on a network, use the computer name that already exists, to avoid confusion. Otherwise, invent a name for the computer.

Set Up Session Configuration Options

The next window (see Figure 10-4) offers options that you can accept or reject to configure the way you want to work when you're accessing your QuickBooks files from another computer (your remote session).

Following are some guidelines for configuring your remote sessions. When the word "this" is used, it refers to the server—the computer you're using for these tasks.

Automatically Reduce Screen Resolution To Match Client Computer

Select this option if the remote computer you'll use to connect to this computer has a lower screen resolution than this computer. If so, the Access Anywhere software will reduce this computer's resolution automatically whenever you connect. This means you won't have to use the scroll bar to see all the contents of the windows you open.

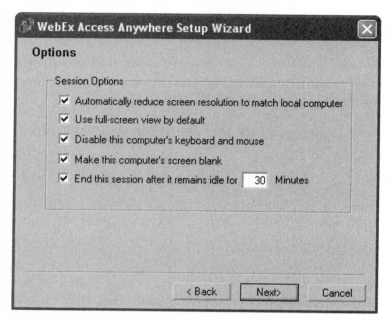

Figure 10-4: Set options for the way you want to work from the
remote computer.

Use Full-screen View By Default

Choose this option to specify that the QuickBooks windows on this computer will appear in full-screen mode on the client computer you're
using.

Disable This Computer's Keyboard And Mouse

Choose this option to disable this computer's keyboard and mouse while
you are connected from a client computer. This means that if people are
in your office, they can't use this computer while you're working on your
QuickBooks files from the client computer.

Make This Computer's Screen Blank

Select this option to force the screen on this computer to go blank when
you're connected from the client computer. This means that if people are
in your office, they cannot see the data in your QuickBooks files.

End The Session After It Is Inactive For [X] Minutes

Choose this option to force the Access Anywhere software to break the connection between the computers if there hasn't been any keyboard or mouse activity on the client computer for the amount of time you specify for X.

Select the Software to Access

The next window lets you select the applications installed on this computer that you can run from the remote client computer when you're away from your office. Because you're using a version of Access Anywhere that's connected to your QuickBooks Premier edition software, the wizard only lists your QuickBooks Premier edition software. Click Next.

NOTE: If you want to run other software that's installed on this computer from a remote computer, you can sign up for Gold Services.

Set Security

The next wizard window covers authentication options. The settings you specify here will be used to invoke security measures when you attempt to access this computer from a remote client computer. The software offers two methods of authentication:

- Access Code authentication, which is available with the free trial version of Access Anywhere.
- Phone authentication, which is grayed-out and inaccessible unless you've signed up for Gold Services.

Access Code authentication works by storing an authentication code that you create on this computer, and the code is stored on this computer. When you connect to this computer from a remote computer via the WebEx website, you're asked to enter this code before you can gain access to the QuickBooks files.

The access code is nothing more than a password for entering the computer from a remote location. If you have a problem remembering all your passwords, you can use the same password you created for logging in to the WebEx Access Anywhere website.

Enter an access code in the Access Code field in the Authentication dialog. The characters you enter aren't displayed in the dialog; instead, you see bullets so your entry is hidden from anyone who may be able to view your monitor. Enter the same access code in the Confirm Access Code field. If the characters you type aren't exactly the same in both fields, you'll see an error message. Try again, or choose an access code that's easier for you to type without making mistakes.

When you connect to this computer from the remote computer over the WebEx site on the Internet, you have to enter this code to get into the computer and use QuickBooks.

Phone authentication (for Gold Services) is a bit more complicated, and requires more work to connect to your computer from a remote site, but it also provides tighter security. Briefly, it means that after you connect the remote computer to this computer via the WebEx website, an automated phone dialer at WebEx calls a phone number you specify. That phone number must be available to you at the remote site. You must answer the phone and use the phone buttons to enter a pass code to connect to the computer and access your QuickBooks files.

Finish the Setup Process

When you click Next, the Setup Complete window informs you that you've finished configuring your Remote Access feature. Click Finish to end the setup program. You return to the Remote Access web page, where your computer is now listed. Click Log Out, and close Internet Explorer.

The Access Anywhere software that makes this computer available for remote access automatically opens, and an icon appears In the Notification Area of your Windows taskbar (the Notification Area is the right side of the taskbar, where the current time is displayed, along with other icons).

If you have another computer that holds QuickBooks Premier Edition data files (perhaps you're running another company on a different computer), you can set up that computer as a server for Access Anywhere, too. Go to that computer and repeat all the steps you performed to set up this computer. When you're finished, your Access Anywhere log in website window will list both computers, and when you're working from a remote client computer you can choose the computer you want to work on.

Using the Access Anywhere Taskbar Icon

If you hover your mouse pointer over the Access Anywhere icon on the taskbar, a pop-up displays the current status of your connection:

- Available means your computer is connected to the Access Anywhere website, and a remote user can access your QuickBooks files.
- Offline means this computer is not available for access via the Access Anywhere website.
- Blocked means you have blocked access to this computer from remote users.

To change the status of your Access Anywhere connection, right-click the icon and select one of the options from the menu that appears. The menu choices vary, depending upon the current status, and I'll go over them here.

Log Out

Click Log Out to disconnect your Access Anywhere software from the website. Remote users (including you) who go to your Access Anywhere website are notified that you are not logged in, so no remote access is available.

When you log out, the icon remains on your taskbar so you can easily log in again by right-clicking the icon and choosing Log In.

Log In

If you've logged out, you can log in again by right-clicking the Access Anywhere icon and choosing Log In. A Log In dialog appears, displaying the WebEx website URL, your login name (the e-mail address you used when you signed up for Access Anywhere), and a blank Password field. Fill in the password and click OK to log in.

Remember, the password you enter to log into Access Anywhere is your login password for the WebEx Access Anywhere service, not the password that is the access code for the server computer (unless you used the same password for both logins).

Block the Computer

Click Block This Computer to remain connected to the WebEx website while preventing anyone from accessing the QuickBooks files on this computer. A red circle with a line (the traditional NO symbol) appears over the Access Anywhere icon.

If a remote user tries to use this computer via Access Anywhere, the website window will say the computer is blocked, and the user will not be able to continue the session.

You should block the computer if you're working on the computer, and a remote session would interfere with that work. For example, block the computer if you're performing a backup. To make the computer available to remote users again, right-click the Access Anywhere icon and select Unblock This Computer.

Close the Access Anywhere Agent

The last option on the right-click menu for the Access Anywhere icon is Close Access Anywhere Agent. This shuts down the Agent's connection to the WebEx website, and closes the software. To start the Access Anywhere Agent again, select it from the Programs menu.

Change Configuration Options

You can view your configuration options by right-clicking the Access Anywhere icon on the taskbar, and choosing Preferences from the shortcut menu. The Preferences dialog opens, displaying a tab for each of the configuration options and features of Access Anywhere.

- The Account tab displays the information required to log on to the WebEx site.

- The Options tab holds the configuration options for remote sessions that you established during setup.
- The Applications tab lists the applications on this computer that are available to remote users. The Access Anywhere account you open through QuickBooks does not permit remote users to open any other software except QuickBooks.
- The Authentication tab contains the access code you created when you configured the computer.
- The Log tab contains the log that Access Anywhere keeps. This log tracks everything that happens, such as any changes you make in the computer's status (e.g. changing Available to Block This Computer). The log also contains an entry for every Access Anywhere session.

You can change all your configuration options, with the exception of your WebEx account information, from the Preferences dialog. Open the Preferences dialog, make the appropriate changes and click Apply.

A dialog appears, displaying your WebEx account ID (your e-mail address), and asking for your Access Anywhere password (not the authentication password you created for access to the computer). Enter your password so the changes can be sent to the WebEx website. Once that's done, your information on the site matches the information in the local Preferences dialog.

Changing WebEx Account Information

You can change your account information on the WebEx website. Your account information includes your login name, password, and your credit card information after your free account expires and you sign up for the service.

To make changes to your account information, open Internet Explorer and travel to the URL you use to log in to the site. After you log in, click the My Profile link and make any necessary changes.

Launching the Access Anywhere Software

By default, the Access Anywhere software configures itself to start automatically whenever you boot your computer. This means a listing for

Access Anywhere Agent should appear in the Startup folder of your Programs menu. It also means that after your computer is up and running, the Access Anywhere icon automatically takes up residency on your taskbar.

If you don't want the software to start automatically whenever you start your computer, you can right-click the Access Anywhere Agent listing in the Startup folder, and choose Delete from the shortcut menu. This action doesn't delete the software; it merely deletes the shortcut in the Startup folder.

A program listing for WebEx Access Anywhere appears on your Programs menu. The listing has a right-facing arrow, indicating the presence of a submenu. The following submenu items are available:

- Access Anywhere Agent, which you click to start the software if you've removed it from the Startup folder, or if you've closed the software by choosing Close The Access Anywhere Agent from the taskbar icon's right-click menu. Starting the software puts the Access Anywhere icon on the taskbar.
- Uninstall Access Anywhere, which you click to uninstall the software if you don't want to use it any more.

NOTE: *If you uninstall the software during your free trial period, there's nothing more you have to do. If you signed up for Access Anywhere after the free trial period, you must contact WebEx and cancel your account in order to stop the automatic charge to your credit card.*

Using QuickBooks from a Remote Computer

To use Access Anywhere to work on your QuickBooks files, the following requirements must be met:

- The server (the computer that holds your QuickBooks files) must be available so remote users can gain access to it. Check the status on the Access Anywhere icon on the server's taskbar.
- The remote user must be working at a computer that can access the Internet.

The remote user could be you if you are traveling, you're at a client site, or you just feel like working from home. The remote user could also be a free-lance bookkeeper that prefers to work from home, or from his or her own office. On the other hand, perhaps your on-staff bookkeeper is an employee who telecommutes.

Starting a Remote Session

As long as the server is available, you can work with your QuickBooks files from a remote computer. You'll need the following information to initiate the session:

- The URL for your WebEx Access Anywhere sessions.
- The Login ID for your Access Anywhere account (the e-mail address you used when you created the account)
- The password for the Login ID
- The name of the server that holds the QuickBooks file you want to work with (if you have more than one computer set up for Access Anywhere)
- The authentication password to enter the server

Log In to Access Anywhere

To begin, open your browser on the client computer, and enter the URL for the WebEx Access Anywhere website. Enter your login ID and password. You can automate the login process by checking the option Save My User Information For Automatic Login, but don't do so if other people have access to the computer.

Connect to the Server

Go to the list of the computers you've configured for remote access. Select the computer you want to work on by clicking its check box to insert a check mark. Then click Connect to establish a remote connection to the computer.

For most people, only one computer is running QuickBooks Premier, so the Access Anywhere window looks similar to Figure 10-5. However, if you registered and configured multiple computers for your Access Anywhere account, they'll all be listed.

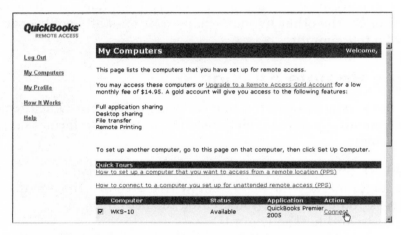

Figure 10-5: Select a computer and click Connect.

The first time you connect to the Access Anywhere website from a remote computer, the WebEx Client software is automatically downloaded and installed on that computer. A Security window appears, asking if it's okay to download files from WebEx. Accept the file transfer, and select the option to download from WebEx automatically in the future. Then wait a moment while the files are transferred.

WARNING: As soon as you begin the connection process, you must dedicate your browser to your Access Anywhere session. Do not click the Back or Forward buttons on the browser, do not click the Refresh button, do not enter another URL in the Address Bar, and don't select a website from your Favorites menu. Performing any of these actions closes the Access Anywhere connection.

You must authenticate yourself before you can gain access to the computer. The Access Code dialog opens (see Figure 10-6), and you must enter the access code you created to permit access to the server. After you enter the code, click OK.

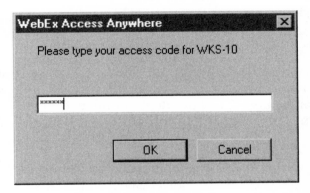

Figure 10-6: Enter the authentication code you created to access this computer.

Working in QuickBooks

After you're authenticated, Access Anywhere establishes a connection to the server computer. Then the Access Anywhere software automatically launches QuickBooks on the server computer (if QuickBooks isn't already open), and displays the QuickBooks window on your computer.

If you configured your QuickBooks company file for user logins, nothing changes just because you're working from a remote computer. The same QuickBooks Login window appears that you see when you're working directly on your QuickBooks computer. You must enter your QuickBooks login name, enter the password, and click OK to open the password-protected company file.

When the QuickBooks window opens, it looks almost exactly the same as it would if you were working at the server computer. The only difference is the presence of the Access Anywhere title bar, because your QuickBooks window is displayed inside the Access Anywhere window.

Back at the server, unless you selected the option to make the computer screen black during a remote connection, the QuickBooks window is also displayed on the monitor. This means every QuickBooks transaction or report window you open while you're working remotely is visible to anyone near the server. In addition, on the server computer the Access Anywhere icon on the taskbar displays the status "In Session".

Changing the View

If your preconfigured options did not specify that the QuickBooks window should display on your client computer as a full screen window, you can change the option in order to have the QuickBooks window fill your screen during this session. This means that only the QuickBooks window appears on your monitor.

Click the arrow next to the Access Anywhere icon on the Access Anywhere title bar. In the drop-down list, select Show Full Screen View. The Access Anywhere icon moves to the lower left corner of your screen, because the title bar is no longer visible. When you click the arrow next to the icon, you see that the command changed to Restore View, so you can reverse the action.

Manipulating the Server

While you're working from the remote computer, you have quite a bit of power over the server computer. Click the arrow next to the Access Anywhere icon. The available commands (covered next) are on a submenu under the Remote Computer command on the Access Anywhere drop-down list. These are the configuration options you set when you set up the server.

Make Screen Blank

If you don't want anyone who is in the same room as the server computer to see what you're doing while you work, select Make Screen Blank. A check mark appears next to the command, and to reverse the process, click the command again to remove the check mark (it's a toggle).

This command doesn't always work, and if it fails, you have either (or both) of the following problems on the server computer:

- The video controller in the server computer is not capable of supporting this function (called *video overlay*). If the video controller on your server cannot perform this function, you may want to replace it.
- The remote computer is not running the appropriate version of Microsoft DirectX, which is a Windows utility that manages graphics capabilities. On Windows 9X, ME, 2000, and XP, screen blanking requires DirectX 6.5 or a later version. For Windows NT, screen blanking requires DirectX 6.0. You can download updates to Direct X from Microsoft's website.

Disable Keyboard and Mouse

To prevent anyone who is working on the server computer from working in QuickBooks, select the command Disable Keyboard And Mouse. To reverse the action, select the command again to remove the check mark.

The keyboard and mouse aren't totally disabled; they just don't work in QuickBooks. The person working at the server computer can continue to work in any other application, and can perform any operating system task.

Reduce Screen Resolution To Match This Computer

If you find you need to use the scroll bar to see all of the items in a QuickBooks window, the screen resolution of the server computer may be set at a higher specification than the resolution of the computer you're using.

Click Reduce Screen Resolution To Match This Computer to reduce the server computer's screen resolution to match that of the client computer for the duration of the Access Anywhere session. When you end the session, the server computer's screen resolution is automatically restored.

You could also reconfigure the remote computer you're using to match the server's settings (in the Settings tab of the Display Properties dialog), but that may retard the performance level of an Access Anywhere session.

Send Ctrl+Alt+Del

If someone is available to work with the server computer, and if the server computer is running Windows 2000/NT/XP, you can open the Windows Security dialog on the server computer by clicking the command Send Ctrl+Alt+Del. Then, the person in front of the computer can log you in or out of your computer or network, or lock/unlock the computer.

Bring Shared Application to Front

If an application window was left open on the server computer, and the application window is in the foreground of the server computer's screen, your remote computer displays a shaded box that interferes with your ability to work in QuickBooks.

Click the command Bring Shared Application To Front to make the QuickBooks window the foreground window. This command also works if another application window is in the foreground because a user is working on the server computer.

However, after a moment of confusion, the user will probably click the taskbar button for the other application to bring that window to the foreground. To avoid a foreground/background windows duel with the user, tell users not to work on the server computer during remote sessions.

Ending the Remote Session

When you're finished working with QuickBooks, you should close the QuickBooks window before you end your Access Anywhere session. If you don't take this step, the QuickBooks software window remains on the screen at the server computer. This can be dangerous, especially if QuickBooks is configured for user logins, and you logged in with Admin rights.

After you close the QuickBooks window, select End Access Anywhere Session from the Access Anywhere drop-down command list. Then click Yes to confirm your action. You're returned to the WebEx Log In window. You can select another computer that you've set up for Access Anywhere, or log out and close the browser.

Accountant Edition Remote Access

The Premier Accountant Edition has a special version of Remote Access that's designed to help you support your QuickBooks clients over the Internet. As a user of QuickBooks Premier Accountant Edition, you automatically qualify for a free year of Remote Access.

You can use Remote Access to work directly in a client's copy of QuickBooks, and make adjusting entries, view or change transactions, and generate reports. You can also use this Internet connection to train clients; showing them how to perform tasks, and explaining what to do, and when to do it.

Whether you visit your client sites, or you send QuickBooks support personnel, using Remote Access lets you eliminate all the down time that isn't billable. You don't lose time and money driving from client to client (and you also save parking fees).

Getting started with Remote Access is quick and easy. You must set up a Remote Access account, and then download a small software program. After that, you're ready to go online and work directly in your clients' QuickBooks files.

Signing Up for an Account

To use Remote Access, you must first sign up for an account. Be sure your computer is connected to the Internet, open any QuickBooks company file, and choose Accountant → Remote Access. In the QuickBooks Remote Access window that opens, click Register Now to open the Sign Up window seen in Figure 10-7.

TIP: *When you use any QuickBooks function that's connected to the Internet, the software may display a message telling you it must open your Internet browser. Click OK and select the option Don't Display This Message Again to avoid encountering this message in the future.*

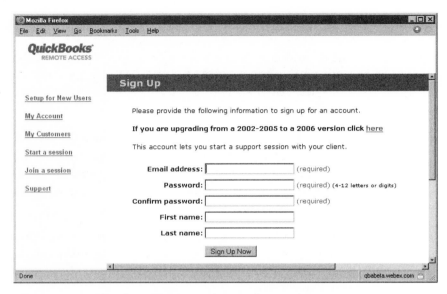

Figure 10-7: The first step is to sign up for an account.

Enter your e-mail address (which becomes your login name) and a password. When you enter your password, you won't see the characters you type; instead, the window displays bullets, preventing anyone who happens to be hanging around from learning your password.

Enter the same password in the Confirm Password field. If the characters you type don't match the characters you entered in the Password field, QuickBooks displays an error message. If this error occurs, you may have selected a password that's difficult for you to type, so you should create a different password—one that you can type without making mistakes.

After you fill out the information, click Sign Up Now at the bottom of the window. The data you entered in the form is sent to the WebEx database, and the QuickBooks Remote Access window displays a message telling you that you've successfully signed up for the service. The on-screen message displays the following information:

• Your login ID (your e-mail address)
• Your password

- The expiration date for your free trial
- The website address (URL) you must use for your Remote Access sessions

Be careful! The message shows your password in plain text, so anyone who can view your monitor can get your password. The message also includes a directive to print the page, and if you do, remember that the printed document contains your password. Don't print the document if you use a shared printer that is in a hallway or another office, unless you want to share your password with anyone who happens to be near the printer (giving away a password is never a good idea).

You don't really have to print the window, because you'll be sent a confirmation of your registration via e-mail in a matter of minutes. The e-mail message includes the same information: your login ID (which is the e-mail address you entered in the Sign Up form), your password, and the URL for Remote Access sessions. You should copy this information to a file, or print it and store it in a safe place.

You won't be asked for a credit card number nor for any other payment information at this point, because you have a free account for a year (one of the perks of purchasing QuickBooks Premier Accountant edition). When the free account service ends, you'll have to pay a monthly fee, and at that time, you'll be asked to provide credit card information. In the meantime, this period of free access lets you decide whether the service is useful enough to buy it later.

On the client side, there's no need to sign up for the service, because your clients will never incur any fees for this feature.

Installing the Software

You must install the Remote Access software (named WebEx Meeting Manager), which is an add-on (a *plug-in*) for Internet Explorer. If you are planning to run Remote Access sessions from the computer on which you installed QuickBooks Premier Accountant edition, you should install Meeting Manager on that computer.

However, I advise clients to access the Remote Access website from a computer other than the computer that contains your own QuickBooks Premier Accountant edition installation. If you use another computer to use Remote Access, it means other people in your office can use QuickBooks to enter transactions, get reports, etc.

If you have a laptop, you can use Remote Access to support clients even when you're away from the office.

You can start a Remote Access session from Internet Explorer, or from within QuickBooks. Choose Accountant → Remote Access from the QuickBooks menu bar, and the QuickBooks Remote Access feature will automatically direct you to the right Web site.

TIP: To increase your efficiency, put the Remote Access website URL on the Favorites list of Internet Explorer on every computer you might use for Remote Access.

Travel to the Remote Access website and log in (unless you're still there now that you've finished signing up). Click Set Up For New Users to open the Setup For New Users window (see Figure 10-8). Click Set Up to download the software to your computer.

Internet Explorer may display a Security Warning message that asks if you want to install software from this website. WebEx provides the security features that Internet Explorer and Microsoft Windows requires, so it's okay to click Yes. In fact, it's okay to put a check mark into the check box that says Internet Explorer can always trust content from WebEx.

The software is transferred to your computer. You don't have to go through an installation or configuration process for the software, all of that is taken care of automatically.

When you see the message Setup Is Complete, click OK. The Log In window appears so you can initiate a support session with a client. If you're not ready to run a Remote Access session now, just close the Remote Access window.

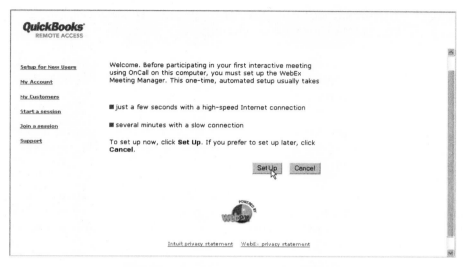

Figure 10-8: Set up Meeting Manager on your computer.

Your clients also must have the Webex Meeting Manager plug-in. The client version of the software is installed automatically when your client connects to the WebEx website for a Remote Access session.

Maintaining Your User Profile

During your free trial of Remote Access, your user profile consists of your login name (which is your e-mail address) and your password. After a year, when the free trial period ends, you'll probably sign up for Remote Access. At that point, your user profile also includes your credit card information.

If you want to change your password, or change the credit card information, log on to the Remote Access website and click My Account. Follow the instructions to make your changes, and click Update.

Starting a Remote Access Session

To start a Remote Access session, open Internet Explorer (or QuickBooks) and travel to the Remote Access website address you were given. Because you're traveling to a secure website, you'll see the usual Internet

Explorer warnings about entering and leaving secure sites. (If you wish, you can select the option to stop showing the warning.)

NOTE: Your Remote Access URL starts with https:// instead of http://. The letter s stands for secure.

When you reach the Web site, you see the WebEx Log In window. Fill in your e-mail address (which is your Log In User ID), and the password you created when you signed up.

You can also select the option Save My User Information For Automatic Login, which eliminates the need to fill in the Email Address and Password fields in the future. However, if other people access your computer, an automatic login is a security risk.

After you log on, the WebEx Support Session window opens, as seen in Figure 10-9. You can use the utilities available on the window, such as updating your account information, signing up for Platinum services, or setting up a customer list.

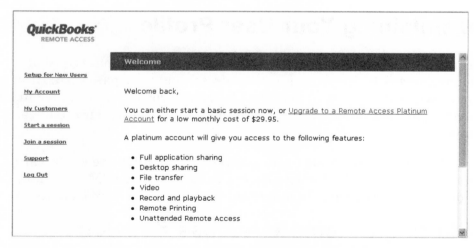

Figure 10-9: Before you start a support session, you can use the tools available on the Support Session window.

Creating a Customer List

You can maintain a customer list on the Remote Access site to make it easy to contact your clients when you want to use a Remote Access support session. (I think of accountant's customers as "clients", but Remote Access calls them customers).

To take advantage of this nifty feature, click My Customers (in the left pane) after you log in. The first time the My Customers window opens, no customers are listed (of course). To add a client to your customer list, click Add Customer to open the blank Customer Form seen in Figure 10-10.

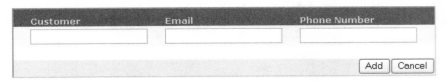

Figure 10-10: Create client records to store on the Remote Access website.

Fill in the Add Customer form as follows:

- The Customer field is for the name by which you refer to the client. You can use a first or last name, a full name, or a nickname. The name appears in the support window during a Remote Access session, but it's unrelated to logins or authentication.
- The E-mail field is for the e-mail address of the person at the client site you work with when you're running a Remote Access session. Remote Access uses the e-mail address to send an invitation to join a session.
- The Phone Number field is a handy reference so you can call the customer to set up a Remote Access support session. This field is optional.

Click Add to place this client in your Remote Access Customer List. Then repeat the process for all the other clients with whom you'll use the Remote Access service.

To edit customer information, select the listing by clicking the check box to place a check mark within it. Click Edit and make the needed changes. Then click Update to save the new data. To delete a customer, select the listing and click Delete.

Initiating a Support Session

Initiating a support session means reserving space on the WebEx secure website where you and your client can "meet". At the meeting place, your client's QuickBooks software is available (which is much easier, safer, and more convenient than entering your client's computer by using a remote control software application).

To work in a client's QuickBooks files, click Start a Session (in the left pane) to open the Remote Access Support Session window. The window displays the unique Session ID for this session in the left pane. Your client needs this session number to meet you on the WebEx site.

Until your client joins the session, the commands on the left side of the Support Session window are inaccessible.

Notifying Your Client

Your client must access the Remote Access website from the computer that has QuickBooks installed. In order to join you in the support session, the client must know the Support Session Identification number. You have two ways to provide this information to your client:

- Send e-mail with a link to the URL and Session ID (either using the automated e-mail feature, or using the client's entry in your Customer List)
- Call or fax the client and provide the URL and the Session ID

Sending the Client an Automatic E-mail Message

You can have Remote Access automatically send an e-mail message to your client. The message contains a link to the URL for the session, as well as the Session ID. All the client has to do is click the link to open

Internet Explorer and travel to the website to join you. To send the message, use one of the following methods:

- If the client is on your customer list, click the arrow to the right of the field with the text Select From Customer List and select the client. The name and e-mail address fills in automatically.
- If the client isn't on your customer list, fill out the Name and Email Address fields.

After the fields are filled in, click Invite. The message is sent immediately from the website—you don't have to open your own e-mail software to send it.

The recipient should check his or her e-mail at the appointed time (or you should call and report the fact that you're sending the message).

This only works properly if your client is expecting the e-mail, and is ready for the session, so be sure to make your arrangements beforehand. In addition, the client's e-mail software must be on the same computer as QuickBooks. Otherwise, clicking the link in the e-mail message to join the session automatically would be useless.

Phoning the Client with the Session Information

If the client's e-mail software isn't on the same computer as QuickBooks, the advantage to an e-mail message with a link you can click is lost. In that case, you can transmit the information about the support session on the telephone. Give the client the URL and the Session ID. (Faxing works just as well.)

Client Login

At the client site, a designated user should be working at the computer that contains the QuickBooks program and files. All software applications, except QuickBooks, should be closed.

QuickBooks can be open on the client computer, but it's not a requirement. If QuickBooks is not open when the two computers connect, Remote Access will automatically open the software.

If the client received an e-mail message with a link that automates the client login, clicking the link automatically opens the client's browser. The browser, in turn, automatically travels to the WebEx Log In website (see Figure 10-11). The client's name and the Session ID are already filled in, and all the client has to do is click Join.

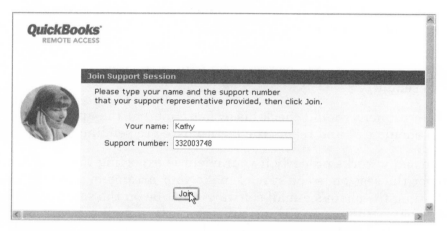

Figure 10-11: Your client needs to log in with a name and the ID
number for this session.

If you didn't send an e-mail message with an automatic link, the client must open a browser and manually enter the Remote Access URL. The Remote Access website displays the Join Support Session window, where the client must enter a name in the Your Name field, and also enter the Session ID for this session in the Support number field.

> **TIP**: The name the client enters in the Your Name field can be any name. It is not a login ID, and it does not need to be authenticated. It's merely a way of letting you know who is on the other side of the Remote Access connection.

After the client user clicks Join to enter the session, the Remote Access Manager browser plug-in is automatically downloaded to the client's computer. The client waits for the support representative (that's you), to begin the session (see Figure 10-12).

Figure 10-12: The client has no chores and must wait for you to
make contact.

When the client computer is connected to the session, the commands
in the left pane of your Remote Access Support Session window become
available (they're grayed out until the client computer connects to the
session). You can open and view the client's QuickBooks files (or open
any other application on the client computer, if you've signed up for
Platinum service). You and your client can interact in a variety of ways,
and these options are discussed in the following sections of this
chapter.

Understanding Client Permissions

By default, Remote Access asks the client's permission to perform the following tasks during a support session:

- View the client's QuickBooks files—select Request Application
  View.
- Take control of the client's QuickBooks software window—select
  Request Application Control.

Each time you select one of those commands in the Remote Access
window, a dialog appears to tell you that Remote Access has requested
permission from the client to perform the task.

On the client's computer, a message appears to ask if the support representative can perform the task. When the client clicks OK, you're notified of that fact, and you can continue with the task.

If the client also selects the check box Don't Request Permission Again During This Session, any future commands you issue from your computer are automatically launched without sending a permission request message to the client.

This wholesale permission makes the support session faster and more efficient. It also means the user at the client site is free to leave the computer and perform other work in the office. The wholesale permissions are not permanent, they exist for the current support session only; they do not carry over to future support sessions with this client.

If your client is unwilling to provide wholesale permissions for the support session, a user must remain in front of the client's computer throughout the support session in order to grant permission for each command you want to implement.

Opening the Client's QuickBooks File

The first step is to gain access to the client's QuickBooks file. To accomplish this, click Request Application View from the command list in the left pane.

Remote Access sends a message to the client computer, asking if the support representative can view the client's application (see Figure 10-13). The message dialog on the client's computer also includes the option to give wholesale permissions for this Remote Access session. A message telling you that the client been sent your request appears on your computer.

When the client clicks OK, a dialog appears on the client computer, listing the applications that can be shared. If you haven't upgraded to Platinum services, and your use of Remote Access is the result of your purchase of QuickBooks Premier Accountant edition, that list is limited to QuickBooks. The client must select QuickBooks and then click Share.

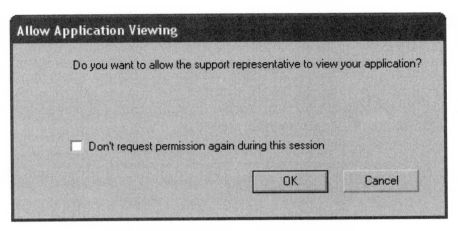

Figure 10-13: The client must agree to let you open
QuickBooks.

If QuickBooks isn't already open on the client's computer, Remote Access opens it. Both your screen and your client's screen display the client's QuickBooks window.

Client View of the Shared QuickBooks Window

On the client's computer, a Sharing icon appears in the upper right corner of the screen. Clicking the down-arrow to the right of the icon displays the client's sharing menu, which contains the command Stop Sharing. If the client selects this command, your permission to view the application is revoked, and you must re-initiate the request to share the application. In addition, the client is returned to the Remote Access Support Session window. (The client's drop-down menu also includes a command to change the annotation color, which can only be used after the accountant turns on annotation.)

The client has control of the QuickBooks window, which is useful if you're on the telephone for a training session, or you just want to walk the client through a specific activity. However, you can take control of the QuickBooks application, so that your own mouse and keyboard controls the software. See "Taking Control of QuickBooks" later in this chapter.

Accountant View of the Shared QuickBooks Window

On your computer, the QuickBooks software window is displayed inside the Application Control software window. You can see the client's mouse pointer in addition to your own mouse pointer, and as the client works, the results are displayed on your screen.

Both the Application Control window and the QuickBooks window have a Sharing icon in the upper right corner. Each of these icons contains a drop-down list of commands.

If you use the Sharing icon on the Application Control software window to switch to Full Screen View, the QuickBooks application window fills your screen (the title bar for the Application Control software window disappears and the QuickBooks title bar is at the top of the window).

In Full Screen View, the Sharing icon for the Application Control window moves to the lower left corner of your screen. The definition of "Full Screen" is literal; the QuickBooks window fills your screen, and your taskbar disappears. To return to the original view, choose Restore View from the Sharing icon's drop-down command list.

TIP: Press the Windows key on your keyboard to see your taskbar.

Taking Control of QuickBooks

If you want to perform tasks directly in the client's QuickBooks file, you can take control of the shared application, by returning to the Remote Access Support Session window (the original window in which you selected the command to start a session) and selecting the command Request Application Control.

Returning to the Remote Access Support Session window isn't always a cakewalk. You may have some trouble finding it, because it's hidden behind other Remote Access windows. You may see multiple taskbar buttons related to the support session, but they're not clearly labeled. I find it easiest to minimize the Application Control window to reveal the Support Session window.

If the client didn't select the option to give you wholesale permissions, you must wait for the client to agree to give you control of the QuickBooks software window. Once you gain control of the client's QuickBooks window, you can use your mouse and keyboard to manipulate the client's QuickBooks file.

However, the term "control" isn't terribly accurate because you and the client user are really sharing control of the client's QuickBooks window. If the client clicks the mouse, the client takes back control. You can click your mouse to regain control whenever the client takes control.

This paradigm can become silly, frustrating, or annoying if you end up in a "battle of the mouse clicks". As control passes to one user, the other user is notified, along with instructions to click to take back control of the window.

There is no way to take absolute control for the session, and then turn control back to your client when you're finished. As a result, you must reach an accommodation with your client about who controls what, and when.

Using the Chat Window

You can open a chat window so that you and the client user can exchange messages. This is useful if you don't have a telephone connection running simultaneously with your Remote Access session (perhaps because calling the client results in long distance charges).

To open a chat window, return to the Support Session window and click Start Chat. A chat window that can be used by both sides of the connection opens on both computers.

Enter text in the bottom of the chat window and press Enter (or click Send) to move the text into the main part of the Chat window. As each person sends a message, the chat window displays the text along with the user's name (see Figure 10-14). Either participant can close a chat window by clicking the close button (X) in the upper right corner of the Chat window.

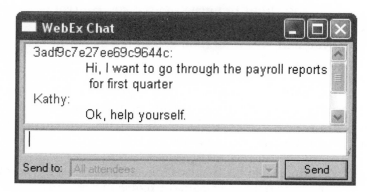

Figure 10-14: Use the Chat window to communicate with your client.

Annotating the QuickBooks Window

If you want to point out an element in a QuickBooks window, or show the client some significant entry or change you've made, you can annotate the QuickBooks window. Your client can also use annotation mode to point out elements to you. Turning on annotation mode affects both computers.

To turn on annotation mode, click the Sharing icon, and choose Annotate from the drop-down command menu. Your mouse pointer turns into a pen point and you can begin drawing on the screen (see Figure 10-15).

To change the color of the annotations, choose Annotation Color from the Sharing icon's drop-down menu. The annotation palette appears and you can select a new color.

When you turn on annotation mode, an Annotation icon appears in the client's window. Clicking it displays a drop-down list that has only a command to change the annotation color. The client can (and should) select a different color for annotation so you can both easily identify who drew what.

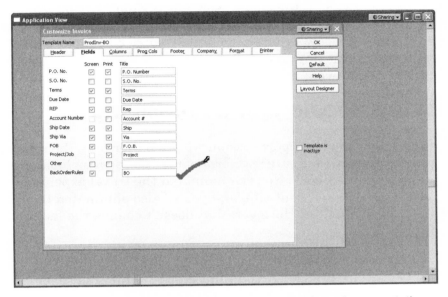

Figure 10-15: Draw attention to screen elements by using annotation mode

To stop annotating, and return your mouse pointer to its normal mode, select Stop Annotating from the Sharing icon's menu. This command also clears all the annotations from the software window.

Ending the Support Session

Either party can end a Remote Access Support Session. When one side of the connection ends the session, the other side of the connection receives a message indicating that fact.

On the accountant's side, you can end the session by returning to the Remote Access Support Session window and choosing End Support Session. You're asked to confirm your action, and after you click OK, the client sees a message that the session has been terminated by the support representative. You're returned to the original Log In window, where you can start another session, log out, or close Internet Explorer.

On the client side, if the client user selects Stop Sharing from the Sharing icon drop-down list, he's returned to the client Remote Access Support Session window, where the only available command is End Support Session. Clicking that command ends the session, and sends notification of that event to you.

Tracking Session Time for Billing

As soon as you begin a support session, you're performing the same tasks you (or a member of your staff) perform when you're on a client site, working in a client's books. You've eliminated the travel expenses incurred for travel to a client site, and you've also eliminated the downtime between client sites. However, that doesn't change the fact that the work is billable.

You should consider using the Timer program that came with your copy of QuickBooks Premier Accountant edition. Start the timer clock when you begin your online support session, and you'll have an accurate record of billable time. The Timer doesn't require QuickBooks, it's an independent application, so even if you're supporting clients from a computer that doesn't have QuickBooks installed, you can track your time and print reports.

Chapter 11

Accountant Edition Features

Using Accountant Edition to run your practice

Supporting clients with Accountant Edition tools

The Premier Accountant Edition differs from all the other Premier editions. It contains features, tools, add-on programs, and third-party offers that aren't included in the other Premier editions. The Premier Accountant Edition is designed to serve two purposes:

- Provide a robust accounting application for running an accounting practice.
- Provide tools and features that make it easy to support QuickBooks clients.

In this chapter I'll go over some of the most important and most useful features in the Premier Accountant Edition.

All QuickBooks Editions Included

The best part of purchasing QuickBooks Premier 2006 Accountant Edition is that you've really bought all the QuickBooks 2006 editions. In addition to the Premier Accountant Edition, you can also run QuickBooks Pro, QuickBooks Simple Start, QuickBooks Premier (not industry specific), and all of the QuickBooks Premier industry specific editions (Contractor, Manufacturing & Wholesale, Nonprofit, Professional Services, and Retail). To switch among QuickBooks editions:

1. Choose File → Toggle To Another Edition to open the Select QuickBooks Edition dialog.
2. Select the edition you want to use, and click Next. QuickBooks displays a window confirming the edition you've selected.
3. Click Toggle to close the currently loaded edition and load the selected edition.

NOTE: *The company file that is open at the time you toggle is loaded in the new edition.*

Running Your Practice

In this section, I'll go over some of the features in Premier Accountant Edition that you'll find helpful for running your own practice in

QuickBooks. Most of the information will also help you work with client files.

Company Data File

QuickBooks provides a wide range of options for tracking clients, projects, and income. The flexibility built into QuickBooks lets you set up your company data file in the way that best meets your needs.

Proving the old legend of the shoemaker's children, I've found many accounting firms that spent years operating without full-featured accounting software. They have a time and billing program for receivables and payments, and they use write-up software to record revenue totals and disbursements.

Fixed assets and liabilities are tracked in spreadsheets, and a variety of other software documents keep track of other financial details. They have an outside payroll service, but they don't track the weekly payroll (at the end of a quarter or year, they enter the totals provided by the payroll service). Preparing the firm's tax return must be a real joy!

Many of these firms, especially those who support clients using QuickBooks, have begun installing QuickBooks for their own use—and I find the Premier Accountant Edition in use at many accounting practices. When I visit these firms to help them tweak their QuickBooks software, I often find configuration options that aren't helping accountants make QuickBooks truly useful.

As a result, a lot of after-the-fact work (especially the calculation of subtotals and the process of analyzing revenue) continues to be performed in spreadsheet applications. Very little of the work done outside of QuickBooks would be required if the configuration options were more carefully considered, and some training sessions were held. I guess old habits are hard to break.

Creating a New Company File

If you're new to QuickBooks, after you launch the software for the first time, you're offered an opportunity to create a new file. You can create a company file by using the EasyStep Interview (a wizard), or by creating the file manually.

EasyStep Interview

To use the EasyStep Interview, click Start Interview when the first wizard window opens. Go through the wizard windows, answering questions and providing information.

If you've created company files with the EasyStep Interview in prior versions of QuickBooks, you'll find the 2006 version much different. It's much shorter, which is nice; but you can't leave the interview. If you click the Leave button, QuickBooks displays a message telling you that you can finish the interview the next time you open the company file.

Then QuickBooks abruptly closes the file, leaving you to stare at the No Company Open window. The next time you open the company, the EasyStep Interview picks up where you left off—and it will keep doing that until you finish the entire interview. Luckily, as I said, this is a short interview compared to previous years. (I've complained about this to Intuit, and hopefully by the time you bought your copy of QuickBooks, they'd changed this behavior).

The EasyStep Interview does not ask about the type of business organization (corporation, partnership, proprietorship, etc.), and as a result, you'll have to add the equity accounts you need.

The only opening balance the EasyStep Interview asks about is the bank account. You can enter zero as the balance, or answer No to the question about setting up a bank account at all. Either solution avoids the problem of QuickBooks posting an amount to the Opening Bal Equity account (for more discussion on equity accounts, see "Organizing Equity Accounts" later in this chapter).

Creating the Company File Manually

To create your company file manually, click Skip Interview, and fill out the ensuing dialogs. The company name is required, but everything else can be added later if you're in a hurry to get started with QuickBooks.

The Creating New Company dialog (see Figure 11-1) offers a field for selecting the type of tax form your company files. The selection you make determines the equity accounts QuickBooks automatically adds to the chart of accounts.

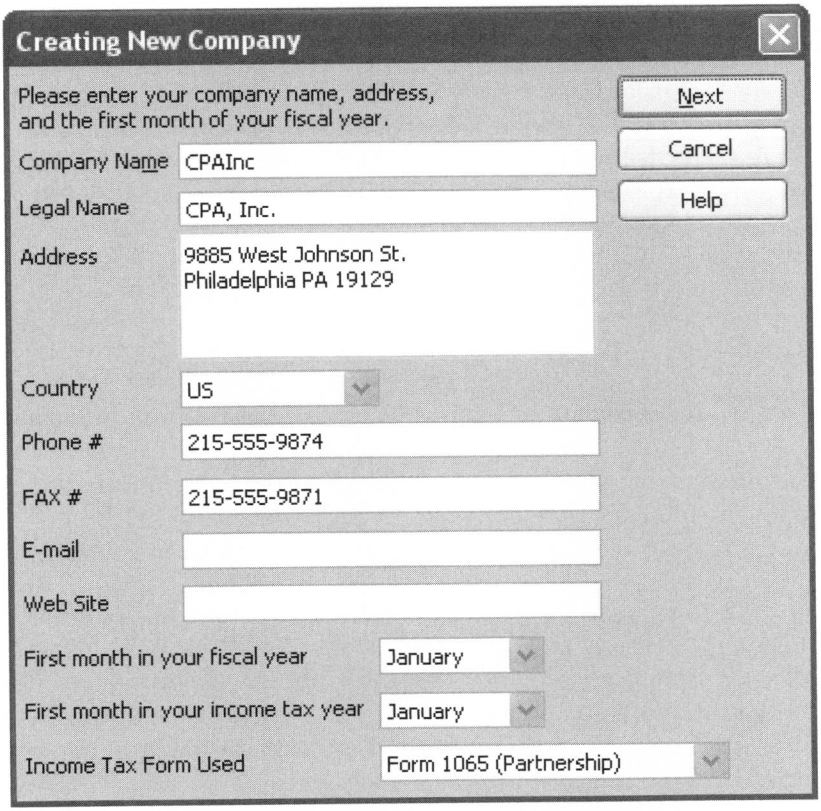

Figure 11-1: Setting up a company file manually lets you enter information the EasyStep Interview skips.

Configuring the Chart of Accounts

QuickBooks creates a partial chart of accounts for accounting firms, but it's missing many accounts. In addition, the accounts are not numbered (and I've never met an accountant who didn't prefer numbered accounts).

Using Numbered Accounts

To number your accounts, choose Edit → Preferences and select the Accounting category in the left pane of the Preferences dialog. In the Company Preferences tab, select the option Use Account Numbers, and also select the option Show Lowest Subaccount Only.

If you added any accounts to the chart of accounts that was installed automatically by QuickBooks, they will not be automatically numbered, and selecting the "Show Lowest Subaccount Only" option produces an error message that tells you that you must create numbers for all accounts before you can enable this option.

Enable account numbers, open the chart of accounts, and enter account numbers for the accounts you added manually. Then return to the Accounting category of the Preferences dialog to enable the Show Lowest Subaccount Only option.

Incidentally, the reason selecting Use Account Numbers works automatically is that QuickBooks actually provides account numbers for the chart of accounts it establishes automatically during company setup. Even though numbers are attached to every account, QuickBooks sets the default configuration for the chart of accounts so it doesn't display those numbers. I have never figured out why—the numbers are there, most accountants prefer account numbers, why not display them?

When you've enabled account numbers, check the number scheme to make sure it matches your own preferences. With one exception (equity accounts), QuickBooks uses the standard numbering paradigm for an Accountant/CPA chart of accounts:

- 1000 starts the asset accounts
- 2000 starts the liability accounts
- 3000 is a bit confusing—see the next section, "Organizing Equity Accounts".
- 4000 starts the income accounts
- 6000 starts the expense accounts
- 7000 starts the "other" income accounts
- 8000 starts the "other" expense accounts

Organizing Equity Accounts

All QuickBooks company files have an equity account for Retained Earnings, and for Opening Bal Equity. If you created the company file manually, and selected a tax form, QuickBooks adds equity accounts to match the tax form.

- For a partnership, QuickBooks creates two equity parent accounts, named Partner One Equity and Partner Two Equity. There are subaccounts for each parent account for draws, investments, and earnings. You can add accounts to match the number of partners.
- For a proprietorship, QuickBooks creates one parent equity account (Owner's Capital), with subaccounts for investments and draws.
- For corporations (both C and S), QuickBooks creates a Capital Stock equity account.

Except for Opening Bal Equity, which is in the 3000 number range, all the equity accounts are linked to numbers in the 1000 range. This doesn't affect your reports, but it may affect your sensibilities. Moreover, it causes the chart of accounts to display in an inconsistent manner—the numbers don't set the sorting pattern, because QuickBooks sorts by account type, not by number.

If the numbering system bothers you, edit the equity accounts so they fall in the 3000 range. Select an account and press Ctrl-E to open the Edit Account dialog. Change the account number, and click OK.

In addition, if the equity account you're editing is for a partner, change the account name so it reflects a partner's name. Otherwise, every time you want to post to the account you have to ask yourself "Who is partner 1?"

You must also edit any subaccounts for the equity accounts you change—give each subaccount a new number, and make other changes as needed.

Opening Bal Equity Account

The Opening Bal Equity account you see in the chart of accounts is a QuickBooks invention. It doesn't have any connection to the phrase "opening balance" the way that term is usually applied in accounting.

QuickBooks uses the Opening Bal Equity account as the offset account when users enter opening balances during setup. Those opening balances might have been entered during the EasyStep Interview, or when users manually created accounts, customers, or vendors (the dialogs have a field for an opening balance).

TIP: In my books, articles, and seminars, I always advise users to avoid filling in any opening balance fields during setup. Instead, I suggest they create transactions that predate the QuickBooks start date to establish those balances (and post the amounts to the appropriate accounts). I advise accountants to take the same attitude when they work with QuickBooks users.

Any accountant who supports QuickBooks clients needs to learn to deal with the Opening Bal Equity account. After a user has entered an opening balance for a bank account in the EasyStep Interview, and then entered opening balances while creating accounts, customers, and vendors, the Opening Bal Equity account can have a rather large balance.

This can create an accounting problem, because users often use the current date to apply opening balances, not a date that precedes the QuickBooks start date. Even if the user understands the concept of the QuickBooks start date, how often do businesses start using QuickBooks on the first day of the year?

Very often the QuickBooks start date is not the first day of the fiscal year. This means that some amounts that should appear in P & L accounts are inappropriately sitting in the Opening Bal Equity account, which is, of course, a balance sheet account. Accountants have to move amounts that are applicable to the current fiscal year out of the Opening Bal Equity account.

You can open the Opening Bal Equity account and see the postings. If a posting seems mysterious, double-click its listing to see the original transaction window—although you may still have a mystery on your hands if you don't understand the way QuickBooks handles these transactions.

For example, a user creates a bank account in the chart of accounts, and enters an opening balance in the New Account dialog. QuickBooks posts the amount to the bank, and to Opening Bal Equity. You can see the transaction in both the bank account register and the Opening Bal Equity register. If you double-click on the account register listing, the transaction window that appears is the Make Deposits window—the same transaction window QuickBooks uses for standard bank deposits. The only clue that this is a deposit that resulted from a new account setup is that the offset account is Opening Bal Equity.

You can (and should) use a journal entry to move the balance in the Opening Bal Equity account to Retained Earnings, or to Retained Earnings-Previous Years (an account that does not exist by default, but is a good candidate for the first new equity account you should create).

After you clear out the balance in the Opening Bal Equity account, you can't relax. Any of the following user actions will put funds back into the account:

- Entering an opening balance when creating a new account (for those account types that have an Opening Balance field).
- Entering an opening balance when creating a new customer.
- Entering an opening balance when creating a new vendor.
- Telling QuickBooks to make an adjustment when bank reconciliation doesn't work.

You can train your clients to avoid the first three items on this list, but there's no way to avoid an adjustment when a bank rec fails to balance. Most failed bank reconciliations are eventually resolved. Usually, the error is discovered, and an adjusting journal entry removes the amount from the Opening Bal Equity account. Sometimes, an equal and opposite error occurs the following month, and the QuickBooks automatic adjustment sets everything back the way to zero. (When this occurs, it usually means the user missed an item during the first reconciliation and failed to clear it, and sees the item the next time the bank account is reconciled).

All balance sheet accounts except Retained Earnings display their current balances when you open the Chart of Accounts window. Train your users to look at the balance of the Opening Bal Equity account, and contact you if a balance exists. In fact, to make it easier to spot, and to discourage any user from posting to it, have your clients rename the account CALL BOB (unless your name is Mary, in which case the account should be named CALL MARY). Use all capital letters to make it easier to spot the account in the list. When your clients give you the information on the postings, you can give them instructions to create the appropriate journal entry (or send a bookkeeper to the client's site to perform the task).

Adding Missing Accounts

The chart of accounts that QuickBooks creates lacks many accounts you need. This isn't peculiar to the chart of accounts created for accountants; it's true of all business types in QuickBooks, which means you'll find the same problem in the chart of accounts at your client sites.

Chief among the missing are cash accounts, so you'll have to add bank accounts. However, you may find that the chart of accounts has no asset accounts at all. You'll also find that many times, the chart of accounts has no liability accounts except Payroll Liabilities.

You cannot delete the payroll liabilities account, even if the company is configured for no payroll activities. In fact, if a company is doing payroll in house, most accountants prefer to use specific payroll liability accounts (FICA, Medicare, FTW, state withholdings, and so on). The same is true for payroll expenses, but you won't be able to remove the Payroll Expenses account that QuickBooks automatically puts in the chart of accounts.

If you don't need either or both of those accounts, make them inactive so they don't appear on the account list, and nobody can accidentally post amounts to them.

Adding accounts one at a time is onerous, and accountants should create preconfigured chart of accounts lists to import into company files—their own files and their clients' files. Appendix A and Appendix B cover importing lists.

Configuring Customers and Jobs

Many accountants track only customer names, omitting jobs from the configuration of their company data files. Specific types of work for clients are tracked by items, or by posting revenue to specific income accounts.

Using Jobs

If you use service items or revenue accounts to track types of services, analyzing any individual client's history requires quite a bit of work. You have to customize a report so it filters items and/or revenue accounts.

All of the information is available, without customization, on a job report. If you want to view individual client histories to analyze your work and income stream, you should consider tracking clients by jobs.

Incidentally, jobs are not restricted to projects with a start and end date; a job can be defined as a definition of work. For example, you might decide to create the following jobs for clients:

- Business tax preparation
- Personal tax preparation
- Audits (performing or attending)
- Planning (preparing pro formas, business plans, and so on)

If some or all of your clients are on retainers, create a job for special work that isn't covered by the retainer, such as the work involved in dealing with an IRS audit.

Using Customer Types

If you choose the CPA business type during company file setup, QuickBooks prepopulates the Customer Types list for specific business types. For an Accountant/CPA business, you can view and manipulate those customer types by choosing Lists → Customer & Vendor Profile

Lists → Customer Type List. Figure 11-2 shows the customer types that QuickBooks automatically adds to your data file.

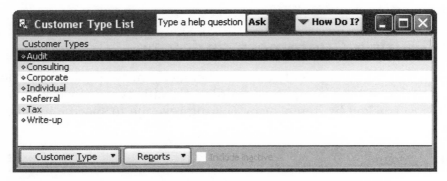

Figure 11-2: The prepopulated customer types may not suit your practice.

If these types work for you, assign a type to each customer. However, many accountants find that these customer types don't work, because many, if not all, clients occupy multiple types.

You may not need customer types at all. Customer types are handy when you need to produce a report of your clients sorted by some particular commonality (the type). For example, you may want to use the QuickBooks Write Letters feature to send a note or a newsletter to certain clients.

At many accounting firms, I install what my clients think is an extremely useful design for customer types—the month of the fiscal year end for business clients. Create twelve customer types, from January to December. Then assign the appropriate type to each customer record. Every month, run a report for the customer type two months hence, and begin the steps for year-end work, which could encompass any of the following:

- Use the Write Letters feature in QuickBooks to send a note reminding clients of the things they must do to close their books and produce reports. Include a request to call the office to make an appointment.

- If you use pretax preparation worksheets (a copy of last years figures and a line for clients to enter the current totals), use the Print Labels feature to send the packages to the appropriate customer type.
- Print a Customer listing of only the appropriate type, and have a staff member set up the appointments.

Add your own end of year protocols to this list of chores, and you'll find that it's easy to identify the right clients because almost all QuickBooks reports let you filter for a customer type.

Managing Items

Items are the services and products a company sells. As an accountant, you sell services, and your item list can be as simple or as complex as your client services and invoicing standards require.

Most accounting firms need service items such as tax preparation (both personal and business), audits, tax planning, business planning, write-up or other bookkeeping services, and special services such as preparing business plans or projections. Create an item for each service you provide.

You can create subitems to refine your items list. For example, if your tax preparation processes involve partners, associates, bookkeepers, or other multiple types of personnel, you may charge a different rate for each type. Create a subitem for each parent item service that involves multiple billing rates. Don't assign a rate to the parent item; assign rates only to the subitems.

Using Price Levels

Price levels provide a way to fine-tune your pricing in situations where you want to pass along a discount (or a higher rate) on an item. QuickBooks Premier editions offer two types of price levels:

- Fixed percentage price levels
- Per item price levels (not available in QuickBooks Basic and Pro editions)

To use price levels, you must first set up your items. If your items have no assigned rates, you can use price levels to set all rates for the item. If your items have been assigned a rate, you can create price levels based on that rate. (Chapter 4 contains the information you need to create and apply price levels.)

Using Billing Rate Levels

The Billing Rate Level List lets you assign a billing rate to a person performing a specific service. This list is only available in the following Premier Editions:

- Accountant Edition
- Contractor Edition
- Professional Services Edition

After you create billing rate levels, and associate them with service providers, invoicing for services becomes almost automated. Every time you create an invoice with billable time, QuickBooks automatically fills in the correct rate for the service, based on the person who performed the work.

For instance, you can have one rate for audit activities that are performed by a senior partner, and another rate for audit activities performed by a junior partner. The senior partner rate for audits may be different from the senior partner rate for creating business plans. The permutations and combinations are almost endless, which makes this a very powerful feature. Learn how to create and apply billing rate levels in Chapter 4.

Adjusting Journal Entries

This feature, available only in QuickBooks Premier Accountant Edition, lets you specify a journal entry as "adjusting". The GJE window includes a check box labeled Adjusting Entry, which is enabled by default. To create a journal entry choose Company → Make General Journal Entries.

TIP: *If you used QuickBooks previously, be aware that the Make General Journal Entries command is no longer available on the Banking menu.*

However, the way QuickBooks tracks adjusting entries, compared to journal entries that aren't designated "adjusting", is inconsistent. After you create an adjusting entry, when you view the registers of the affected accounts, the transaction type is GENJRNL. That's the same transaction type that QuickBooks records for a journal entry that's not configured as an adjusting entry.

You can view a report of adjusting entries by choosing Reports → Accountant & Taxes → Adjusting Journal Entries (a report that's only available in Premier Accountant Edition).

If you upgraded to QuickBooks Premier Accountant Edition, all the existing journal entries in your company file are marked as adjusting entries. In addition, if you perform a file cleanup (File → Clean Up Company Data) QuickBooks condenses closed transactions by creating JEs. All of those JEs are marked as adjusting entries. (File Cleanup, called Archive and Condense in previous versions of QuickBooks, is discussed in QuickBooks 2006: The Official Guide.)

I must say, discussing adjusting entries always makes me want to ask, "What's the difference between an adjusting entry and any other type of journal entry; aren't all JEs adjustments?" So, I literally asked the question of my own accounting firm, and the answer I received indicates that the difference is subtle, but apparently understood by all accountants. One of the accountants replied, "It's really a distinction without a difference; an adjusting journal entry is posted to correct or update an account in the general ledger." Another accountant told me, "Often when referring to an adjusting entry, the term is used in the sense of preparing a financial statement and not as a permanent entry". (Thanks, Craig and Steve.)

History and Reports in the JGE Window

In the Premier Accountant edition, the Make General Journal Entries transaction window displays existing (prior) GJE transactions. Each time you open a GJE window, you can quickly check the existing journal entries. This means you won't re-enter a journal entry you already made, which is an occasional problem during end-of-period activities.

By default, the list includes all the journal entries created in the last month, but you can change the time period. Click the arrow to the right of the List Of Selected General Journal Entries text box to select a different time interval for displaying journal entries (see Figure 11-3). All journal entries that match the date range are displayed.

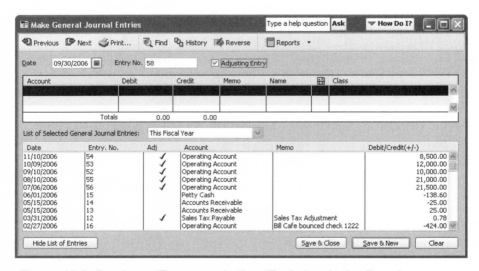

Figure 11-3: Previous JEs appear in the JE window in the Premier Accountant Edition.

When the previous entries are displayed, the number of lines that appear in the GJE window is reduced. If you have a long journal entry to record, click the Hide List Of Entries button to reveal a full GJE transaction window. The button label changes to Show List Of Entries, so you can bring back the list with a click of the mouse.

When you close the GJE window, QuickBooks remembers its state (whether the list of previous journal entries is displayed, and if so, which time interval is selected), and the next time you open the window you see that same state.

Viewing and Editing Existing Journal Entries

The journal entries in the history list display the account you used in the first line of the JE, along with the amount posted to that account. To see the other account(s) in a JE, click the appropriate item in the history list. The contents of that JE are loaded into the GJE transaction window, and the transaction becomes the current transaction. You can edit the JE, making changes to any part of the transaction, and selecting/deselecting the Adjusting Entry designation.

Quick Reports from the GJE Window

The GJE window also has a Reports button at the top of the transaction window. Click the arrow to the right of the button and select one of the following reports from the drop-down menu:

- Adjusting Journal Entries
- Entries Entered Today
- Last Month
- Last Fiscal Quarter
- This Fiscal Year to Date
- All Entries

When you open one of these reports, the report is collapsed, which means a total is displayed for each account used in each JE. Click the button labeled Expand to display each posting of any account that has multiple postings in the JE. (The button changes its name to Collapse).

Supporting QuickBooks Clients

The Premier Accountant Edition is built from the ground up to help you support QuickBooks clients. You can create report templates that provide the information you need, and send them to clients (see Chapter 7). You can access your clients' QuickBooks files over the Internet and perform tasks, or run a training session (see Chapter 10).

In addition, the Premier Accountant Edition has preconfigured data files for specific industries. These are the same preconfigured company files that are available in the other industry-specific versions of Premier editions. If you have clients using industry-specific Premier editions, you can duplicate their environments in your own copy of Premier Accountant Edition. More important, you can use the industry-specific company files to prepare company files for all your QuickBooks clients.

Predefined Company Files

Many of the industry-specific Premier editions offer predefined company files for businesses in that industry. When a Premier edition user starts the process to create a company file, he or she can select one of the predefined files. Most of the predefined company files for the entire range of Premier editions are also available in the Premier Accountant edition.

You can use the predefined files for your QuickBooks clients when they need to create or tweak their company data files. The client does not have to be running the Premier edition for that industry. In fact, the client does not have to be running any Premier edition. If you have a client in the construction industry running QuickBooks Pro, use the contractor's predefined company file, and give it to your client. As long as the QuickBooks edition is the same version (the same year), the client can use the file.

However, the predefined files aren't identified as such; you have to know what they are. Table 11-1 lists the predefined company files that are buried innocuously in the Type of Business list you see when you create a new company file.

If you have clients who are using an earlier version of QuickBooks, you can export the data from a predefined file and have the client import the data. This requires a minor adjustment in the export file, which is covered later in this chapter, in the section "Creating Export Files".

These features provide a value added service for your clients that is very easy to administer. The workload at your office isn't onerous, and you save the client the long, often confusing, process of creating or tweaking a company file. That's worth something!

Industry	Subcategory
Construction	All subcategories
Retail	All subcategories
Consulting, Professional and Technical Services	Advertising Architecture Building Inspection Consulting-Professional Consulting-Personal Drafting Engineering Graphic Design Industrial Design Interior Design Legal Services Other Consulting, Professional and Technical Services Other Design Services Surveying & Mapping

Table 11-1: Industry choices that are really predefined company files.

Components of Predefined Files

The predefined industry-specific company data files contain the following components:

- A start-up chart of accounts configured for the industry.
- An items list reflecting common products and services for the industry.
- Preferences configured for the industry.
- Classes configured for the industry.
- Customer and Vendor Type lists configured for the industry.
- Sales transaction templates configured for the industry.

The chart of accounts for most of the predefined company files contains income and expense accounts that are suitable for the specific industry. However, you'll have to add some asset and liability accounts. The following balance sheet accounts may be missing:

- Bank accounts
- Fixed assets
- Current liabilities (although a Payroll Liabilities account always exists)

Most of the industry-specific predefined files have the account number preference disabled. Open the Preferences dialog, go to the Accounting category, and enable account numbers. Take this step before you add any accounts, because QuickBooks only automatically adds numbers to predefined accounts, and won't add a number to an account that was created manually. After you enable account numbers, the account number field is available in the New Account dialog.

In addition, when you create the industry-specific company file, the equity accounts reflect the type of tax return you specify during setup (only if you create the company file without the EasyStep Interview).

For example, choosing a partnership creates equity accounts and subaccounts for two partners in addition to Retained Earnings, but choosing a corporate return results in only a Retained Earnings account.

I specify a corporate return for my generic company file, and add all the other equity accounts to the chart of accounts. When I prepare a company file for a client, I remove the unneeded equity accounts. Removing accounts is faster and easier than adding accounts.

Using the Predefined Company Files

There are two ways to make use of the predefined industry-specific company files, and each method has a specific advantage for the various scenarios you may encounter with your clients.

- Create the file, give it a generic company name (e.g. Contractor), tweak it, and give it to your client. This works best for clients who are just starting with QuickBooks.
- Create the file, give it a generic company name, tweak it, and export the components. Give the export file to your client with instructions on importing the file. This is useful for clients who have set up their basic QuickBooks company file and need to refine the chart of accounts, and add components such as items, customer types, and so on.

NOTE: *Guidelines for tweaking predefined files are presented later in this section.*

I've found that I can improve the efficiency of these processes by preparing folders on my hard drive that help me store files appropriately. I created the following folders:

- GenericQBFiles. This folder holds the industry-specific company files I created and tweaked.
- ClientQBFiles. This folder holds the client-specific files I prepare.
- Client Export Files. This folder holds the export files I prepare for clients.

Here are the steps to take when you want to turn a generic file into a client file:

1. In Windows Explorer or My Computer, open the folder that holds the generic company files (GenericQBFiles in the above example).
2. Copy the appropriate generic file to the folder you use to store company files for specific clients (ClientQBFiles in the above example).
3. Rename the copied file (the file in the ClientQBFiles folder) to match the client name.
4. Open QuickBooks and load the client-named file. When the company file opens, the title bar still uses the generic company name you applied when you created the file.
5. Choose Company → Company Information and change the company name from the generic name to the client's company name.
6. Enter the income tax form used by this client.
7. Enter the EIN or SSN for the client.
8. Click OK.

The QuickBooks title bar now displays a company name that matches the client's name, and is related to the name you gave the file. (The filename doesn't have to be an exact match for the company name.)

If the income tax form the client uses is different from the income tax form you used when you created the generic file, QuickBooks issues a message that warns you that tax related information will be removed from the accounts. That's fine, you don't mind if the tax information disappears. The tax information is established for each account so that users can do their own taxes. Because this company is a client, you'll be doing the taxes.

Creating Generic Client Files

To create an industry-specific generic file, choose File → New Company. In the EasyStep Interview window, click Skip Interview. Fill out the company information using a generic company name that reflects the industry type you're creating. Click Next and select the industry type for this client. If the type of business matches one of the predefined files listed in Table 11-1 earlier in this chapter, select it.

Tweak the file as described earlier in this section, paying attention to the following:

- Enable account numbers.
- Set other preferences to suit the majority of your clients in this industry. For example, enable sales tax if the industry for which you're creating the file usually collects sales tax.
- If most of your clients use outside payroll services, disable the payroll preference.
- Add missing accounts to the chart of accounts.
- Go through the all the lists to add, remove, and change entries to match the needs of the majority of your clients in this industry.

TIP: If you've created report templates, import them into this company file (see Chapter 7).

The file is now ready to be sent to your clients who are just starting to use QuickBooks. The client must have installed an edition (any edition) of QuickBooks 2006.

To use the file, the client must choose File → Open Company, and select the file you sent. It's easier to do this if you instruct the client to place the file in the folder that holds the QuickBooks software.

If you're e-mailing the file to the client, and either you or the client lacks a fast Internet connection, you can reduce the size of the attachment by sending a portable file (see "Using Portable Files", later in this chapter).

Creating IIF Import Files

If your client is already using QuickBooks, and you want to tweak the company file, you can create an import file. To accomplish this, you must first export all or some of the contents of the generic file you prepared. Choose File → Utilities → Export → Lists To IIF Files. In the Export dialog (see Figure 11-4), select the components you want to include in the client's import file.

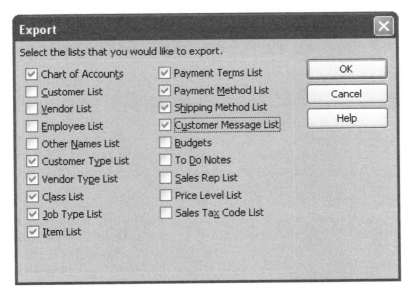

Figure 11-4: Export the components you want your clients to import.

Click OK and save the file with a name that reminds you of its contents. For example, if you exported all the lists from your generic file for contractors, name the file ContractorAll.iif. If you exported only the Items list, name the file ContractorItems.iif.

TIP: Create a folder to hold import files.

You can also use the exported file as a template, creating customized import files for specific clients. Open the file in Excel and add, remove, or change any items. Then save the file with a new name (the client's name) and send the file to the client with instructions for importing it.

Creating IIF Files for QuickBooks 2006

If the clients to whom you send import files have installed QuickBooks 2006 (any edition), you don't have to do anything more to the export file. It's automatically an import file that will work.

Send the file to the client, and instruct the client to import the file by choosing File → Import → IIF Files

Creating IIF Files for Earlier Versions of QuickBooks

If you want to send the import file to clients who are using an earlier version of QuickBooks, you must make some changes to the export file in order to create an import file that will work. Open the file in Excel (or another spreadsheet application).

The first two rows of the exported file contain version-specific information for QuickBooks 2006. Delete those rows by selecting the row numbers and choosing Edit → Delete.

Choose File → Save As, and save the file with a filename that indicates you've adapted the file for earlier versions of QuickBooks. For example, you can name the file ContractorListsAll-Pre2006.iif. Be sure the Save As Type field in the Save As dialog specifies Text (Tab delimited).

When you click Save, Excel issues a message to remind you that text files lack Excel features. Click Yes to continue to save the file as a text file. When you close Excel, you're given another opportunity to save the file as an Excel file, but don't accept the invitation.

TIP: An IIF import file designed for pre-2006 versions works in QuickBooks 2006 too. You can make these changes in your main import file, and send the file to all clients, regardless of the version of QuickBooks they've installed.

IIF Files for Specific Business Types

Some of the preconfigured files need more work than others. For example, the contractor predefined company has a long list of items. Many of the items may not be useful to certain types of contractors, and the Item List may lack items needed for some types of contractors.

To create useful company files for plumbers, electricians, carpenters, and so on, it's better (and less confusing to the client) to have only the items related to the specific client type. You could create multiple generic company files, each containing the right settings, but that's too much trouble. Instead, create import files. For example, to create customized Items Lists for specific types of contractors, follow these steps:

1. Export the Items List from the Contractor predefined company file.
2. Open the file in Excel, and remove, change, and add items for a specific type of contractor (for instance, a plumber).
3. Save the file with an appropriate filename (e.g., PlumberItems).
4. Close the file, and open the original export file.
5. Repeat steps 2 and 3, modifying the list for a different type of contractor.

You can use this approach for any type of specialized import file, including the chart of accounts as well as lists. After a while, you'll have an enviable collection of import files that will help your clients use QuickBooks more efficiently without the need to create components manually. Don't forget to delete the two rows of version information, or you won't be able to give the file to pre-2006 users.

TIP: You can use import files to perform mass updates of existing data in QuickBooks lists. See Appendix C for more information.

Using a Portable Company File

A portable company file is a copy of a QuickBooks company file that has been condensed to save disk space. Portable files not only take up less room on a disk, they also save upload and download time if you send the file as an attachment to an e-mail message.

Clients can send a portable company file to their accountants. You can also use a portable company file to move data between computers (such as your home computer, and your office), so you can work at home, and then bring the updated file back to the office.

A portable company file is not a backup; it's a smaller version of your company file. The smaller size is the result of the condensing process, and in fact, most portable company files are small than backups of QuickBooks files that have been in use for enough time to accumulate many transactions. A portable company filename has the extension .QBM.

Portable Company File Vs. Accountant's Copy

A portable company file is not the same thing as the accountant's copy. An accountant's copy has two properties that the portable company file lacks:

- The changes made in an accountant's copy can be merged back into the company file from which it came.
- The accountant's copy has limited functions available.

> **NOTE**: *Chapter 15 of QuickBooks 2006: The Official Guide explains the function limits of the accountant's copy. A copy of the book is in your Premier Edition software box.*

Because the changes an accountant makes to the file (if it's an accountant's copy) can be merged into the client's company file, the client can continue to work in the company file while the accountant is working in the accountant's copy.

A portable company file is a copy of a company file. When anyone works in a portable company file, any work done in the original company file will be lost when the portable company file is re-installed. The original company file is overwritten (totally replaced) by the portable company file being installed.

Creating a Portable Company File

To create a portable company file, choose File → Portable Company File → Create File. QuickBooks displays a message telling you it must close and reopen the company file to perform this task. Click OK.

In the Create Portable Company File dialog (see Figure 11-5), select a name for the file. By default, QuickBooks uses the company filename (changing the extension to .QBM), and there's usually no reason to change it.

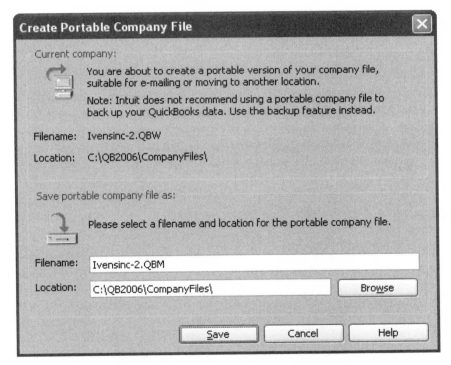

Figure 11-5: Save the file in a convenient folder, so you can find it when you want to transfer it to a disk or attach it to an e-mail message.

Select a location for the file (by default, QuickBooks chooses the folder or subfolder in which you store the company file). If you're taking the file home (or back to the office), select a Zip Disk or USB stick drive. If you don't have a zip drive in the other location, use a USB stick drive, which you can easily install on any computer.

If you're going to copy the file to a CD or e-mail it to your accountant (or back to the client if you're the accountant), choose an easy-to-find location (such as the root of your hard drive).

TIP: *If you're moving the file between your home and office, and you don't have a Zip drive or a USB stick drive (or you need those drives for a nightly backup), you can e-mail the file to yourself.*

When you've set the location, click Save. It takes a while to create the file, and when it's done, QuickBooks issues a success message. Your company file is reopened, and you can go back to work.

But, wait! If you do any work in the file, when you re-install the portable file (which will have been modified by the work performed in that file), you'll lose the work you do in the file now. Close the company file and don't open it again until you're ready to reinstall the portable company file.

Installing a Portable Company File

Before performing this step, back up your company file. In fact, my advice is to copy your company file. Open My Computer or Windows Explorer and copy your company file (the one with the .QBW extension) to another location on your hard drive. Bet you can guess why I'm providing these dire warnings.

To install a portable company file you've received or brought back to your computer, choose File → Portable Company File → Open File to open the Import From Portable Company File dialog.

In the top section of the dialog, click the Browse button to find and select the filename and location of the portable company file you want to install (it has a .QBM extension).

In the bottom section of the dialog, enter the filename and location of the regular QuickBooks company file you want to create. The first time you do this, the company file doesn't exist. After that, you'll be replacing the existing company file with this portable company file.

If the company file already exists on your computer, QuickBooks issues a warning that you are about to overwrite an existing file. Click Yes to confirm the replacement (because the new company file is up-to-date and the existing file isn't). Then, QuickBooks issues another warning, telling you that you're going to delete the existing file. Type yes, and click OK, to confirm that you want to replace the existing file with the contents of the portable company file.

After the portable company file is uncompressed and loaded in the software window, QuickBooks issues a dialog suggesting that you back up this file immediately. When you click OK, QuickBooks opens the Backup dialog.

Industry Specific Reports

Each industry-specific version of QuickBooks Premier has a group of reports that are useful for the industry type in which the reports are installed. The reports are built in to the industry-specific editions of QuickBooks Premier software, avoiding the need to customize standard reports to get industry-specific information.

QuickBooks Premier Accountant Edition contains some of the industry-specific reports that are included in industry specific Premier editions. Choose Reports → Industry Specific to see the list.

For a more comprehensive list, use the Toggle feature to switch to each of the Premier industry specific editions, and examine the reports installed in the edition.

Being able to access reports that are available in the other Premier editions is valuable for supporting your QuickBooks Premier edition clients. You can open a report and discuss its settings with your clients, or customize one or more of these reports for a client with particular needs. After you customize the report, send the report template to the client (see Chapter 7 to learn about exporting report templates).

However, the real value in these reports is your ability to use them to provide report templates that are specifically designed for clients who are not using Premier editions. It's a worthwhile added value service to provide customized reports that are industry specific for client businesses running QuickBooks Pro. You can even export a template group that contains the entire range of the industry-specific reports for any industry type. Chapter 7 explains how to create report templates and report template groups.

Working Trial Balance

The Working Trial Balance is a spreadsheet-like display of general ledger activity over a specified period (see Figure 11-6). You can use it with a client's company file, or with the Accountant's Review copy of a client's file. To access this tool, choose Accountant → Working Trial Balance.

For each account, the report displays the opening balance, the closing balance, and the transactions and adjustments that created the closing balance. In addition, this tool has the following powerful options:

- You can hide the display of accounts that have no activity.
- Double-clicking an account listing opens the account's record so you can edit it.
- You can create a journal entry for any account by selecting the account and clicking the Make Adjustments button.
- You can use the Workpaper Reference column for notes if you make any changes.

Fixed Asset Manager

All versions of QuickBooks have a Fixed Asset Item list, which you can use to store information about fixed assets. This list is meant to track data about the assets you depreciate. Except when it's opened in QuickBooks Premier Accountant Edition, this is merely a list, and it doesn't provide any method for calculating depreciation, nor does it link to any depreciation software. It's designed only to keep a list of assets.

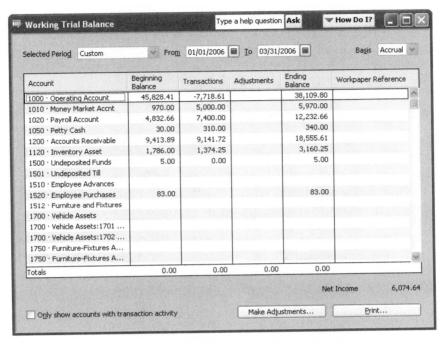

Figure 11-6: Use the Working Trial Balance to view and manipulate account activity.

QuickBooks Premier Accountant Edition has a nifty tool, Fixed Asset Manager that can synchronize data with the Fixed Asset Item list.

Fixed Asset Manager also works independently of the Fixed Asset Item list, so if your client hasn't used the list, you can still manage fixed asset depreciation.

Fixed Asset Manager calculates depreciation for fixed assets, and lets you create journal entries using the calculated amounts. It works with the currently open QuickBooks company data file, which is usually a client's company file.

TIP: *Fixed Asset Manager integrates with Intuit's ProSeries Tax products, so you can automatically pass asset data from QuickBooks to ProSeries Tax.*

In the following sections, I'll provide an overview of the Premier Accountant Edition Fixed Asset Manager. The program is complex and powerful, and it's beyond the scope of this book to go over all its functions. You can use the Help files to learn the step-by-step procedures for all the functions in Fixed Asset Manager.

Creating a Fixed Asset Manager Client File

Fixed Asset Manager must know the type of tax form a business files. Before you open Fixed Asset Manager, make sure the right tax form is configured for the company file that's open. In fact, make sure the tax form information isn't blank, which is often the case. To see the tax form information, choose Company → Company Information.

With the QuickBooks company file (the client file) you want to work with open, choose Accountant → Manage Fixed Assets. When the Fixed Asset Manager software opens for the first time, it attempts to open a Fixed Asset Manager client data file for the company. If no client data file exists you must create one.

> **NOTE**: You can also use Fixed Asset Manager with an Accountant's Review Copy provided by your QuickBooks client, but you lose some of the functionality of Fixed Asset Manager. Details are available in the Help files.

In the opening software window, select the option Create A New Fixed Asset Manager Client, and click OK. The Fixed Asset Manager New Client wizard launches. As with all wizards, you must click Next to go through all the windows.

Configuring Company Information

The wizard takes information from the QuickBooks file that's open, displays the company information, and then queries the accountant about the following data:

- Current fiscal year
- Prior short years
- Qualification for the "small corporation" exemption from AMT

- Depreciation bases
- Default depreciation method for each selected basis

The wizard also asks how you want to synchronize fixed asset data between the company file and the Fixed Asset Manager client file it's creating. The first question asks how you want to bring data from QuickBooks into Fixed Asset Manager. The following window asks how you want to move data from Fixed Asset Manager into QuickBooks. What all of this is doing is setting up synchronization options between the company file and Fixed Asset Manager.

The last wizard window is a summary of the QuickBooks company information. If any information is incorrect, use the Back button to return to the appropriate wizard window and make changes. When all the information is correct, click Finish.

Importing the Fixed Assets

Fixed Asset Manager finds the Fixed Asset Item List, and displays a log report. Fixed Asset Manager identifies the assets using the text in the Purchase Description field of the QuickBooks Fixed Asset Item list—not the name assigned to the asset.

NOTE: *If an asset isn't transferred to Fixed Asset Manager, the log report indicates that fact. Usually, the reason is a date of purchase that is later than the end date of the fiscal year you indicated in the wizard. For example, if you're setting up Fixed Asset Manager in 2006 for 2005 depreciation, assets purchased in 2006 are not transferred.*

Click OK to close the log report and view the Fixed Asset Manager software window, seen in Figure 11-7. A robust set of functions is available on the menu system, and in the various tabs.

Entering Fixed Assets Manually

If the client's company file has no entries in the Fixed Asset Item List, but has maintained information about the purchase of fixed assets, you can enter the data manually. Click the Add icon on the toolbar, and enter the appropriate data by scrolling through both sections of the window.

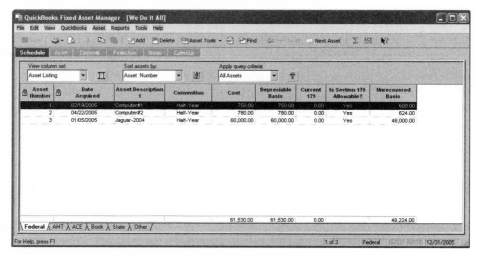

Figure 11-7: The QuickBooks Fixed Asset Manager client file is
loaded and you can begin your work.

Importing Data from Other Software

If asset and depreciation records are tracked in another software application, you can import the data to Fixed Asset Manager. In the Fixed Asset
Manager window, choose File → Import. The only import file format on
the submenu is Comma Separated Value (CSV) file.

If the other program can't export data to a CSV file, but can save
data in a file format that is readable by Microsoft Excel, open the file in
Excel, and then save the file in CSV format.

> **NOTE**: *You must map the fields in the import file to the fields
> in Fixed Asset Manager. Fixed Asset Manager provides help
> for this task during the import. (See Appendix A to learn about
> mapping fields.)*

If you've been managing fixed assets for the client in ProSeries tax
software, you can import data directly from that software to Fixed Asset
Manager. If ProSeries is available (installed), the File → Import submenu
includes the listing ProSeries Tax.

Viewing and Editing Assets

As I said earlier in this section, I'm not going over all the features and functions of Fixed Asset Manager (because it would fill a separate book), but I'll present a few guidelines that should help you get started.

Schedule Tab

In the Schedule tab, Fixed Asset Manager identifies the assets using the text in the Purchase Description field of the QuickBooks Fixed Asset Item list—not the text in the Name field. In fact, Fixed Asset Manager doesn't even import the name field from the QuickBooks Fixed Asset Item list.

Fixed Asset Manager assigns a number to each asset, and that number becomes the asset's name (you can think of it as a code) in the Fixed Asset Manager client file. If the assets were obtained automatically from a QuickBooks Fixed Asset Item list, the numbers represent the order of assets in that list.

The asset that's currently selected in the Schedule tab is the asset used when you visit any of the other tabs at the top of the software window.

Asset Tab

Use the Asset tab to enter information about tax forms, posting accounts, and other data about the selected asset.

The upper section of the tab is the place to enter general information for the selected asset, including any classification fields. The bottom section of the Asset tab is the Basis Detail section. Enter the cost, date acquired, tax system, depreciation basis, recovery period, and other information needed to calculate the asset's depreciation. You can also configure Section 179 deductions here, if appropriate for this asset.

Disposal Tab

Use the Disposal tab to dispose of assets. Fixed Asset Manager displays the cost basis, and any Section 179 deductions. Enter the sales price, the expense of sale, and any other relevant information about the disposal.

For ProSeries client file exports, select a property type from the drop-down list to determine where the disposal information will appear on Form 4797, Sales of Business Property.

Projection Tab

Use the Projection tab to determine the best depreciation method for the selected asset by reviewing its projected depreciation. Use the Bases tabs at the bottom of the window to see the projections.

TIP: You can change information in the Asset tab to alter the projections available in the Projection tab.

The other tabs on the Fixed Asset Manager window are informational. The Notes tab is a blank window where you can write notes and reminders. The Calendar tab displays information about an asset on the selected date (select date acquired, date of disposal, or both).

Configuring Depreciation

Use the Tools menu to set up depreciation, using the following tools:

- **Prepare For Next Year**. This process removes disposed assets from the asset list, adds the current year depreciation to each asset's record, updates unrecovered basis fields for each asset, and calculates depreciation for next year. Be sure to print reports on the current status of each asset before using this tool.
- **Recalculate All Assets**. This process recalculates the current depreciation for each asset. Prior depreciation is calculated and posted according to the rules you configure in the dialog.
- **179/40% Test**. This process applies the Section 179/40% test to the appropriate assets. You can select the convention you want to use for the test.

Using the Section 179/40% test

To determine whether the Section 179 deductions claimed for the current year are within allowed limits, or to calculate the percentage of assets acquired in the last three months of the year, use the Section 179/40% test.

Perform these diagnostics after you enter client asset information and before you print reports or link the file to the client's tax return. To perform these tests, choose Tools → 179/40% Test. Review the Section 179 test, then click the 40% test tab to review mid-quarter totals.

Reviewing Section 179 limitations

The Section 179 test determines the total cost of all eligible Section 179 property, the total Section 179 expense deduction made, and how much of the deduction exceeds federal limits for the active year

Reviewing the Mid-Quarter 40% test

Fixed Asset Manager totals the cost of all assets purchased in the active year and all assets purchased in the last quarter of the active year. If the percentage of assets purchased in the last quarter is greater than 40%, you can convert these assets to the mid-quarter convention.

Using the Client Totals Summary

Use the Client Totals Summary to review the accumulated cost and depreciation before and after current-year calculations for each basis supported in a client file. To see the Client Totals Summary, choose View → Client Totals.

Calculating Depreciation

When the selected asset is properly configured, go to the Asset tab and choose Asset → Calculate Asset. If the command is grayed out, Fixed Asset Manager does not have all the information it needs to perform the calculation. Check all the fields to make sure you've entered the required information about this asset.

TIP: You can configure Fixed Asset Manager to automatically calculate assets after making modifications. To select this setting, choose Tools → Program Options. Select the Automatically Calculate Assets option, and click OK to save the change.

Posting a Journal Entry to QuickBooks

Fixed Asset Manager automates the process of creating a journal entry for depreciation expense and/or accumulated depreciation. Choose QuickBooks → Post Journal Entry To QuickBooks, and then enter the appropriate information.

Creating Reports

Fixed Asset Manager provides a variety of report options, including pre-configured report templates. Choose Reports → Display Reports to view the available reports.

To organize a report list, choose Reports → Report List Organizer (see Figure 11-8). Select the reports you want to associate with your client (you're creating a custom report list). You can also opt to print reports in batches.

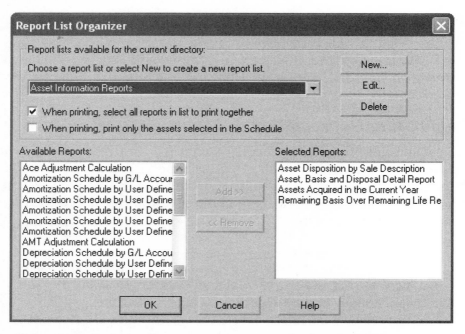

Figure 11-8: Organize the appropriate reports for the client file.

Select a report list from the drop-down list (or create a new report list by clicking New). Then select and deselect the reports you want to include.

Exporting Depreciation Data

Fixed Asset Manager has built in tools for exporting depreciation data, and then importing the data to another software application. The following file formats are supported:

- ProSeries
- Microsoft Word
- Microsoft Excel
- ASCII (text) file
- CSV file
- Tax Worksheets

Creating Tax Worksheets

Fixed Asset Manager automatically creates tax worksheets, using the information in the client file. Choose Reports → Display Tax Worksheet to open the Print Preview dialog. Select the worksheets you want, and click OK to preview them, and then print them. The following tax worksheets are available:

- Form 4562 Part I — Section 179 Summary Copy
- Form 4562 Part II & III— Lines 15, 16 and 17
- Form 4562 Part III — Lines 19 and 20
- Form 4562 Part IV — Summary
- Form 4562 Part V — Listed Property
- Form 4562 Part VI — Amortization
- Form 4797 Part I — Property Held More Than One Year
- Form 4797 Part II — Ordinary Gains and Losses
- Form 4797 Part III — Gains from Disposition of Depreciable Property
- Form 4626— Depreciation Adjustments and Tax Preferences
- Form 4626— ACE Worksheet
- Form 4626— Gain/Loss Adjustments

Understanding Fixed Asset Manager Synchronization

When you open and close Fixed Asset Manager, data is synchronized between the software and the QuickBooks company file (and a log is displayed). You can also manually update the asset information between QuickBooks and Fixed Asset Manager. The commands, and the default settings for automatic synchronization, are on the QuickBooks menu.

Before you synchronize, be sure to print reports about the asset list from both software applications, so you have a way to track changes. Remember, if you dispose of an asset in Fixed Asset Manager, the synchronization process removes the asset from the QuickBooks Fixed Asset Item list.

Financial Statement Designer

The Financial Statement Designer (FSD) gives you the power to customize financial statements that are directly linked to a client's QuickBooks data. This means you don't have to export financial data to other programs when you want to create a customized statement. This is a powerful and robust program, and in the following sections, I'll give you an overview of the program.

As a built-in program, FSD opens from within QuickBooks, and uses the data in the currently open QuickBooks company file (usually a client's file). To open the program, choose Accountant → Financial Statement Designer (the program is also listed on the Reports menu).

When the Financial Statement Designer opens, the program window offers two options:

- Create A New Financial Statement Designer Client, which creates a file for the current company.
- Reconnect To An Existing Financial Statement Designer Client, which opens a client file you previously created.

For this discussion, I'm assuming you selected a new client file, and I'll go over some of the tools and features you'll find as you create that file.

Financial Statement Designer Components

The FSD has three components:

- Financial Statement Organizer
- Financial Statement Editor
- Supporting Document Editor.

Financial Statement Organizer

The Financial Statement Organizer is the "front end" of the FSD. It's the component you see when you start using the FSD (see Figure 11-9). This is where you select the options for the financial statement(s) you're building.

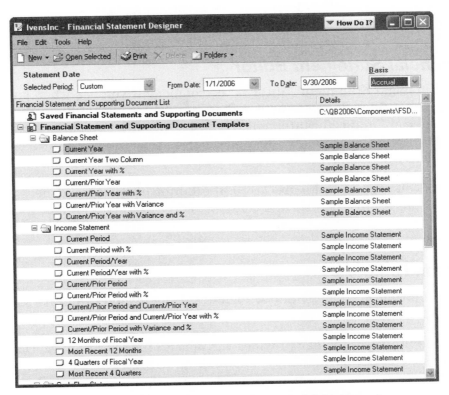

Figure 11-9: Make your selections in the Financial Statement Organizer.

All of the following tasks are performed in the Financial Statement Organizer:

- Creating a new set of financial statements and supporting documents.
- Setting the date range for the statement.
- Setting the statement basis.
- Selecting a template for the new financial statement.
- Printing financial statements and supporting documents.
- Saving statements and supporting documents as PDF files.
- Editing saved financial statements and supporting documents.
- Viewing the list of saved financial statements and supporting documents.
- Creating folders to organize your statements and documents.

Financial Statement Editor

The Financial Statement Editor is the component you use when you're designing a financial statement. When you double-click a financial statement in the Financial Statement Organizer window, QuickBooks fetches the data from the company file, and displays the statement in the Financial Statement Editor.

As you can see in Figure 11-10, the Editor uses a spreadsheet paradigm. You can insert rows and columns, add accounts and formulas, attach supporting schedules, and change the formatting of your financial statements.

Editor Toolbars

The Financial Statement Editor includes three toolbars that are similar to the toolbars you use in Excel.

The Standard toolbar provides the normal file operation functions, such as New, Open, Cut, Copy, Paste, Save, Print, Print Preview, Undo, and Redo. In addition to these familiar icons, the Standard toolbar offers a Refresh icon (to refresh the data in the statement), and a Statement Date icon (to set a different date range).

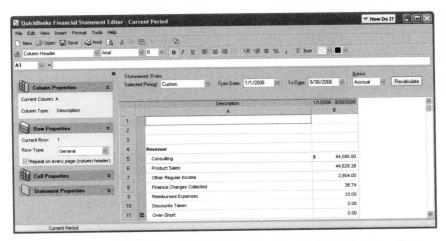

Figure 11-10: I selected an Income Statement, and now I can edit it
in the Financial Statement Editor.

The Format toolbar contains icons to apply fonts, font color, indentations, alignments, cell underlines, formats (for decimals, percentage, and currency), and AutoSum functions.

The Formula bar identifies the current location of the cursor, and provides a text box for entering formulas.

Design Grid

The Design Grid is the area that displays the account descriptions, balances, report headers and footers, column headers, and the results of the formulas you've entered.

You can customize statements by inserting columns or rows to show prior year balances, percentages, and variances between other columns and sub-totals. You can also insert rows for sub-totals to group accounts, or add blank rows for spacing between account types.

To enhance the appearance of the document, or add information, click the Insert menu and select one of the following commands:

- Page Break inserts a page break at the location of the cursor.
- Page Number prints the page number.

- Current Date and Time prints the date and time of printing (actually two separate fields; you must insert both fields to print both on the report).
- Statement Date prints the statement ending date.
- Statement Basis prints the statement basis (cash or accrual).
- Client Information prints a selected field from the Client Information window (such as company name, e-mail address, URL for the company's web site, etc.).
- Accountant Information prints a selected field from the Accountant Information window (such as firm name, e-mail address, URL for the accounting firm's web site, etc.).

Properties Panel

The Properties panel is on the left side of the Editor window. This panel consists of four sections: Column Properties, Row Properties, Cell Properties, and Statement Properties. You can use the Properties panel to view or change the properties for a particular area of the financial statement.

Use the Column Properties to set the date range for account balances in a specific column. For example, you can configure one column for prior period balances, and another column for current period balances.

Row Properties affect a variety of settings, depending on the element you select in the Design Grid. You can use the Row Properties to do the following:

- Repeat column headers on every page
- Change the account description that appears on the financial statement
- Add or remove accounts for a combined account row
- Reverse the sign of an account balance
- Print an account row even if the account balance is zero.

The Cell Properties let you to set a date range that overrides the column's date range for account balances. The change affects only the selected cell.

The Statement Properties allow you to set the column spacing.

Attaching Supporting Schedules

Supporting schedules are used to report the details for major account categories (such as inventory, or operating expenses) in a condensed financial statement. To attach a supporting schedule, choose Tools → Attach Supporting Schedules.

When you attach a supporting schedule to a financial statement, both the financial statement and the select supporting schedule(s) are printed. You can choose the order of printing on the General tab of the Print window.

Previewing and Printing Financial Statements and Documents

You can preview and print a complete set of financials statements and supporting documents. You can export and e-mail the documents, and even save them as PDF files. Previewing financial statements and documents lets you see how they will look when they're printed, giving you a chance to make sure they're formatted correctly.

- To preview the financial statement, choose File → Print Preview.
- To print the financial statement, choose File → Print.

The Options tab on the Print dialog includes selections that apply to financial statements (see in Figure 11-11).

You can configure the way account balances appear on the financial statements, as follows:

- Divided by 1000.
- Use whole numbers (numbers are rounded to the nearest dollar). Select the account to which rounding errors are posted from the drop-down list on the Options tab of the Print dialog.

You can suppress the printing of accounts with a zero balance, and you can replace the zeros with another character (enter the character in the box).

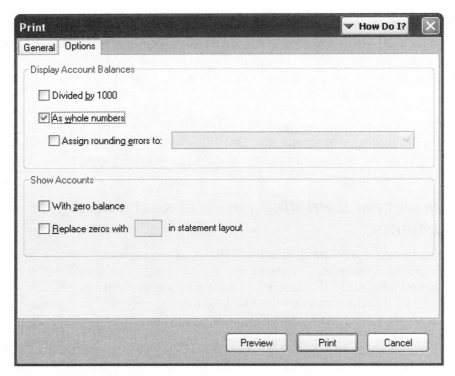

Figure 11-11: Set print options for the financial statements.

TIP: *The settings on the Options tab of the Print window can also be set in the Options window of the Financial Statement Editor (choose Tools → Options).*

Exporting FSD Files

You can export your financial statements to an FST file format, which is the format used by the Financial Statement Editor. You can then import the FST files into another client's company so statements provided by your firm use the same organization and appearance.

You can export the financial statements to the following file formats:

• ASCII and tab-delimited text files (.txt)

- Comma-delimited files (.csv)
- Excel files (.xls).

You can export your supporting documents to the following file formats:

- RTF (.rtf)
- ASCII and tab-delimited text (.txt)
- Comma-delimited files (.csv)

Saving FSD Files as PDF Files

You can save your financial statements and supporting documents to PDF files. These files preserve the text formatting of your financial statements and can be viewed using Adobe Acrobat Reader (which can be downloaded from the Adobe Web site at http://www.adobe.com).

Of course, like all PDF files, they print beautifully, maintaining the formatting, design, and layout you want. In addition, you can e-mail the files to any user, regardless of the operating system that user runs.

Chapter 12

Contractor Edition

Contractor company files

Tweaking your company file

Managing materials

Handling customer deposits

Job costing

Estimates

Handling change orders

Managing retainage

Payroll issues

Customized reports

Q uickBooks Premier Contractor Edition includes features and functions designed for businesses in the construction and contracting
industries. My experience with contractor clients includes gener-
als, subs, and independent trade businesses (plumbers, electricians, and
so on). QuickBooks Contractor edition has features for all of those construction types. In this chapter, I'll cover the issues that arise most frequently.

Predefined Contractor Company File

If you're just starting with QuickBooks, you have to create a company
file. QuickBooks Premier Contractor Edition has a predefined company
file for contractors that works extremely well.

The predefined company file for contractors isn't marked as such
when you create a new company file. It's merely listed as an industry
type, with no indication that it contains a suitable chart of accounts, and
some prepopulated entries in lists.

To create a company file using a predefined file, choose Create A New
Company File from the Welcome window you see when you first launch
QuickBooks. Alternatively, you can choose File → New Company.

As explained in Chapter 1, you can create your file with the
EasyStep Interview, or click Skip Interview on the opening window of the
EasyStep Interview, and create the file manually.

If you use the EasyStep Interview, in the Select Your Industry window, choose either of the subcategories under Construction:

- Construction Trades
- Land Subdivision and Development

If you create your file manually, choose Construction/Contracting.

Because you chose a preconfigured file, many of your preferences are
already set up appropriately, and quite a few of the lists are populated
with entries. Open the lists so you can delete the entries that aren't specific to your business, and rename the entries you need if the names
aren't appropriate.

Tweaking an Existing Company File

If you're upgrading a previous version of QuickBooks to the Premier Contractor edition, you already have a company file, lists, and configuration settings. However, you should consider creating a new file using the predefined file, just to gain ideas for tweaking your chart of accounts, your settings, and your lists. Go through the EasyStep Interview to create the file, which you can name ContractorTest or something similar.

TIP: Creating a second company file is a great way to experiment with complicated transactions—it becomes a "test file". If you're not sure how you want to handle a transaction in your real company file, open the test file and create transactions, then look at the reports.

QuickBooks also provides a sample file for contractors. The sample file is not the same as the predefined company file. The predefined file is meant to be used as a real company file, while the sample file is designed to let you experiment with QuickBooks processes. You can open the sample file by following these steps:

1. Choose File → Open Company.
2. In the Open A Company dialog, choose the file named **sample_contractor-based business.qbw**, and click Open.
3. Click OK in the message dialog that warns you this is a sample file.

When the sample file opens, look at the chart of accounts, the Items list, and other components of the file, so you can compare them to your own company file. You can print any list, including the chart of accounts, by pressing Ctrl-P while the list window is open.

You can also export the lists you think would be useful from the contractor test company you created, or the sample contractor company. After you export the lists, import them into your existing company file (your real file).

Billing Rate Level List

The QuickBooks Premier Contractor Edition offers a feature called Billing Rate Levels, which lets you link a billing rate to a specific person who is performing a specific service.

This means you can automate some of your invoicing, so you don't have to keep paper notes on the rates you charge for different types of work performed by specific people.

For example, you can have a journeyman's rate for a specific type of work, and a lower apprentice's rate for the same type of work. You can apply these rates to employees and subcontractors.

If a worker who is a journeyman (and is billed as a journeyman when he performs that job) sometimes acts as a supervisor, or performs some other task that involves more responsibility, you can assign a higher billing rate to that different job, for that same person. Chapter 4 explains how to set up and use billing rate levels.

Classes for Contractors

The predefined company file for contractors contains classes that are deemed desirable for contractors. As you can see in Figure 12-1, these classes track job related revenue and costs.

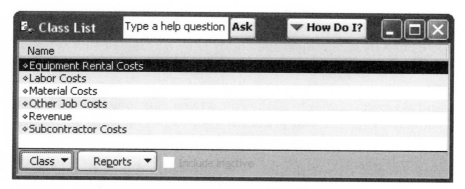

Figure 12-1: The predefined classes may not suit your needs.

I've never had a construction client where these classes were useful. These predefined classes are for tracking costs, and there are two things wrong with that approach:

- The best use of classes is to provide separate Profit & Loss Statements for each class. I've never met a business owner or an accountant who wanted to see a Profit & Loss Statement based on costs.
- You already track costs by posting transactions to expense accounts in the chart of accounts. If your chart of accounts is well designed, you can learn everything you need from standard QuickBooks reports.

In the following paragraphs, I discuss some of the scenarios I've encountered with contractor clients, and the way we set up classes to meet their reporting needs.

Creating Virtual Branch Offices with Classes

If you perform work in more than one city, town, county, or state, you probably have expenses (usually tax expenses) for each location. For example, you may have to pay taxes based on gross receipts or net profits earned in that locality, as well as payroll taxes for employees (including yourself) who perform work in that locality.

If the local income taxes are based on gross receipts or net profits, you need to track local costs, such as permits, licenses, and other specific costs of doing business in those localities.

Some accountants take the total gross or profit for the company, and then report these local earnings by applying a percentage. For example, if you have a net income of $100,000, and you tell your accountant you do 15% of your work in East Overcoat Township, your accountant files a tax return with the East Overcoat tax authority that assumes a tax liability based on $15,000.

I've had calls for help from contractors who couldn't defend the numbers that approach produced when they were called in for an audit by a local taxing authority. Besides, suppose the work you do in East Overcoat isn't as profitable as the work you do in Hollow Spoon Township, but the East Overcoat tax rate is much higher?

If you treat each local authority as a branch office (by using a class), you can produce Profit & Loss reports for each class. Furthermore, you can assign a percentage of your overhead expenses to each class, using a formula that's based on the real numbers produced by your P & L By Class reports.

Here are some guidelines for using classes for this purpose:

- Create a class for every taxing authority, and create a class named Administration (for general overhead expenses that aren't specific to any job).
- Post every income transaction to the appropriate class.
- Post every expense that is specific to the local authority to the appropriate class (such as permits, licenses, and taxes).
- Assign classes to expenses that are job related. For example, if you write a check to a supplier for something you purchased for a job, link the expense to the appropriate class for that job.
- Split expense postings when you write a check that covers costs for multiple jobs. Each line of the vendor bill or check should be assigned to a class, and the line items must total the payment to the vendor.
- Create payroll items to match your classes, and track the hours your employees spend in each locality. If you use a payroll service, ask them to help you set up a way to track employee time by locality. Remember to post your employer payroll costs to classes, too.

Tracking the Source of Work with Classes

If you want to know the profit margins of work that you obtain in different ways, you can use classes to track the source. Then, your P & L By Class reports provide a way for you to analyze where the best profits are.

For example, perhaps you get customers who call you directly (usually referred by one of your happy customers), and customers who are referred by hardware stores or do-it-yourself chain stores with whom you've registered your services (or you put a sign on a corkboard). And then, of course, there's advertising such as the local yellow pages, or ads in the community newspaper.

If you track profits by source for a while, you may discover a pattern, and you can adjust the way you look for work to match the pattern. If you learn that referrals from the local hardware stores turn out to provide more profit than referrals from any other place, visit more hardware stores to arrange for referrals.

Using classes for this purpose only lets you track profits (and assign overhead intelligently) by broad general categories. If you want to track the profit by each referring entity (specific hardware stores, or specific advertising contracts), you need to track customers and jobs by type (covered later in this chapter).

Tracking the Type of Work with Classes

Depending on your specific type of business, you might want to track the profitability of different types of jobs. For example, you may have some jobs that are new construction, and some that are restoration or rehab. To track profits and losses for each type of work, create the appropriate classes.

The class-based reports you create can provide more than just the P & L figures you need for tax forms. These reports give you insight on the financial advantage (or disadvantage) of each division of your business. If you learn that your bottom line for rehab work is much better than your bottom line for new construction, perhaps it's time to turn your company into a rehab specialty business.

Tracking General Vs. Sub Profits with Classes

If you act as a general contractor for some jobs, and as a subcontractor for other jobs, you can track the profitability over the year(s). To report net profits from your general contractor work separately from your subcontractor work, create classes for each type of work.

Customer Types for Contractors

You should create entries representing the customer types you want to track, and then apply the appropriate type to each customer. The predefined customer types in the QuickBooks contractor company file are:

- From Advertisement
- Referral

These customer types provide an excellent method of tracking the way you obtain jobs. You can easily use the information you gain to increase business. Of course, these customer type entries don't work unless you specifically ask each customer how they learned about your business.

Whether tracking referrals shows you get more business that way, or less business that way, test the referrals paradigm. Do something to increase referrals (besides the obvious ploy of doing a good job and making your customers happy), and then track the results.

For instance, when you send your final invoice, enclose a flyer that offers something for every referral that turns into a job. Buy merchandising gifts that fit your business, and send a gift to each customer that refers a new customer. Depending on the type of contractor business you have, a suitable gift may be a tape measure, a stud-finder, polish for plumbing fixtures, a flashlight, or any other inexpensive and useful gift. Print small labels with your name, logo, and telephone number, and affix one to the gift.

If referral business increases, continue to reward referring customers. If referral business doesn't grow, and advertisements continue to be more effective, increase your advertising budget. Test one new medium at a time, and track the results.

You can also use these predefined customer types as the basis of more complex, and more meaningful, customer types. For example, you could have the following customer types:

- Ad-yellow pages
- Ad-local paper

- Ad-cable TV
- Ad-broadcast TV
- Refer-Joe's hardware
- Refer-Bob's hardware
- Refer-customer

NOTE: *You can use up to 31 characters for a Customer Type entry.*

Sometimes, the source of business isn't import to you. Perhaps you don't feel you need to spend money on advertising, or you don't need to track the source of business because all your business comes from a store or a general contractor. In that case, use customer types that provide another quantifying description for customers, and track those descriptions in reports.

For example, you may find it useful to sort customers by the type of work. Depending on your type of contractor business, you could use New and Rehab as customer types. Alternatively, examine the list of suggestions for using classes earlier in this section, and use one that isn't suitable for your own class list, but may work nicely as your customer type list.

Job Types for Contractors

Use the Job Type list to sort jobs in some manner that's useful for analyzing the work you do, and the profits from each type of work. The QuickBooks predefined company file for contractors contains several job type entries, seen in Figure 12-2.

If you're an electrician, plumber, or stonemason, or some other type of contractor far removed from carpentry, the predefined job types don't work for you. Delete those job type entries and create your own descriptive types, based on the types of jobs you take on.

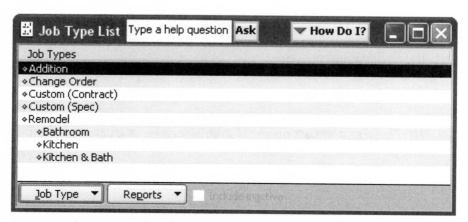

Figure 12-2: The pre-loaded job types are useful for some types of construction businesses.

Vendor Types for Contractors

You can track vendors by type, to analyze the categories in which you spend your money, and to contact vendors appropriately. The QuickBooks predefined company file contains some built-in vendor types, but I usually advise clients not to use them. Most of the categories they represent can be tracked automatically in QuickBooks. For example, expense accounts in the chart of accounts provide the same information.

I prefer to use vendor types to quantify vendors in a way that makes it easier to contact them for specific reasons. For example, vendors who are your subcontractors need to be contacted when you need bids for a potential job. In that case, I use vendor types that sort appropriately when my client needs to send an RFP. For example, the following examples illustrate the possible vendor types for a plumber:

- Sub-digging/back hoes
- Sub-gas line install
- Sub-high tech controls

My clients then create a vendor report filtered by type, displaying the vendor contact name, address, phone number, fax number, and e-mail address. This makes it easy to send out an RFP. Additionally, my clients use the QuickBooks Write Letters feature to create mail merge letters that are RFPs.

Items for Contractors

The entries you put into the Items list should be well thought out, because you use them constantly. You need an item for every category of sale you make, but not for every single individual product or service—the word "category" is the important keyword to consider.

Many independent contractors keep an inventory of parts and want to track inventory in QuickBooks. That's not a good idea, because it's more trouble than it's worth. You don't have inventory in the sense that a wholesaler or retailer has inventory. You don't resell your inventory as discrete items, over the counter. You're merely keeping a store of supplies that you use often, to avoid having to drive to your supplier to purchase what you need every time you show up at a job. See the next section "Managing Materials" for some guidelines about tracking parts.

The predefined company file for contractors has an Items list you should examine. If you upgraded to the Premier Contractor edition from a previous version of QuickBooks, and you didn't create a company to have access to the predefined file, open the sample company and examine the Items list. This Items list probably doesn't match your exact needs, but you can get a sense of the way an Items list can be put together. If you're using the predefined company file, delete the items you don't need, and add the items you need.

Managing Materials

Most contractors don't need to track inventory formally, because they don't buy parts for resale, the way a retail store does. Instead, they keep parts in stock for use in jobs. However, I find that many independent contractors have a long list of inventory parts in their Item lists. Frequently, the list contains multiple entries of the same item.

For example, I've seen item lists in electrician's files that included Plate Covers-2hole, Plate-Covers-4hole, and so on. Plumbers have listings such as PVC-4', PVC-8', and so on. Plumbers who do this probably add a new inventory item every time they buy a different length of PVC. This is almost always totally needless, and makes the time you spend on record keeping longer than necessary.

It's much better to keep a short list of items. For example, use an item named Pipe in your invoices. If your customer cares about the number of feet of pipe you used, enter that information in the Description column (I'll bet most customers don't care). Even better, use an item named Materials in your invoices, and then use the Description column to inform your customer that it was pipe.

When you create your items, use the Non-inventory Part item type, and select the option This Item Is Purchased For And Sold To A Specific Customer:Job. Fill out the cost and the price, along with the posting accounts.

When appropriate, use a per-unit cost and price. For example, you can have an item named 2x4 Pine, and enter the per-running-foot cost and price. Then, when you use 25 feet of that wood on a job, enter the item, enter a quantity of 25, and let QuickBooks do the math.

Handling Customer Deposits

When you receive a deposit from a customer, you cannot record the money as income. You haven't yet earned the money; it still belongs to the customer. You can turn it into income by completing the work (or a portion of the work, as agreed to with the customer). Until that time, that money is a liability to your company.

Creating Accounts for Customer Deposits

To track the money you receive as deposits separately from money you earn as income, you need to set up an account to track the deposits. The earned revenue is automatically posted to an income account.

Creating a Liability Account for Customer Deposits

You need a liability account to track customer deposits, and you use this account when you receive a deposit from a customer.

To create this account, open the chart of accounts and press Ctrl-N to create a new account. Select the account type Other Current Liability, and name the account Customer Deposits, or something similar. If you used the predefined company file for contractors, the account already exists.

When you earn the money by doing the work, you credit the customer's invoice for the amount of the deposit (or a portion of it), and that action moves the funds from the liability account to the income account you use to track revenue.

Creating an Item for Customer Deposits

You need an item for customer deposits, which you use when you create transactions involving those deposits. If you used the predefined company file for contractors when you set up your company file, the item already exists.

If you're not using the predefined company file for contractors, you have to create the item. Open the Items List, and press Ctrl-N to open the New Item dialog. Then create the item using the following guidelines:

- The type of item is Service.
- The rate is zero, because it's customer-specific, and is therefore entered at the time you create the transaction.
- The account to which it's linked is the liability account you created to track customer deposits.

Creating a Virtual Bank Account for Customer Deposits

You don't need to open a separate bank account to hold customer deposits (only businesses that keep escrow funds, such as lawyers, need to do that). However, if most of your jobs are long-term, and you're holding on to customer deposits for an extended period of time, you might want to think about opening a money market account (or another type of business bank account that pays interest).

If you deposit customer deposits into your regular business bank account, you must make sure you don't spend down into the deposit money. You can keep a post-it note that tracks the total of customer deposits you're holding, and maintain that balance in the bank.

Or, you can configure your bank account so that it tracks two sets of totals; the total funds for customer deposits, and the total funds for the money you can spend.

If your customer deposits and regular funds are co-mingled in a single account, you should consider using virtual bank accounts to separate deposit funds from operating funds. When you use the operating account to pay your business expenses, the balance won't include the deposit amounts you're holding. This makes it easier to avoid spending the money you're holding as customer deposits.

In addition, having a bank account for customer deposits (whether real or virtual) provides a quick way to check the status of those funds. The amount in the bank account should always equal the amount in the customer deposit liability account.

Virtual bank accounts are subaccounts of your business bank account. Create a bank account if your chart of accounts doesn't already have one (this becomes the *parent account*). Then, open the chart of accounts window and create subaccounts as follows:

1. Press Ctrl-N to open the New Account dialog.
2. Select Bank as the account type.
3. Enter a number for the virtual operating account (if you're using account numbers). Use a number one digit higher than the number of your bank account. For example, if your bank account number is 1010, make the new account 1011.
4. Enter a name for the new account, such as Operating Funds.
5. Select the option Subaccount Of, and select your bank account from the drop-down list in the text box.
6. Optionally, enter a description of this account.
7. Click Next to open a blank New Account dialog, which has Bank selected as the account type.
8. Enter the next highest number as the account number.
9. Enter a name, such as Customer Deposit Funds.
10. Select the option Subaccount Of, and select your bank account from the drop-down list in the text box.
11. Optionally, enter a description.
12. Click OK.

In the chart of accounts window, your new subaccounts are listed (and indented) under your bank account.

Transferring Funds to Subaccounts

After your bank subaccounts are created, you need to transfer the appropriate amounts into each subaccount. The main bank account should have a zero balance, although it displays the total of the balances of the subaccounts when you view the chart of accounts.

Create a journal entry to transfer the funds. Credit the entire current balance of the bank account, and debit the appropriate amounts for each subaccount (see Figure 12-3).

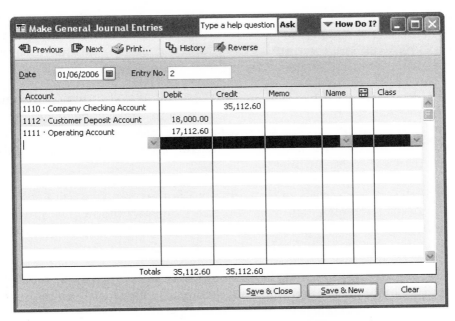

Figure 12-3: Empty the parent bank account, and fill the subaccounts.

When you open the chart of accounts window, the balance displayed for the main bank account is the total of the balances in the subaccounts. Balance sheet reports and trial balance reports display the balances of the subaccounts (with no balance in the parent account).

Depositing Funds to Subaccounts

Your QuickBooks company file configuration probably enables the Undeposited Funds account. This means when you create transactions for received funds (customer payments of invoices, or cash receipts), the money is deposited into the Undeposited Funds account.

When you deposit the funds in the bank, you use the Make Deposits feature to transfer the funds into a bank account. This is the best way to manage bank deposits, because it matches the way your bank statement reports deposits. However, if you're using virtual bank accounts via subaccounts, it complicates your life.

When you move revenue from the Undeposited Funds account into the appropriate bank account, you have to separate regular income from customer deposit income. Select all the regular income, and deposit that in the operating bank account. Select all the customer deposit receipts, and deposit them in the customer deposit bank account.

Often, this isn't an easy task, because you can't tell which income is for regular earned income, and which is for customer deposit payments. As you can see in Figure 12-4, nothing in the Payments to Deposit transaction window tells you which receipts are for customer deposits, and which are for regular income.

The only way to resolve this dilemma is to come up with a solution that announces itself in the Payments to Deposit window. Using the Memo field in a customer payment transaction window doesn't work, because memo text isn't displayed in this window.

For my clients, I solved the problem with a new payment method. I created a payment method named CustomerDeposit, with a payment type of Other (see Figure 12-5).

When customer deposits arrive, either as a payment against an invoice, or as a cash receipt, the sales transaction window is marked with the Customer Deposit Payment type. The transaction window continues to accept the customer's check number (always important to record in case of any disputes with the customer).

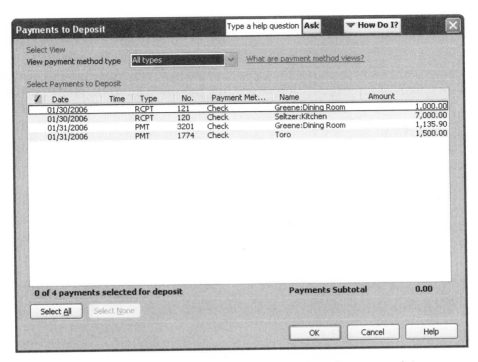

Figure 12-4: How do you deposit these receipts into the appropriate bank?

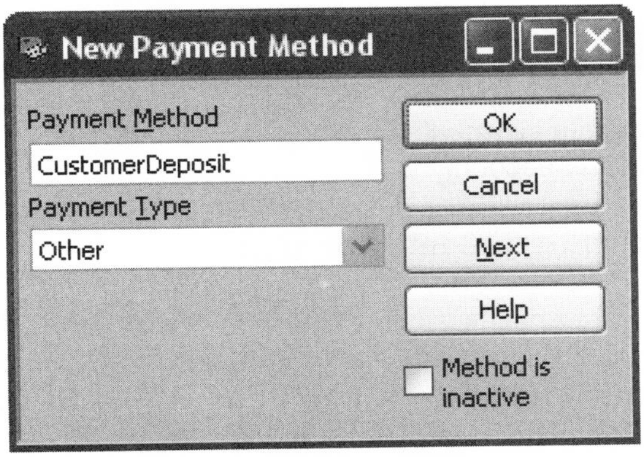

Figure 12-5: Create payment methods that help you identify which bank account should get the deposits.

- In the Receive Payment transaction window, when you select Customer Deposit (or any other payment method classified as Other), the Check # field changes its name to Reference #.
- In the Enter Sales Receipts transaction window, when you select Customer Deposit (or any other payment method classified as Other), the Check No. field doesn't change its label.

When you use the new Customer Deposit payment method in transactions, the Payments to Deposit window is much easier to work with. As you can see in Figure 12-6, customer deposits are clearly discernable.

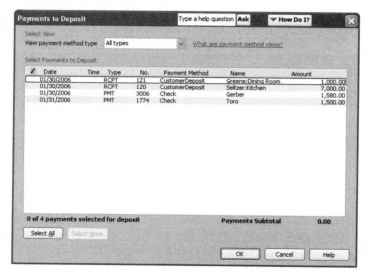

Figure 12-6: You can separate payments by type when depositing funds into a bank account.

To deposit different payment types into different bank accounts, use the following steps:

1. Click the arrow next to the View Payment Method Type field at the top of the Payments to Deposit window, and choose Selected Types from the drop-down list.
2. In the Selected Types dialog, choose Other.
3. Click OK to return to the Payments to Deposit window, where only your customer deposit payments are displayed.

4. Click Select All to select all your customer deposit funds, and then click OK to open the Make Deposits window.
5. Select the Customer Deposit bank subaccount, and click Save & New to return to the Payments to Deposit window.
6. Select All Types at the top of the window, and click Select All to select the remaining payments.
7. Click OK to open the Make Deposits window, and select the Operating bank subaccount.
8. Click Save & Close.

Reconciling Bank Accounts with Subaccounts

When you reconcile the bank account, use the parent account. Because your subaccounts are virtual bank accounts, instead of real separate bank accounts, the parent account actually maintains all the activity in the bank register.

After you fill out the Bank Reconciliation window displays all the transactions for both accounts. In fact, as you can see in Figure 12-7, the parent account doesn't pay any attention at all to the fact that there are subaccounts; this is just a regular bank reconciliation and no transaction shows any indication of being initiated from a subaccount.

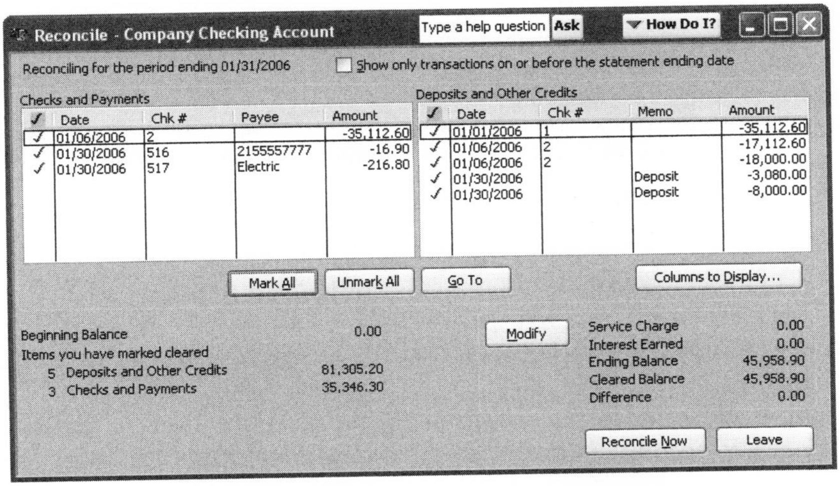

Figure 12-7: When you reconcile the parent account, the system ignores the fact that subaccounts exist.

Applying a Customer Deposit to an Invoice

To create the invoice against which you need to apply the upfront deposit, open the Create Invoices transaction window. Fill out the invoice with the items you've sold the customer. For the last item, use the upfront deposit item you created, and enter the amount of the deposit with a minus sign (see Figure 12-8).

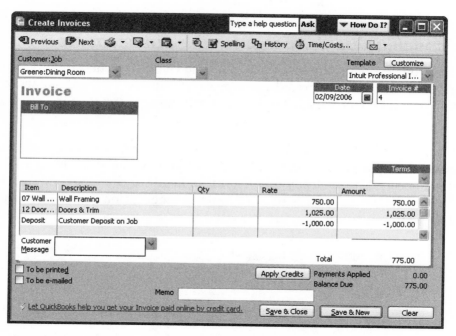

Figure 12-8: Apply the deposit against the total of the services or products you sold.

QuickBooks posts the invoice in the following manner:

- The income account(s) attached to the item(s) on the invoice are credited.
- The liability account attached to the discount item is debited.
- The A/R account is debited for the balance due.

If you're maintaining subaccounts of your bank account to separate deposits from operating funds, transfer the amount of the discount you applied from the customer deposit subaccount to the operating funds subaccount. This money is now yours, not the customers.

To transfer funds between subaccounts, choose Banking → Transfer Funds, and fill out the dialog as follows (see Figure 12-9):

- The From account is the customer deposits subaccount.
- The To account is the operating funds subaccount.
- The Transfer Amount is the amount of the deposit you released by applying it to the customer's invoice.

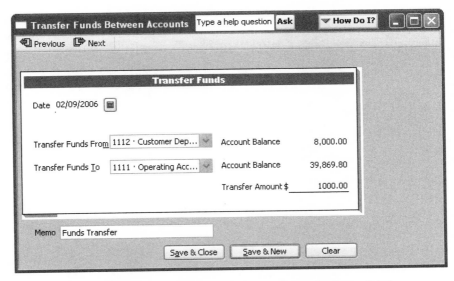

Figure 12-9: Now that you've turned the customer's deposit into income, move the funds into the operating subaccount.

The balance in the customer deposit subaccount should now equal the balance of the liability account for customer deposits.

Deposits that are Just Payments in Advance

Sometimes, a customer deposit is nothing more than an advance payment. This usually means that the job is completed in a short time. (You shouldn't hold deposits for long jobs unless you treat the deposits as liabilities.)

In this circumstance, you can create an invoice upfront (before beginning the job), apply the advance payment, and then hold the rest of the invoice until you finish the job. You don't have to treat the advance payment as a liability.

Creating an Advance Payment Item

To use an advance payment, you must create an item for it. In the New Item dialog, select Payment as the Item type, and name the item Advance Payment or Payment in Advance. As you can see in Figure 12-10, items of the type Payment don't have a lot of fields to fill out.

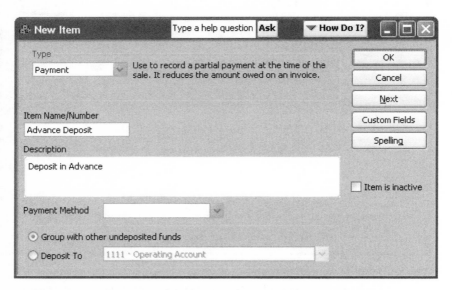

Figure 12-10: Set up an item to handle payments in advance on an invoice.

The description field is optional, but you should enter the text you want to appear in the invoice, to make it clear to the customer that the advance has been applied to the invoice. The payment type is also optional.

Select the Undeposited Funds account as the account that receives the deposit. If you don't use the Undeposited Funds account, select the operating account.

Applying an Advance Payment to an Invoice

In QuickBooks, you receive an advance payment and create an invoice at the same time. The advance is not treated separately as a sales receipt or a payment against an existing invoice. You can create the scenario for the advance payment in any of several ways:

- Create the invoice, including the advance payment, and take it to the customer. Get the check at the same time. (This assumes you've made these arrangements with the customer.)
- Ask the customer to send you the advance, and when it arrives don't use a Sales Receipt transaction to record it. Instead, create the invoice with the advance payment included.

To create the invoice, enter the item(s) you're selling the customer, and then enter the Advance Payment item. Do *not* enter a minus sign; Payment type items are automatically deductions, so QuickBooks automatically enters the minus sign.

The invoice total is the net of the sale less the advance payment (see Figure 12-11).

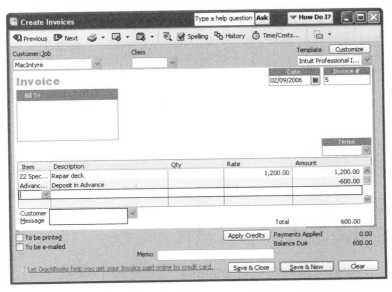

Figure 12-11: Create an invoice and apply the advance payment.

When you finish the job, send or take the invoice (with its remaining balance) to the customer.

Depositing Advance Payments

When you apply an advance payment to an invoice, QuickBooks automatically deposits the money. If you linked the advance payment item to the Undeposited Funds account, the next time you use the Payments to Deposit window, the advance payment is there (see Figure 12-12). The payment is differentiated by the code INV in the Type column.

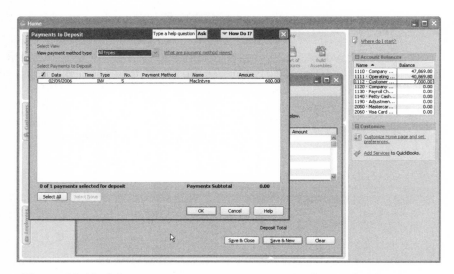

Figure 12-12: Advance payments are automatically received and deposited.

Select the payment for deposit, and if you're using subaccounts, deposit the funds into the operating fund subaccount, not the customer deposits subaccount. This type of advance payment is not treated as a liability.

Job Costing

Job costing is tracking the costs of each job so you can keep an eye on your costs and your profits. In QuickBooks, if you use estimates, you can also use job costing to track your estimated costs against your real costs (see the section "Estimates", later in this chapter).

Going over all the processes involved in setting up and implementing job costing involves far more information than I could present here. Each type of construction business has different needs, and you'll find that as you continue to use QuickBooks, and create reports, you'll think of other job-costing details you want to track. As a result, you'll be continuously tweaking your company file and creating new rules for entering transactions. In the following sections I'll present an overview of some of the things to think about as you implement job costing.

For job costing to work properly, every job should be a job. If you have a customer that you believe is a one-time-only customer, create a discrete job anyway.

Items and Job Costing

To track job costs effectively, you need to make sure you have all the items you need in your Items list. That means items that describe the materials and services you provide, as well as the materials and services you purchase. Use the following guidelines when you set up items:

- Create an item for each type of work you perform, and for materials you sell as part of that work.
- Create an item for each phase of work, when the work you perform has multiple phases. (This is especially useful if one phase is subcontracted.)
- Use subitems to refine both your invoicing and job costing activities. For example, if you have an item for Permits & Licenses, create subitems for the specific types of permits and licenses you need to perform your work.
- All the items you create should be of the Service type (even if the item covers materials).
- Items for materials should be generic; use lumber as an item instead of creating multiple items for different types or sizes of lumber.

- Don't enter cost and sales prices for items unless it's an item or a subcontracted service that you always buy and resell at a specific cost and price.

When you create your service items, select the check box labeled "This service is performed by a subcontractor, owner, or partner" (even if the item doesn't seem to fit that definition). Selecting this option changes the New Item (or Edit Item) dialog by adding fields for tracking both costs and sales (see Figure 12-13).

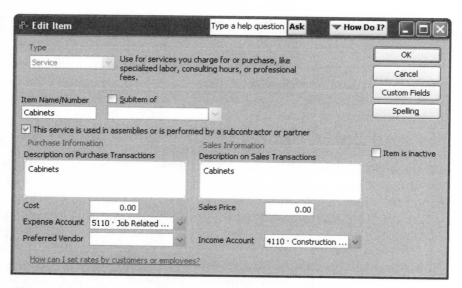

Figure 12-13: Set up your item to track both costs and sales.

In the Expense Account field, select the account to which you post job-related costs. This account should be of the type Cost of Goods. In the Income Account field, select the income account to which you post job revenue.

Linking Expenses to Jobs

When you pay a vendor, either by entering the vendor's bill in the Enter Bills transaction window, or by using the Write Checks transaction window, you should link the expense to both an item and a job. This means you move to the Items tab, instead of entering accounts in the Expenses tab.

Enter the item connected to the expense, the amount of the expense, and the job for which you incurred this expense.

If the vendor bill covers more than one job, enter the information over multiple lines, to make sure that postings for each item and job are applied properly (see Figure 12-14).

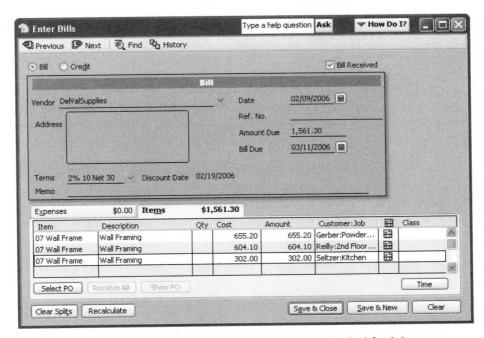

Figure 12-14: Split a vendor bill as many times as needed for job costing.

When you invoice the customer, the charges will be waiting in the Time and Costs dialog (click Time/Costs at the top of the invoice window), and you can add them to the invoice.

Tracking Material That Isn't Specifically Purchased

If you purchase materials or services for a job, you link the purchase to the job by entering the job in the Customer:Job column of the vendor bill or the Write Checks window.

However, when you use warehoused materials on a job (the stuff you buy just to keep because you use it on jobs), you should track that usage in QuickBooks, so you can keep track of your job costs.

To track these generic parts and materials, you can use a system I call "paying yourself for the consumed parts". As you pay yourself (which doesn't involve any real payments), you assign the cost to a job.

To accomplish this, create a new account in your chart of accounts named Adjustment Register. The account type is Bank. If you're using numbered accounts, use a number that falls at the end of the number range for your other (real) bank accounts.

You'll use this account to record a zero amount check by creating two entries—one positive entry and one negative entry, which cancel themselves out. During the entry process, you allocate the cost to a customer or job, and to a class (if you're tracking classes). Here are the steps:

1. Choose Banking → Write Checks to open the Write Checks window.
2. In the Bank Account field, select the Adjustment account.
3. In the Date field, enter the date you used the material.
4. Don't enter anything in the payee field.
5. Click the Items tab at the bottom of the window, and select the appropriate item, such as pipe, clamp, nails, brackets, etc. Or, you can enter a generic item, such as Materials, if you don't care about tracking the specific items.
6. In the Description column, optionally enter a description of the material you used.
7. Enter the Amount.

8. Select the Customer:Job (and select a Class if you're using classes).
9. On the next line, fill in the exact same information for all columns except the Customer:Job and Class columns, using a negative quantity. (If you filled out the Customer:Job and Class columns, you'd be setting the charge to the customer and class to zero, which you don't want to do).
10. Repeat the process in the next two lines if you have additional material to allocate. Continue to repeat the two-line entries until you've accounted for all the materials you used on this date.
11. Click Recalculate. The amount of the check changes to zero (see Figure 12-15).
12. Click Save & Close.

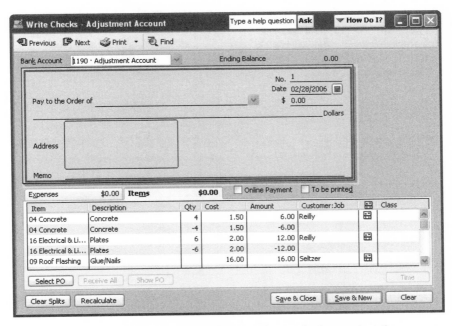

Figure 12-15: The bank account still has a zero balance, but the customer has been charged for materials.

When you invoice the customer, the charges will be waiting in the Time and Costs dialog, and you can add them to the invoice.

> **NOTE**: Read Chapter 6 of QuickBooks 2006: The Official
> Guide to learn how to invoice customers for time and cost
> expenses. A copy of the book is in your QuickBooks Premier
> edition software box.

Estimates

Estimates are a necessity for contractors, and creating an estimate in
QuickBooks is a straightforward process. Enter the item, the cost, and
the markup. QuickBooks calculates the total (see Figure 12-16).

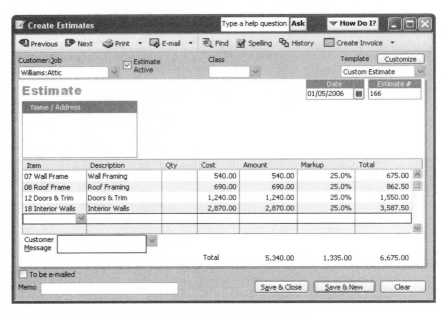

Figure 12-16: Most jobs start with an estimate.

When you print the estimate for your customer, only the total
amounts appear; the cost and markup rate are not printed.

If the job has phases, you should think about creating separate estimates for each phase. This makes progress billing less complicated, and
also provides a way to track estimated-to-final costs on a phase-by-phase

basis (which is valuable information to have when you create an estimate for another job with the same work load).

NOTE: Chapter 3 of QuickBooks 2006: The Official Guide has a full discussion of estimates, and progress billing.

Change Orders

Change orders are a common fact of life for both general and sub contractors. QuickBooks Premier Contractors Edition supports this feature, which makes your business life easier. If you're using QuickBooks Pro, you can always change an estimate, but you end up with a changed estimate. With the change order feature, you see all your change order items on the estimate form

Unfortunately, many independent contractors don't bother to create or track change orders, and sometimes this leads to misunderstandings (and occasionally, serious disputes) with customers.

It only takes a few seconds to create a change order, and you should get into the habit of using this feature for any changes to the original estimate. In fact, if you're not bothering to create estimates for every job, you should change that habit, too.

Creating a Change Order

To create a change order, you must have saved an estimate. Change orders don't exist by themselves; they're linked to estimates. To create a change order, follow these steps:

1. Open the original estimate.
2. Make changes to the quantity, price, or other line item components.
3. Click Save & Close (or Save & New if you need to create another estimate).
4. QuickBooks displays a message asking if you want to record your changes. Click Yes.

5. QuickBooks displays the Add Change Order dialog (see Figure 12-17) asking if you want to add this change order to the estimate. Click Add.

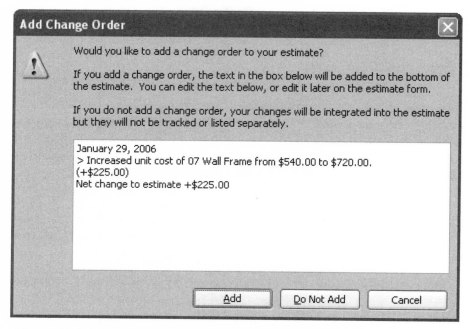

Figure 12-17: Track your changes by adding them to the estimate.

Making Additional Changes to an Estimate

It's not uncommon to require multiple changes to an estimate, especially if the estimate has many entries. Frequently, you may have to add services or items, due to some unexpected event as you complete the job.

You can continue to add items to the original estimate, creating an audit trail of the job's changes. However, you have to be careful about the way you add further items.

When you view the original estimate, the change order(s) appear below the line items. A blank line sits between the line items and the change order(s), as seen in Figure 12-18.

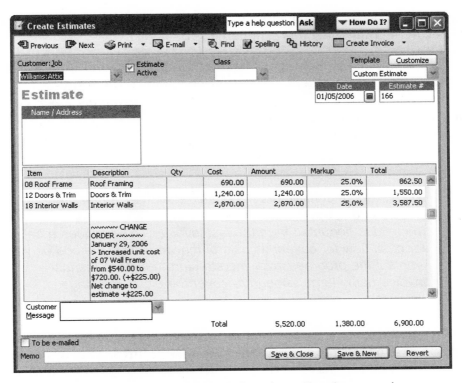

Figure 12-18: Add items in the blank line above the change order.

You should use the blank line above the change order to add items, because you want your change orders to remain below the items list. If you click the Item column in the same line that contains the change order to use that row, the change order is deleted.

If you need more than one new line, right-click the Item column of the existing new line, or the line in which the change order appears, and choose Insert Line. A new blank line appears above the line your cursor is in.

Managing Retainage

Construction contracts frequently contain a *retainage* clause (sometimes called a *retention* clause). This clause specifies that a certain percentage of the total price of the job will not be invoiced to the customer until all parties agree that the job is completed satisfactorily.

The retainage percentage is usually ten percent, and it means that you can only invoice ninety percent of the job until the terms governing retainage are met. If you use progress invoicing (invoicing a percentage of the contract price as the appropriate percentage of the work is completed), you must deduct the retainage percentage from the total of each invoice.

> **NOTE**: Some contractors negotiate retainage so that progress invoices don't deduct retainage, and the entire ten percent of the total is deducted from the last invoice. This provides a better cash flow for covering costs of the work. This method only works if the progress invoicing structure results in the last invoice being large enough to cover the entire retainage amount.

If your business encounters a retainage clause, you have to configure QuickBooks to track and report the retainage figures. This means creating accounts and items, and then entering the appropriate transactions.

Configuring QuickBooks for Retainage

The money involved in retainage is part of the contract you signed, and is your money. It's yours contractually, and it's yours because there's an expectation that you'll earn it. That makes the retainage amount an asset, so you need an asset account in your chart of accounts to track retainage.

Creating a Retainage Account

If you're using the predefined company for contractors, the retainage asset account already exists; it's account number 1320, named Retentions Receivable. The account type is Other Current Asset.

If you're not using the predefined company, you need to create the account. You can use an account type of Other Current Assets, or

Accounts Receivable (this means a separate Accounts Receivable account, in addition to the existing Accounts Receivable account). Check with your accountant to see which account type to use.

Use an account number that is appropriate for the account type (see Chapter 2 for information about designing the chart of accounts). Name the account appropriately, e.g. Retainage Receivable, or Retentions Receivable.

Creating Retainage Items

You need several items to include on your sales forms to implement retainage. You need an item to deduct the percentage, an item to subtotal the sales form before deducting the percentage, and an item to use when it's time to collect the retainage due to you.

Retainage Deduction Item

To create the retainage deduction item, follow these steps:

1. Choose Lists → Item List to open the Item List window.
2. Press Ctrl-N to open the New Item dialog.
3. Select Other Charge from the drop-down list in the Type field.
4. Enter Retainage Deduction (or Retention Deduction) in the Item Name/Number field.
5. Enter Deduction for Retainage (or something similar) in the Description field.
6. Enter -10% in the Amount or % field (note the minus sign and the percent sign).
7. Enter a non-taxable tax code in the Tax Code field (which only exists if you've enabled Sales Tax).
8. In the Account field, select your retainage asset account.
9. Click OK.

NOTE: If you have contracts with a different retainage percentage, create another item and configure it for the appropriate percentage.

Retainage Subtotal Item

The retainage item is a percentage, and QuickBooks calculates percentages against the line immediately above the percentage item on the sales form. Therefore, you must subtotal all the items on your sales form before you enter an item that calculates a percentage. This requires a discrete subtotal item in your items list.

Create a new item, using the following configuration settings:

- The item type is Subtotal.
- Name the item Subtotal (or something similar).
- Optionally, enter a description that will appear on your sales forms.

Retainage Collection Item

After the job is approved, you bill the customer for the retained amount, so you need an item to include on your invoice form. Use the general instructions described earlier to create the retainage deduction item. However, use the following configuration settings:

- The item type is either Service or Other Charge. I prefer Other Charge because it keeps the listing near the retainer deduction charge.
- Name the item Retainage Collection (or something similar).
- Optionally, enter a description to appear on your sales forms.
- Do not enter a rate or amount—you'll fill that in when you create the sales form.
- In the Account field, select the retainage asset account.

Using the Retainage Item in Sales Forms

You must use your retainage items whenever you create a sales form for a customer that has a retainage clause in the contract.

During the course of the job, create invoices as usual. After all the applicable line items are entered for each invoice, insert the subtotal item in the next line. Then, insert the retainage deduction item in the line after the subtotal item. QuickBooks will use the percentage figure and calculate the invoice correctly.

When the job is finished, and the contractual terms for collecting the retainage amount are met, the retainage can be released to you. Create an invoice, and use the retainage collection item to bill the customer for the withheld funds. Enter the amount due in the Amount column of the invoice.

Of course, to enter the amount due, you have to discover the correct amount. No built-in QuickBooks report exists to provide this amount, so you must create a report for this purpose. Use the following steps to determine the retainage amount you've deducted for a specific customer or job:

1. Choose Reports → Customers & Receivables → Customer Balance Summary.
2. Click Modify Report.
3. Go to the Filters tab.
4. Select Account in the Filter list.
5. In the Account list, scroll down the list to find and select your retainage asset account.
6. Click OK.
7. In the report window, locate the customer or job, and note the amount (which is the total amount you deducted over the course of all invoicing for this customer or job).

Memorize this report to avoid the need to set the filters next time you need this information for a customer. Click the Memorize button and name the report Retainage Totals (or something similar).

Depositing Checks with Two Payees

If you're in the construction business, and you're a subcontractor, the checks from the general contractor frequently arrive with two payees.) This scenario often occurs when you're working in a "time and materials" environment. You sell a customer (general contractor) a product or a service you sub out. The vendor charges you $1000.00. You enter the vendor's bill and send the sub or the product to the job.

You send the customer an invoice for $1000.00. The check arrives from the customer, and there are two payees: you and the vendor.

You can't deposit the check in your regular checking account, and then write a check to the vendor, because your bank won't take a check that isn't endorsed by both payees. Here's the solution:

1. Create a fake bank account named "Passthrough Payments" (or something similar).
2. Open a Receive Payments window and pay off the customer's invoice with the check. Be sure to note the check number for later reference.
3. Select the option to deposit the check to a specific account, and select the fake bank account. In QuickBooks, don't use the option to group with other undeposited funds.
4. Select Pay Bills, and choose the fake bank account in the Payment Account field. Select the appropriate vendor bill and use the same check number to pay the bill.
5. Endorse the check and send it to the vendor with a copy of the vendor's bill.

The transactions you entered "wash" the fake bank account, so it has a zero balance. If that account shows a balance, you've forgotten to take one of the steps:

- If it has a positive (debit) balance, you paid off the customer invoice, but you didn't pay the vendor's bill.
- If it has a negative balance, you paid the vendor's bill, but you didn't pay off the customer's invoice.

When you open the bank account, you can see a history of every check you treated in this manner.

Payroll Issues for Contractors

If you do your own payroll, you have to make sure you set up your company file to manage all the payroll issues. All the information you need to set up in-house payroll is in Chapters 8 and 9 of *QuickBooks 2006: The Official Guide*.

Timesheets

QuickBooks has a built-in program for tracking time. You can track employee hours by customer:job, and by class. To learn how to use timesheets, read Chapter 18 of *QuickBooks 2006: The Official Guide*. To learn how to turn timesheets into paychecks, read Chapter 19.

Workers Comp

If you sign up for QuickBooks Enhanced Payroll, QuickBooks can manage workers comp automatically. The setup options are available in the Payroll & Employees category of the Preferences dialog. Click the Set Preferences button to open the Workers Comp dialog. Select Track Workers Comp to enable the feature.

When workers comp is enabled, you can also opt to see reminder messages to assign workers comp codes when you create paychecks or timesheets. In addition, you can select the option to exclude an overtime premium from your workers comp calculations (check your workers comp insurance policy to see if you can calculate overtime amounts as regular pay).

To set up the workers comp calculations, choose Employees → Workers Compensation → Set Up Workers Comp. Follow the prompts to set up your workers comp expenses.

Certified Payroll

Most construction projects funded by public funds require certified payroll reports. Occasionally, privately funded projects require certified payrolls. You can manage payroll certification within QuickBooks by performing the tasks described in this section.

Creating a Prevailing Wage Rate Payroll Item

You must create payroll items for the prevailing wage rates. Open the Payroll Items list and press Ctrl-N to create a new item, and then follow these steps to move through the wizard, clicking Next as you enter data in each wizard window:

1. Select Custom Setup in the Add New Payroll Item Wizard.
2. Select Wage as the payroll item type.
3. Select Hourly Wages as the wage type.
4. Select Regular Pay as the hourly wage type.
5. Name the item Prevailing Wage Rate.
6. Enter the account for posting these wages.
7. Click Finish.

If you don't have an exclusion from overtime calculations, repeat this process to create an Overtime Prevailing Wage Rate.

Applying the Prevailing Wage Rate Payroll Item

When you create a timesheet and/or paycheck for an employee's work on a certified job, use the Prevailing Wage Rate payroll item you created. If all your work requires certified payroll, or if certain employees only work on certified payroll jobs, edit the Payroll & Compensation data in the employee records. Enter the Prevailing Wage Rate item instead of the generic hourly item.

Creating Certified Payroll Reports

You can view the application of certified payroll rates by selecting the payroll item and pressing Ctrl-Q. Change the date range of the QuickReport that opens to meet your needs.

QuickBooks Premier Contractor Edition includes a report that provides all the information you need to fill in Box 1 of a Certified Payroll Form for employees. Choose Reports → Contractor Reports → Certified Payroll - Box 1 Employee Information.

Job Costing Center

One of the best reporting tools available in QuickBooks is the Job Costing Center. Choose Contractor → Job Costing Center to open the window that contains a great deal of at-a-glance information (see Figure 12-19).

TIP: The jobs that aren't showing a profit are usually not yet invoiced—if the invoice has gone out, then it's time to worry.

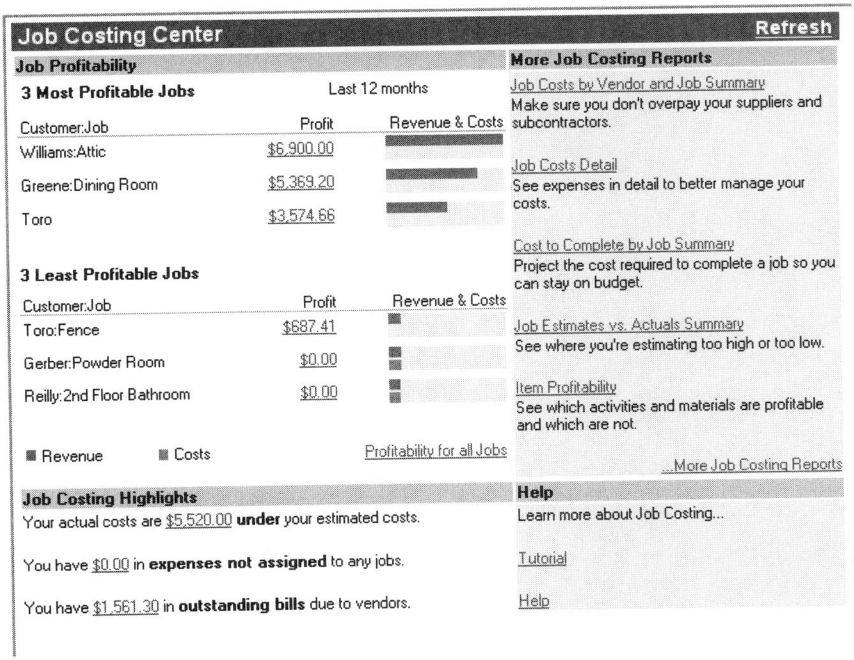

Figure 12-19: The Job Costing Center provides all the information
you need to track your job profitability.

Click the links to get in-depth information about all the facets of
your jobs, your job costs, and your profits.

Customized Reports for Contractors

QuickBooks has included a great many preconfigured reports of use to
contractors. You can view the list by choosing Reports → Contractor
Reports. The list of reports is quite comprehensive (and self-explanatory).

Chapter 13

Manufacturing and Wholesale Edition

Advanced inventory and sales order features

Customer RMAs

Returning products to a vendor

Tracking damaged and missing inventory

Customized reports

Like most computer consultants who specialize in accounting software installations, I spend the majority of my time with manufacturing and wholesale clients. When I started consulting, a million years ago, these were the first business types to install computerized accounting systems.

Many companies purchased software systems designed specifically for their type of business. The systems are called "vertical applications" and they're written specifically for certain types of manufacturing or distribution businesses. The software packages are extremely expensive, because they're designed for businesses that gross many millions each year, and have extremely complicated process that the software tracks.

For smaller businesses, it's certainly possible to track the same accounting processes with QuickBooks, and the Premier Manufacturing and Wholesale Edition includes features to help you do just that.

If you think about it, the paradigm is always the same. You buy stuff at a certain price, and you sell it at a higher price (distribution), or you use the stuff to build stuff you sell (manufacturing). Many businesses do both; they resell products, and they assemble their own products for resale.

This is all very straightforward, and small manufacturing and wholesale business can easily manage their finances with QuickBooks.

TIP: Chapter 6 has instructions for using the Premier editions features that help you run your business, such as automatic generation of purchase orders, managing back orders, creating assembled products, and so on.

Stock Status Information for Sales Orders

The QuickBooks Premier Manufacturing & Wholesale Edition offers advanced functions for tracking sales orders. Two important and useful advanced features are built into this edition of QuickBooks Premier:

- Stock shortage warnings during the creation of a sales order.
- One-click access to stock status reports in the Create Sales Orders transaction window.

These features are only available in the Manufacturing & Wholesale, Retail, and Accountant Premier editions. The other Premier editions don't advise you about stock shortages until you convert a sales order to an invoice.

Stock Status Configuration Options

By default, QuickBooks warns you about inventory stock shortages when the Quantity on Hand (QOH) is at zero. However, when you're creating a sales order, the QOH isn't necessarily the only time you need to be warned about shortages.

If the QOH of a product is 10, and you want to sell 5, the math isn't as simple as it seems. If existing sales orders include that product, and those sales orders add up to 6 units, you don't really have 5 units available when you're creating a new sales order.

Similarly, if the QOH is 10, and the people in the warehouse have begun assembling products that use that inventory part, a substantial number of the QOH may be in the process of going into an inventory assembly.

Therefore, you need to configure QuickBooks to track the quantity available, not the quantity on hand. To access this configuration option, choose Edit → Preferences, and select the Purchases & Vendors category in the Preferences dialog. Move to the Company Preferences tab, and make the appropriate adjustments to the configuration options (see Figure 13-1).

- Control the way QuickBooks calculates available stock by selecting either or both of the options in the dialog (include quantity used in assemblies and sales orders).
- Specify the conditions in which QuickBooks should warn you about insufficient stock levels by basing the calculation on QOH or Quantity Available.

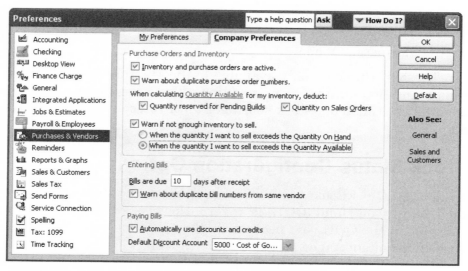

Figure 13-1: Configure the stock status algorithms that help you
manage inventory efficiently.

Out of Stock Warnings

If an item is out of stock (QOH is zero), QuickBooks issues a warning as
soon as you select the item in the sales order, even before you enter the
quantity (see Figure 13-2). You can continue with the sales order, and
wait until stock is available before converting the sales order to an
invoice.

If you configured stock status warnings to occur when Quantity
Available (instead of QOH) is insufficient, the definition of "out of stock"
includes inventory that is still on the shelves, but sales orders exist for
the item. (If the sales orders had been turned into invoices, the stock
would have been removed from the shelves, and therefore from the quantity on hand.)

As you can see in Figure 13-3, the warning message explains clearly
that no quantity is available, so the item is deemed "out of stock".
Because insufficient stock is available, the warning is displayed as
soon as you enter the item in the sales order (before entering a quantity).

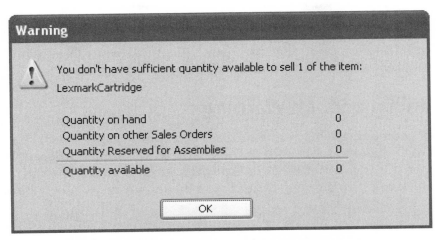

Figure 13-2: When there's no stock left, QuickBooks tells you as soon as you enter the item in the sales order.

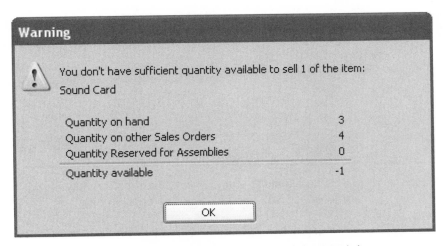

Figure 13-3: This item isn't out of stock, but all the stock is promised.

You can continue with the sales order and wait until stock is available before converting the sales order to an invoice, or negotiate an exchange of stock with the person who created the other sales orders. This is one of those times when you need to consider whether one customer should take priority over another customer.

To free up stock that's available but promised, change the quantity on the earlier sales order, then re-enter the sales order for the customer you think should receive the stock (see "Modifying Sales Orders to Obtain Promised Stock", later in this section).

Insufficient Stock Warnings

If stock is on hand, when you enter the item in the sales order, you may not have sufficient stock to fill the quantity the customer ordered. When you enter the number of units in the Ordered column, if there isn't sufficient stock to fill this order, QuickBooks displays a message explaining the stock status (see Figure 13-4).

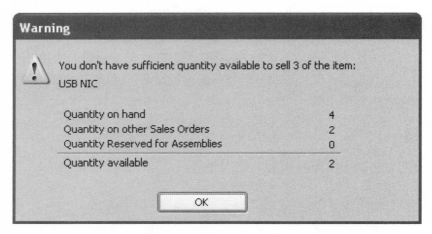

Figure 13-4: This item's stock status is less than the quantity ordered, so you can't invoice this order in full.

You can continue with the sales order, and create an invoice to ship the available stock, creating a backorder for the remaining items. Or, you can hold the invoice until sufficient stock is available to fill the entire order.

Checking Stock Status Details

One of the nifty enhanced functions in the Premier Manufacturing & Wholesale Edition is the ability to check stock status, in detail, right from the sales order transaction window. After you enter the item in the sales order, whether you receive a stock status warning or not, click the icon that appears on the right side of the Ordered column.

QuickBooks calls this icon and resulting report "Available to Promise". This is a report on the current status of this item. As you can see in Figure 13-5, this report has more information than the stock status warnings QuickBooks displays.

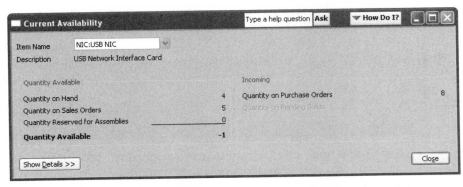

Figure 13-5: There's no available stock, but a purchase order exists, which means stock should arrive soon.

You can learn even more about the stock status of this item by clicking the Show Details button. Then choose the type of information you want to see by selecting one of the following topics from the drop-down list:

- **Sales Orders**. This choice displays all the current sales orders that contain this item. See "Modifying Sales Orders to Obtain Promised Stock" to remove items from one of those sales orders so you can invoice and ship the current sales order.
- **Pending Builds**. This choice displays all the pending bills that include this item.
- **Purchase Orders**. This choice displays all the current purchase orders for this item, including the expected date of arrival (see Figure 13-6).

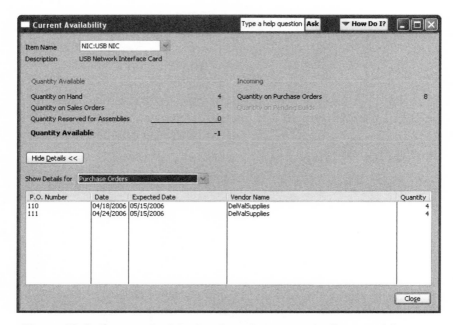

Figure 13-6: If more stock is due to arrive soon, don't convert the sales order to an invoice until that date.

Modifying Sales Orders to Obtain Promised Stock

When you click the Show Details button, and select Sales Orders, QuickBooks displays a listing of the sales orders that include the item you want to include in the sales order you're creating.

If the sales order you're creating is for a customer you think should be shipped product faster than the customers on the existing sales orders, you can modify any of the displayed sales orders to reduce the item's quantity.

Double-click the listing for the sales order you want to change. However, since you have a sales order in process in the Create Sales Orders window, and QuickBooks can neither open a second sales order in the window, nor open another instance of the Create Sales Orders window, you have to decide how to remove the current sales order from the window. QuickBooks displays a message that offers three choices for handling the current sales order:

- **Save Changes**. Save the current sales order with its current items and quantities, and open the selected existing sales order in the Create Sales Orders window. You can return to the sales order you saved to adjust the quantity, after you finish modifying the older sales order.
- **Discard Changes**. Close the current sales order without saving it, and open the selected existing sales order. You can create the new sales order after you've adjusted the quantities in the existing sales order.
- **Continue Editing**. Forget about opening an existing sales order, and return to the sales order you're currently working on.

Unless the sales order you're trying to create is for an important customer who doesn't accept back orders, and no additional stock is expected in the near future, it's best to continue editing the current sales order.

When stock arrives, you can ship to this customer first by converting this sales order to an invoice before the earlier sales orders are converted. See the next section, "Sales Order Fulfillment Worksheet, to learn how to allocate stock to sales orders.

Sales Order Fulfillment Worksheet

The QuickBooks Premier Manufacturing & Wholesale Edition has a Sales Order Fulfillment Worksheet that you can use to decide how to fill sales orders if there is insufficient stock to fill all sales orders.

To open the worksheet, choose Customers → Sales Order Fulfillment Worksheet. When the worksheet opens (see Figure 13-7), its appearance is determined by the availability of the stock entered in sales orders, and the way you sort the data. You can sort the display of sales orders by selecting a sort order from the drop-down list.

In the sales order listing at the top of the window, QuickBooks uses symbols to indicate the fulfillment status of each sales order:

- A solid green circle means there is sufficient stock to fill the order.

• A half filled amber circle means there is sufficient stock to ship a partial order. This could mean that less stock than ordered is available for the items in the sales order, or one (or more) items on the sales order is out of stock (even though there is sufficient stock to fill the order on another item.

• An empty square with a red X means there is no stock available to fill the order.

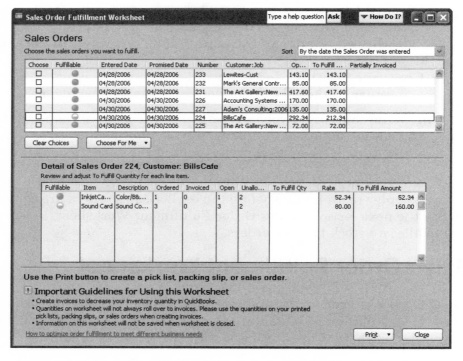

Figure 13-7: A worksheet is available to help you decide which sales orders to fill when stock is limited.

Click any order to display stock status details for that order in the bottom of the window. QuickBooks uses the same symbols to indicate the fulfillment capabilities of each item in the sales order.

The fact that more than one sales order has a green circle doesn't mean you can fulfill all the "green circle" sales orders. Depending on stock availability, it could mean that you can fulfill one order, and when you do, the stock is used and the other sales orders won't be able to ship (and their symbols will change).

Click the button labeled Choose For Me to display a variety of choices you can select to have QuickBooks automatically select the sales order to fill (see Figure 13-8).

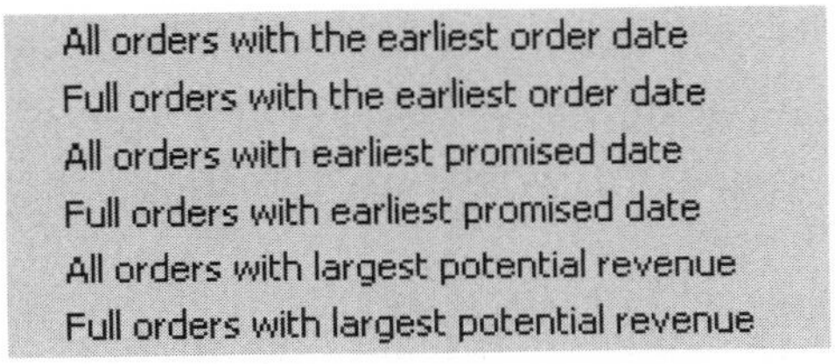

All orders with the earliest order date
Full orders with the earliest order date
All orders with earliest promised date
Full orders with earliest promised date
All orders with largest potential revenue
Full orders with largest potential revenue

Figure 13-8: Select the stance you want to take about filling sales orders.

To choose sales orders manually, select a listing and click the check box in the first column. The bottom of the window inserts the number of items required to fill the order (or partially fill the order if the sales order does not have a green circle) in the Fulfill Qty column. If this action uses up the available stock, the symbols for other sales orders that include this stock change to an empty square with a red X.

Selecting a sales order does not turn it in to an invoice, nor does it lock the available stock so that it belongs to this sales order. This is a worksheet, an informational window. However, you can begin the process of converting a sales order to an invoice from the worksheet window.

The first step is to make sure that the reported availability numbers match what's actually on the shelves. Select the sales order you want to fill, and click the Print button at the bottom of the window. Select Print Pick Lists and then send the printed pick list to the warehouse to make sure the sales order can be filled to match the quantity in the Fulfill Qty column.

TIP: If you're on a network, install a printer near the stock shelves, and select that printer when you print pick slips.

If enough stock is available to fill the order, double-click the sales order listing to open the original sales order. Then click the Create Invoice button at the top of the Create Sales Orders window and follow the prompts to turn the sales order into an invoice.

When you return to the worksheet, the symbols on the worksheet change to indicate the new status of order fulfillment, now that you've actually removed product from inventory.

You could also close the worksheet window, convert the appropriate sales orders to invoices, and then check the worksheet stats again when new product arrives. This worksheet is an ad-hoc document, which means that any information you entered in the window wasn't saved, and each time you open the worksheet the data in the window displays real time information as of the moment you open it.

Customer RMAs

RMAs (sometimes called RAs) are a fact of life in your business. You have to deal with customer returns, but you can, and should, impose rules and protocols; otherwise, tracking the financial consequences becomes extremely difficult.

One rule that most distributors impose is that no merchandise can be returned unless an RMA number that you provide is on the packing slip and/or the shipping label.

Creating RMAs

QuickBooks has built in a way to assign an RMA number, and track it, using a Microsoft Word document. Of course, you must have Word installed on your computer to take advantage of this feature.

Choose Mfg & Whsle → Inventory Activities → Customer Return Materials Authorization Form. Microsoft Word opens with the form loaded in the software window (see Figure 13-9). The document doesn't really exist as a discrete file (you can see that the title bar lacks a file name), so the first thing to do is save this document so you can access it from Word.

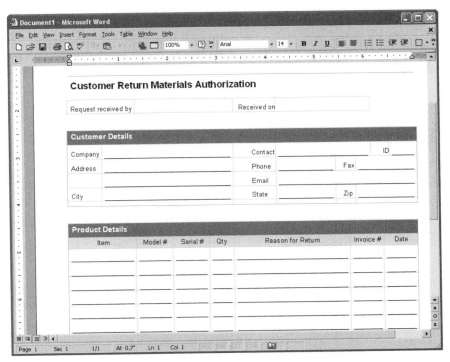

Figure 13-9: QuickBooks provides a form for tracking RMAs.

Choose File → Save As and name the document. By default, Word saves the document in your My Documents folder. You could create a folder for your QuickBooks documents and forms, either directly on the root of your hard drive (e.g. C:\QBForms), or as a subfolder in your My Documents folder.

Save the document before you fill anything out, so you have a boilerplate you can open directly in Word. This means the person managing RMA forms doesn't have to be a QuickBooks user, nor does it matter if he has QuickBooks software installed on his computer (see "Manipulating the RMA Form", later in this section).

You can use this form whenever you need a customer RMA. The form is configured as a Word table, so you can enter data into all the appropriate cells. Every time you fill out the form, use the Save As command to save the document, using a new filename.

Print a copy of the form for your bookkeeper, who can issue a credit in QuickBooks when the material comes back from the customer. You should also print a copy for your warehouse personnel, so they know the material is due.

TIP: If you name each RMA document with the format XXXX-<CustomerName> (where XXXX is the RMA number), when you open the folder in which you're storing RMAs, you can automatically determine the next RMA number.

This form is inert, which means it has no automatic functions connected to QuickBooks or your QuickBooks company file. You have to track RMA numbers manually, outside of QuickBooks.

Additionally, the form provides fields that make it easy for you to create a credit memo for the customer when the products are returned. However, the data in your QuickBooks file, such as Item Name and Invoice #, don't automatically appear—no drop-down lists exist of course, because you're not working in QuickBooks.

Manipulating the RMA Form

The RMA form that QuickBooks installs and uses is a Word template file, which means its file extension is .DOT instead of .DOC (the extension for Word documents).

If you're comfortable editing Word templates, you can open it directly in Word, make changes to it, and then save it using a different filename. It's best to copy the file to the My Documents folder of the person in your organization who tracks RMAs. You can find the file in \<*QuickBooks Installation Folder*>\Components\Vertical Forms. Substitute the folder into which you installed QuickBooks for <*QuickBooks Installation Folder*>. The file name is:

CustomerReturnMaterialsAuthorizationForm.dot.

In fact, even if you're not going to change the form, you should copy it to the My Documents folder of the person who manages RMAs. Have that person open the file, and use File → Save As on the Word menu bar to save the document as a Word document file (a file ending in the extension .DOC).

Processing Customer Returns of Inventory

When a customer returns inventory, you have to track the inventory return and the customer's financial information in a way that fits the scenario. For example, the customer may have already paid for the inventory and is returning it because it's damaged. Or the customer may not have paid for the inventory, and is returning it "just because".

The condition of the inventory (whether it is damaged, or is fine and can be resold), and the state of the customer's indebtedness to you determine the transactions you create.

Providing Credits for Damaged Inventory

If the inventory being returned by your customer is damaged, you cannot put it back into your warehouse. However, you need to credit the customer's account, which automatically puts the inventory back into stock. To accomplish this, credit the customer's account, and then create an inventory adjustment, as explained in the following sections.

Creating a Credit for a Paid Invoice

If the customer paid the invoice that covers the damaged returns, you must enter a credit memo, or issue a refund check. The credit memo/refund should cover only the returned items, not the entire invoice (unless the only item on that invoice was this product).

When you create the credit memo, use the returned items in the line item section of the transaction window. You should also credit any shipping charges (proportionately, if the credit memo is for an invoice that included more items than those being returned).

When you save the credit memo, QuickBooks asks if you want to save the credit for future use by the customer, create a refund check, or apply the credit to an existing invoice.

If you opt to save the credit or apply it to an existing invoice, QuickBooks makes the following postings:

- Debits the Inventory Asset account (puts the product back into inventory).
- Credits the COG account (removes the cost expense).
- Debits the sales account connected to the item (lowers your income).
- Credits the A/R account (lowers the total receivables).

In addition, appropriate changes are made to your sales tax liability account (if the item and the customer are both taxable), and to any shipping charges you included in the credit.

If you create a refund check, QuickBooks makes the following additional postings:

- Debits Accounts Receivable (reversing the action taken when you saved the credit memo)
- Credits the bank account (removes the money from the bank).

After the customer's record is updated, you must adjust your inventory to remove the damaged goods that QuickBooks put back into inventory. See the section "Adjusting Inventory for Damaged Goods".

Voiding an Unpaid Invoice

If the customer has not yet paid the invoice, and the invoice only contains the product being returned, void the invoice. QuickBooks makes the following postings:

- Debits the Inventory Asset account (puts the product back into inventory).
- Credits the COG account (removes the cost expense).
- Debits the sales account connected to the item (lowers your income).
- Credits the A/R account (lowers the total receivables).

If the invoice contains additional items, do not void it. Instead, issue a credit for the returned item, and when you save the credit choose the option to apply the credit to a specific invoice, and then choose the invoice that contains the damaged inventory.

Adjusting Inventory for Damaged Goods

You must remove the damaged inventory that QuickBooks put back into your system when you created the customer's credit memo. To do this, choose Vendor → Inventory Activities → Adjust Quantity/Value on hand to open the Inventory Adjustment transaction form seen in Figure 13-10.

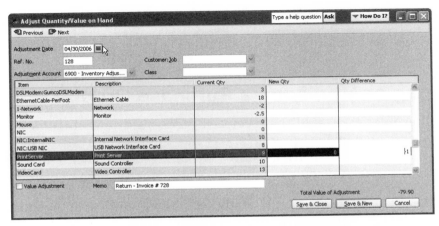

Figure 13-10: Adjust your inventory to remove damaged products.

In the Adjustment Account field, select the inventory adjustment account (in the Expense section of your chart of accounts). Locate the item in the listings and adjust the number of units by the number of returned damaged units. You can either enter data in the Net Qty column (mentally subtracting the returned number from the displayed Current Qty number), or enter the number of returned items in the Qty Difference column (don't forget the minus sign). It's a good idea to use the memo field for details, so when you see this transaction in reports (or your accountant sees it) you can explain it.

In addition, if you purchased this inventory, you must return it to your vendor (usually the manufacturer), and you can also track the details by using the Damaged Goods Log. All of these functions are discussed in the next section.

Returning Products to a Vendor

When you return products to a vendor you have to enter the appropriate transaction in QuickBooks. The actions you take differ, depending on the scenario:

- You have a P.O. in the system, but haven't entered the receipt of goods or bill (because you noticed damage when the product arrived).
- You have a receipt of goods in the system, but have not yet entered the bill (because it didn't arrive in the package).
- You have entered both a receipt of goods and a bill into the system.

Voiding or Modifying a Purchase Order

If you haven't yet created the receipt of goods/bill transaction for the P.O. that covers the damaged products, you can void the purchase order. This only works if the P.O. contains only the damaged products, and all of the products were damaged (which would be an unusual occurrence).

If the P.O. contains a quantity larger than 1 of the item, and some of the items aren't damaged, you can void the P.O. and create a new one with the correct data. Be sure to notify the vendor about this action, telling them to ignore the original P.O. and look for a new P.O.

You can also modify the P.O. by reducing the quantity to reflect the number of items you're returning. Notify the vendor that you've changed the P.O. and ask them to adjust their records.

Voiding or Modifying a Receipt of Items

If you received the items into inventory (without the bill), you can void or modify the Receipt of Goods transaction. The quickest way to locate the original Item Receipt is to open the Vendor Center, select the vendor, and select Item Receipts in the Show field.

If the receipt covers only this item, and if the entire quantity of items is damaged, void the receipt. If the receipt covers multiple items, and/or only some of the quantity received of a single item is damaged, adjust the data in the Qty column, and click Recalculate to adjust the total.

Voiding or Modifying a Receipt of Items and Bill

If you received the items into inventory and also entered the vendor's bill, adjust your transactions according to the contents of the receipt and bill. If everything covered in the receipt of items/bill is damaged, void the transaction.

If you only need to adjust the quantity of an item to reflect the damaged goods you're returning, adjust the data in the Qty column, and click Recalculate to adjust the total.

Entering a Vendor Credit for a Paid Bill

If you paid the vendor before returning damaged goods, you need to create a credit with this vendor. Use the following steps to accomplish this:

1. Choose Vendors → Enter Bills
2. Select the Credit option at the top of the Enter Bills window.
3. Select the vendor.
4. Use the Items tab in the line item section of the window to enter the item and the amount of the credit.
5. If appropriate (meaning if you and the vendor agree), use the Expenses tab to enter a credit for any shipping costs you incurred for the delivery or will incur for the return of goods.

You can use the credit against existing bills or future bills from this vendor.

Entering a Vendor Refund

If the vendor agreed to send you a refund check, enter a credit as described in the previous section. The credit applies the appropriate postings to your inventory and A/P accounts. When the check arrives, use the following steps to enter it into your QuickBooks system:

1. Choose Banking → Make Deposits to open the Payments to Deposit window.
2. If there are deposits listed that you want to make, select them.
3. Click OK (even if you haven't selected any deposits) to open the Make Deposits window.
4. In the first blank line make the following entries:
   - Enter the Vendor in the Received From column.
   - Enter Accounts Payable in the From Account column (this washes the A/P posting you entered when you created the vendor credit memo).
   - Optionally, enter a note in the Memo column, enter a check number, and select the payment method in the appropriate columns.
   - Enter the amount of the check in the Amount column.

Saving the credit memo and depositing the check into the bank created all the right postings to your general ledger. However, the postings to A/P did not specifically affect this vendor.

To take care of this last step (matching the credit to the vendor's check), choose Vendor → Pay Bills to open the Pay Bills window. When the window opens, in addition to any bills that are currently due, you see a bill for this vendor, in the amount of the check you deposited.

It's easy to spot this transaction since unlike the other listings in the Pay Bill window, this bill has no due date. That's because it's not really a bill, it's a credit waiting to be assigned to itself. Select the bill for payment by clicking in the leftmost column to insert a check mark. QuickBooks immediately displays the message seen in Figure 13-11.

Click OK, and then click Pay & Close in the Pay Bills window. QuickBooks displays a message telling you that you should track the details of the bills that were paid entirely by a credit, in case your vendor asks why a bill wasn't paid. Since the bill was never a real bill, such a conversation won't occur.

Creating a Non-Conforming Materials Report

After you have an RMA number from your vendor, you can track detailed information about the return of damaged goods with the Non-conforming

Material Report, which is a Word document QuickBooks installs for this purpose.

Figure 13-11: QuickBooks pays this ersatz bill by crediting it against itself.

Choose Mfg & Whsle → Inventory Activities → Non-conforming Material Report to open the document in Word (see Figure 13-12). Fill out the appropriate cells, and use Word's Save As command to save the document with an appropriate name for this return. Print a copy to use as a packing slip.

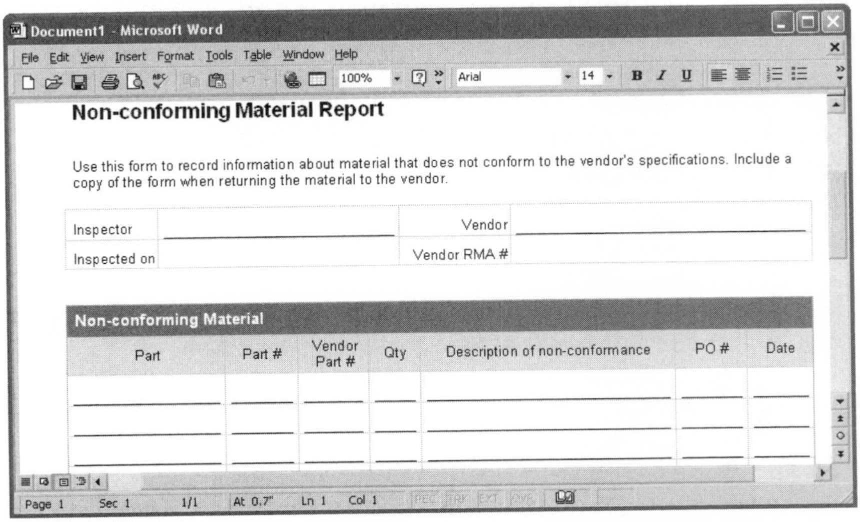

Figure 13-12: Track details for merchandise you return to the vendor.

You can copy this template to the My Documents folder of the person in charge of handling vendor returns, and access it directly from Word, instead of working through QuickBooks. Save the document as a Word document, instead of a Word template, as described in the preceding section on the Customer Return Materials Authorization Form.

Tracking Damaged and Missing Products

If you want to keep a log on inventory products that are damaged internally (or go missing) you can use the Damaged Goods Log that QuickBooks installs. This is a Word template that you can use directly from Word, as explained in the previous sections on other Word documents.

To open the log from within QuickBooks, choose Mfg & Whsle → Inventory Activities → Damaged Goods Log. When the Word document opens (see Figure 13-13), you can fill it in.

Use the instructions presented earlier to copy this Word template to the My Documents folder of the person who tracks damaged and missing inventory. You should create a second document, changing the name to Missing Goods Log, so you can track damaged and missing goods separately.

> **NOTE**: *Damaged inventory that isn't returned to vendors should be physically removed from inventory so it's not accidentally counted the next time you do a physical count.*

When inventory is damaged, or disappears, you must adjust your inventory, using the following steps:

1. Choose Vendors → Inventory Activities → Adjust Quantity/Value On Hand.
2. In the Adjust Quantity/Value On Hand dialog, select the Adjustment Account from the drop-down list (it's usually an expense account named Inventory Adjustment).
3. Select the listing for the missing or damaged item.

4. In the Qty Difference column, enter the number of missing or damaged units of this item with a minus sign. QuickBooks automatically calculates the New Qty column.

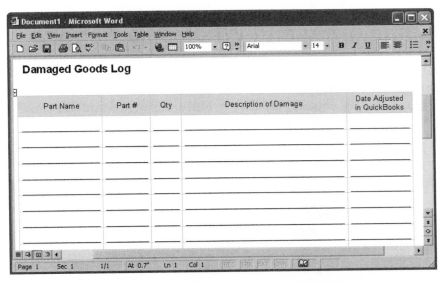

Figure 13-13: Track details about damaged or missing inventory items.

If inventory is missing, it could be the result of a miscount or an item being placed on the wrong shelf, or in the wrong room. However, if this happens more than a couple of times, you need to look for another reason. I've found two common scenarios to explain missing inventory items:

- Sales personnel take inventory and hide it in their own offices to make sure they can service their customers. This is common for inventory items that have high turnover and are frequently out of stock before the next order arrives from the vendor.
- Employees are helping themselves to inventory items. Yes, I mean "stealing". Employee theft of inventory items is a common occurrence, and the jargon for this is *shrinkage*.

No software can solve either problem, although it's been my experience that when accounting software is installed, and inventory tracking is part of the software, shrinkage slows down. To accomplish the change in attitude (the attitude that nobody will notice if you steal), you need to make an announcement that when there's a difference between the software's inventory numbers and the physical count, you're going to believe the software's numbers.

Manufacturing and Wholesale Reports

QuickBooks includes many customized and memorized reports that are designed to be useful to your type of business. To view the list of reports (see Figure 13-14), choose Reports → Manufacturing and Wholesale Reports. The report titles are self-explanatory.

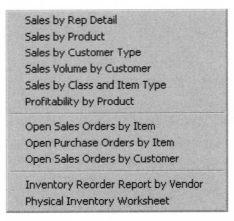

Figure 13-14: These reports are designed with your industry in mind.

You can customize any of these reports to suit your own needs, and memorize them for frequent use.

Chapter 14

Nonprofit Edition

Unified chart of accounts for nonprofits

Using Classes

Equity accounts

Customized templates for transactions

Memorized reports for nonprofits

The Premier Nonprofit Edition has some special problems, because it isn't designed properly for nonprofit use. However, the Premier Nonprofit Edition includes the Unified Chart of Accounts for nonprofits, customized templates you can use to record specific types of income, and some useful customized reports.

You have to adapt your use of QuickBooks to use it successfully for nonprofits. In this chapter, I provide an overview of some of the basic issues involved in using QuickBooks for nonprofit transactions.

> **NOTE**: Adapting QuickBooks for nonprofit accounting is a rather complicated endeavor. Due to the demand for this information, we've published a book on the topic. Look for Running QuickBooks in Nonprofits from CPA911 Publishing at your favorite bookstore, or at www.cpa911publishing.com.

Unified Chart of Accounts (UCOA)

Most nonprofits have to file a great many detailed reports about their financial activities. Federal and state governments have filing requirements, and grant-givers frequently require financial information. Except for the Form 990 model on the federal level, there's no particular across-the-board standard you can take for granted (although most states will accept the Federal Form 990).

The Unified Chart of Accounts (UCOA) is an attempt to standardize the way nonprofits keep financial records, and report them. The UCOA is based on Form 990, but it's useful and efficient even for nonprofit organizations that don't file Form 990. Developed by the California Association of Nonprofits and the National Center for Charitable Statistics (NCCS), UCOA provides a way to unite all of your reporting needs into one set of accounting records. By using UCOA as a model for your own chart of accounts, you'll find it easier to produce reports for all who demand them.

When you create a new company file and select nonprofit as your type of business, QuickBooks offers to install a chart of accounts suitable for nonprofit organizations. The file that's installed is the UCOA.

Using the UCOA

Starting with QuickBooks 2006 Premier Nonprofit Edition, the chart of accounts (which is the UCOA) is ready-to-use.

In versions of Premier Nonprofit Edition prior to 2006, the accounts are marked Inactive (hidden). When you open the Chart of Accounts window, if the option Include Inactive isn't selected (at the bottom of the window), you'll see only a few accounts that QuickBooks automatically defined during company file setup, not the entire chart of accounts.

When the option Include Inactive is selected, all the accounts in the UCOA have a large X in the left column, indicating the accounts are inactive, and therefore hidden.

Hidden accounts don't appear in the drop-down list of accounts when you create transactions in QuickBooks, so you won't be able to get any work done until you change the status of your accounts to Active.

You must go through the list to activate the accounts you want to use. To activate an account, click the X in the left column, and your action automatically removes the X (it's a toggle).

A subaccount can't be activated until the parent account is activated. If you click the X of a subaccount, nothing happens. When you activate a parent account, QuickBooks asks if you want to activate all the subaccounts. Click Yes to save yourself a lot of mouse clicks.

Renaming Accounts

Some of the accounts have generic names, and you should go through the account list to rename the accounts to fit your circumstances. Select each account you want to rename, and press Ctrl-E. The account record opens in Edit Mode, and you can change the name.

Importing the UCOA

If you updated an existing QuickBooks company file (that did not have the UCOA) to QuickBooks 2006 Premier Nonprofit Edition, you can import the UCOA. Then you can edit and merge accounts to make sure your current balances are properly transferred to the UCOA accounts you want to use.

When you installed QuickBooks Premier Nonprofit Edition, the UCOA file was installed on your computer. To import it, follow these steps:

1. Choose File → Utilities → Import → IIF Files.
2. In the Import dialog, if the folder in which QuickBooks is installed isn't selected, navigate to that folder.
3. Select UCOA.IFF and click Open.

When the file is imported, QuickBooks issues a success message. Open the chart of accounts and see if you have duplicate, or nearly duplicate, accounts (your original chart of accounts may have the same, or similar, accounts as the UCOA). If so, delete unneeded duplicate accounts, or merge your original accounts with the new accounts that were installed with the UCOA. (See Chapter 2 for instructions on merging accounts).

Accounts Receivable

For nonprofits, tracking income source and income type is far more complex than it is in the for-profit business world. Tracking accounts receivable means creating transactions and reports about money owed or expected. That money has to be categorized by the type of income.

Using Multiple A/R Accounts

If you're using the UCOA, you have multiple A/R accounts, so you can track receivables by type. Depending on the type of income you generate, you may need to add more A/R accounts to your chart of account (and remove those you don't need).

If you're not using the UCOA, be sure to add the A/R accounts you need. Following are some of the A/R accounts I've entered in client files. These may not mirror your needs, but they should stimulate your thinking as you plan the A/R section of your chart of accounts.

- Accounts Receivable: Used for invoices for services or goods you sell.
- Grants Receivable: Used for invoices entered to track expected grants.
- Contracts Receivable: Used for invoices entered to track expected service contracts (commonly from government agencies).
- Tuition Fees Receivable: Used for invoices for tuition (if you are a school, or if you offer classes).
- Pledges Receivable: Used for invoices for pledges from individual donors.
- Dues Receivable: Used for invoices for membership dues.

Using A/R Accounts in Invoice Transactions

If you have multiple A/R accounts, all invoice transaction windows have a field named Account at the top of the window. You have to remember to enter the appropriate A/R account for the invoice you're creating.

NOTE: *Of course, as a nonprofit organization, your invoices are really records of pledges from individual donors, or of expected grants or contracts.*

Entering the A/R account does more than post the transaction to the right account—it affects the invoice numbering system. Invoice numbers are automatically incremented, using the last invoice number in the A/R account being used for the invoice transaction. This means each of your invoice types has its own, discrete, numbering system, which is quite handy.

Reporting on Receivables

Maintaining multiple A/R accounts means you can create reports on the money you're expecting (called an *aging report*), and display the information by category. This lets you determine how much money you're expecting, and the source of that money.

You can see how much money is due from grants, contracts, membership fees, pledged donations from individuals, and so on.

You can also customize an aging report for a particular category by filtering the report for a specific A/R account.

1. Choose Reports → Customers & Receivables → A/R Aging Summary.
2. Click the Modify Report button at the top of the report window.
3. Move to the Filters tab, where the Account field displays All Accounts Receivable.
4. Click the arrow in the Account field, and select the specific A/R account you need for this report.
5. Click OK.

The report displays the aging for the A/R account you selected (see Figure 14-1). You can customize a detail report in the same way, producing subtotals by donor.

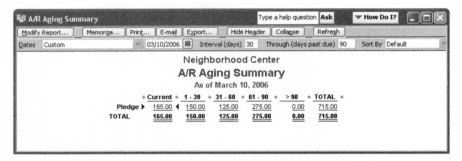

Figure 14-1: This report is an aging summary for pledges that haven't yet been received.

Using Classes

Nonprofit organizations can't use QuickBooks without using classes to track transactions. Without classes, getting the reports you need for funding agencies, government agencies, and your board of directors is extremely difficult. You either have to spend many hours (or days) analyzing each transaction and creating tallies outside of QuickBooks, or spend a lot of money to have your accountant perform tasks that wouldn't be necessary if you'd used classes.

You can think of a class as a division, or department. In the for-profit world, a business that has a main office in Philadelphia, and a branch office in Camden, would create classes named Phila and Camden. Every transaction would be assigned to a class, so the business owner can tell what the income and expenses are for each location. Because that business owner tracks income and expenses by class, she can create a Profit & Loss Statement (also called an *Income Statement*) for each class.

In the nonprofit world, we do the same thing, using classes to break down income and expenses by the categories we need to track. We can produce a Statement of Activities (the nonprofit term for an income statement) for each class.

At the very least, when you create reports and tax returns, you must provide the total amount for expenses in each of the following three categories:

- Program services
- Management (administration)
- Fundraising

In addition to preparing reports and tax returns with these categories, these are the expense breakdowns that funding agencies want to see when they consider your organization for grants. And, your board of directors probably wants to see expenses broken down by these categories.

Therefore, these are the classes to start with. You can create any additional classes and subclasses you need. For example, many nonprofit organizations create classes for special events, and for capital improvement projects.

In addition, you should create a class named Restricted or Restricted Funds, so you can track restricted income. Later, as the funds are moved to unrestricted use, you can track the movement by program (using the program classes).

"Program services" is a generic category that applies to the programs you run (the services you provide). You should have a specific class for each program, and you can accomplish that either by creating subclasses, or by using a discrete class for each program.

Having a class for each program lets you create a Statement of Activities for each class, and present the appropriate report to the funding agencies for programs. Figure 14-2 is a sample Class List for a community organization.

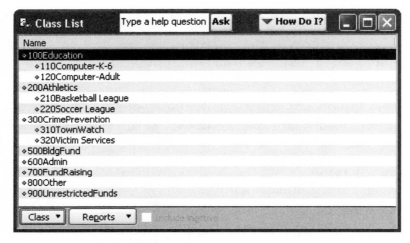

Figure 14-2: This community organization can track income and expenses for each funded program.

Customers and Jobs

QuickBooks didn't bother to change any component names or field names for the Premier Nonprofit Edition, so you have to live with the terms "customers" and "jobs".

- A customer is a donor, and a donor is any entity (individual or organization) from whom you receive revenue.
- A job is a grant or a contract. Each grant/contract that requires reporting must be entered as a discrete job.

Customers that don't require reports don't need jobs. This definition fits any entity that provides unrestricted funds, such as individual donors, tuition-payers, or members who pay fees.

Equity Accounts

QuickBooks provides two equity accounts automatically: Retained Earnings, and Opening Bal Equity. These equity accounts don't work properly for nonprofits.

A nonprofit organization requires multiple equity accounts (called *net asset* accounts), to wit:

- Permanently Restricted Net Assets
- Temporarily Restricted Net Assets
- Unrestricted Net Assets

If you're using the Unified Chart of Accounts, these equity accounts are available. If you're creating your own chart of accounts, or updating an existing chart of accounts, you must add the equity accounts required for nonprofits.

Many organizations add subaccounts to these equity accounts, in order to track details. As you post transactions to the subaccounts, you can link the transactions to programs or donors. The subtotals of the subaccounts are displayed as the total for the parent account when you create reports.

For example, you might want a structure similar to the following set of equity accounts:

- The Permanently Restricted Net Assets parent account could have subaccounts for endowments or restricted gifts.
- The Temporarily Restricted Net Assets parent account could have subaccounts named Restricted By Type and Restricted by Time.
- The Unrestricted Net Assets parent account could have a subaccount for Transfers. This account receives postings as you use transaction forms to bring funds in and out. Using transaction windows (invoices, sales receipts, vendor bills, direct disbursements, or journal entries) lets you assign classes and customers to the postings.

Even after you create all the net asset accounts you need, QuickBooks won't post transaction amounts to them. You have to create journal entries to move money from the Retained Earnings account to the appropriate net asset accounts.

Customized Templates for Transactions

QuickBooks Premier Nonprofit Edition includes some templates you can use for tracking income. Both of these templates are for donations from individuals, not for grants.

Pledges

Many donations start out as pledges, and nonprofit organizations have a number of creative methods for obtaining pledges from friends of the organization. You may have a pledge form that you hand out, a sign-up sheet that's passed around at an event, or even a website that contains a form to make a pledge.

Whatever you do to get pledges, when a pledge is promised you should record it in QuickBooks to make sure your financial reports are complete (a pledge, like an invoice in the for-profit world, is part of your accounts receivable assets).

QuickBooks Premier Nonprofit edition provides a template for a pledge, which is a standard QuickBooks invoice that's been customized. Open a blank pledge transaction window using one of these actions:

- In QuickBooks 2006 and later, click the Pledges icon in the Customers section of the Home page, or choose Nonprofit → Enter Pledges from the menu bar.
- In QuickBooks versions earlier than 2006, choose Nonprofit → Enter Pledges from the menu bar, or press Ctrl-I and select the Standard Pledge template from the drop-down list of templates in the Create Invoices window.

When the Standard Pledge form opens, it looks like Figure 14-3. If you're using the UCOA, select the Pledges Receivable account in the Account field at the top of the form. If you're not using the UCOA, you should add a Pledges Receivable account to your system. Notice that the title bar of the Pledge window contains the name of the A/R account you've assigned to the transaction.

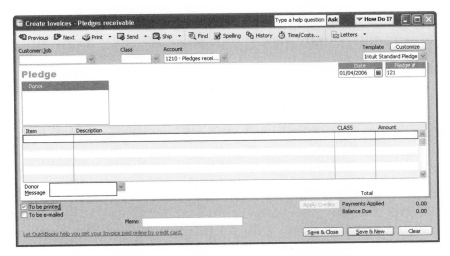

Figure 14-3: A Pledge is an accounts receivable transaction.

Using Pledges Efficiently

Unlike high-end (expensive) accounting software, QuickBooks isn't designed to provide an unlimited amount of data in its files. As QuickBooks files get large, the software operates more slowly.

TIP: Chapter 4 has information about the maximum number of entries in QuickBooks lists.

Many organizations receive pledges from hundreds, or thousands, of donors. Some of these donors are one-time givers, others give periodically (especially if you stay in touch with them).

If you receive a great many pledges, you don't have to track customer information for donors who pledge money within QuickBooks. You can track the names and other important information in another software application, such as a spreadsheet or database program. Then use the data in that software to correspond with to the people who made pledges.

The work you do in QuickBooks is designed to get the financial totals into the system, and it's not a good idea to try to keep customer records on a great many individuals. You probably have no reporting requirements that insist on listing every individual who pledges money.

Using a Generic Pledge Customer

Create a generic customer for pledges. Enter the generic name you want to use (e.g. Pledge) in the Customer Name field in the New Customer dialog. Don't enter any other information.

If you want to print and send pledge forms (as reminders), you still don't have to create a customer to get a name and address entered on the form. Instead, when you receive a pledge, open the Pledge form and follow these steps:

1. Select the generic customer.
2. In the Bill To section of the form, enter the donor's name and address.
3. Fill out the line detail with the appropriate item. If the donor indicated a pledge for a specific program, enter the program in the Class column; otherwise, assign the pledge to unrestricted funds.
4. Click the Print icon on the form window to print the pledge form.
5. Click Save & New to create another pledge, or click Save & Close if you're finished.
6. When QuickBooks displays the message asking you if you want to change the customer record to include the address you typed in the form, click No to prevent any changes in the generic customer record.

Incidentally, when you view the pledge later (by opening it from a report or by using the Previous button to move back through the pledges you entered), the name and address you entered on any individual form remains on the form.

If you use a generic customer for pledges, you don't have to enter each pledge individually. If you received twenty pledges on a given day enter the total amount in a single pledge template to record the total A/R (see Figure 14-4).

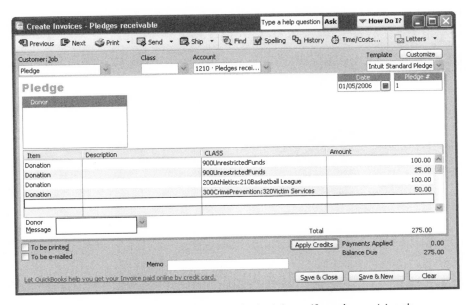

Figure 14-4: You can record pledges in batches, if you're not tracking information about each donor.

Donations

Donations differ from pledges because a donation is money. It's cash, a
check, or a credit card number (if you take credit cards). There's no
receivable; you can take the money right to the bank.

When you want to record a donation, QuickBooks Premier Nonprofit
Edition has a template named Intuit Standard Donation, which is better
suited to this situation than the regular sales receipt template (which is
named Custom Sales Receipt). To open this template, take one of the following actions:

- Click the Donations icon on the Home page.
- Choose Nonprofit → Enter Donations (Sales Receipts) from the
  menu bar.

When the Enter Sales Receipt window opens, click the arrow in the
Template field and select the template named Intuit Standard Donation.

The Donation template looks like the Custom Sales Receipt template, but it differs in two ways (see Figure 14-5):

- The word Donation appears at the top of the form, instead of Sales Receipt.
- The address block is labeled Donor instead of Sold To.

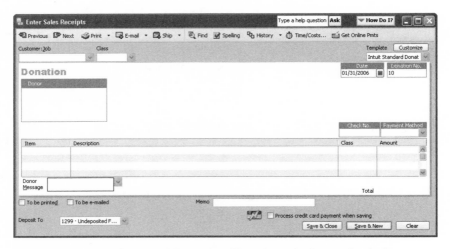

Figure 14-5: The Standard Donation Template works perfectly for cash donations.

You don't have to add each donor to your QuickBooks file. You can keep those names in another software application. Create a generic customer name (such as Donor), and post all donations to that customer.

If you want to print and mail a receipt to a particular donor, enter the name and address of the donor in the Donor address box. Then, print the form by clicking the Print icon on the form's window. When you save the transaction, QuickBooks asks you if the Donor record should be updated with this new address. Select No, because you don't want to add the address to the customer record of your generic donor.

Letter Templates

QuickBooks builds in some boilerplate documents you can use to send letters to your donors and potential donors. You can edit the letters to match your specific needs, and then use the mail merge feature in Microsoft Word to send the letters to customers (or people in your Other Names list). The following letters are included:

- Nonprofit Fund Raising Letter
- Nonprofit Thank You Letter

TIP: *After you fill out a Pledge form, click the Letters icon on the transaction window to automatically merge the data in the transaction to one of the predefined letters. This is a good way to thank a donor who has made a pledge, or to remind the donor to honor the pledge.*

Memorized Reports for Nonprofits

The Premier Nonprofit Edition provides useful reports that have been customized and memorized for this QuickBooks edition. Choose Reports → Memorized Reports → Nonprofit, and select one of the following memorized reports:

- Biggest Donors/Grants
- Budget vs. Actual by Donors/Grants
- Budget vs. Actual by Program/Projects
- Donors/Grants Report
- Programs/Projects Report
- Statement of Financial Income and Expense
- Statement of Financial Position
- Statement of Functional Expenses (990)

You can further customize any of these reports to meet your own needs, and then memorize them (using a new name for the memorized report).

Chapter 15

Professional Services Edition

Configuring your company file

Managing retainers

Managing customer deposits

Managing escrow

Customized templates

Customized reports

This is an interesting Premier edition. QuickBooks is extremely well suited for service businesses, and the Premier Professional Services Edition extends that innate strength. QuickBooks has built in transaction templates, customized reports, and other features that are designed with professional service providers in mind.

Company File

If you're new to QuickBooks, you have to create a company file, and QuickBooks offers several predefined files you can adopt as your own file. The predefined files aren't marked as such; you have to know what to choose during the company setup procedure to select a file that's built for professional service providers.

A predefined file has a chart of accounts, list entries, and configuration preferences preset to make it easier to manage your business with QuickBooks.

If you've upgraded to Premier Professional Services Edition from another version of QuickBooks, you should tweak your company file to take advantage of the features available in this Premier edition.

Creating a Company File

If you're just starting to use QuickBooks, the first time you launch the software, the Welcome to QuickBooks window offers an option to create a new company file. Alternatively, you can choose File → New Company. Either action opens the EasyStep Interview.

You can use the interview to set up your company file, or create the file manually. However, if you want to locate one of the predefined company files geared for professional service providers, the EasyStep Interview makes it easier to locate the selection you need.

Using the EasyStep Interview

Click the Start Interview button to begin setting up your company. In the first window (see Figure 15-1), the only required entry is your company name. However, some documents you produce in QuickBooks print your company information, so it's best to fill in all the fields. (You can also complete the information later, by choosing Company → Company Information from the QuickBooks menu bar.)

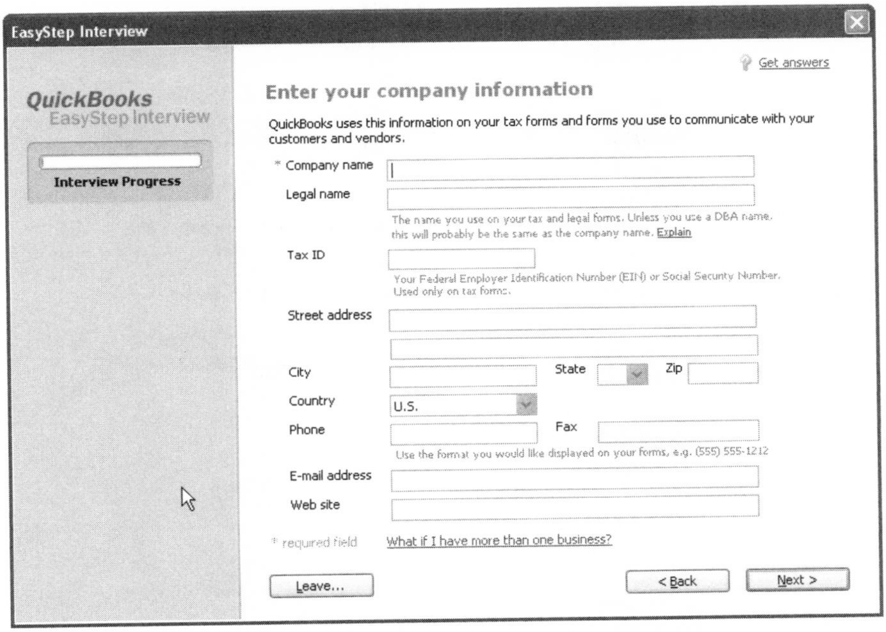

Figure 15-1: The first step is to enter basic information about your company.

In the next window, you can create a password for the QuickBooks administrator. You're the administrator, because you're the one setting up the company file, and also because you're the one who knows the password.

A password isn't necessary if you don't share the company file with other users, either on this computer or over a network. If you do share the company file with other users, you can establish the password later.

Follow the prompts in the next wizard windows to save your company file. QuickBooks automatically names the file to match the company name you entered in the first wizard window, but you can change the filename if you wish.

In the next window, the wizard offers a list of industries and specific businesses within those industries. Because you're running the Premier Professional Services Edition, the wizard displays the section of the list that covers professional services (see Figure 15-2). Scroll through the list of business types to find the listing that's closest to your company's mission.

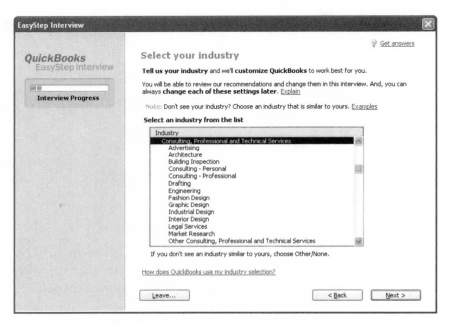

Figure 15-2: Choose an industry and a business type that matches your business.

No matter which business type you select, the chart of accounts that QuickBooks automatically loads for the company file will be a good starting point for developing the chart of accounts you need.

However, some of the selections in the listings under Consulting, Professional and Technical Services are really predefined company files, even though they're not marked or highlighted to point that out.

The following business type listings have additional entries and configuration options that make it easier to set up your QuickBooks system.

If your business matches one of these categories, you can save a lot of time in company setup:

- Advertising
- Architecture
- Building Inspection
- Consulting—Professional
- Consulting—Personal
- Drafting
- Engineering
- Graphic Design
- Industrial Design
- Interior Design
- Legal Services
- Other Consulting, Professional and Technical Services
- Other Design Services
- Surveying & Mapping

Continue to click Next to move through the wizard, answering questions and making selections.

WARNING: Don't enter an opening balance for your bank account if you opt to create the bank account during the interview. Enter the bank account's opening balance by following the instructions in Chapter 2.

Creating the Company File Manually

You can skip the EasyStep Interview, and configure your company file manually. When the first wizard window appears, click Skip Interview to display the Creating New Company dialog seen in Figure 15-3.

When you create a company file manually, you can enter the income tax form you use, and QuickBooks will add tax form information to the accounts in your chart of accounts. This is helpful if you do your own taxes (each account that requires entries on tax forms is identified by the form and line number).

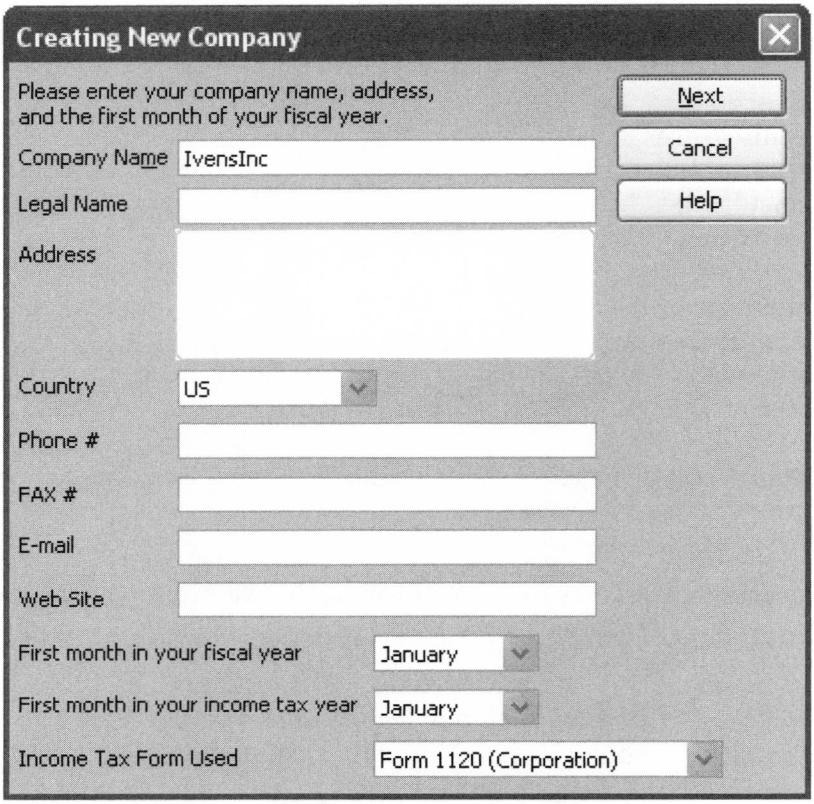

Figure 15-3: Enter company information to begin the company file setup.

Click Next and select the type of business you operate from the left pane of the dialog (see Figure 15-4). Refer to the list in the previous section to choose a business type that produces a file that has predefined entries.

QuickBooks saves the company file, using the company name you entered in the first dialog (which you can change). Use the instructions in Chapters 2, 3, and 4 to tweak your company file settings so they work perfectly for your business.

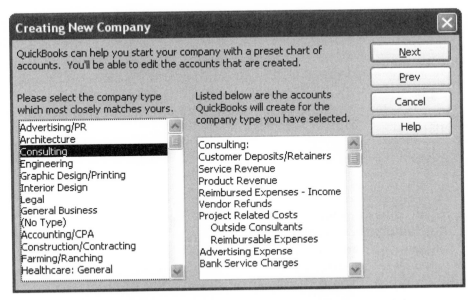

Figure 15-4: Select the business type that comes closest to matching your company.

Tweaking an Existing Company File

If you're updating an existing company file to Premier Professional
Services Edition, you should look at the configuration settings and list
entries that QuickBooks provides in the predefined company files, and in
the sample files.

To use a predefined company file as a reference, create a new company as described in the previous section. Then, examine the settings and
lists to see if there are any ideas you can use in your own file.

You can also open one of the sample files to see how it's configured.
You may find some good ideas for tweaking your chart of accounts, lists,
or preferences. To open a sample file, choose File → Open Company and
select one of the sample professional services files:

- Sample_Consulting Business.QBW
- Sample_Engineering Firm.QBW

- Sample_Graphic Design Agency.QBW
- Sample_Law Firm.QBW
- Sample_Service-Based Business.QBW

You can make notes about the configuration options you think would be useful in your file. You can export a list that seems appropriate for your business, and then import it into your own company file.

Lists

If you created your company file from a preconfigured file, many of your preferences are already set up appropriately, and some of the lists (such as the Customer & Vendor Profile Lists) are populated with entries. If you upgraded from another version of QuickBooks, you've probably developed the list entries you need. In this section, I'll discuss some of the concepts you should consider for developing lists in a service business.

Customers and Jobs List

Most professional service businesses should track jobs for customers. Even if the work you do for a customer doesn't seem to fit the description of a "job", it's best to set up a job, so you can later track special projects with additional jobs.

Even if some customers don't want reports and invoices on a job basis, tracking jobs gives you internal information about your business. You can track job costs and profitability, and analyze the types of jobs or projects that generate the most income.

TIP: Lawyers who have personal injury practices often provide advance money for doctors and other expenses before a case is settled. A job cost report works well as a settlement sheet when the insurance check arrives.

Items

Most of the items you create for a professional service company are of the item type Service. You should plan your items to make sure you can track each type of service for job costing, and for profitability reports.

If you have services that are provided by non-employees, be sure to set up service items for that scenario. Create a service item for this circumstance, and select the option This Service Is Performed By A Subcontractor, Owner, Or Partner. Selecting that option changes the New Item dialog to include fields for tracking both costs and revenue. This means you can track profitability for the item.

If you're going to track time, remember to set up service items for unbillable time, so you can track those totals. Create a parent item named unbillable time, and then create subitems to cover meetings, proposal writing, sales calls, administrative tasks, and so on. Using those services with the QuickBooks Timesheet feature lets you track your expenses, including overhead, quite closely.

NOTE: Most professional service businesses bill for time. To learn how to use all the timekeeping features in QuickBooks, read chapters 18 and 19 of QuickBooks 2006: The Official Guide, a copy of which is in your Premier edition software box.

Customer and Vendor Types

Create Customer Types and Vendor Types to match the way you want to separate customers and vendors when you produce reports. In addition, bear in mind the types you need for analyzing your business—where your business comes from, and where you spend money. For example, you may want to track customers by referral type, which lets you analyze the effects of your advertising and marketing.

On the other hand, you may prefer to use business types as your customer types, separating lawyers, doctors, engineers, and so on. Then, you can contact customer types if you expand your service offerings to match a need of a specific business type. You can create reports on profitability and receivables by type, and if you discover that some types of customers don't pay well, or aren't profitable, you can adjust the way you plan sales calls.

If you selected a predefined company file during setup, your file may already have entries in the Customer Type and Vendor Type lists. Some of these preloaded entries may not suit your purposes, so you can remove them and create your own.

Billing Rate Levels

The Premier Professional Services Edition includes the Billing Rate Level List, which lets you assign a billing rate to a person performing a specific service. This means you can bill the time of a senior associate at a different rate than a junior associate who is performing the same service.

All the instructions you need to create, assign, and apply billing rate levels are in Chapter 4. After you create billing rate levels, and associate them with service providers, invoicing for services becomes automatic. Every time you create an invoice with billable time, QuickBooks automatically fills in the correct rate for the service, based on the person who performed the work.

Classes

Classes let you track your business in a divisional manner, and then produce divisional Profit & Loss Reports. The way you use classes depends on the organization of your business. Here are a few of the common class tracking scenarios for service businesses (to stimulate your thinking):

- Tracking multiple offices. In recent years, I've seen this class structure applied in companies that run virtual offices (everybody works from home and the company pays some of the home office expenses).
- Tracking partners.
- Tracking service divisions. A law firm may have a domestic relations division and a personal injury division. An advertising agency may have a creative division, and a media buying division.

Income is linked to the appropriate class when creating invoices or sales receipt transactions. Expenses that are specific to a class are linked to that class during vendor transactions (bills, checks, or credit card purchases).

Allocating Overhead with Classes

Create a class for general administration, so you can allocate overhead among the divisions you're tracking with classes. Allocations are performed with a journal entry at a regular interval. You can allocate expenses monthly, quarterly, or at the end of your fiscal year.

General office expenses are posted through normal transaction entries (vendor bills, checks, or credit card purchases). All of these transactions are posted to the Administration class. These expenses can include rent, payroll (including employer payroll expenses), utilities, insurance, web hosting, online services, and so on.

Creating Allocation Journal Entries

To allocate overhead expenses, create a journal entry that moves the funds from the Administration class to the divisions you're tracking by class. For example, Table 15-1 shows a portion of a typical allocation journal entry (the portion that allocates the monthly $900.00 rent). Originally, a check for $900.00 was sent to the landlord, and the transaction was linked to the Administration class. The allocating journal entry has two parts:

- It washes out the expense (credits the debit) and links that action to the Administration class (the original posting class).
- It creates a debit for each class, and the total of those debits equals the amount of the credit.

Account	Debit	Credit	Class
Rent		900	Administration
Rent	300		Partner #1
Rent	300		Partner #2
Rent	300		Partner #3

Table 15-1: Allocating overhead among classes.

You don't have to allocate 100% of an overhead expense; you can allocate some of the expense and leave the remaining amount in the Administrative class. Some companies allocate different amounts to each class, using a formula that reflects a logical allocation. For example, I have clients who first determine the percentage of income each class provided to the business for the month, and then allocate overhead by a matching percentage.

Memorizing Allocation Journal Entries

If you have a sizeable list of overhead expenses, building your journal entry from scratch every month is too onerous. Instead, create a journal entry for this purpose (see Figure 15-5), and memorize it, using the following steps:

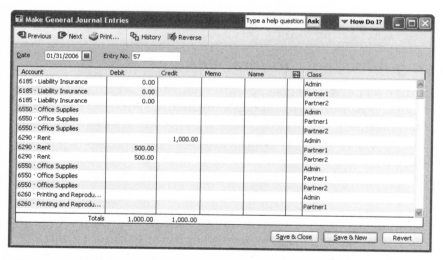

Figure 15-5: Preload a journal entry with your allocations, and memorize it.

1. Enter each expense account as many times as needed (the number of classes including the administrative class).
2. In the Debit and Credit columns, enter the amounts that are constant (such as rent), and leave the amounts that vary blank (you fill them in each month).
3. In the Class column, enter the class name.

4. After all the accounts and classes are entered, memorize the journal entry by pressing Ctrl-M.

5. Enter a name for this memorized transaction, such as Allocations.

6. Specify whether you want QuickBooks to remind you to create the journal entry, and if so, set the reminder.

7. Click OK to return to the Make General Journal Entries window.

8. Close the window by clicking the X in the upper right corner—do not click Save & Close, do not click Save & New.

9. When QuickBooks asks if you want to record the transaction, click No (you're building a template, you're not entering a transaction, and you don't have to save a journal entry to memorize it).

When it's time to allocate overhead, press Ctrl-T to open the Memorized Transaction list. Select this allocation journal entry, enter the appropriate data, and save it.

Managing Retainers

Many professional service providers work with some, or all, customers on a retainer basis. The customer sends a certain amount of money that is held as a deposit against future invoices.

When you receive a payment for a retainer, it isn't income. It becomes income when you earn it, at which point you create an invoice or a cash receipt to turn it into revenue.

To manage retainers, you need to set up the following components in your company file:

• A liability account to track the retainer funds.
• A retainer item.

Ideally, you should create a bank account to hold retainer funds. The bank account doesn't have to be a real, separate, bank account; instead, you can use a virtual bank account to make sure you don't spend customers' funds inappropriately.

Lawyers are required to maintain separate bank accounts for client funds, but in most states, that rule doesn't cover retainers. However, escrow funds for clients have to be deposited into a separate escrow account. Other service businesses, such as real estate professionals and agents, also maintain escrow accounts. See the section "Managing Escrow", later in this chapter.

Liability Accounts for Retainers

You need a liability account to track retainers. If you used one of the pre-defined company files included with Premier Professional Services Edition, the account exists.

Depending on the specific type of business you chose when you set up your company file, the account may be named Customer Deposits/Retainers, Customer Deposits, or Client Retainers. If your chart of accounts doesn't have this account, create a new Other Current Liability account and name it Retainers or something similar.

Some businesses prefer to separate retainers from other types of upfront deposits. If your chart of accounts has the Deposits/Retainers liability account, you can rename the account Deposits, and create another Other Current Liability account named Retainers.

Even better, create an account named Client Funds, and then create subaccounts for deposits and retainers. Only use the subaccounts in transactions. When you view the chart of accounts, or create reports that include your liability accounts, the parent account reports the total of the amounts in the subaccounts.

Retainer Items

You need an item for retainers, which you use when you create transactions involving retainers. If you installed a predefined company file, the item exists, although the name of the item differs depending on the specific business type you selected. For example, you may see an item named Upfront Deposits.

The pre-populated Upfront Deposits item is an Other Charge type, because it's assumed you'll use it to collect deposits on products you purchase for your customers. Retainers are usually Service items. If you manage both retainers and upfront deposits, you should have two items, so you can track them (and create reports about them) separately.

To create an item for retainers, use the following guidelines:

- The type of item is Service.
- The rate is zero, because it's customer-specific, and is therefore entered at the time you create the transaction.
- The account to which it's linked is the liability account you use to track retainers.

Virtual Bank Accounts for Retainers

Most users put retainer funds into the business bank account. Separate escrow accounts are used to hold customer escrow money (covered later in this chapter), but retainer funds are often deposited to the regular business account.

If your retainer and regular funds are co-mingled in a single account, you should consider using virtual bank accounts to separate retainer funds from operating funds. When you use the operating account to pay your business expenses, the balance won't include the retainer amounts you're holding. This makes it easier to avoid spending retainer money.

In addition, having a bank account for retainer funds (whether real or virtual) provides a quick way to check the status of retainer funds. The amount in the bank account should always equal the amount in the retainer liability account.

Creating Subaccounts as Virtual Accounts

Virtual bank accounts are subaccounts of your business bank account. Create a bank account if your chart of accounts doesn't already have one (this becomes the *parent account*). Then, open the chart of accounts window and create subaccounts as follows:

1. Press Ctrl-N to open the New Account dialog.
2. Select Bank as the account type.

3. Enter a number for the virtual operating account (if you're using account numbers). Use a number one digit higher than the number of your bank account. For example, if your bank account number is 1010, make the new account 1011.
4. Enter a name for the new account, such as Operating Funds.
5. Select the option Subaccount Of, and select your bank account from the drop-down list in the text box.
6. Optionally, enter a description of this account.
7. Click Next to open a blank New Account dialog, which has Bank selected as the account type.
8. Enter the next highest number as the account number.
9. Enter a name, such as Retainer Funds.
10. Select the option Subaccount Of, and select your bank account from the drop-down list in the text box.
11. Optionally, enter a description.
12. Click OK.

In the chart of accounts window, your subaccounts are listed (and indented) under your bank account.

Transferring Funds to Subaccounts

After your bank subaccounts are created, you need to transfer the appropriate amounts into each subaccount. The main bank account should have a zero balance, although it displays the total of the balances of the subaccounts when you view the chart of accounts.

Create a journal entry to transfer the funds. Credit the entire current balance of the bank account, and debit the appropriate amounts for each subaccount (see Figure 15-6).

When you open the chart of accounts window, the balance displayed for the main bank account is the total of the balances in the subaccounts. Balance sheet reports and trial balance reports display the balances of the subaccounts (with no balance in the parent account).

Managing Deposits to Subaccounts

Your QuickBooks company file configuration probably enables the Undeposited Funds account. This means when you create transactions for received funds (customer payments of invoices, or cash receipts), the money is deposited into the Undeposited Funds account.

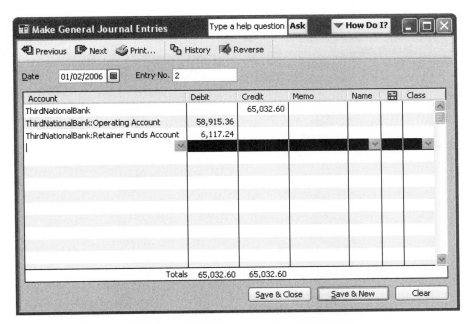

Figure 15-6: Empty the parent bank account, and fill the subaccounts.

When you deposit the funds in the bank, you use the Make Deposits feature to transfer the funds into a bank account. This is the best way to manage bank deposits, because it matches the way your bank statement reports deposits. However, if you're using virtual bank accounts via subaccounts, it complicates your life.

When you move revenue from the Undeposited Funds account into the appropriate bank account, you have to separate regular income from retainer income. Select all the regular income, and deposit that in the operating bank account. Select all the retainer receipts, and deposit them in the retainer bank account.

Often, this isn't an easy task, because you can't tell which income is for regular earned income, and which is for retainer payments. As you can see in Figure 15-7, nothing in the Payments to Deposit transaction window tells you which receipts are for retainers, and which are for regular income.

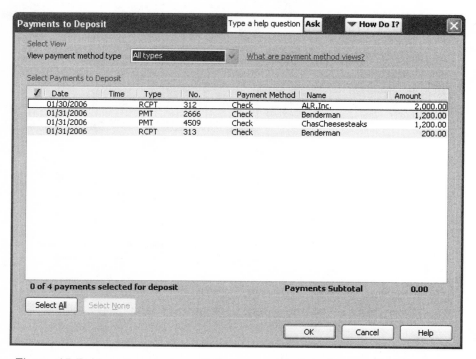

Figure 15-7: How do you deposit these receipts into the appropriate bank?

The only way to resolve this dilemma is to come up with a solution that announces itself in the Payments to Deposit window. Using the Memo field in a customer payment transaction window doesn't work, because memo text isn't displayed in this window.

For my clients, I solved the problem with a new payment method. I created a payment method named Retainer, with a payment type of Other (see Figure 15-8).

When retainers arrive, either as a payment against an invoice, or as a cash receipt, the sales transaction window is marked with the Retainer

Payment type. The transaction window continues to accept the customer's check number (always important to record in case of any disputes with the customer).

- In the Receive Payment transaction window, when you select Retainer (or any other payment method classified as Other), the Check # field changes its name to Reference #.

- In the Enter Sales Receipts transaction window, when you select Retainer (or any other payment method classified as Other), the Check No. field doesn't change its label.

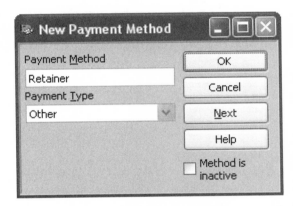

Figure 15-8: Create payment methods that help you identify which bank account should get the deposits.

When you use the new Retainer payment method in transactions, the Payments to Deposit window is much easier to work with. As you can see in Figure 15-9, retainers are clearly discernable.

To automate the deposit of different payment types to different bank accounts, use the following steps:

1. Click the arrow next to the View Payment Method Type field at the top of the Payments to Deposit window, and choose Selected Types from the drop-down list.
2. In the Selected Types dialog, choose Other.
3. Click OK to return to the Payments to Deposit window, where only your retainer payments are displayed.

4. Click Select All to select all your retainer deposits, and then click OK to open the Make Deposits window.
5. Select the Retainer bank account, and click Save & New to return to the Payments to Deposit window.
6. Select All Types at the top of the window, and click Select All to select the remaining payments.
7. Click OK to open the Make Deposits window, and select the Operating bank account.
8. Click Save & Close.

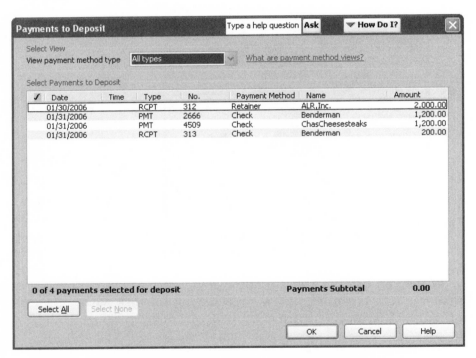

Figure 15-9: You can separate payments by type when depositing funds into a bank account.

Reconciling Bank Accounts with Subaccounts

When you reconcile the bank account, use the parent account. Because your subaccounts are virtual bank accounts, instead of real separate bank accounts, the parent account actually maintains all the activity in the bank register.

After you fill out the Bank Reconciliation window displays all the transactions for both accounts. In fact, as you can see in Figure 15-10, the parent account doesn't pay any attention at all to the fact that there are subaccounts; this is just a regular bank reconciliation and no transaction shows any indication of being initiated from a subaccount.

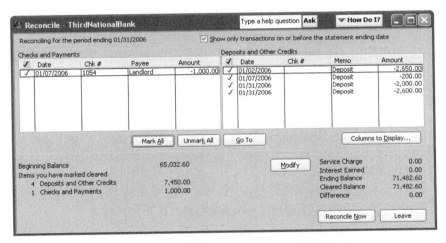

Figure 15-10: When you reconcile the parent account, the system ignores the fact that subaccounts exist.

Invoicing a Retainer Customer for Services

The retainers you hold aren't your funds; they belong to your customers. They become your funds when you earn them, at which point they become revenue. When you invoice your customer for services performed, you transfer retainer funds to income.

To invoice a retainer customer, create an invoice as usual, using the following guidelines:

- Enter the appropriate items in the line item section of the invoice (including discounts).

- The last line item in the invoice is the retainer item, which you enter with a minus sign.
- If the retainer balance is larger than the invoice amount, apply a retainer amount equal to the invoice amount.
- If the retainer balance is smaller than the invoice amount, apply the entire retainer balance.
- In the Memo field, enter text to indicate retainer funds were applied to the invoice.
- Save the invoice.

You can print and send the invoice to the client, but many businesses don't bother sending individual invoices to retainer customers (especially because the invoices almost always have a zero total). Instead, they periodically send a report on the retainer balance.

There's a big problem with the scenario I just described. You have no indication on the invoice form of the client's retainer balance. You must ascertain that information before you create invoices. To do that, you have to create a report on retainer balances (see the section "Tracking Retainer Balances").

Postings for Applying Retainer Funds

When you create an invoice and apply retainer funds to the invoice, QuickBooks posts the amounts as follows:

- The income account(s) attached to the items in the invoice are credited, and Accounts Receivable is debited.
- The Customer Retainers liability account is debited, and Accounts Receivable is credited (because the line item is a negative amount).

NOTE: If the amount of the retainer applied equals the invoice total, the invoice is a zero amount invoice. If you view the invoice, you'll see the PAID stamp in the transaction window.

Moving Retainer Funds

After you invoice retainer customers, the retainer amounts you applied to the invoices are no longer the customers' funds, they're your funds, and you can spend them. In addition your retainer liability account balance no longer matches the retainer bank subaccount balance.

Both of these circumstances are resolved by transferring the funds in the liability account to the operating account. You have two methods at your disposal:

Use a journal entry (on the Company menu) to credit the liability subaccount and debit the operating subaccount.

Use the transfer funds transaction feature (on the Banking menu), as seen in Figure 15-11.

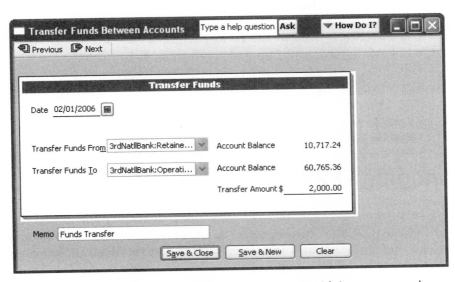

Figure 15-11: Move funds from the retainer account into your operating account.

> **NOTE**: *If you're keeping retainer funds in a separate bank account instead of using subaccounts, write a check or use an online transfer function to move the funds to your operating account.*

Tracking Retainer Balances

You need to keep an eye on customer retainer balances, so when you create invoices you know whether there are sufficient funds to apply against an invoice. To do this, you must create a Retainer Report, using the following steps:

1. Choose Reports → Customers & Receivables→ Customer Balance Detail.
2. In the report window, click Modify Report.
3. In the Filters tab, select Account in the Filters List.
4. In the Account field, select the Customer Retainers liability account.
5. Click OK to return to the report window (see Figure 15-12).
6. Click Memorize and name the report (e.g. Retainer Balances).

> **TIP**: *You can make the retainer balance report cleaner and easier to read (and print) by deselecting the Class and Balance columns in the Columns list on the Display tab.*

Managing Upfront Deposits

Under certain circumstances, you may ask a customer for an upfront deposit against a job. This is particularly important if the job requires you to lay out substantial funds, perhaps to hire a subcontractor, or purchase a product.

> **NOTE**: *Some companies collect a certain percentage of the estimated cost of a job up front as a standard policy.*

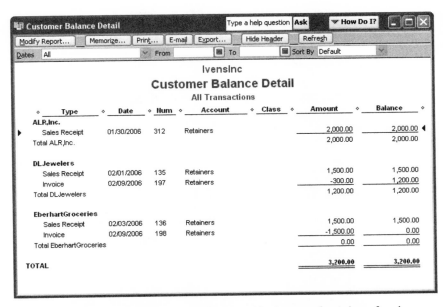

Figure 15-12: Track the use and current balance of retainer funds.

To open the memorized report in the future, choose Reports →
Memorized Reports List, and select this report.

When you receive a deposit, you cannot record the receipt as income.
You haven't yet earned the money; it still belongs to the customer.
Therefore, it's a liability to your company.

Creating Accounts for Upfront Deposits

You need a liability account to track customer deposits, of the type Other
Current Liability. Name the account Customer Deposits, or something
similar.

If you also collect retainers from clients, you can use a single account
for both types of funds. However, I tend to be a purist about these things,
so I prefer separate liability accounts.

If you have both retainers and upfront deposits to track, you can also
set up virtual bank accounts for both types of customer funds, as well as

a subaccount for operating funds. See the discussion on creating virtual bank accounts with subaccounts in the previous section on tracking retainers.

TIP: In fact, the best way to handle a mixture of retainers and upfront deposits is to create a liability account named Customer Funds, and then create separate bank subaccounts for retainers and upfront deposits.

Creating Items for Upfront Deposits

You need to create an item for upfront deposits, so you can record the deposit activities in sales forms. The type of item you create depends on the circumstances under which you ask customers for deposits.

- For upfront deposits on services, create a Service item.
- If you only ask for upfront deposits when you have to purchase products, create an Other Charge item.
- If you collect deposits under both circumstances, choose either type of item—flip a coin.

Link the item to the liability account you created for customer upfront deposits.

Receiving Upfront Deposits

Most of the time, the receipt of an upfront deposit is the result of a conversation or a written proposal. It's not common to create an invoice for a deposit, so when the customer's check arrives it's a sales receipt.

Whether you use an invoice or a sales receipt, the way you fill out the transaction window remains the same. Enter the upfront deposit item, and enter the amount.

If you use an invoice, QuickBooks posts the transaction as follows:

- Debits Accounts Receivable
- Credits the Upfront Deposit liability account.

If you use a sales receipt, QuickBooks creates the following postings:

- Debits the Undeposited Funds account.
- Credits the Upfront Deposit liability account.

If you don't use the Undeposited Funds account, and instead you deposit the funds to a bank account (the subaccount you created for customer deposits), that bank account receives the debit posting.

If you use the Undeposited Funds account, and you want to deposit the funds into the Customer Deposits subaccount of your bank account, use the instructions earlier in this chapter for separating the funds in the Payments to Deposit window. Create a new Payment Method named Upfront Deposit and make it a type Other, and use the drop-down list in the Payments to Deposit window to display only the type Other.

However, the display of payment methods of the Other type includes both retainers and upfront deposits (if you happen to have both types of customer receipts on the same day). This doesn't work well if you have two separate subaccounts to track these customer advance payments. There are two solutions:

- Keep notes on what each cash receipt is for, select only the retainers, and deposit them to the retainers bank account. Then select the upfront deposits, and deposit them to the upfront deposits bank account.
- When you enter the customer's check number in the original transaction window (either a Sales Receipt or a Receive Payments transaction), put a letter in front of the check number: R for retainer, U for upfront deposit. Because the check number appears in the Payments to Deposit window, this makes it easier to select the right listings in that window.

Applying an Upfront Deposit to an Invoice

To create the invoice against which you need to apply the upfront deposit, open the Create Invoices transaction window. Fill out the invoice with the items you've sold the customer. For the last item, use the upfront deposit item you created, and enter the amount of the deposit with a minus sign (see Figure 15-13).

QuickBooks posts the invoice in the following manner:

- The income account(s) attached to the item(s) on the invoice are credited.
- The liability account attached to the discount item is debited.
- The A/R account is debited for the balance due.

If you're maintaining subaccounts of your bank account to separate deposits from operating funds, transfer the amount of the discount you applied to the operating funds. (See the instructions earlier in this chapter for transferring funds between bank subaccounts.)

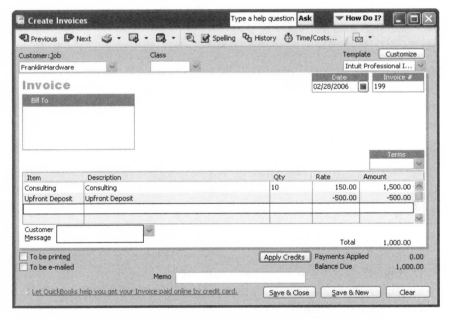

Figure 15-13: Apply the deposit against the total of the services or products you sold.

Upfront Deposits that are Just Payments in Advance

Sometimes, a customer deposit is nothing more than an advance payment. This usually means that the job or product is delivered to the customer in a short time. (You shouldn't hold deposits for long jobs unless you treat the deposits as liabilities.)

In this circumstance, you can create an invoice, apply the advance payment, and then hold the invoice until you deliver the services or products. You don't have to treat the advance payment as a liability.

Creating an Advance Payment Item

To use an advance payment, you must create an item for it. In the New Item dialog, select Payment as the Item type, and name the item Advance Payment or Payment in Advance. As you can see in Figure 15-14, items of the type Payment don't have a lot of fields to fill out.

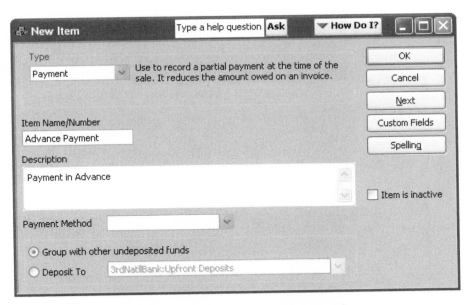

Figure 15-14: Set up an item to handle payments in advance on an invoice.

The description field is optional, but you should enter the text you want to appear in the invoice, to make it clear to the customer that the advance has been applied to the invoice. The payment type is also optional.

Select the Undeposited Funds account as the account that receives the deposit. If you don't use the Undeposited Funds account, select the operating account.

Applying an Advance Payment to an Invoice

In QuickBooks, you receive an advance payment and create an invoice at the same time. The advance is not treated separately as a sales receipt or a payment against an existing invoice.

Enter the item(s) you're selling the customer, and then enter the Advance Payment item. Do *not* enter a minus sign; Payment type items are automatically deductions, so QuickBooks automatically enters the minus sign.

The invoice total is the net of the sale less the advance payment (see Figure 15-15).

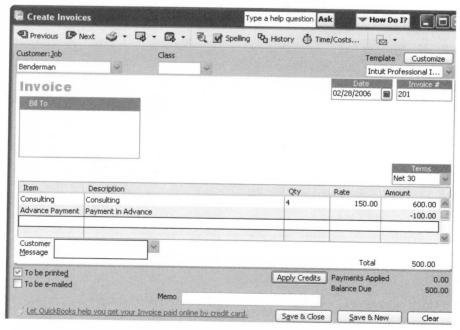

Figure 15-15: Create an invoice and apply the advance payment.

Depositing Advance Payments

When you apply an advance payment to an invoice, QuickBooks automatically deposits the money. If you linked the advance payment item to the Undeposited Funds account, the next time you use the Payments to Deposit window, the advance payment is there (see Figure 15-16). The payment is differentiated by the code INV in the Type column.

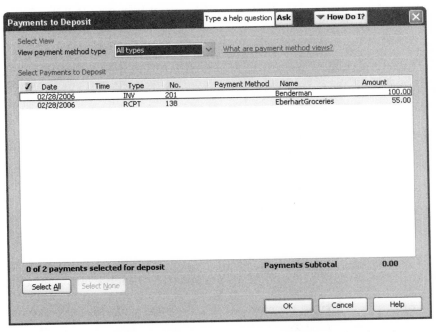

Figure 15-16: Advance payments are automatically received and deposited.

Managing Escrow

Managing escrow funds differs from managing retainers and deposits in two respects:

- The funds belong to your client, but are not collected from that client. Instead, they're collected from a third party on behalf of your client.

• The rules for managing escrow funds are mandated by state law and the rules of your professional association.

All states require attorneys to maintain a separate bank account for escrow funds, and to impose bookkeeping procedures for tracking escrow funds as liabilities.

Professional associations and general conventions impose similar rules on other professions, such a realtors, agents, and others who collect funds on behalf of clients.

To manage escrow you must open a separate bank account for escrow funds. In QuickBooks, you must create the following accounts in your chart of accounts:

• A bank account for the escrow account.
• A current liability account to track escrowed funds (usually named Funds Held In Trust).

TIP: *If you used the predefined file for law practices to set up your company file, the accounts you need to track escrow transactions are already in the chart of accounts.*

If you need more than one "real" escrow bank account, you must create a bank account in your chart of accounts for each escrow account.

If you have multiple escrow bank accounts, you can still use one liability account for escrowed funds. Because all transactions are linked to a customer, your customer reports make it easy to ascertain which funds belong to which customer. On the other hand, you may be more comfortable using subaccounts to separate the liability account by category.

Customized Templates

The Premier Professional Services Edition offers several customized templates you can use to create transactions. You can use these templates as-is, or as the basis of further customizations.

Customized Invoice Templates

The customized invoice templates are designed to tweak standard Intuit invoice templates so they use the right jargon (which is a slick professional touch). For example, the Time & Expense invoice template has a column named Hours/Qty instead of the standard Qty heading that's more appropriate for product sales. The Fixed Fee invoice template has a simplified design that omits any columns for quantity, and adds a Date column.

Customized Proposal Template

If you create proposals, QuickBooks has a Proposal template available when you choose the Create Estimates command from the Customers menu (or the Create Proposals & Estimates command from the Professional menu).

This Proposal template has a column titled Est. Hours/Qty. If you wish, you can customize this template to eliminate the text Qty from the column heading.

TIP: Use the Invoice button on the Proposal template to create an invoice automatically.

Customized Reports

The Premier Professional Services Edition includes a well thought out list of reports that have been customized for service providers. Choose Reports → Professional Services Reports to display the list.

Chapter 16

Retail Edition

Predefined company files

Advanced inventory features

Upfront deposits

Layaways

Gift certificates

Selling on consignment

Point of Sale add-ons

Customized reports

The Premier Retail Edition is designed to help you track retail sales efficiently. While I wouldn't try to use QuickBooks to run a supermarket that has to track thousands of inventory items, the Premier Retail Edition works well for small retailers.

In this chapter, I'll go over some the features and functions available in your copy of QuickBooks Premier Retail Edition software.

Using Predefined Company Files for Retailers

If you're new to QuickBooks, the first time you launch the software, the Welcome window offers an option to create a new company file. Alternatively, you can choose File → New Company. Either action opens the EasyStep Interview wizard, which walks you through the process of setting up your company.

During the company file setup process, QuickBooks asks you to describe the type of business you have. The retail industry offerings are predefined company files (even though the wizard doesn't indicate that fact). Predefined company files have had Preferences set to match the predefined industry type you selected. The files also contain the following prepopulated components:

- Chart of Accounts
- Item list (including sales tax items)
- Class list
- Tax Code list
- Customer Type list
- Vendor Type list
- Terms list
- Customer Message list
- Payment Method list
- Ship Via list

Some of the list entries lack specific settings (such as the entries in the Items list), and others have generic names you'll want to change.

Using the EasyStep Interview

If you want to use a wizard to set up your file, click Start Interview. Then step through the wizard windows, answering questions and providing information. The questions and fill-in fields are self-explanatory.

The wizard creates a QuickBooks company file, named to reflect the information you entered about your company name. After you save your company file, the wizard offers the opportunity to select your industry type (see Figure 16-1).

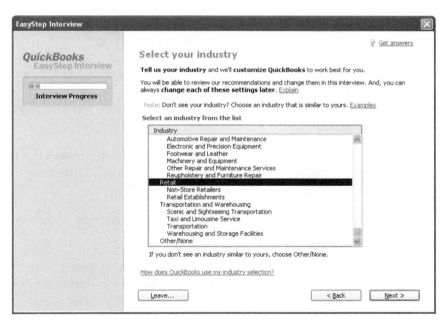

Figure 16-1: The wizard displays the Retail industry choices automatically, because you're running the Premier Retail Edition.

TIP: The wizard offers two business types for the retail industry, and it doesn't really matter which you choose; the resulting predefined file settings are the same.

In the ensuing windows, the wizard asks you to provide some details about your business, such as whether you sell services in addition to products, and whether you want to track customers by name, or merely summarize daily sales.

You don't need to give a great deal of thought to answering these questions, because your responses aren't etched in stone. For example, if you tell the wizard you don't create invoices because you sell for cash, you can still create invoices when needed. QuickBooks does not turn any feature on or off permanently as a result of your responses.

Creating the Company File Manually

If you don't want to work your way through the EasyStep Interview wizard windows, click Skip Interview on the opening window. The Creating New Company dialog opens so you can supply information about your business (see Figure 16-2).

Only the Company Name field is required, but you should fill in the address and contact information because it's displayed on transaction forms and reports.

Click Next, and select the business type that matches your company (see Figure 16-3).

The predefined company file that's installed when you create your company file manually is similar to the file that's installed when you select a retail business in the EasyStep Interview.

Tweaking an Existing Company File

If you're updating an existing company file to Premier Retail Edition, you should look at the configuration settings and list entries that QuickBooks provides in the predefined company files, or in the sample files.

To use a predefined company file as a reference, create a new company as described in the previous section. Then, examine the settings and lists to see if there are any ideas you can use in your own file.

Figure 16-2: Enter the basic information about your company.

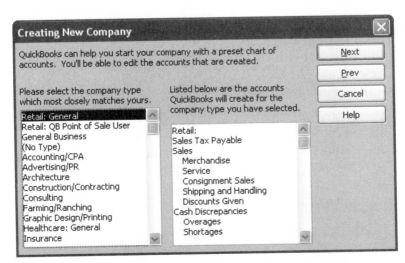

Figure 16-3: Select either of the retail business types to install a predefined company file.

You can also open one of the sample files to see how it's configured. You may find some good ideas for tweaking your chart of accounts, lists, or preferences. To open a sample file, choose File → Open Company and select one of the sample retail company files:

- Sample_Retailer_who_tracks_individual_sales.QBW
- Sample_Retailer_who_tracks_summarized_sales.QBW

You can make notes about the configuration options you think would be useful in your own file. If you find a list that seems appropriate for your business, export the list and import it into your company file.

NOTE: *See Appendix A to learn how to export and import Excel and CSV files; see Appendix B to learn how to export and import IIF files.*

Stock Status Information for Sales Orders

The QuickBooks Premier Retail Edition offers advanced functions for tracking sales orders. Two important and useful advanced features are built into this edition of QuickBooks Premier:

- Stock shortage warnings during the creation of a sales order.
- One-click access to stock status reports in the Create Sales Orders transaction window.

These features are only available in the Retail, Accountant, and Manufacturing & Wholesale Premier editions. The other Premier editions don't advise you about stock shortages until you convert a sales order to an invoice.

Out of Stock Warnings

If an item is out of stock, QuickBooks issues a warning as soon as you select the item in the sales order, even before you enter the quantity (see Figure 16-4). You can continue with the sales order, and wait until stock is available before converting the sales order to an invoice.

Warning
You don't have sufficient quantity available to sell 1 of the item:
Widget-3
Quantity on hand 0
Quantity on other Sales Orders 0
Quantity Reserved for Assemblies 0
Quantity available 0
OK

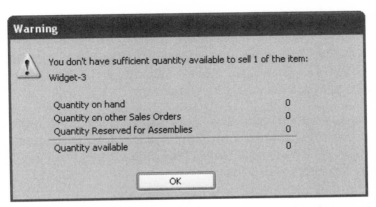

Figure 16-4: When there's no stock left, QuickBooks tells you as soon as you enter the item in the sales order.

Because QuickBooks tracks inventory on current sales orders in the Premier Retail Edition, the definition of "out of stock" includes inventory that is still on the shelves, but sales orders exist for the item. (If the sales orders had been turned into invoices, the stock would have been removed from the shelves, and therefore from the quantity on hand.)

As you can see in Figure 16-5, the warning message explains clearly that no quantity is available, so the item is deemed "out of stock". Because this is an out of stock item, the warning is displayed as soon as you enter the item in the sales order (before entering a quantity).

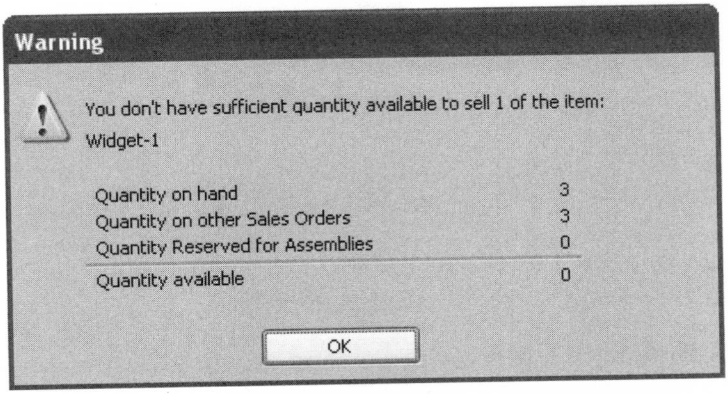

Warning
You don't have sufficient quantity available to sell 1 of the item:
Widget-1
Quantity on hand 3
Quantity on other Sales Orders 3
Quantity Reserved for Assemblies 0
Quantity available 0
OK

Figure 16-5: This item is not out of stock, but it's promised.

You can continue with the sales order and wait until stock is available before converting the sales order to an invoice, or negotiate an exchange of stock with the person who created the other sales orders. This is one of those times when you need to consider whether one customer should take priority over another customer.

To free up stock that's available but promised, change the quantity on the earlier sales order, then re-enter the sales order for the customer you think should receive the stock (see "Changing Sales Orders to Obtain Promised Stock", later in this section).

Insufficient Stock Warnings

If stock is on hand, when you enter the item in the sales order, you may not have sufficient stock to fill the quantity the customer ordered. When you enter the number of units in the Ordered column, if there isn't sufficient stock to fill this order, QuickBooks displays a message explaining the stock status (see Figure 16-6).

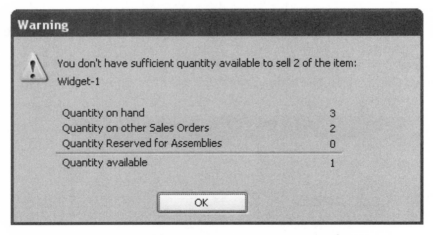

Figure 16-6: This item's stock status is less than the quantity
ordered, so you can't invoice this order in full.

You can continue with the sales order, and create an invoice to ship the available stock, creating a backorder for the remaining items. Or, you can hold the invoice until sufficient stock is available to fill the entire order.

Checking Stock Status Details

One of the nifty enhanced functions in the Premier Retail Edition is the ability to check stock status, in detail, right from the sales order transaction window. After you enter the item in the sales order, whether you receive a stock status warning or not, click the icon that appears on the right side of the Ordered column.

QuickBooks calls this icon and resulting report "Available to Promise". This is a report on the current status of this item. As you can see in Figure 16-7, this report has more information than the stock status warnings QuickBooks displays.

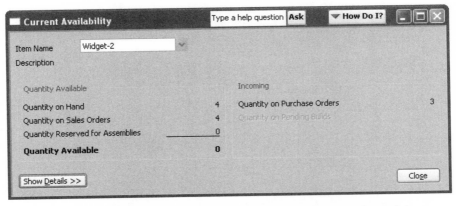

Figure 16-7: There's no available stock, but a purchase order exists, which means stock should arrive soon.

You can learn even more about the stock status of this item by clicking the Show Details button. Then choose the type of information you want to see by selecting one of the following topics from the drop-down list:

• **Sales Orders**. This choice displays all the current sales orders that contain this item. See "Changing Sales Orders to Obtain

Promised Stock" to remove items from one of those sales orders so you can invoice and ship the current sales order.

- **Pending Builds**. This choice displays all the pending bills that include this item.
- **Purchase Orders**. This choice displays all the current purchase orders for this item, including the expected date of arrival (see Figure 16-8).

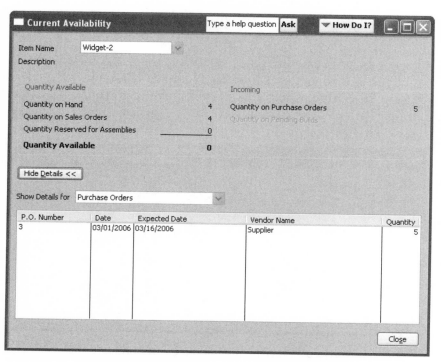

Figure 16-8: If more stock is due to arrive soon, don't convert the sales order to an invoice until that date.

Changing Sales Orders to Obtain Promised Stock

When you click the Show Details button, and select Sales Orders, QuickBooks displays a listing of the sales orders that include the item you want to include in the sales order you're creating (see Figure 16-9).

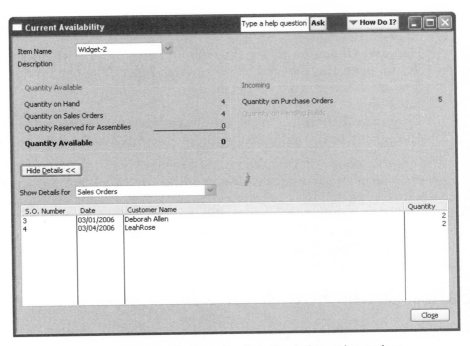

Figure 16-9: QuickBooks displays the list of existing sales orders
that include the product you need.

If the sales order you're creating is for a customer you think should
be shipped product faster than the customers on the existing sales
orders, you can modify any of the displayed sales orders to reduce the
item's quantity.

Double-click the listing for the sales order you want to change.
However, since you have a sales order in process in the Create Sales
Orders window, and QuickBooks can neither open a second sales order in
the window, nor open another instance of the Create Sales Orders window, you have to decide how to remove the current sales order from the
window. QuickBooks displays a message that offers three choices for handling the current sales order:

- **Save Changes**. Save the current sales order with its current
  items and quantities, and open the selected existing sales order in
  the Create Sales Orders window. You can return to the sales order

you saved to adjust the quantity, after you finish modifying the older sales order.

- **Discard Changes**. Close the current sales order without saving it, and open the selected existing sales order. You can create the new sales order after you've adjusted the quantities in the existing sales order.
- **Continue Editing**. Forget about opening an existing sales order, and return to the sales order you're currently working on.

Unless the sales order you're trying to create is for an important customer who doesn't accept back orders, and no additional stock is expected in the near future, it's best to continue editing the current sales order. When stock arrives, you can ship to this customer first by converting this sales order to an invoice before the earlier sales orders are converted. See the next section, "Sales Order Fulfillment Worksheet, to learn how to allocate stock to sales orders.

Sales Order Fulfillment Worksheet

The QuickBooks Premier Retail Edition has a Sales Order Fulfillment Worksheet that you can use to decide how to fill sales orders if there is insufficient stock to fill all sales orders.

To open the worksheet, choose Customers → Sales Order Fulfillment Worksheet. When the worksheet opens, its appearance is determined by the availability of the stock entered in sales orders, and the way you sort the data. As you can see in Figure 16-10, the default setting is to display the sales orders by creation date. You can sort the display of sales orders by selecting a sort order from the drop-down list.

In the sales order listing at the top of the window, QuickBooks uses symbols to indicate the fulfillment status of each sales order:

- A solid green circle means there is sufficient stock to fill the order.
- A half filled amber circle means there is sufficient stock to ship a partial order. This could mean that less stock than ordered is available for the items in the sales order, or one (or more) items on the sales order is out of stock (even though there is sufficient stock to fill the order on another item.

- An empty square with a red X means there is no stock available to fill the order.

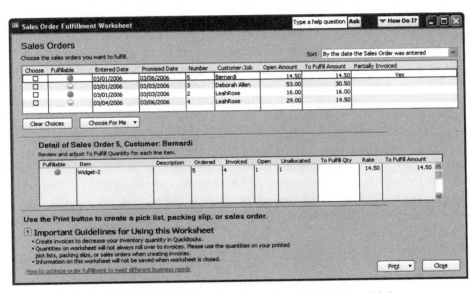

Figure 16-10: A worksheet is available to help you decide which sales orders to fill when stock is limited.

Click any order to display stock status details for the order that's selected in the bottom of the window. QuickBooks uses the same symbols to indicate the fulfillment capabilities of each item in the sales order.

The fact that more than one sales order has a green circle doesn't mean you can fulfill all the "green circle" sales orders. Depending on stock availability, it could mean that you can fulfill one order, and when you do, the stock is used and the other sales orders won't be able to ship.

Click the button labeled Choose For Me to display a variety of choices you can select to have QuickBooks automatically select the sales order to fill.

To choose sales orders manually, select a listing and click the check box in the first column. The bottom of the window inserts the number of items required to fill the order (or partially fill the order if the sales order does not have a green circle) in the Fulfill Qty column. If this action uses up the available stock, the symbols for other sales orders that include this stock change to an empty square with a red X.

Selecting a sales order does not turn it in to an invoice, nor does it lock the available stock so that it belongs to this sales order. This is a worksheet, an informational window. However, you can begin the process of converting a sales order to an invoice from the worksheet window.

The first step is to make sure that the reported availability numbers match what's actually on the shelves. Select the sales order you want to fill, and click the Print button at the bottom of the window. Select Print Pick Lists and then send the printed pick list to the warehouse to make sure the sales order can be filled to match the quantity in the Fulfill Qty column.

TIP: *If you're on a network, install a printer near the stock shelves, and select that printer when you print pick slips.*

If enough stock is available to fill the order, double-click the sales order listing to open the original sales order. Then click the Create Invoice button at the top of the Create Sales Orders window and follow the prompts to turn the sales order into an invoice.

When you return to the worksheet, the symbols on the worksheet change to indicate the new status of order fulfillment, now that you've actually removed product from inventory.

You could also close the worksheet window, convert the appropriate sales orders to invoices, and then open the worksheet again when new product arrives. This worksheet is an ad-hoc document, which means that any information you entered in the window wasn't saved, and each time you open the worksheet the data in the window displays real time information as of the moment you open it.

Handling Upfront Deposits

Deposits are funds a customer gives you before taking delivery of a product. It's common to ask for a deposit when you're selling a customized product that you have to build or special-order.

Theoretically, upfront money is money you've collected that continues to belong to the customer. Because the money isn't yours, it's a liability, and you must create a liability account to track those funds.

However, you can make your life easier if you treat upfront deposits as accounts receivable transactions. This means entering the upfront deposit when you create the invoice. (This assumes the entire transaction is completed in a timely fashion—unlike a layaway, covered later in this chapter.)

The easiest way to manage a sale that has an upfront deposit is to create a standard invoice, and then immediately accept a deposit against it.

Asking for a deposit is an acceptable and common way of doing business when a customer wants a special item. To make the bookkeeping more accurate, and make sure the customer understands the terms, I usually have clients perform the following tasks:

- Create an item to cover upfront deposits.
- Create Terms to cover a sale that is waiting for you to deliver the product.
- Customize the transaction template to reflect the special circumstances of the sale.

Creating an Item for Upfront Deposits

You need a way to enter the deposit you received from the customer in QuickBooks, and also let the customer know you've acknowledged the deposit. To create an item for this transaction type, open the Items list and press Ctrl-N to open a New Item dialog (see Figure 16-11). Then take the following steps:

1. Select Payment as the item type.
2. Name the item Customer Deposit (or something similar).
3. Enter a description that makes the transaction clear to the customer.

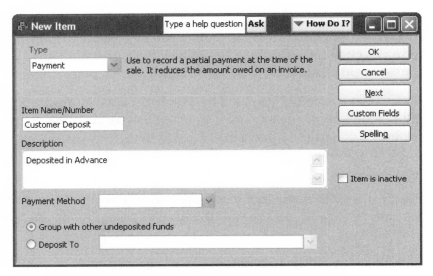

Figure 16-11: Create a payment item for upfront deposits.

Creating Terms for Sales with Upfront Deposits

If you're sure of the delivery date of the special order, you can use terms that reflect the expected time lapse between the deposit and the product delivery date. For example, if you take a deposit on a product you know you can deliver within a month, use the standard 30 days terms on the invoice.

However, if you're not sure of the delivery date, you don't want to consider the customer overdue in 30 days, or 60 days, etc. In addition, if you send statements to overdue customers, you certainly don't want to risk having a statement sent to a customer who is waiting for you to deliver the product.

To cover uncertain delivery dates, create new terms named On Delivery, as follows:

1. Choose Lists → Customer & Vendor Profile List → Terms List to open the Terms List window.
2. Press Ctrl-N to open a New Terms dialog
3. Select Standard as the type of terms.
4. Enter 120 days (or even a longer period) in the Net Due field.

The invoice displays "On Delivery" instead of a specific number of days, and aging reports won't show this customer overdue until the number of days you specified has elapsed.

TIP: When you apply the new terms to an invoice, QuickBooks asks if you want to change the customer's default terms in the customer record. Unless this customer only buys special order items, click No.

Applying an Upfront Deposit to an Invoice

In QuickBooks, when you receive an upfront deposit, you create an invoice at the same time. The upfront deposit is not treated separately as a sales receipt or a payment against an existing invoice.

Enter the item(s) you're selling the customer, and then enter the Upfront Deposit item you created. Do *not* enter a minus sign; Payment type items are automatically deductions, so QuickBooks automatically enters the minus sign. The invoice total is the net of the sale less the advance payment.

When you apply an advance payment to an invoice, QuickBooks automatically deposits the money. If you linked the advance payment item to the Undeposited Funds account, the next time you use the Payments to Deposit window, the advance payment is listed (it's differentiated by the code INV in the Type column).

Creating a Special Order Invoice Template

For a special order, it's a nice touch to have the status of special order clearly indicated on the invoice. You can add a field to the invoice to indicate that this is a special order sale requiring a deposit, and even change the title of the invoice. In the Create Invoices window take the following steps:

1. Click Customize to open the Customize Template dialog.
2. Select the template you want to use as the basis of the new template (I found the Professional Invoice template the most suitable), and then click New.
3. Name the template (e.g. Special Order).
4. To change the title of the invoice, go to the Header tab and change the text in the Default Title field to Invoice - Special Order, or something similar.
5. To add a field, move to the Fields tab and select Screen and Print for the Other field. Then enter the text you want to use for the field, such as Special, or Special Order. (You fill in the appropriate text when you're creating the invoice.)
6. Click OK when you have finished customizing the template.

I have several clients who have made both changes (see Figure 16-12). The Special Order field is used to specify terms of the sale. For example, if the invoice is mailed to the customer before an upfront deposit is received, the Special Order Field text is Deposit Reqd. If the customer paid the upfront deposit at the time the invoice was created, the Special Order field says "Will Notify" (if the delivery date is uncertain), or June 30 (to indicate a promised delivery date).

Managing Layaways

Layaways require you to take an item out of stock for the period of time that the customer makes payments. You should have a policy on layaways that clearly spells out the payment schedule, and what happens if the customer stops making payments. That policy should be printed and given to the customer along with the invoice or sales order.

Using Invoices for Layaways

The easiest way to manage layaways is with an invoice. Create an invoice for the sale (use the Memo field to indicate the sale is a layaway). As each payment arrives, use the Receive Payments transaction window to apply it.

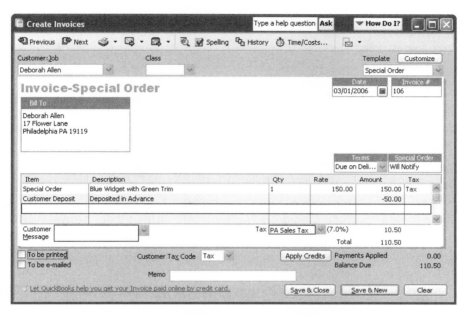

Figure 16-12: A slick, professional, invoice is good for your image,
and makes the terms clear to your customer.

If the item is an inventory part, the invoice decrements the inventory
and increments cost of goods. Because the item isn't on the shelves, that's
a logical approach. If the item is something you're likely to run out of,
you should move the item from the stock shelves into a special area for
layaways.

However, your accountant may suggest that the item isn't really
sold, and would prefer you didn't treat the layaway as a real sale. A real
sale decrements the inventory quantity, applies the amount of the invoice
to income, and applies the cost of goods. None of those things really occur
for a layaway transaction. In that case, read the next section on using
Sales Orders for layaways.

Using Sales Orders for Layaways

Technically, since a layaway isn't a completed sale until all the payments
are made, you can consider a layaway a sales order. A sales order is a
pending order, and doesn't post any amounts to accounts. The item isn't

removed from inventory, but inventory reports display the item as linked to a sales order.

> **NOTE**: *To use sales orders, you must enable the sales order feature in the Sales & Customers category of the Preferences dialog (choose Edit → Preferences).*

If you selected Retail as your industry type during company setup, QuickBooks included a Layaway Sales Order template (see Figure 16-13). If you didn't select Retail as your industry type, or you updated a previous version of QuickBooks, you can create a Layaway Sales Order by creating a new template based on the Custom Sales Order template. Name the new template Layaway, and change the template title in the Header tab to Layaway Sales Order.

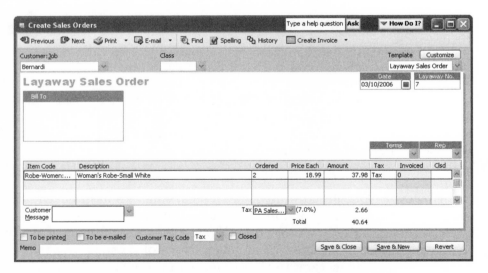

Figure 16-13: A Layaway Sales Order template makes it easy for you and your customers to remember that this is a layaway sale.

After you create the sales order, you have two methods for tracking layaway payments:

- Enter a payment against the sales order, and let the payments pile up until you create the invoice, at which point you can apply the payments to the invoice.
- Create a credit memo for each payment, and then apply all the credits against the invoice you create when the product is paid for.

Creating a Layaway Payment Method

I've found it easier to track a customer's layaway payments by applying a specific layaway payment method. This makes it easier to generate reports on customer layaway payment activities.

To create a payment method for layaways, choose Lists → Customer & Vendor Profile List → Payment Method List. Press Ctrl-N to open the New Method Payment dialog, and use the following guidelines to create the payment method:

- Name the new payment method LayawayPayment.
- Select a payment type. Most of my clients select cash or check as the payment type.

Applying Payments Against a Sales Order for Layaways

You can enter each layaway payment as a payment receipt, even though there's no invoice. Use the following steps to accomplish this:

1. Choose Customers → Receive Payments.
2. Select the customer from the drop-down list in the Received From field.
3. Enter the amount of the payment.
4. Enter LayawayPayment in the payment method field. (If the payment is a check, enter the check number in the Reference # field.)
5. Enter Layaway Payment—SO # XXX in the Memo field (substitute the sales order number for XXX).
6. If unpaid invoices that are not layaways are displayed for this customer, QuickBooks automatically selects them. Deselect the invoice(s)—this is not a payment against an invoice.

Since no invoice is selected, you've entered a customer payment that is larger than any invoice being paid. When you save the transaction,

QuickBooks displays a message telling you a credit has been established for the customer (see Figure 16-14).

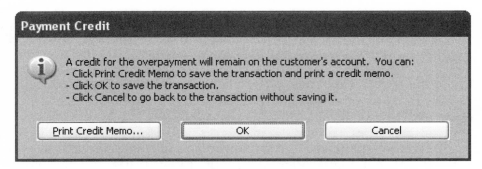

Figure 16-14: A customer payment that's not applied to an invoice is the same as a credit memo.

If the customer paid in person, definitely print a credit memo. You might also want to print and mail a credit memo if the customer's check arrived by mail.

Each time the customer sends a payment repeat this process. QuickBooks displays the total of the existing (past) credits in addition to presenting the current credit amount in the Overpayment message.

When the customer has finished paying off the layaway, or shows up to make the last payment, turn the sales order into an invoice. You apply the credits to the invoice, using the following steps:

1. Open the original sales order.
2. Click the Create Invoice button on the transaction window to open the Create Invoice Based On Sales Order dialog.
3. Select Create Invoice For The Entire Sales Order, and click OK.
4. In the Create Invoices window, click Apply Credits.
5. QuickBooks displays a dialog telling you the transaction has changed and must be saved. Click Yes to save the transaction.
6. In the Apply Credits dialog (see Figure 16-15), select the credits to apply to this invoice (usually all of the credits, unless the customer has multiple layaway sales orders), and click Done.

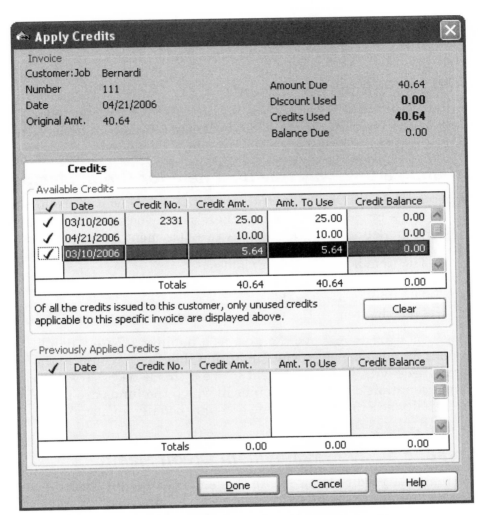

Figure 16-15: Apply the customer's credits as payments against the invoice you're creating.

The bottom of the invoice displays the total of payments applied to the invoice, as well as any balance due. (Often, layaway customers come in with the last payment when they're ready to pick up their merchandise.)

Save the invoice. If a balance exists, take the money, and then use the Receive Payments transaction window to apply it against this invoice. Then give the customer the merchandise.

Using Credit Memos for Layaway Payments

You can also create credit memos for the customer, and let them "float" until the layaway is paid for. A credit memo requires an item, so you have to create the item before you can use this method.

Creating a Layaway Payment Item for Credit Memos

To accomplish this you have to create an item for layaway payments. The item is not a prepayment, because there's no invoice yet. Instead, use the following guidelines to create the layaway payment item:

- The item is a type Other Charge.
- Do not enter an amount.
- The item is non-taxable.
- Link the item to the revenue account you use when you sell items.

If you want to manage the item as a liability, create a liability account for customer layaway funds, and link that account to the new item. Check with your accountant to see if this is necessary. If so, have your accountant design the manner in which the funds are moved from the liability account to an income account (usually a journal entry that contains the customer's name).

Creating a Layaway Payment Credit Memo

To create the credit memo choose Customers → Create Credit Memos/Refunds to open the Create Credit Memos/Refunds transaction window. Select the customer; enter the layaway payment item, and the amount of the payment.

When you save the credit memo QuickBooks asks you how to handle the credit. Choose the option labeled Retain As An Available Credit.

When the customer finishes paying for the layaway, open the original sales order, convert it to an invoice, and apply the credits as described in the previous section.

Tracking Customer Layaway Payments

If you posted customer layaway payments as payments (instead of credit memos), you can keep an eye on the total payments in the Customer Center.

Open the Customer Center, and select the customer of interest in the Customer & Jobs tab. Then, in the right pane of the Customer Center, select the following options from the drop-down lists:

- In the Show field, select Received Payments.
- In the Filter By field, select Layaway Payment
- In the Date field, select whatever date range is appropriate.

The resulting display (see Figure 16-16) provides a quick look at the payments that have arrived against a layaway.

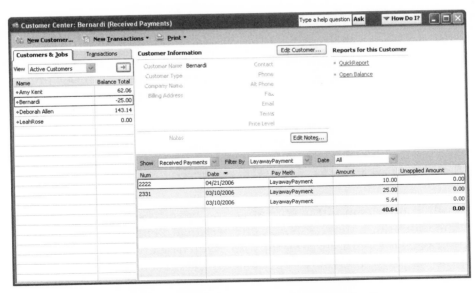

Figure 16-16: If a customer asks about layaway payments, the details are easy to find.

NOTE: *You can also filter the right pane for credit memos, if that's how you're accepting layaway payments. However, because credit memos don't have a payment method, you can't tell whether a credit memo is for a layaway or returned goods.*

You can also customize a Customer QuickReport, or a sales report on all customers, to show layaway payments. In a customized report, you can also opt to print the memo field, so the specific sales order number you entered in that field is displayed in the report.

Service Charges for Undelivered Layaways

It's common, and perfectly acceptable, to assess a service charge if the customer doesn't finish paying for the layaway. When the customer shows up to tell you "I've changed my mind", you return the customer's money, less the service charge. (Some businesses call this a *restocking charge*, or a *handling charge*.)

If you want to assess a service charge, you must create an item for it. Make the item a Service or Other Charge item, and link it to an income account for service charges. Don't specify a price for the item; instead, when you invoice the customer for the charge, you can enter an amount that matches your layaway policy.

If you are returning a customer's money, and assessing a service charge, you should do both on the same invoice.

Managing Gift Certificates

To sell and redeem gift certificates, you need to set up accounts and items to manage those sales. A gift certificate isn't a real product, so when you sell a gift certificate, you haven't received money that qualifies as income. Instead, you've put cash on the street that can be redeemed for a product in the future.

You need to set up a liability account to track your gift certificates, and you also need items for selling and redeeming the gift certificates.

Creating an Account for Gift Certificates

The funds you received for the sale of the gift certificate aren't yours; they belong to the certificate holder. Because you're holding funds that belong to someone else, you've incurred a liability.

You must create a liability account to track the sale and redemption of gift certificates. The account type is Other Current Liability, which you should name Gift Certificates.

Creating Items for Gift Certificates

To sell a gift certificate, you need two items: one for the certificate, and another for the income you receive when you sell a certificate (so you can deposit the money you receive into your bank account).

Create the item for gift certificates with the following configuration options:

- The item type is Other Charge
- The item name is GiftCert, Gift Certificate, or something similar.
- Do not enter text in the Description field (you use that field when you sell the gift certificate).
- The item is not taxable.
- In the Account field, select the liability account you created for gift certificates.

Because the item isn't linked to an income account, you don't record income when you sell a gift certificate. Now you need a way to post the money you received to your bank account without creating a sale. QuickBooks offers an item type of Payment for this purpose.

Create another item, of the type Payment. Name it Paymt-GiftCert (or something similar). Configure the item for deposit to a bank account, or to the Undeposited Funds account, depending on the way you usually handle bank deposits.

Selling Gift Certificates

You can use an invoice or a sales receipt to record the sale of a gift certificate, using the following steps:

1. Enter the gift certificate item in the Item column.
2. Enter the gift certificate number in the Description column.
3. Enter the amount of the gift certificate in the Amount column.
4. On the next line, enter the payment item you created for gift certificates.
5. In the Amount column, enter the amount of the payment. Don't enter a minus sign, because QuickBooks automatically assigns a minus sign to payment items.
6. Save the transaction.

As you can see in Figure 16-17, the transaction has a zero balance. When you save the transaction, QuickBooks makes the following postings:

- The gift certificate liability account is credited.
- The bank (or the Undeposited Funds account) is debited.

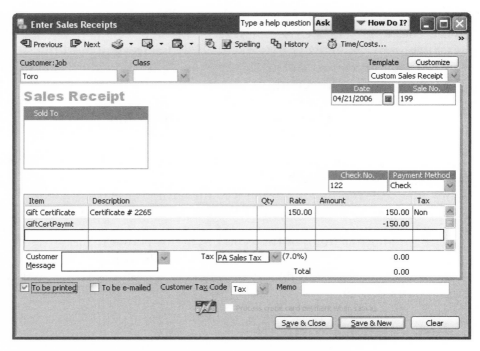

Figure 16-17: Create a sales transaction for a gift certificate.

If the customer ordered a gift certificate, but didn't pay for it, issue an invoice using the gift certificate item. When payment arrives, treat it the same way you handle any invoice payment.

TIP: If you don't want to track the customers who purchase gift certificates, create a generic customer named GiftCertificate.

Redeeming Gift Certificates

When a customer redeems a gift certificate, you can use either a sales receipt or an invoice as the transaction type. Use the following steps to redeem the gift certificate during a sale:

1. Fill out the transaction window with the item(s) the customer purchased and the prices.
2. In the last line of the transaction, enter the gift certificate item.
3. Enter a negative amount for the gift certificate. Do not exceed the amount of the sale if the gift certificate is larger than the total sale.
   - If the total sale is more than the amount of the gift certificate, the customer must pay the balance.
   - If the total sale is less than the amount of the gift certificate, you should issue a new physical certificate for the balance (do not enter that certificate in QuickBooks).

When you save the transaction, QuickBooks makes the following postings:

- The gift certificate liability account is debited.
- The income accounts connected to the items you sold are credited.

If the gift certificate was larger than the sales total, and you entered an amount equal to the sales total, but smaller than the certificate, you didn't "wash" the entire amount of the certificate in the liability account.

Issue a new physical certificate for the balance due on the original certificate. When that certificate is redeemed (assuming it's not larger than the next sale), entering its amount will wash the rest of the original posting to the liability account.

Consignment Sales

A consignment sale is a sale you make on behalf of another seller. Instead of purchasing goods from the seller, you offer the products to your customers, acting as an agent for the seller. When (or if) the goods are sold, the seller is paid, and you get your commission.

You have several choices about the way you want to track consignment sales in QuickBooks. You should ask your accountant to help you decide which paradigm to follow. In the following sections, I'll go over some of the options available to you.

Configuring QuickBooks for Consignment Sales

To track consignment sales accurately, you need to create components in your company file that let you separate consignment transactions from the transactions involving your purchased products. You need the following components:

- A vendor record for each consignor.
- Items for consigned products (see the following sections regarding inventory and non-inventory consignment items).
- A custom field for items, to track the consignor.
- An income account to track consigned item sales.

TIP: In addition to setting up QuickBooks for consignment sales, you need to establish an identification system for consigned products. Each product must have a sticker or tag that identifies it as a consigned item, and identifies the consignor by name or by a code you've created.

Custom Fields for Consigned Items

To facilitate transactions and reports, you should add a custom field to your Items list, and use it for consigned items. When you create a custom field in any item, it's available for all items and all item types. Use the following steps to accomplish this:

1. Double-click any item in the Item list to open its record.
2. Click Custom Fields. If this is the first custom field you're creating, QuickBooks displays a message telling you there are currently no custom fields. Click OK.
3. In the Custom Fields dialog, click Define Fields.
4. In the Define Custom Fields For Items dialog (see Figure 16-18), enter the text for the field's label, and select the Use check box.
5. Continue to click OK until you close all dialogs and return to the Item list.

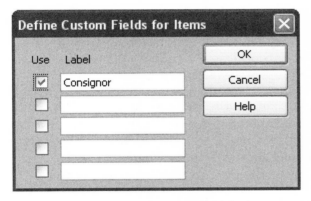

Figure 16-18: Create a custom field for items so you can track the consignor.

As you create consignment items, you can use the custom field to enter the name of the consignor. You should also add the custom field to the transaction templates you use to sell those items. See the section "Customizing Templates for Consignment Sales".

Consigned Products as Inventory Parts

If you want to track consigned products as inventory parts, you must separate the consigned inventory from your regular inventory (the inventory you purchased and own).

It's not a good idea to track consigned products as inventory if you have a large variety or volume of consignment sales. You'll find the amount of work involved is onerous if you sell more than a few consigned items a month.

Before you can set up consigned items as inventory parts, you have to create the following accounts:

- A separate inventory asset account named Consigned Inventory. (Inventory accounts are Other Current Assets.)
- A separate Cost of Goods account.

You assign those accounts to the inventory parts you create for consigned items.

Inventory Items for Consigned Products

If you want to track inventory for consigned products, each product must have its own discrete item listing. Use the following guidelines when you create the inventory part:

- Use a special convention for the Item Name/Number to make it easy to identify consignment items in the drop-down list. For example, start each item name with **X-**. (If you only sell consignment items, you can ignore this suggestion.)
- In the Cost field, enter the amount you have to pay the consignor.
- In the COGS Account field, enter the COGS account to use for this item.
- In the Preferred Vendor field, enter the name of the consignor.
- In the Sales Price field, enter the price of the item.
- In the Tax Code field, enter the appropriate tax code.
- In the Income Account field, enter the income account for consignment sales.
- In the Asset Account field, enter the inventory account for consignments.
- Click Custom Fields, and in the Custom Field labeled Consignor, enter the consignor's name, and click OK. (The data appears on your customized transaction templates.)

Click Next to create another consigned inventory part, or click OK if you're finished.

Receiving Consigned Products into Inventory

If you're tracking consigned products as inventory, you must receive the products into inventory. This action increments the value of your consignment inventory asset, and updates the quantity available for the items. Use the following steps to receive the items:

1. Choose Vendors → Receive Items to open the Create Item Receipts transaction window.
2. Select the vendor (consignor).
3. Move to the Items tab and select the item from the drop-down list in the Item column.
4. Enter the number of items in the Qty column. The cost should appear automatically from the item's record. If you didn't enter a cost when you created the item, enter the cost per item in the Cost column. (QuickBooks automatically calculates the quantity and cost to enter data in the Total field at the top of the transaction window.)
5. If necessary, continue to receive items for this shipment.
6. Click Save & New to receive another shipment. Click Save & Close if you're finished.

When you sell the items, QuickBooks automatically posts the cost of goods, and decrements the inventory asset.

Consigned Products as Non-inventory Parts

To manage your consigned items outside of inventory, use a Non-inventory Part type for the items. If you selected a predefined company file for a Retail business when you created your company file, this item is already in your items list.

You can create a special naming convention, such as a prefix of **X**, to separate your consignment items from your purchased items. Or, you can create a parent item, and make all your consigned items subitems. I think the subitem paradigm is easier to manage, and it also makes it easier to see totals in reports.

In the Non-inventory Part dialog, select the option This Item Is Purchased For And Sold To A Specific Customer:Job. Even though the option doesn't fit the way you sell consigned items, selecting the option changes the dialog by adding the cost fields you need (see Figure 16-19).

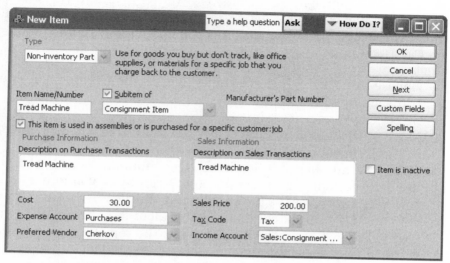

Figure 16-19: Track cost and sales configuration for consigned items.

Fill in the information about the item, and click Custom Fields to enter the consigner name for each item.

If you're using subitems, when you create the parent item don't enter any information except the expense and income account. Then, for the subitems, enter information about cost, price, description, and vendor.

Customizing Templates for Consignment Sales

You need a customized template for sales transactions, so you can track consignor information. Most retailers use a sales receipt template, so I'll go over the customizations for that form. However, if you use invoices, you can make the same changes to an invoice template.

To create a customized template, open the Enter Sales Receipt transaction window, and click Customize to open the Customize Template dialog. The Custom Sales Receipt template is selected (highlighted). Follow these steps to create your new template:

1. Click New to open the Customize Sales Receipt dialog.
2. In the Template Name field, enter **Consignment Sale**.
3. On the Header tab, you can change the heading (title) of the template to include the word Consignment.
4. In the Columns tab, go to the Consignor entry (the custom field you created for items), and click the Screen option. This puts the column on the on-screen version of the template so you can enter the consignor's name in order to track sales for this consignor.

Selling Consigned Items

When a customer purchases a consigned item, open the template you created for consignment sales. Enter the item, and the rest of the row should be filled in automatically, using the information in the item's record (see Figure 16-20).

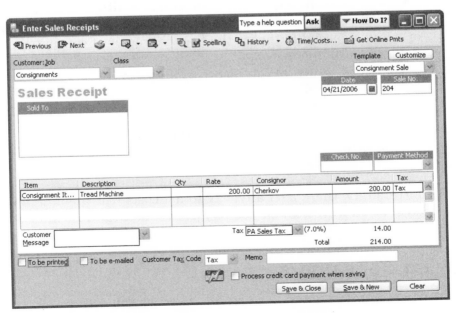

Figure 16-20: A consignment sale is like any other sale, except you track the consignor.

Tracking Consigned Item Sales

You need a consignment sales report in order to pay your consignors. Several reports can be modified to produce information about your consignment sales. Here are the instructions for creating the customized report I install at client sites:

1. Choose Reports → Custom Transaction Detail Report.
2. In the report window, click Modify Report.
3. In the Display tab, go to the Columns list and select Consignor. Then deselect all the selected columns except for the following:
   - Date
   - Item
   - Amount
4. In the Filters tab, make the following changes:
   - Select Account in the Filter box. Then select the account to which you post your consignment sales.
   - Select Item in the Filter box, and choose Multiple Items. Then select all your consignment items. (This is where using subitems or using a special letter for the first character of consignment item names comes in handy.)
5. Click OK to return to the report window.
6. In the Total By field, select Totals Only.
7. In the Sort By Field, select Consignor.

My customization actions create the report seen in Figure 16-21. Memorize the report to avoid going through all these customizations again.

Unfortunately, there isn't any way to list costs (the amount you owe the consignor). However, when you pay the vendor, the cost information is available (see the next section on paying consignors).

Paying Consignors

The way you pay consigners depends on whether you set up your consigned items as inventory parts, or non-inventory parts. Regardless of your method, use the customized report you created as your basis of information.

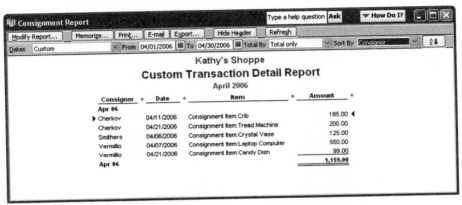

Figure 16-21: Create an easy-to-use report of consignment sales so you can pay the consignors.

Paying for Inventory Parts

If you use inventory parts, you received the items with the inventory item receipt transaction. To remit payment, choose Vendors → Enter Bill For Received Items. In the Select Item Receipt dialog, choose the Vendor, and the list of item receipt transactions appears in the dialog.

Choose the appropriate receipt and click OK to open the Enter Bills window. All of the data is filled in automatically.

The Qty column displays the Qty received. If you received more items than you sold, change the number to reflect the sold items, and click Recalculate. Then follow the usual procedures to create or print the check.

Paying for Non-inventory Parts

To remit payment to consignors for non-inventory parts, you can enter a vendor bill, or you can write a check.

To enter a bill, choose Vendors → Enter Bills. In the Enter Bills transaction window, select the vendor. Move to the Items tab and enter the items and quantities of the products you sold.

To write a check, choose Banking → Write Checks. Enter the vendor, and move to the Items tab. Enter the items and quantities of the products you sold.

Point of Sale Add-ons

For most retailers, it's difficult to track everything you want to track without a robust POS add-on. In fact, I don't think it's possible to run anything beyond a small boutique retail business without help from a POS. There are two common POS approaches:

- A powerful cash register that provides detailed reports about sales. You manually enter the totals into your QuickBooks company file.
- A software add-on that runs the "front end" of your sales. The software should be able to integrate with QuickBooks, so you can transfer data into the general ledger of your company file.

A POS software program is more convenient, of course, and many applications are available for QuickBooks.

QuickBooks POS

Start by investigating QuickBooks POS, which is built from the ground up to integrate with your company file. QuickBooks POS runs the sales activities (sales and inventory), while QuickBooks Premier Retail Edition tracks your accounting data.

QuickBooks POS transfers sales totals to your general ledger. In addition, as you add vendors, customers, and items into the POS software, that data is transferred to your company file.

QuickBooks POS is available in three versions: Basic, Pro, and Multi-store. You can learn more about this software by visiting www.QuickBooks.com, and following the links to the products.

Third Party POS Applications

A number of third-party developers have created POS applications that integrate with QuickBooks. You can investigate their offerings by traveling to www.marketplace.intuit.com.

Customized Reports

The Premier Retail Edition is chock-full of reports that have been customized for you. To see the list of available reports, choose Reports → Retail Reports. The report names listed on the submenu are self-explanatory. You can, of course, modify any of these reports to create memorized reports that provide exactly the information you need.

Appendix A

Importing Excel and CSV Files

Importing the contents of your lists is an efficient way to get the data you need into your QuickBooks company file, without going through all the work of entering each entry by filling out a dialog one entry at a time.

You can import data into QuickBooks directly from Excel or a CSV file (unless your version of QuickBooks is earlier than 2004), or a from tab-delimited text file that's been configured properly for importing to QuickBooks. In this appendix, I'll go over the steps for importing Excel/CSV files. Tab-delimited text file imports are discussed in Appendix B.

Importing Excel or CSV Files

While the ability to import data directly into QuickBooks from Excel is attractive, it's a limited feature. You can only perform a direct import for the following lists:

- Chart of accounts
- Customer list
- Vendor list
- Items list

Additional limitations include the inability to import complex listings, such as nonposting accounts, or detailed information about entries (for example, custom fields). After you import your list, you have to open each list entry and fill in those details. However, if you hadn't been tracking that information anyway, this is an easy way to populate your QuickBooks company file with the important basic lists.

Configuring an Excel or CSV File as an Import File

The data format of your Excel/CSV file must follow a set of conventions and rules in order to be recognized as an import file by QuickBooks (see the section Header Row).

In addition, some of the data in the import file must contain text that matches QuickBooks keywords (see the Section Data Keywords).

> NOTE: Each worksheet (or spreadsheet, if only one worksheet exists) must contain data for a single list. Other lists you want to import must be in their own discrete worksheets or spreadsheets.

Header Row

The top row must contain headers that categorize the data in each column. You can enter the header text that QuickBooks requires (header keywords), or leave the header text from the export file you created, and map that text to the QuickBooks keywords when you perform the import.

If your worksheet doesn't have a header row, insert a blank row at the top of the worksheet, and enter the QuickBooks column heading keywords. For Excel and CSV files, QuickBooks uses plain English phrases for keywords. All of the keywords are documented in this appendix.

> NOTE: For IIF files, QuickBooks requires specific (less user-friendly) keywords for each category. IIF files are covered in Appendix B.

It's possible to import an Excel/CSV file without having a header row, because QuickBooks will use the Column Names that Excel displays (Column A, Column B, and so on) when it maps the categories. However, this means you either have to memorize the type of data in each column, or print at least one row of the spreadsheet to use as a reference.

Understanding Mapping

Mapping is the process of matching the text in your file that describes categories to the specific text QuickBooks requires. Specifically, it means matching the titles of your columns (column headings) to the field names in the QuickBooks list.

For example, QuickBooks uses the text "Name" for an entry's name in the list. Your exported file may use different text for that category, such as CustName for a customer list. QuickBooks needs to know which column holds the data for the category Name, but your exported file has the column heading CustName. When you import the file, you map "CustName" to "Name". QuickBooks uses the data in the column named CustName as if the column were named Name.

Data Keywords

Mapping, the ability to match your text to the text QuickBooks needs, is only available for column headings (categories). Certain data in your file must match the text QuickBooks is expecting, called *keywords*.

> **WARNING**: The keywords for an Excel or CSV import file are different from the keywords for an IIF file. Importing IIF files is covered in Appendix B.

The data categories that require keywords vary, depending on the list you're importing. For example, QuickBooks requires specific text for account types in the chart of accounts, and requires a Y or N (for Yes and No) in some fields of other lists (such as whether a vendor is configured for Form 1099). See the section "Keywords for Excel/CSV Import Files", later in this appendix, for details.

When your file is ready (with the data arranged in columns by category, and the data that requires keywords appropriately entered), save the file with an .xls extension or a .csv extension, depending on the spreadsheet program you use.

To import the data, open QuickBooks, and open the company file for the company into which you want to import the list. Before you begin the import, back up the company file (just in case something goes wrong during the import process).

Selecting the Import File and Worksheet

Select the file you want to import by choosing File → Import → Excel Files to open the Import a File dialog seen in Figure A-1. Even though the command seems to be exclusively for importing Excel files, it also works for CSV files.

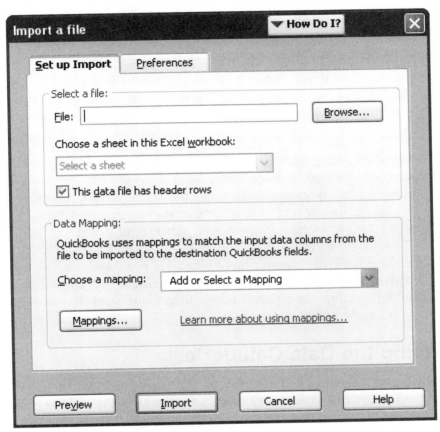

Figure A-1: The Import a File dialog can handle XLS and CSV files.

Click the Browse button and locate the file you saved. When you select the file, QuickBooks enters the filename in the File field of the dialog.

If the file is an XLS file, click the arrow to the right of the field labeled Choose a Sheet in This Excel Workbook. Then choose a worksheet from the drop-down list. (If the file is a CSV file, it only has one worksheet, so you can skip this step.)

Many Excel workbooks have multiple worksheets, so even if you only used one worksheet the other worksheets still exist (unless you deleted them). The drop-down list displays the names of all the worksheets in the selected file.

If you renamed the worksheet you used for your list, you'll see it on the drop-down list. If you didn't rename the worksheet you used, you see Worksheet1, Worksheet2, and so on. Select the Worksheet that contains the data for the list you're importing.

TIP: *If you have multiple worksheets that contain data, open your spreadsheet in Excel before importing the list. Either rename each worksheet to specify the contents (e.g. Chart of Accounts, Customers, and so on), or make yourself a note about the contents of Worksheet1, Worksheet 2, etc.*

If the XLS/CSV file doesn't have a header row, deselect the option labeled This Data File Has Header Rows. During the mapping process, QuickBooks will map the column labels (e.g. Column A, Column B, etc.) to the appropriate keyword text.

Mapping the Data Categories

A QuickBooks mapping is a set of data that links the text in the heading row of an import file to category names that match the fields of the list being imported. For example, if you're importing an Excel or CSV file that has a column named VendorName (because that's what your previous application used for vendor names), you must map that text to the QuickBooks text "Name" (which is the field name QuickBooks uses for the vendor name).

QuickBooks mappings are created for specific lists, so you must create a mapping for each type of list you're importing. You can save your mappings and use them again for re-importing the same type of list.

To create mappings for the list you're currently importing, click the arrow to the right of the Choose a Mapping field, and select <Add New> to open the Mappings dialog seen in Figure A-2.

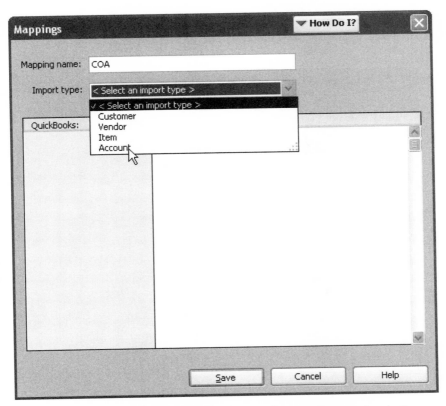

Figure A-2 Name the mapping scheme you're creating, and select the type of list you're importing.

Give the mapping scheme a name (make sure the name is a hint about the list it's intended for), and select the list you're importing from the drop-down list in the Import Type field.

TIP: Once you create a mapping scheme and name it, you can select it in the future for importing the same QuickBooks list. If a list you want to import in the future has different column headings in your XLS/CSV file, you can edit this mapping scheme to change the text that maps to the appropriate QuickBooks fields. This is easier than building the mapping scheme from scratch.

QuickBooks displays the text used for the field names in the list you're importing in the left pane of the dialog (see Figure A-3).

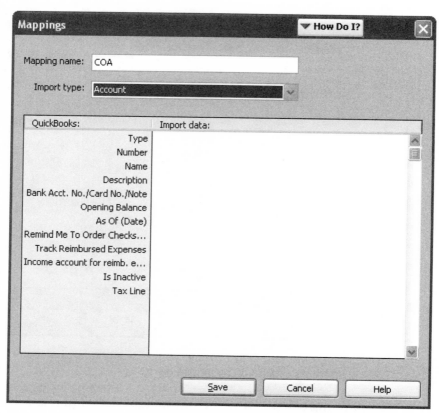

Figure A-3: The field names QuickBooks uses are displayed, and you need to link each field name to the text in your worksheet.

Click inside the Import Data column, to the right of the first QuickBooks field name for this type of import file. QuickBooks displays the column headings of your worksheet (or the column labels if you don't have a heading row).

Select the column heading that matches the QuickBooks field (see Figure A-4).

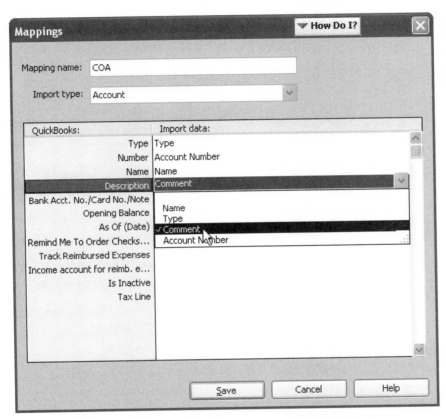

Figure A-4: Map the text in your column headings to the text
QuickBooks requires for the list you're importing.

Continue to map your worksheet column headings to the QuickBooks text for the fields in this list.

Usually, QuickBooks offers more fields than your worksheet contains, because you weren't tracking all the information available in QuickBooks. If you decide to enter data for the fields you haven't been using, you can edit each record after you import the file.

Click Save when you've finished mapping your column headings to the QuickBooks field names. Your mappings are saved, using the name you provided, and you're returned to the Import A File dialog.

Setting Preferences for Importing Data

Move to the Preferences tab of the Import a File dialog to specify the way you want QuickBooks to manage duplicate records and errors (see Figure A-5).

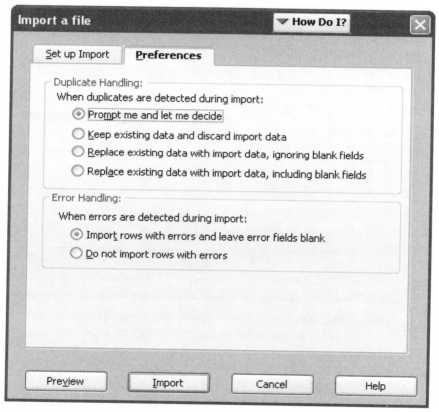

Figure A-5: Specify the way to manage problems.

- Duplicate records occur if your list already has entries that are also in your import file.
- Errors occur if any data is incorrectly configured. For example, you may have the wrong text for a field that requires a QuickBooks keyword, or your data may use more characters than QuickBooks permits in a given field.

Managing Duplicate Records

Here are the guidelines for selecting your options for duplicate records:

- **Prompt me and let me decide**. Don't select this option because the message you see (the prompting message upon which you're expected to make a decision) doesn't name the record in question. Blind guesses don't work well as a problem solving technique.
- **Keep existing data and discard import data**. This tells QuickBooks to skip the imported data and keep the existing record.
- **Replace existing data with import data, ignoring blank fields**. Existing data is replaced, and a blank field in the import file won't overwrite any existing data in that field.
- **Replace existing data with import data, including blank fields**. Existing data is totally replaced with imported data. If an existing field has data, but the import file field is blank, the blank field overwrites the existing data.

Managing Duplicate Records When You're Importing a List

If you're importing a list to get all your records into QuickBooks, the option **Keep existing data and discard import data** is the best choice. It means that the import won't disturb any records you've already created.

If you don't have any records, and you're using the Import function to create a list from scratch, it doesn't matter which option you choose for managing duplicate records.

Managing Duplicate Records When You're Modifying a List

If you're importing a list for the purpose of modifying the data in an existing list, then use either of the options that start with **Replace existing data**. You can decide which of those options to select depending on the current state of your QuickBooks list, and the data in your import file.

For example, you may be changing the numbering scheme for a chart of accounts, or you may be adding or changing the Type field in a customer or vendor list.

If you're changing the data in a list, it's often easier to export your original list, make changes in Excel, and then import the list back into QuickBooks. Excel has handy features for sweeping changes such as "Search and Replace". Importing the modified data back into QuickBooks is quicker and easier than opening every record in the list and making changes.

Managing Error Handling

Use the following guidelines for managing errors:

- **Import rows with errors and leave error fields blank**. This option works best. It means that, except for any fields that have data errors, your records are imported. You can edit the imported records later to enter the data that wasn't imported.
- **Do not import rows with errors**. If you select this option, the entire record is skipped if any field has an error. You'll have to enter the entire record manually.

Previewing the Import

It's always better to preview the import to see if your data has any problems. Click Preview to have QuickBooks test the data and display the results in the Preview dialog, which also tells you how many rows (records) were processed, and how many errors were found.

TIP: Unfortunately, the Preview feature doesn't catch all errors, just some data entry errors. You could still have errors when you import the file.

Managing Preview Errors

QuickBooks displays the results of the test import in the Preview dialog, along with the row number, and an explanation of the problem. By default, the Preview dialog shows all the import data, not just the errors, and you have to scroll through the list to find the errors. To make it easier to locate errors, select Only Errors from the drop-down list in the field labeled In Data Preview Show, at the top of the dialog.

Figure A-6 shows the result of a preview of an import of the chart of accounts. QuickBooks found two records with data errors.

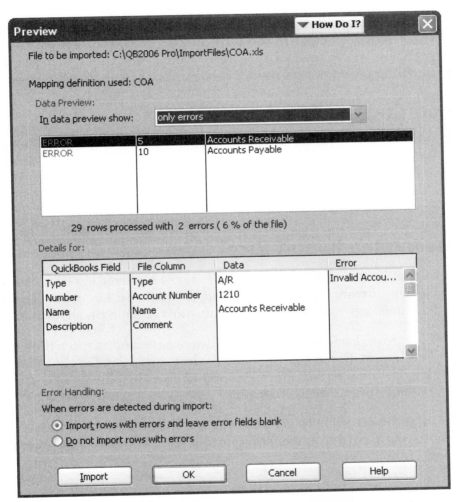

Figure A-6: In two records, the data in the Account Type field didn't match the text required by QuickBooks.

In this case, I have to change the text "A/R" to "Accounts Receivable" (the QuickBooks keyword), and change the text "A/P" to "Accounts Payable (the QuickBooks keyword).

You can correct the problem right in the Preview dialog, instead of canceling the import, opening your worksheet, changing the data, and starting the import again.

To correct an error, select the record in the top part of the dialog, and then change the text in the Data column in the bottom part of the dialog. When you've made all the corrections, click Preview to see if any errors still appear (and fix them). If the errors are gone, click Import.

Importing the File

When there are no errors in your file, click Import. QuickBooks displays a message asking if you want to continue with the import, rather than cancel it in order to back up your company file. If you've just backed up the file, as suggested here, click Yes to continue. Your list is imported into your QuickBooks company file.

Viewing the Import Error Log

After QuickBooks imports your data, it saves an error log that contains details about errors, or warnings about problems (if any were encountered). A message appears to ask if you want to save the error log.

Click Save, because you should always save and inspect the log. In the Save Import Error Log As dialog, select a location for the error file, and give the file a name. The file is saved as a CSV file, which you can open in your spreadsheet program.

Open the error log to examine the problems. In many cases, an error prevents the record from being imported. Here are some of the common errors:

- A required field had no data
- The record name (or number, if the file is a chart of accounts with account numbers) is already in use
- The format of the data did not match QuickBooks requirements, which is frequently a problem with the way you enter dates
- The number of characters your data uses exceeds the number of characters allowed in the field

- A job or subaccount was not imported because the parent account did not exist. This means the parent account may have had a data problem and was not imported, or it was listed below the subaccount in your worksheet—it must be listed first.

You can correct the problems in your worksheet, and re-import, but unless the majority of your records had errors, it's easier to open the list in QuickBooks and manually edit or enter records.

Re-using Mappings

Once you save a mapping, you can use it again for another import of the same list. As long as the worksheet you're importing uses the same columns, and has the same heading text as the existing map, QuickBooks will import the data to any company file.

If you plan to import lists to multiple companies (a common task for accountants), use a generic name when you save the mapping. For example, you can name the mapping for a chart of accounts "COA". Essentially, you're creating a mapping template.

Editing a Mapping

If a new worksheet is slightly different from the saved mapping, you don't have to create a whole new mapping. Instead, you can edit an existing mapping. For example, if you receive the data for a list from your client you may face one or more of the following scenarios:

- The worksheet uses different text for one or more of the column headings.
- The worksheet omits a column that exists in your mapping.
- The worksheet has a column that doesn't exist in your mapping.

To edit a mapping so it matches the worksheet you want to import, follow the steps enumerated earlier in this appendix to import an Excel/CSV file. When all the fields on the Import a File dialog are populated with data, follow these steps:

1. Choose Edit from the drop-down list in the field labeled Choose a Mapping to open the Mappings dialog.

2. Select the mapping you want to edit.
3. Change whatever needs to be changed.
4. Click Save to return to the Import a File dialog.
5. Preview, and then import, the list.

Deleting a Mapping

To delete a mapping, click the Mappings button on the Import a File dialog to open the Mappings dialog. Select the appropriate mapping name and click Delete. QuickBooks asks you to confirm the fact that you want to delete the mapping. Close the Mappings dialog to return to the Import a File dialog, where you can create a new mapping, editing an existing mapping, or close the dialog if you're not ready to import a file.

Keywords for Excel/CSV Import Files

Two types of keywords are required for a direct import of an Excel or CSV file:

- Heading keywords, which are category names, and they match the names of the fields in the list. In your worksheet, these appear as column headings. You don't have to use the keywords in your spreadsheet document, because you can map your text to the keyword text QuickBooks needs.
- Data keywords (only for certain fields), which are the text entries that must match text that QuickBooks expects (keywords).

The heading keywords are the name of the field for each component of the data record. When you import a list using an Excel/CSV file, QuickBooks uses plain English that matches the text you see if you're creating list entries directly in QuickBooks. If the heading row of your import file doesn't match the text QuickBooks requires, you can map your text to the QuickBooks text (as described earlier in this appendix).

For the data keywords (which are actually the choices you see in drop-down lists in the dialog when you're creating an entry directly in QuickBooks), you must be sure to use the keyword text in your worksheet data. In the following sections, I'll provide the data keywords you need for each list you can import via an Excel or CSV file.

Chart of Accounts Excel/CSV Headings

When importing the chart of accounts, you must enter data in all required fields, and can optionally enter data in the other fields. Table A-1 describes the headings and data requirements for the chart of accounts.

Heading	Data
Account Type (Required)	The type of account. You must use the text QuickBooks expects for the account type (covered in the next section).
Account Number	The account number you want to assign to the account.
Account Name (Required)	The account name.
Description	A description of the account.
Bank Acct. No/Card No./Note	The assigned number for a bank account, credit card, or loan.
Opening Balance	Don't use this field; see the discussions in this book about the reasons to avoid opening balan ces.
As Of (Date)	The date for the opening balance you're not going to enter.
Remind Me To Order Checks	The check number you'll be entering at the point you want to be reminded to order checks.
Track Reimbursed Expenses	Enter Yes or No to specify whethe r you want to track reimbursed expenses for this account. See the section "Understanding Reimbursed Expenses Accounts".
Income Account For Reimb. Expenses	The name of the income account to use to track reimbursed expenses.
Account Is Inactive	Enter Yes or Not-Active to hide the account; Enter No or Active to make the account active.

Table A-1: Headings and data requirements for importing the chart of accounts.

Account Type Keywords for Excel/CSV Files

The chart of accounts dialog has only one drop-down list, Account Type. The data in the Account Type column must match the text QuickBooks uses in the drop-down list. Use the following text for account types:

- Accounts payable
- Accounts receivable

- Bank
- Credit card account
- Cost of goods sold
- Equity
- Other expense
- Other income
- Expense
- Fixed asset
- Income
- Long term liability
- Other asset
- Other current asset
- Other current liability

QuickBooks also supports an account type of non-posting, but it's not in the drop-down list of the New Account dialog, so you cannot import non-posting accounts with an Excel/CSV import file (you can import non-posting accounts with an IIF file).

Understanding Reimbursed Expenses Accounts

When you're posting expenses, either by entering vendor bills or direct disbursements, you can assign the expense to a customer:job, and invoice the customer for the expense. In addition, QuickBooks provides a feature that lets you post the income from those reimbursements to an income account, instead of "washing" the expense account. In order to implement the feature, you have to take the following steps:

- Enable the ability to track reimbursed expenses as income. This option is in the Company Preferences tab of the Sales & Customers section of the Preferences dialog.
- After the option is enabled, when you create or edit an expense account you see additional fields: a check box to track reimbursements to this expense account as income, and a text box in which you enter the name of the income account that receives the postings for reimbursed expenses.

You must create an income account for each expense account you've marked as tracking reimbursements as income. That means a separate income account for each expense account so marked; you cannot post all reimbursed expenses to a single income account. (Chapter 6 of QuickBooks 2005: The Official Guide has detailed instructions on configuring this feature and implementing it during customer invoicing.)

Tips for Importing the Chart of Accounts from Excel/CSV Files

Data in your chart of accounts import files should follow certain protocols in order to ensure a successful import, and/or to make sure the data in the list is consistent and easy to work with.

Using Account Numbers

If you're planning to use account numbers, and have entered account number data in the appropriate column, QuickBooks imports the account numbers and saves them, even if account numbers aren't enabled.

By default, QuickBooks does not enable account numbers, and if you haven't changed the setting in the Accounting section of the Preferences dialog, you won't see your account numbers when you open the chart of accounts after you import the file. Don't panic, QuickBooks stored the account numbers you imported, and as soon as you enable account numbers, they'll show up.

Import the Chart of Accounts First

If you're planning to import the Items list, you must import the chart of accounts before you import the Items. Some of the data connected to an item includes account numbers (income account, cost of goods sold for inventory items, and so on).

Importing Subaccounts

If you want to import subaccounts, you must list the parent account first, and then list the subaccount(s) in the format **ParentAccountName:SubaccountName**. Be sure there are no spaces before or after the colon.

If any subaccounts are listed above the parent account, when you preview the import you won't see any errors. However, when you perform the import, any subaccounts listed above the parent account aren't imported. The error log indicates that the parent account didn't exist, so the subaccount wasn't imported.

TIP: *Remember that the colon means "subaccount" to QuickBooks, so don't use colons in account names. It's a common writing technique to make text clear by using a colon, and you may find it logical to name an account Insurance:Automobile. However, because QuickBooks only uses a colon to indicate a subaccount, the account won't be imported because you don't have a parent account named Insurance. Instead, use a hyphen (Insurance-Automobile).*

Retaining Leading Zeroes

Many users like to enter the account number in the Bank Acct.No/Card No./Note field of bank accounts, current liabilities (loans), and credit card accounts. If the account number begins with one or more zeroes, after you enter the number and move to the next cell, the leading zeroes are removed, because the default format for cells is General (which doesn't support leading zeroes).

Before you begin entering data, select the entire column for this heading and change the format of the cells to Text. The data in Text cells is retained exactly as it's typed.

Customer:Job Headings for Excel/CSV Files

The QuickBooks headings that map to your column headings are represented in Table A-2, along with the data requirements.

Customer:Job Data Mappings for Excel/CSV Files

Customer and job records have quite a few keywords that are useful for defining customers, or for tracking information about customers so you can create transactions quickly. Unfortunately, the keywords aren't preconfigured in QuickBooks; instead, they are the data entries in other lists. The other lists cannot be imported with an Excel/CSV file; instead, you must enter everything manually (or import the list with an IIF file).

Heading	Data
Job or Customer Name (Required)	The customer name, or the job name.
Opening Balance	Don't use this field; see the discussions in this book about the reasons to avoid entering opening balances in lists.
Opening Balance As Of	The As Of date for the opening balance you aren't going to enter.
Company Name	The company name.
Salutation	Mr., Mrs., etc.
First Name	Customer's first name.
Middle Initial	Customer's middle initial.
Last Name	Customer's last name.
Contact	Your contact name for the customer.
Phone	Phone number.
Fax	FAX number.
Alternate Phone	Alternate phone number.
Alternate Contact	Alternate contact name.
Email	Contact's e-mail address (used to e-mail transactions if you choose that Send Method).
Billing Address 1 Through Billing Address 5	Each line of the customer's billing address.
Shipping Address 1 Through Shipping Address 5	Each line of the customer's shipping address.
Customer Type	Customer type.
Terms	Terms for this customer.
Sales Rep	Sales rep assigned to this customer.
Preferred Send Method	Preferred send method for invoices, estimates,

Table A-2: Columns (categories) for importing customers and jobs.

Your text must match the text of the entries in the lists described in Table A-3. The list entries must have been created before you import the customer list. Except for the Sales Tax items, all of the lists are in the Customer & Vendor Profile Lists submenu. The Sales Tax Code list is on the Lists menu, and Sales Tax Items must be predefined in the Items list (or included in an import file for Items).

Heading	List Name
Customer Type	Customer Type List
Preferred Payment Method	Payment Method List
Price Level	Price Level List
Sales Rep	Sales Rep List
Tax Code	Sales Tax Code List
Tax Item	Items List
Terms	Terms List

Table A-3 These lists must be populated before you import customer data that includes entries from the lists.

QuickBooks prepopulates some of the lists (e.g. Terms and Payment Methods). If you use a predefined company file (available in some Premier editions), other lists, such as Customer Type, may also have some prepopulated data. However, you may have added entries to any of these lists, or renamed or removed pre-loaded entries. To have the correct text available when you create your import file, print each list's contents by opening the list window and pressing Ctrl-P.

Job Keywords for Excel/CSV Files

Jobs have two data fields you can use to categorize the job record, and your data must match the text in the associated lists:

- Job Type, which is a list in the Customer & Vendor Profile Lists submenu.
- Job Status, which is a descriptive phrase that appears in the Jobs & Estimates Preferences dialog which you access by choosing Edit → Preferences.

TIP: QuickBooks prepopulates the Job Type list with entries in some of the predefined company files.

Tips for Importing the Customer:Job List from Excel/CSV Files

Your QuickBooks tasks will be easier if your customers and jobs are set up for efficiency, so you need to pay attention to some protocols as you create your import file.

Jobs are Like Subaccounts

Jobs don't stand alone; they're subordinate to customers. To import jobs, the data must be in the format **CustomerName:JobName** (no spaces around the colon). This is similar to the way subaccounts are managed in an import file for the chart of accounts. The customer must exist in order to import a job, so you must be sure to list the customer name before the job name in your import file.

Customer Financial Information

As described earlier, your import file contains columns for financial information about the customer. Here are some guidelines for entering this data:

- **Credit Limit**. Enter the amount without a dollar sign.
- **Credit Card Number**. Don't use this field, it's dangerous. In fact, it's probable that either your merchant account agreement, or state law (or both), makes it illegal to have this information stored in plain text. The laws and rules that govern computer storage of credit card numbers usually limit you to storing the last four digits only (either omitting the other digits or using XXXX to replace them).

Vendor Headings for Excel/CSV Files

QuickBooks will map your column headings to the QuickBooks field names, if your column headings don't match those in Table A-4. Mappings represent the columns that QuickBooks will import, which in turn represent the fields available in the Vendor dialog you work in if you're entering vendors one-at-a-time in QuickBooks.

Mapping	Data
Name (Required)	Vendor name (your vendor code).
Opening Balance	Don't use this field; see the discussions in this book about the reasons to avoid entering opening balances in lists.
Opening Balance (As Of)	The As Of date for the opening bal ance you aren't going to enter.
Company Name	Company name.
Salutation	Mr., Ms., etc.
First Name	Vendor's first name.
Middle Initial	Vendor's middle initial.
Last Name	Vendor's last name.
Address 1 Through Address 5	Each line of the vendor's address.
Contact	Your contact name for the vendor.
Phone	Phone number.
Fax	FAX number.
Alternate Phone	Alternate phone number.
Alternate Contact	Alternate contact name.
Email	E-mail address.
Print On Check As	Vendor's name as printed on a check.
Account Number	Your account number with this vendor.
Vendor Type	Vendor types.
Terms	Terms
Credit Limit	Your credit limit with the vendor.
Tax ID	Tax ID number.
Vendor Eligible For 1099	Yes or No.
Is Inactive	Yes or Not-Active to hide the vendor's listing; No or Active to display the listing.
Note	Your notes about the vendor.

Table A-4: Columns (categories) for importing vendors.

Vendor Data Keywords for Excel/CSV Files

Some of the data referenced in Table A-4 (vendor categories) requires you to enter text that matches existing data in other existing lists, to wit:

- Vendor Type
- Terms

Be sure to populate those lists, before importing your vendor list.

Tips for Importing the Vendor List from Excel/CSV Files

To make sure it's easy to enter transactions and get the reports you need, you must be careful to import your vendor list accurately, using all the data you'll need. While you can always correct or add data by editing each vendor's record, that's a time consuming, annoying task.

Enabling 1099 Tracking

If your vendor data includes references to Form 1099, you must enable 1099 tracking. This option is in the Company Preferences tab of the Tax 1099 category of the Preferences dialog. You must also configure the expense accounts that are associated with Form 1099 tracking. Detailed instructions for setting up, configuring, and printing Form 1099 are available in various chapters of QuickBooks 2005: The Official Guide.

TIP: If a vendor is not eligible for Form 1099, you don't have to fill in data for the Tax ID category.

Account Number Means Your Account Number

The QuickBooks Help files for importing Excel/CSV files say that in the category Account Number you should enter the vendor's account number. That's misleading. You should enter *your* account number (your customer number with the vendor) in this field.

The text you enter in this field is automatically printed on the Memo line of checks (if you print checks), and this is the commonly accepted method of providing your account number to the vendor when you pay bills.

If you use online bill paying, the Account Number field must contain your customer account number with the vendor. The data is included in the online bill paying information, and it's the only way the vendor can identify you as the payer.

TIP: *If you think of the Account Number field as "the text that prints in the Memo line of checks", you can enter messages for those vendors that don't assign you account numbers. Make the messages short, because the memo line isn't very long.*

E-Mail Address is for Sending Purchase Orders

QuickBooks offers a method of sending purchase orders to vendors via e-mail. The e-mail has message text, and the purchase order is attached as a PDF file. If you plan to use this feature, enter the e-mail address of the person who receives purchase orders from you in the Email field of your vendor import file. Complete instructions for setting up and using e-mail for invoices, estimates, purchase orders, and other transaction forms are in Chapter 3 of QuickBooks 2005: The Official Guide.

Vendor Name as Printed on a Check

As I explained in Chapter 4 of this book, the vendor name you assign a vendor should be a code, and your protocols for entering vendor codes should be consistent. However, the name/code probably won't work for addressing mail, nor for printing the payee name on checks. The field Vendor Name As Printed On Checks is a nifty solution.

When you're entering vendors directly in QuickBooks (using the New Vendor dialog), after you enter the text for the Company Name field, QuickBooks automatically copies that text to the Vendor Name As Printed On Checks field. That's almost always appropriate. Therefore, to save a little time when you're creating your import file, use the Copy feature in Excel to copy the Company Name text to the Vendor Name As Printed On Checks field.

Item Headings for Excel/CSV Files

For importing items, the QuickBooks headings that map to your column headings are represented in Table A-5, along with the data requirements.

Mapping	Data	Data Requirements
Type (Required)	Item type.	Must match keywords (see the section "Item Type Keywords")
Name (Required)	Item name	
Is Reimbursable Charge	Yes or No	For services performed by others, item type should be Service. For reimbursable expense, item type should be Other Charge
Description/Description on sales transactions	Item description	
Tax Code	Three character tax code from the Sales Tax Code lists	Data must match existing Tax Code text in the Tax Code list
Account/Income ac count (required)	Name of account linked to this item	Account name must match existing account
Expense/COGS Account	Name of expense account linked to this item	Account name must match existing account
Asset account	Name of asset account linked to this item	Account name must match existing account
Deposit To (Account)	Name of bank account for deposits	Account name must match existing account
Description On Purchase Transactions	Description.	For Inventory Part only
On Hand	Number on hand.	For Inventory Part only
Cost	Cost amount	For Inventory Part only
Preferred Vendor	Vendor's name.	Vendor name must match existing vendor
Tax Agency	Tax agency (vendor)	Name must match existing vendor
Price/Amount Or %/Rate	Price or percentage rate.	To enter a percentage, the Cost category must have data. For inventory items or reimbursable expenses, data must be a dollar amount.
Is Inactive	Yes or No	
Reorder Point	On hand number that kicks in the reorder reminder	
Total Value	The number representing the val ue of this item	Inventory parts only —You can manually enter a number, but it's better to let QuickBooks calculate this amount by multiplying the number on hand by the cost of each item
As Of (Date)	Effective date of Total Value	
Payment Method	Default payment method	Text must match existing entry in Payment Method List

Table A-5: Columns (categories) for importing items.

Item Type Keywords for Excel/CSV Files

For item type, the text in your file must match the keywords for item types. Following are the keywords for item types:

- Service
- Inventory Part
- Inventory Assembly
- Non-inventory Part
- Other Charge
- Subtotal
- Discount
- Payment
- Sales Tax Item

Tips for Importing the Item List from Excel/CSV Files

The Item list is rather complicated, especially if you want to import information over and above the required fields. If you have a product-based company, it might be less complicated to import only inventory parts, and enter other types of items manually.

Import or Create Other Lists First

Be sure you install (or import) the chart of accounts before you import the Item list. The accounts linked to items are required entries, and the account names in your Item list file must already exist in your company file. Otherwise, the import fails.

WARNING: The data for the account names in your Items list import file must be exactly the same text as the account name in your already-installed chart of accounts.

Table A-5 notes the other lists that impact the Item list. You must either import those lists with an IIF file, or enter the data manually.

Importing Subitems

If you want to import subitems, you must list the parent item first, and then list the subitems(s) in the format **ParentItemName:SubitemName**. Be sure there are no spaces before or after the colon. QuickBooks recognizes the colon as the format for a subitem.

If any subitems are listed above the parent account, when you pre-view the import you won't see any errors. However, when you perform the import, any subitems listed above the parent account aren't imported. The error log indicates that the parent account didn't exist, so the subaccount wasn't imported.

Group Items Cannot be Imported

If you check the drop-down list for item types in the New Item dialog, you'll notice that when I listed the keywords for item types earlier in this section, I omitted two item types: Group, and Sales Tax Group. You cannot import a group item type with an Excel/CSV file. Import the items, and then manually create the group items you need.

Appendix B

Importing IIF Files

Understanding IIF file formats

IIF file keywords documentation

You can import data into QuickBooks directly from a tab-delimited text file that has the filename extension .iif. The file must be configured properly for importing to QuickBooks.

In this appendix, I'll go over the steps for creating and importing IIF files into a QuickBooks company file. I'll also provide the keywords and format information for the commonly imported lists.

IIF import files are a bit complicated to create, but they are more powerful as an import tool than the Excel or CSV files discussed in Appendix A. You can create an IIF file in a spreadsheet program, save it as a tab-delimited text file, and name the file, giving it the extension.iif.

Unlike importing an Excel or CSV file, QuickBooks does not preview or error-check the contents of a tab-delimited text file. If the import fails at some point, it just fails. Therefore, you must be careful about the way you create the file.

On the other hand, using a tab-delimited file means you can import all the data you need to set up a company, instead of being restricted to the few lists provided in the Excel/CSV import feature, each of which is limited in the number of fields it accepts. An IIF file can contain data to populate every list in QuickBooks, including detailed information about each record in the list.

Accountants and IIF Files

An IIF file is a great way for accountants to provide all the data required for a client's company file. It's like creating a perfect company file from scratch in QuickBooks, and delivering the file to the client.

Entering data in a spreadsheet is faster and easier than going through all the work involved in creating a company file in QuickBooks. Entering data in rows and columns in an Excel worksheet is faster than opening one QuickBooks list window after another, and then opening one dialog after another within each list.

Most accountants are extremely comfortable working in a spreadsheet application, and after they've created a series of boilerplate import files for different types of companies, they can zip through the process of customizing a boilerplate for any particular client. Do your work in a regular spreadsheet file, saving it as an Excel file, so you can avoid all those reminders from Excel about text files not having all the features of a regular spreadsheet file. Then, save the file as a tab-delimited text file (with the extension .iif) when you're ready to create an import file for QuickBooks.

Format of an IIF File

To work correctly as an import file, an IIF file has to follow a certain format. Figure B-1 is an Excel worksheet for the chart of accounts that displays the proper format.

	A	B	C	D	E	F
1	!ACCNT	NAME	ACCNTTYPE	DESC	ACCNUM	EXTRA
2	ACCNT	Operating Account	BANK		1000	
3	ACCNT	Money Market Accnt	BANK		1010	
4	ACCNT	Payroll Account	BANK		1020	
5	ACCNT	Petty Cash	BANK		1050	
6	ACCNT	Accounts Receivable	AR		1200	
7	ACCNT	Inventory Asset	OCASSET		1120	
8	ACCNT	Undeposited Funds	OCASSET		1500	UNDEPOSIT
9	ACCNT	Vehicles	FIXASSET		1300	
10	ACCNT	Furniture and Fixtures	FIXASSET		1512	
11	ACCNT	Accounts Payable	AP		2000	
12	ACCNT	Payroll Liabilities	OCLIAB		2100	
13	ACCNT	Payroll Liabilities:FWT	OCLIAB	Federal Taxes Withheld	2110	
14	ACCNT	Payroll Liabilities:FICA Withheld	OCLIAB	FICA Withheld	2120	
15	ACCNT	Payroll Liabilities:Medicare Withheld	OCLIAB	Medicare Withheld	2130	
16	ACCNT	Payroll Liabilities:PA Income Tax Wit	OCLIAB	PA Income Tax Withhel	2140	
17	ACCNT	Payroll Liabilities:Phila Wage Tax	OCLIAB	Phila Wage Tax Withhe	2150	
18	ACCNT	Sales Tax Payable	OCLIAB		2200	SALESTAX
19	ACCNT	Opening Bal Equity	EQUITY		3000	OPENBAL
20	ACCNT	Owner's Capital	EQUITY	Owner's Capital	3130	
21	ACCNT	Owner's Capital:Draws	EQUITY	Draws	3150	
22	ACCNT	Retained Earnings	EQUITY		3900	RETEARNING

CustJob | COA | Items | Vendors | Employ | OtherNames | ShipMeth

Figure B-1: This file is formatted properly.

Notice the following characteristics of this sample IIF file:

- The list being imported is identified by that list's keyword in Cell A-1 (identified by the exclamation point)
- Each record (row) indicates the list into which the data is being imported (keyword in Column A).

- Each category (column header) has the keyword for the field into which the data in that column is imported.

To create an IIF file from scratch, make sure you've set up your columns properly, with the appropriate headings (using keywords). When you enter data, remember that some data requires special handling (keywords again). The documentation for those keywords is in this appendix.

Unlike the Excel/CVS column heading text covered in Appendix A, an IIF file doesn't use the field names you see when you're entering entries into a list in QuickBooks. Instead, the column headings (field names) are indicated by specific keywords. The keywords for each list are documented in this appendix.

Exporting Data into an IIF File

You can export data from another application and specify a tab-delimited file for the exported file format. The application could be another accounting software application, or a spreadsheet in which you've been keeping customer information, inventory information, and so on.

To open a tab-delimited file in your spreadsheet application, right-click the file's listing in My Computer or Windows Explorer and choose Open With. Then choose Microsoft Excel (or another spreadsheet application if you don't use Excel).

Creating Multiple Lists in One IIF File

You can actually create an entire company in one IIF file, by having all the entries for all the lists you want to import in one worksheet. If you're an accountant, this is a good way to deliver a "company in a worksheet" to your clients.

Each list must be in its own contiguous section of rows, with the appropriate keyword headings as the first row of each section. To make it easier to work with the file, insert a blank row between each section (list).

Many accountants who work in Excel save the file as a standard Excel (.xls) file while they're building import files. It's common to create a separate worksheet for each list being created. This method is more efficient, and lets you build boilerplate worksheets for each QuickBooks list.

However, you can't save multiple worksheets when you save a document as a tab-delimited file. When you're ready to turn your Excel document into QuickBooks import files, you can either save each worksheet as a separate IIF file, or you can copy the contents of every worksheet into a single worksheet in a new Excel document. Then, save the new combined document as an IIF file.

Importing an IIF File

Importing an IIF file is an uncomplicated process, and takes only a few easy steps. It's even easier if you copy the file to the folder in which QuickBooks is installed, so you don't have to navigate through the computer to find the file. Use the following steps to import an IIF file:

1. In QuickBooks, open the company that needs the imported file.
2. Choose File → Utilities → Import → IIF Files.
3. Double-click the listing for the IIF file you want to import.

QuickBooks automatically imports the file and then displays a message indicating the data has been imported. Click OK.

IIF File Keywords for Lists

In the following sections, I'll provide the keywords and instructions for building IIF files for QuickBooks lists. For many lists, I'll provide only the keywords for fields that are commonly imported, instead of covering the full range of possible keywords.

For example, all lists accept data in a field (column) named HIDDEN, and you enter Y or N for each entry (row) to indicate whether the entry is active or inactive. It's normal to omit that column in an import file. (In the absence of information about the active status, QuickBooks assumes the entry is active.)

For lists that permit custom fields in the names lists and the items list, QuickBooks has keywords you can use to import that data. However, it would be unusual to take the trouble to create these in a worksheet. It would also be unusual for a file imported from another application to contain this information.

Profile Lists Import Files

Profile lists are the lists that contain entries to help you categorize and sort major lists. The entries in profile lists are fields in major lists, such as Terms or Vendor Type. You can see the profile lists by choosing Lists → Customer & Vendor Profile Lists.

I'm starting the discussion of importing lists with the profile lists, because if you import the profile lists, you can use their contents in other lists. For example, if you import your Customer Type List, you can enter data in the customer type category of your customer import list. However, I'm not covering all the profile lists; instead, I'll discuss those that are commonly imported.

Customer Type List Import File

The Customer Type List has one keyword: Name. Your worksheet needs only two columns:

- Column A contains the list keyword !CTYPE in the top row, and the entry keyword CTYPE on each entry row.
- Column B contains the data keyword NAME on the top row, and the data (the name you've created for a customer type) is in each following row.

!CTYPE	NAME
CTYPE	Name of customer type (e.g. Retail)
CTYPE	Name of customer type (e.g. Wholesale)

Vendor Type List Import File

The Vendor Type List is almost exactly the same as the Customer Type List:

- The list keyword for the first row of Column A is !VTYPE and the entry keyword in Column A for each row of data is VTYPE.
- Column B contains the data keyword (NAME) on the top row, and the data is in each following row.

Job Type List Import File

The Job Type List is also similar to the Customer Type list:

- The list keyword for the first row of Column A is !JOBTYPE and the entry keyword in Column A for each row of data is JOBTYPE.
- Column B contains the data keyword NAME on the top row, and the data is in each following row.

Sales Rep List Import File

The Sales Rep List has the following format:

The list keyword for the first row of Column A is !SALESREP and the entry keyword in Column for each row of data is SALESREP.

- Column B contains the data keyword INITIALS on the top row, and the data (two initials) is in each following row.
- Column C contains the data keyword ASSOCIATEDNAME on the top row, and the data (the name of the sales rep) is in each following row.
- Column D contains the data keyword NAMETYPE on the top row, and the data (a code representing the list the name listed under ASSOCIATEDNAME is a member of) is in each following row.

The NAMETYPE codes are:

- 2 if the rep is in the Vendor List
- 3 if the rep is in the Employee List
- 4 if the rep is in the Other Names List

Note that the QuickBooks help files that document this list are wrong.

Ship Method List Import File

The Ship Method List (which supplies data for the Ship Via field in transactions) is also similar to the Customer Type list:

- The list keyword for the first row of Column A is !SHIPMETH and the entry keyword in Column A for each row of data is SHIP-METH.
- Column B contains the data keyword NAME on the top row, and the data (UPS, FedEx, Truck, etc), is in each following row.

Terms List Import File

The Terms List import file must contain all the information for each named set of terms. The terms you include must cover the terms you need for both customers and vendors (QuickBooks doesn't provide separate Terms files for customers and vendors).

- The list keyword for the first row of Column A is !TERMS and the entry keyword in Column A for each row of data is TERMS.
- The remaining columns contain the data keywords on the top row, and the data is in each following row. The data keywords for columns are explained in Table B-1.

Keyword (Column Title)	Data
NAME	(Required) The name for the terms.
TERMSTYPE	The type of terms. 0 = standard terms (payment within a specific number of days). 1 = date driven terms (payment by a certain date of the month).
DUEDAYS	When TERMSTYPE = 0, t he number of days in which payment is due. When TERMSTYPE = 1, the day of the month by which payment is due.
DISCPER	The discount percentage earned for early payment. The data is a number and the percent sign (e.g. 2.00%).
DISCDAYS	The number of days by which the discount specified by DISCPER is earned.

Table B-1: Terms list import file keywords.

Standard Lists Import Files

The information in the following sections covers the commonly imported lists that are displayed on the Lists menu. After your profile lists are imported, the data in some of the "regular" lists can be linked to the data in the profile lists.

Chart of Accounts Import File

The chart of accounts import file is not terribly complicated:

- The list keyword for the first row of Column A is !ACCNT and the entry keyword in Column A for each row of data is ACCNT.
- The rest of the columns on the first row contain the data keywords. The data is in each following row.

Table B-2 shows the important column headings for importing a chart of accounts. If you don't use account numbers, you can omit the ACCNUM column.

Keyword (Column Title)	Text
NAME	(Required) The name of the account.
ACCNTTYPE	(Required) The type of account. The text must match keywords (See Table B -3).
DESC	Description of the account.
ACCNUM	The account number.

Table B-2: Keywords for the chart of accounts.

The ACCNTTYPE entry is required and your text in that column must match the keywords in Table B-3.

Section	Account Type	Keyword
Assets		
	Bank	BANK
	Accounts Receivable	AR
	Other Current Asset	OCASSET
	Fixed Asset	FIXASSET
	Other Asset	OASSET
Liabilities		
	Accounts Payable	AP
	Credit Card	CCARD
	Other Current Liability	OCLIAB
	Long-Term Liability	LTLIAB
Equity		EQUITY
Income		INC
Cost Of Goods Sold		COGS
Expense		EXP
Other Income		EXINC
Other Expense		EXEXP
Non-Posting Accounts		NONPOSTING

Table B-3: Keywords for account types.

Account Numbers in Import Files

If the company file into which the chart of accounts is imported has enabled account numbers, the numbers in the IIF file are displayed in the chart of accounts window and the drop-down lists in transaction windows.

If account numbers are not enabled in the company file, QuickBooks stores the account number data that was imported. When (or if) the user enables account numbers, the imported account numbers are displayed.

EXTRA Account Keywords

You can include a column named EXTRA to import accounts that QuickBooks automatically creates when such accounts are needed (when specific features are enabled).

For example, when a QuickBooks user enables the inventory feature, QuickBooks creates an account named Inventory Asset Account in the Assets section of the chart of accounts.

To use these accounts in an import file, the text you enter in the EXTRA column must match the required keywords. If the text doesn't match the required keyword, QuickBooks will create another account when the user enables the appropriate feature. Table B-4 contains the keywords required in the EXTRA column when you create these special accounts.

Account	EXTRA Column Keyword
Inventory Asset	INVENTORYASSET
Opening Balance Equity	OPENBAL
Retained Earnings	RETEARNINGS
Sales Tax Payable	SALESTAX
Undeposited Funds	UNDEPOSIT
Cost of Goods Sold	COGS
Purchase Orders	PURCHORDER
Estimates	ESTIMATE

Table B-4: Keywords for configuring the EXTRA column for special accounts.

Although QuickBooks adds these accounts automatically when needed, including them in the import file lets you control their account numbers. If you're an accountant, you can create boilerplate import files by client type, and include the appropriate EXTRA accounts. For example, product-based businesses need inventory and purchase order accounts, and some service-based businesses may need estimates.

Customer:Job List Import File

If you've been keeping a customer list in another software application, you can avoid one-customer-at-a-time data entry by importing the list into QuickBooks. This is only possible if your current application is capable of exporting data to a tab-delimited text file.

Load the tab-delimited text file into a spreadsheet program (I'm assuming you use Microsoft Excel), and use the instructions in this section to create an import file.

A QuickBooks customer import file can contain all the information you need to fill out all the fields in the customer dialog, such as customer type, sales tax status, and so on.

However, it's unlikely you've kept records in a manner that matches these fields. Therefore, I'll provide the keywords and instructions for basic customer information. I'll include some of the additional fields so you can fill them in manually if you wish (or skip the keyword column for any data you don't want to import).

Customer:Job Import File Format

If you're dealing with data from another source, after you import the data to Excel, you need to format the worksheet as follows:

- To make room for the QuickBooks keywords you need, insert a column to the left of the first column, and insert a row above the first row.
- In cell A1, insert the text !CUST (the exclamation point is required). This is the code that tells QuickBooks the import file is a Customer:Job list.
- In the remaining cells in the first column, for every row that has data, insert the text CUST. This identifies the data in that row as data for a Customer:Job list.
- In the first row, starting with the second column (the first column contains !CUST), enter the QuickBooks keywords for customers.

Table B-5 describes the keywords and the text that belongs in the column under each keyword.

TIP: The only required entry is the customer name, which is linked to the keyword NAME. If that's the only information you have, use it to import your customers—you can fill in the rest of the fields as you use each customer in a transaction.

QuickBooks supports multiple shipping addresses for customers, but the import file can only manage one shipping address. When you import the file, the shipping address data becomes the default shipping address. However, there is no keyword for the shipping address name.

Keyword (Column)	Text
NAME	The customer name (the code you use for the customer).
COMPANYNAME	Name of the customer's company.
FIRSTNAME	Customer's first name.
MIDINIT	Customer's middle initial.
LASTNAME	Customer's last name.
BADDR1	First line of the customer's billing address, which is usually a name (customer's name or company name).
BADDR2	Second line of the customer's billing address, which is the street address.
BADDR3	Third line of the customer's billing address, which is either additional street address information, or the city, state, and zip.
BADDR4	Fourth line of the billing address, which is either additional street address information, or the city, state, and zip.
BADDR5	Fifth line of the billing address, which is either a dditional street address information, or the city, state, and zip.
SADDR1	First line of the default shipping address.
SADDR2	Second line of the default shipping address.
SADDR3	Third line of the default shipping address.
SADDR4	Fourth line of the d efault shipping address.
SADDR5	Fifth line of the default shipping address.
PHONE1	Phone number.
PHONE2	Second phone number.
FAXNUM	FAX number.
EMAIL	E-mail address of a contact.
CONT1	Name of the primary contact.
CONT2	Name of another contact .
CTYPE	Customer Type (must match text in the Customer Type import file).
TERMS	Terms (must match text in the Terms import file).
TAXABLE	Y or N
SALESTAXCODE	Tax code (must match text in the Tax Code import file)
LIMIT	Credit limit (e.g. 5000.00)
RESALENUM	Resale number for tax exempt customers

Table B-5: Keywords for a Customer:Job import file.

Having said that, at the time I write this, importing shipping addresses isn't working at all in QuickBooks 2006 (even for the import of

Excel files as discussed in Appendix A). QuickBooks is aware of the problem, so I expect a bug fix to appear in an update. By the time you read this, it may be fixed.

Importing Jobs

A job is like a subaccount, it's linked to a parent, and the text must be in the format customer:job. Notice that no spaces exist before or after the colon.

To import jobs, you must make sure the customer is imported first; the text for the customer must appear in the Name column before the text for the job. For example, if you have a customer named LRAssocs with jobs named Consulting and Auditing, enter the following in the Name column:

LRAssocs

LRAssocs:Consulting

LRAssocs:Auditing

Most jobs have the same basic information (address, taxable status, and so on) as the customer, so you don't have to enter text in the other columns. However, if any specific information is different, such as the name of the primary contact, or the job type, enter the text in the appropriate column.

Vendor List Import File

If you're exporting your vendor list from another software application, follow the formatting rules described earlier for the customer file.

- The list keyword for the first row of Column A is !VEND and the entry keyword in Column A for each row of data is VEND.
- The remaining columns contain the data keywords on the top row, and the data is in each following row.

The data keywords are explained in Table B-6.

Keyword	Data
NAME	The Vendor Name (the vendor code).
PRINTAS	The Payee name that prints on checks.
ADDR1	First line of the vendor's address.
ADDR2	Second line of the vendor's address.
ADDR3	Third line of the vendor's address.
ADDR4	Fourth line of the vendor's address.
ADDR5	Fifth line of the vendor's address.
VTYPE	Vendor Type (must match text in the Vendor Type import file).
CONT1	Your primary contact.
PHONE1	Phone number.
PHONE2	Second phone number.
FAXNUM	FAX number.
EMAIL	E-mail address of a contact.
NOTE	The text you want to print in the Memo field of checks (usually your account number with the vendor).
TERMS	Terms (must match a name in the Terms import file).
TAXID	Tax identification number for a 1099 recipient.
SALUTATION	Salutation or title.
COMPANYNAME	Vendor's company name.
FIRSTNAME	First name.
MIDINIT	Middle initial.
LASTNAME	Last name.
1099	Specifies whether this vendor receives a 1099 -MISC form. Enter Y or N as the data.

Table B-6: Keywords for importing vendors into QuickBooks.

Items List Import File

If you've been keeping your items in a software application (usually this means inventory items only), you can import those items, saving yourself some manual work. Use the instructions earlier in this chapter to format the file.

The required keywords for items import files are the following:

- NAME—the item name
- INVITEMTYPE—the item type
- ACCNT—the income account to which you post sales of this item

Some QuickBooks item types don't have an account (such as prepayments or tax items). However, because most imported items list originally were exported from another application, those item types are rarely imported.

The keyword for the item list is !INVITEM on the heading row, and each record (row) must have INVITEM in the first column. Table B-7 describes the keywords for the rest of the columns on the first row of the import file.

Keyword	Data
NAME	Item Name or Number
INVITEMTYPE	Item type. The data must match the keywords in Table B-8.
DESC	The description that appears on sales forms
PURCHASEDESC	(Inventory part items only) The description that appears on purchase orders
ACCNT	The income account you use to track sales of the item
ASSETACCNT	(Inventory part items only) The inventory asset account
COGSACCNT	(Inventory part items only) The cost of goods account
PRICE	The percentage rate or price of the item (not for Group, Payment, or Subtotal type).
COST	(Inventory part items only) The unit cost of the item.
TAXABLE	Specifies whether the item is taxable —enter Y or N.
PREFVEND	(Inventory part items only) The vendor from whom you

Table B-7: Keywords and data information for an Item List import file.

Several item types have additional options when you create them in the standard dialog while working in QuickBooks. When you select any of these options, the dialog changes to include fields for Cost, Expense Account, Purchase Description, and Preferred Vendor.

- A Non-Inventory Part item type has an option labeled This Item Is Purchased For And Sold To A Specific Customer:Job.
- A Service item type has an option labeled This Service Is Performed By A Subcontractor, Owner Or Partner.
- An Other Charge item type has an option labeled This Is A Reimbursable Charge.

You can set these options in your import file by creating a column with the keyword ISPASSEDTHROUGH. The data for this column is either **Y** or **N** (for Yes or No). For any item that has a Y in this column, you can enter data that is marked **Inventory part items only** in Table B-7.

Keyword	Item Type
ASSEMBLY	Inventory Assembly item
COMPTAX	Sales tax item
DISC	Discount item
GRP	Group item
INVENTORY	Inventory part item
OTHC	Other charge item
PART	Non-inventory part item
PMT	Payment item
SERV	Service item
STAX	Sales tax group item
SUBT	Subtotal item

Table B-8: Item Type keywords.

Employee List Import File

When you import the Employee List, you can only import basic data about the employee. Wage, tax, deductions, and other financial information have to be set up in the Employee record in QuickBooks. However, importing the basic information saves you quite a bit of work.

The keyword for the employee list is !EMP on the heading row (Cell A1), and each record (row) must have EMP in the first column. Table B-9 describes the keywords for the rest of the columns on the first row of the import file.

Keyword	Data
NAME	(Required) Employee's name.
ADDR1	First line of the address.
ADDR2	Second line of the address.
ADDR3	Third line of the address.
ADDR4	Fourth line of the address.
ADDR5	Fifth line of the address.
SSNO	Social Security number (XXX -YY-ZZZZ).
PHONE1	Phone number.
PHONE2	Alternate phone number.
FIRSTNAME	First name.
MIDINIT	Middle initial.
LASTNAME	Last name.
SALUTATION	Salutation (Mr., Ms., Mrs., etc.).

Table B-9: Keywords for Employee List import file.

The Mystery of Employee Initials

QuickBooks' documentation says that the INIT data is a required entry for an employee list import file. It's not; I've imported many Employee Lists without it. In fact, the field doesn't appear in the employee record dialog when you create an employee in QuickBooks, or view an existing employee's record. If you've consulted the QuickBooks documentation to build IIF files, you can ignore this requirement, and omit the column from your import file.

Other Names List Import File

Some companies never use the Other Names list, but this list is necessary for some company types, and handy for others. For proprietorships and partnerships, or any business in which a draw occurs, the owners should be in the Other Names list instead of the Vendors list.

Companies that occasionally issue non-payroll checks (such as loans) to employees must add the employees to the Other Names list. That entry is the payee for loans, or other non-payroll disbursements.

The keyword for the Other Names list is !OTHERNAME on the heading row (Cell A1), and each record (row) must have OTHERNAME in the first column. Table B-10 describes the keywords for the rest of the columns on the first row of the import file.

Price Level List Import File

Price levels are assigned to customers and sales transactions, and the IIF file has the following format:

- The list keyword for the first row of Column A is !PRICELEVEL and the entry keyword in Column A for each row of data is PRICELEVEL.
- Columns B and C contain the data keywords NAME and VALUE.

The data is percentages, such as 10.00%, 5.50%, etc. A discounted price level has a minus sign.

Keyword	Data
NAME	(Required) The name.
BADDR1	First line of the address.
BADDR2	Second line of the address.
BADDR3	Third line of the address.
BADDR4	Fourth line of the address.
BADDR5	Fifth line of the address.
PHONE1	Phone number.
PHONE2	Alternate phone number.
FAXNUM	FAX number.
EMAIL	E-mail address.
CONT1	Primary contact (if a company).
SALUTATION	Salutation, or title (Mr., Ms., Mrs., etc.).
COMPANYNAME	Company Name (if a company).
FIRSTNAME	First name.
MIDINIT	Middle initial.
LASTNAME	Last name.

Table B-10: Keywords for the Other Names List import file.

Sales Tax Code List Import File

Sales tax codes are assigned to customers and items, and indicate whether sales tax should be imposed. These are *not* the sales tax items, which determine the rate (those are in the Item List).

Sales tax codes only need to be imported if you need more tax codes than QuickBooks provides automatically. QuickBooks preloads the entries Tax and Non, which suffice for many businesses. However, for businesses in states that require explanations for nontaxable sales, you need additional codes. Here are some examples of sales tax codes you can assign to customers:

- NPO for nontaxable nonprofit organizations.
- GOV for nontaxable government agencies.
- RES for customers who are nontaxable because they resell products (your customer record should include the resale tax number).

The list keyword for the first row of Column A is !SALESTAXCODE and the entry keyword in Column A for each row of data is SALESTAX-CODE.

The following keywords are used in this import file:

- CODE is the name of the code (and is required data). Data entries cannot exceed three characters.
- DESC is an optional description of the code.
- TAXABLE specifies the taxable or nontaxable status (and is required data). The data is Y or N.

Appendix C

Tips & Tricks for Accountants

Accountants who support QuickBooks users (or users of any accounting software application) spend a lot of time troubleshooting problems. Most of the problems are user-induced rather than software bugs. Some of the predicaments users find themselves in are the result of plunging ahead on a task without calling an accountant first.

In this appendix, I present tips, tricks, workarounds, and troubleshooting techniques that I've used, or learned about from accountants who attend my seminars and CPE classes. It's impossible to cover every possible dilemma, and it's even impossible to cover every possible facet of a particular predicament (users are *so* inventive), so you'll have to view this appendix as a much-shortened course in QuickBooks problem solving techniques.

The topics that are presented are those about which I receive the largest number of queries or comments. They're presented in random order, because it's difficult to create logical groups out of the subject matter offered here.

Updating Lists with Imports

Do any of these scenarios seem familiar?

A client needs to track certain information about customers, and you've suggested a custom field. You created the custom field for the Customers & Jobs list, and added it to sales transaction windows by customizing the templates. The client has 500 customers to update with data for the new field.

A client has created price levels and wants to assign a price level to many of the 200 customers in the system. Or, instead of price levels, it's sales reps (or both).

Tweaking and updating information in lists is a common practice as users become more familiar with QuickBooks, and the additional data can be the solution for producing more sophisticated detailed reports.

Performing these tasks on a customer-by-customer, vendor-by-vendor, or item-by-item basis means opening each record, moving to the appropriate tab, entering the data, closing the record, opening the next record, and... you get the picture.

Not only is this time consuming, but the user is likely to be inconsistent about data entry in the custom field, making it hard to track the needed information. The fastest, most accurate method for upgrading data in lists is to import the information.

Any field in any list can be updated with an IIF file. For example, you may create a Customer Type that you want to use to sort customers in reports, or to prepare mailings. Or, you might create a custom field and have to enter data in that field for most (or all) of the entries in a list. Working in QuickBooks means opening the record for each entry in the list, moving to the right tab in the record's window, typing in the data, closing the record, selecting the next record, etc. etc. This could take days if the list is large.

For some lists, you can use either an IIF file or an Excel XLS file. Only the following lists can accept XLS imports:

- Customer
- Vendor
- Items
- Chart of accounts

However, not all fields are available for import when you use an XLS import file. For example, you cannot import data for custom fields, which is a severe limitation. As a result, I just use IIF files for these tasks.

Creating Import Files to Update Existing Lists

Start by exporting the appropriate list from the company file. Choose File → Utilities → Export → Lists to IIF Files. Do not export multiple lists, even if you want to update more than one list; instead, update the lists one at a time.

Open the resulting IIF file in Excel and look for the first row of "real" data, which has the list name preceded by an exclamation point. Select all the rows above that row and choose Edit → Delete to remove those rows from the worksheet. This data isn't necessary in an import file, and removing it makes it easier to work with columns (because the column names for the rows you're deleting are not the same column names you'll work with as you add data). Figure C-1 displays a customer list where all the rows above !CUST have been selected for deletion.

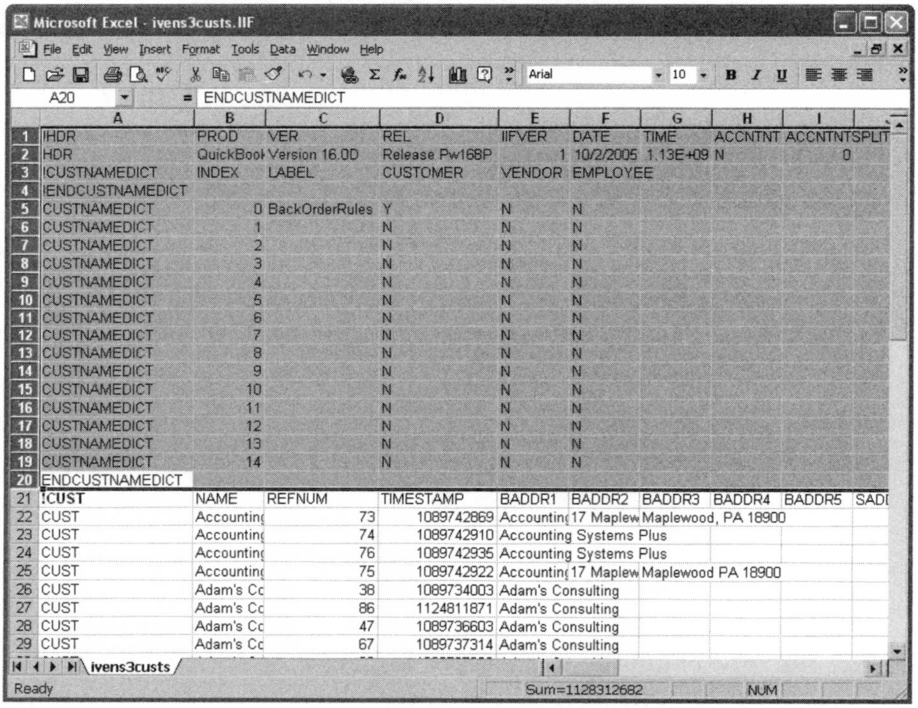

Figure C-1: Find the first row of real data, and eliminate every row above it.

To add data, you must be able to see the NAME column. Freeze the column that holds the names so that as you scroll through the columns the NAME field stays visible. Use the following steps to freeze the column:

1. Click the column heading of the column to the right of the NAME column to select it.
2. Choose Window → Freeze Panes.

Adding and Modifying Data

Except for data going into custom fields (covered in the next section), the data you enter in any column must match the data already in the QuickBooks file. For example, if you're adding Customer Type data to your customers, the data must match the Customer Type entries you created in the Customer Type list. If you created a Customer Type named Stmnt (to indicate customers who should receive statements), the text you enter must be Stmnt; you cannot enter Statement, Stamnt, or any other text. The same is true for Terms, Price Level, and other data contained in QuickBooks lists.

To make sure you enter data correctly, open the list and press Ctrl-P to print the list. Then, with the entries in the Customer Type, Price Level, or whatever list in front of you, you'll be able to enter the text correctly.

WARNING: *If the data you're entering or changing is a QuickBooks Keyword you must use the keyword. Appendix B documents all the keywords for all the list files.*

When you're working in Excel, you can take advantage of the Windows clipboard and the Excel data entry tools to enter data.

1. After you enter data in the first row (record) for which you're entering or modifying text, select the cell and press Ctrl-C (or right-click in the cell and choose Copy) to copy the text to the clipboard.
2. Find the next row that needs the same data, and press Ctrl-V to paste the text (or right-click in the cell and choose Paste).
3. Move to the next row that needs the same data and press Ctrl-V to paste the text there. Continue to paste until you've pasted this text into all the records that should have it. (Once you have text in the Windows clipboard, you can continue to paste it endlessly, as long as you don't stop pasting to perform another task.)
4. Enter the next data text into the appropriate row, and follow the same pattern to paste that text into every row that's appropriate.

If you have a section of contiguous rows that require the same data (e.g. all the jobs listed below a customer), enter the data in the first row, and then select that cell. Position your mouse in the lower right corner of the cell, and when your pointer turns into vertical and horizontal intersecting lines drag down to fill all the cells with the same data.

Working With Custom Fields

The Custom Field columns do not have the name of the custom fields you created. The columns are labeled CUSTFLD1, CUSTFLD2, and so on. Open the custom field list in QuickBooks to see the names of the custom fields you created. The top custom field is CUSTFLD1, the next is CUST-FLD2, etc. Write down the names of the custom fields so you know the type of data you have to enter as you update the list.

- In the Items list, open any item, and click the Custom Fields button to see the custom fields.
- In a Names list, open any entry in the list and move to the Additional Info tab to see the custom fields.

When you enter data into custom fields, you must be consistent, or else it will be difficult to create reports on the contents of the fields. For example, if you have a custom field in your Customer & Jobs list named Backorder (to indicate which customers will accept backorders), devise a protocol for the data. For customers that do not accept backorders, if you use the text NoBO, don't also enter text No BO (note the space), or just No (see Figure C-2).

Saving the Import File

I always use the Save As command in Excel to save the file in order to retain the original exported data (in case I have to repair a mistake I made). I usually add a dash and a number to the original filename (such as custlist-1, if the original exported file was named custlist).

Save the file as a Text (Tab Delimited) file. Excel issues warnings about text files not holding on to formatting, etc. Just ignore the warnings. Then close Excel.

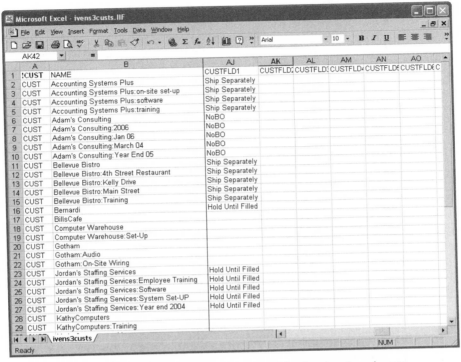

Figure C-2: Entering data for the custom field for backorders keeps
customers happy (the field appears on transaction templates to make it easy to track the information).

Importing Updated Data into QuickBooks

Before you import data in batches with an import file, back up the
company file. If anything goes amiss, you can restore the backup and
continue to work in the file. Then examine your import file to find any
errors, and try again (backing up the file again first, if you've worked in
the file).

To import the file, choose File → Utilities → Import → IIF files.
Select the file you created and click Open. QuickBooks automatically
imports the data. Open the list you tweaked and make sure everything is
as you expected.

Source and Target: Solving the Mystery

Accountants and business owners often use JEs to perform tasks, especially when the task seems to call for a journal entry rather than a series of transactions in individual transaction windows. For example, one common JE is to allocate an expense across jobs to track job costs. It's easy, you just debit the same expense account multiple times in order to select a customer or job for each applicable portion of the expense, and credit the original expense total.

After performing this task, however, it's a common complaint that the job costing reports don't show the expenses that were allocated in the journal entry. In fact, for journal entries that move expenses from one customer to another, often the wrong customer receives the cost posting.

What's going on? The answer is that all transactions in QuickBooks have a source and a target, and if you don't get them right, you end up with unexpected results.

The source is the account where the transaction originates, and the target is the account where it is completed. When you write a check to a vendor, the bank account is the source (it's where the money starts) and the expense account is the target (it's where the money ends up).

If you attach additional information to the check, it travels with its source or target counterpart. For example, assigning a customer to the line that contains an expense account (for job costing) links the customer information and the amount to the target (because the line in which it exists is the target).

For JEs that perform job costing allocations there are two important facts to remember:

- QuickBooks assigns job costing or other information when it's part of the target, and ignores it when it is part of the source.
- The first line of a JE is the source and all other lines are targets.

This means that if you're moving job costing information from one customer to another or, more commonly, from one job to another for the same customer, you will almost certainly end up with one or more incorrect postings.

Creating JEs With No Source Accounts

I've learned that to play it safe, the best way to create a JE is to make every line in the transaction part of the target. Remembering that only the first line is the source, don't use the first line for anything "real".

In the first line of a JE, enter only a memo. Starting with the second line, enter real information (see Figure C-3). Because everything is a target, everything posts appropriately. If you don't want to add the amounts to the customer invoice as reimbursed expenses because you're only performing job costing for your own information, click the icon in the Invoice column to put a red X over it. The costing information is posted to the job whether you invoice the customer or not.

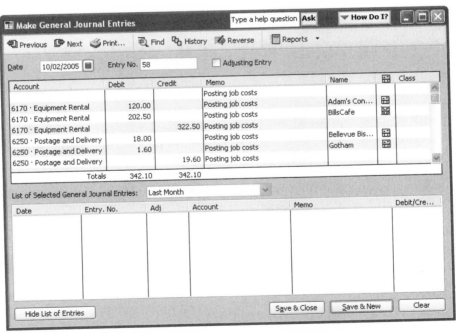

Figure C-3: Guarantee accurate reports with accurate postings.

After I learned to do this, I never had a problem with job costing reports. In fact, I've used this method successfully to make adjustments to 1099 totals (not an easy task without this trick).

If you've already encountered the problem, you don't have to void and re-enter all the journal entries that had a source/target mix up. Just edit the journal entry to change the source line, as follows:

1. Open the JE transaction and click anywhere in the first line to select that line.
2. Press Ctrl+ Ins (or Insert, depending on the label your keyboard uses) to insert a blank line above the current first line.
3. Enter text in the Memo field to create a source line.
4. Close the Make General Journal Entries transaction window.
5. QuickBooks displays a message that you've changed the transaction and asks if you want to save it.
6. Click Yes.

Everything posts correctly.

Disbursements Report Mysteries

Here's another mystery that's solved if you understand the QuickBooks source/target paradigm. Unfortunately, solving the mystery doesn't always remove the problem. Here's a puzzle I was presented with. To guess how I solved it, you have to remember that the target, not the source, has dibs on reports about postings.

An accountant called me from a client site. He was grumpy. Here's the transcript of our conversation.

Him: I'm looking at a trial balance and my client has several expense accounts that have postings for consultants that get 1099s so I'm checking his 1099 payments. When I double-click one of those accounts, I get a QuickReport.

Me: Right, that's what's supposed to happen.

Him: The payees are wrong. I asked my client who Sam Smith is and why he's not listed as a 1099 vendor, and he tells me Sam Smith is a customer. I asked him why he was writing checks to Sam Smith, and he says he's not.

Me: Double-click the listing for the check to Sam Smith - you'll see the original check.

Him: OK, the check is made out to somebody else, why does the report say Sam Smith?

Me: Check the columns in the line item section. I'll bet he linked the expense to a customer named Sam Smith.

Him: That's right. So I have to keep double-clicking every single entry, all hundreds of them, to find out who the payee really is because this report is wrong?

Me: Nope, click Modify Report and deselect the Name listing and select the Source Name listing. But, you have to do this every time you open a QuickReport. You could memorize the report, but then you have to go through all the mouse clicks to open a memorized report and then set the filters for the single account you're checking, so it's faster to modify this report each time.

Him: Why would any software program have a default display that is designed to NOT show you the name of a payee when you're looking at a report of an expense account's disbursements?

Me: Good question.

Reports on disbursements should provide information on the source name by default, saving the use of the target name for job costing reports. I've passed my thoughts on this to Intuit, but I haven't received any response.

You need to be aware of the fact that when you create a report to get information about disbursements and expenses, you may end up with some very confusing data in the report. If an expense is linked to a customer (target data), that's the name that appears on the report. If no expenses are linked to customers or jobs, the payee (source data) appears. Most of the time, modifying the report to display Source Name instead of

Name (which really means target name if a target name exists) cures the problem.

If you have some reason to know both the source and target names, select both from the Display list. For those transactions without a posting to a target name, both columns have the same data (the source name).

Accountant's Review Copy Gotchyas

Even though it's clear what accountants can and cannot do when they're working in a client's Accountant Review Copy, some actions are deceptive.

Can't Enter Opening Balance for New Bank Accounts

Accountants can create new bank accounts in the Accountant's Review Copy, but if you enter an opening balance for that account, QuickBooks ignores it. That's because QuickBooks considers an amount entered in the Opening Balance field of a new bank account a deposit. Entering deposits is one of the "cannot do" actions.

After you create the new bank account (with no opening balance), create a journal entry. Debit the bank account and credit the appropriate account.

A/R and A/P Journal Entries

It's not uncommon for accountants to adjust A/R and A/P totals. However, QuickBooks treats journal entries involving these accounts as transactions, not just adjustments. In addition, QuickBooks won't accept a journal entry that has lines for both accounts; the JE must use only one of these accounts.

You can't use either an A/P or an A/R account in a journal entry without including information about a customer or vendor. Because

QuickBooks treats this as a transaction, you can't change an amount without linking it to the customer that's involved in the transaction.

For example, a simple JE that credits A/R and debits an equity account (or even an income account) isn't possible without selecting a customer. The easiest workaround is to create a dummy customer and a dummy vendor; perhaps InHouseCust and InHouseVend (or, DummyCust and DummyVend).

Inventory Issues

Whether you're helping a client set up inventory, or troubleshooting inventory reports that don't make sense, you need to understand where clients can go wrong with inventory transactions.

Work in Process Inventory

It's possible to set up a QuickBooks system to track WIP and then transfer finished goods to inventory, but QuickBooks doesn't make it easy. The software has no built in "WIP to Inventory" process. That's understandable, because QuickBooks isn't intended for use in complicated manufacturing businesses.

Don't try to do this if the business has more than a few inventory products that are tracked via WIP. In that case, buy a separate software application to track these manufacturing steps. Check the QuickBooks Marketplace Solutions web pages to find a QuickBooks add-on that will work for you.

To track WIP, create a WIP account in addition to the Inventory account QuickBooks creates when you enable inventory tracking. Both accounts are Other Current Assets.

Tracking WIP Transactions

Products or services purchased to create inventory items should be posted to the WIP account, not to COG.

Purchase products and services for WIP without using POs to avoid having to create an item. (Items need COG and income accounts, which makes tracking WIP much more complicated.) Use the Memo field on each transaction to note the product for which you're making the purchase.

If you purchase the same products and services for multiple inventory items, split the purchase amount in order to be able to note each product in the Memo field. This makes it easier to transfer inventory from WIP to the inventory account.

Moving Finished Products into Inventory

When the parts and services have been purchased and you're ready to move a product into inventory, create a report to determine the cost of inventory, and then perform an inventory adjustment to add the product to your inventory at the right cost.

Creating WIP Reports

To gather the information you need about the total cost of parts and services for an inventory product, customize a report to eliminate transactions not included in your WIP system.

Choose Reports → Vendors & Payables → Vendor Balance Detail, and click Modify Report. Make the following changes:

- In the Display tab, select Memo in the Columns drop-down list.
- In the Filters tab, select Account in the Choose Filter list, and then select the WIP account.
- In the Filters tab, select Transaction Type in the Choose Filter list, select Selected Transaction Types, and then select Bill and Check. (The transaction types Bill and Check cover vendor bills, whether or not they've been paid yet, and checks written as direct disbursements.)

The resulting report displays the total cost of an inventory product. If the report covers more than one inventory product (the memo field indicates the product), you can grab a calculator and work out the totals manually, or export the report to Excel, where you can re-sort the data and create formulas for totals.

Adjusting Inventory

With the total cost known, move the product(s) into inventory by choosing Vendors → Inventory Activities → Adjust Quantity/Value on Hand. In the Adjust Quantity/Value on Hand dialog (see Figure C-4), take the following actions:

1. Select the option Value Adjustment (on the bottom left of the window).
2. Select the item you're bringing into inventory.
3. In the New Qty column enter the number of units you're transferring to inventory.
4. In the New Value column enter the total cost of the item.
5. In the Adjustment Account field, enter the WIP account. QuickBooks immediately displays a message telling you it expected an expense or income account. Select the option Do Not Display This Message In The Future and click OK.

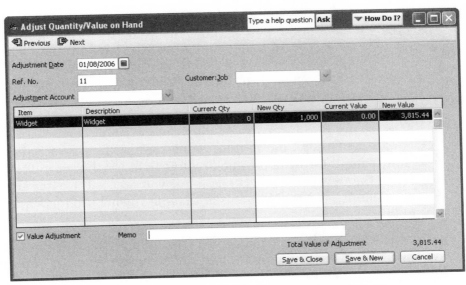

Figure C-4: Enter the new quantity and value of an inventory item you're moving from WIP into inventory.

When you sell the product, QuickBooks divides the total value by the number of units, and posts that amount to COG. In the future, as you move additional units from WIP into inventory, the New Value amount you enter is the total value. That means you must add the results of your new WIP cost report to the existing value.

Customer Credits for Unreturned or Damaged Inventory

Usually, when a customer returns an inventory product for credit, the process of creating and applying the credit is straightforward. When you enter the inventory item in the credit transaction, QuickBooks returns the item by incrementing the inventory account and decrementing the COG account (in addition to the postings to sales and A/R).

If the customer reports a damaged item, most companies tell the customer not to bother returning it to avoid paying the shipping cost for something that can't be resold. Even if the customer returns the damaged item, you can't put it back into inventory.

To create a customer credit without involving the original inventory item, you need to create an account and an item.

- Create an income account named Returns (some accountants prefer the name Returns and Adjustments). I usually make this account a subaccount of the income account that tracks product sales so my P & L reports display the net amount.
- Create an Other Charge item named Adjustments (or Sales Adjustments). In the income account field for this new item, enter the new sales returns account you created. Do not enter an amount, and make the item taxable if your products are taxable.

To create the credit memo, use the new item in the transaction, filling in the amount based on the amount of the unreturned or damaged item. If the customer originally paid for shipping, enter the shipping costs to refund that amount too.

When you save the credit memo, you can apply the amount to another invoice, leave the credit as a floating credit, or issue a refund check.

Purchasing and Selling in Different Lot Sizes

In many accounting software applications designed for wholesale and distribution businesses, an automated conversion chart is available so you can track inventory for a product that you buy in bulk, and sell in individual units. The software automatically converts the bulk purchase cost and price when you sell the individual items.

QuickBooks doesn't support this feature. Some users have created two items: one for the bulk purchase (a gross of items), and one for the sales (an individual item). However, that solution doesn't work, because inventory postings and reports are for two separate items, which is incorrect.

The solution is to make sure that both the purchase of items and the sale of items are decrementing the same inventory item, and applying cost of goods correctly.

In QuickBooks, the only way to accomplish this is to create an item for sales, and then create a group for that item for purchases.

Create the individual item (for sales). Then, create a group item (for purchases) that includes only the individual item, but uses the appropriate quantity. For example, if you sell a widget that you purchase by the gross, the group item is the widget with a quantity of 144.

Inventory Item Quantities Display Half an Item

I've seen quite a few inventory reports in which the amount of available stock for an item is 12.5, or 9.3. How can you have a half or third of a physical item? You didn't sell half an item, or two-thirds of an item.

Inventory quantities end up with this problem as the result of progress invoicing on estimates. When you create a progress invoice, QuickBooks asks you to specify the percentage of the job that's completed so you can send an invoice reflecting that percentage. If products are included in the invoice, the percentage is applied to them, too.

Click the Progress icon on the toolbar of the Create Invoices window. This opens a dialog that allows you to reconfigure the line items. You can change the quantity, rate, or percentage of completion for any individual line item. Use this feature to change line items that contain products, to make sure you're invoicing for "whole" products.

Vendor Transaction Troubleshooting

According to the e-mail I receive, and the questions I'm asked in seminars, it's common to encounter some difficult situations in vendor transactions and vendor balances.

Voided Vendor Checks

An accountant asked me to solve a problem that involved a check sent to a vendor that wasn't cashed, and never would be cashed. The check was written to pay a bill that had been previously entered in QuickBooks.

The accountant voided the check in the bank account, which, of course, put the vendor bill back into the "Bills to Pay" window, and also put the bill into A/P aging reports. When the A/P manager brought this to the accountant's attention, he did what accountants often do—he created a journal entry. (Accountants seem to gravitate to JEs automatically, even though they're frequently not the right tool.).

The journal entry debited A/P and credited the original expense account, and the accountant entered the Vendor name in the JE. Now the A/P aging reports showed correct totals, but the A/P manager reported that the bill continued to appear in the Pay Bills transaction window, and on QuickReports for this vendor. The accountant told her to ignore the bill's listing because the company's books were in balance (the A/P totals were correct).

However, the A/P manager insisted that the bill be removed from the Pay Bills window, and the accountant didn't know how to proceed.

To remove a bill from the Pay Bills window, you have to pay the bill, either with a check or a credit. When the accountant created the JE with the vendor name, a credit was created for the amount posted to A/P.

The credit is floating, so all the bills from this vendor in the Pay Bills window are eligible for the credit. Obviously, the credit should be applied to the bill that was paid with the voided check, and that bill is the same amount as the floating credit (making it easy to select it in the Pay Bills window).

Select the bill, click Set Credits, apply the credit, and click Pay & Close. When the Pay Bill window closes, QuickBooks issues a message telling you that one or more bills were paid by credits and no check was issued. That's what you wanted to happen, so click OK.

The best approach to this is not a JE, which only creates the extra step of the JE. All the postings are correct if you create discrete transactions that are linked to the vendor.

Void the check, which puts the original bill back into its unpaid state. If you're not going to reissue a check to pay this bill, create a vendor credit. Then open the Pay Bills window and use that credit to pay off the bill that reappeared when you voided the check.

Reimbursed Cost of Goods

It's unusual to encounter a situation in which a customer is invoiced for reimbursement of cost of goods, but after receiving several inquiries from business owners and accountants on this subject I figured out a way to do this. In each case, the object was to charge the COG account, not to worry about moving an inventory item in or out of inventory. I'm assuming that these inquiries involve businesses that aren't tracking inventory items, and are posting COG amounts directly when they have an expense directly connected to sales items or services.

Each inquiry I received included the information that when the COG account was selected in the Enter Bills or Write Checks transaction window, QuickBooks did not display the icon representing a reimbursable transaction after the user entered a customer name. Therefore, the amount never showed up in the Time/Costs list when the customer's invoice was created.

The workaround is to create an item that manages this transaction, and use it when you're paying expenses that you want to add to a customer's invoice.

Create the item as an Other Charge type. Name the item (I use Reimbursement as the item name), and select the option labeled This Item Is Used In Assemblies Or Is A Reimbursable Charge.

NOTE: *If your client is using QuickBooks Pro, assemblies don't exist, so the label reads This Is A Reimbursable Charge.*

In the Expense Account field enter the COG account. In the Income Account field, enter an appropriate income account. Do not enter any amounts, and make the item nontaxable.

When you enter the vendor bill, or write a direct disbursement check to the vendor, use the Items tab in the line item section of the transaction window instead of the Accounts tab.

Enter the item you created for this situation, and enter the customer or job that you want to invoice for reimbursement. When you save the transaction, the amount is posted to the Time/Costs for this customer (on the Items tab), and is available for invoicing.

Property Management

If you have clients who are using QuickBooks to manage property, the way you set up the company file depends on how the management business is run.

Property Owners

If the client owns the properties, you want to be able to report on the profit for each property. Use the following guidelines for company file setup:

- Enable Class Tracking in the Accounting category of the Preferences dialog.

- Be sure the option Prompt To Assign classes is checked. This is a reminder to assign a class to every income and expense transaction.
- Create a class for each property.
- Create a class for administration (so that transactions not directly related to a property receive a class assignment).

Every expense directly linked to a property is assigned to that property's class (mortgage, interest, repairs, utilities, and so on). All other expenses are assigned to the administration class.

Each month, or quarter, or year, create a JE to allocate appropriate expenses from the administration class to each property (see Figure C-5). You do not have to clear the original expense account, the amount of expense you allocate is a financial judgment based on knowledge of the way the client's overhead applies to each property.

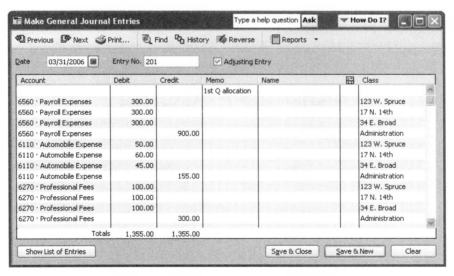

Figure C-5: Allocate appropriate overhead expenses to each property.

You can then create a P & L statement for the properties, as seen in Figure C-6, by choosing Reports → Company & Financial → Profit & Loss By Class.

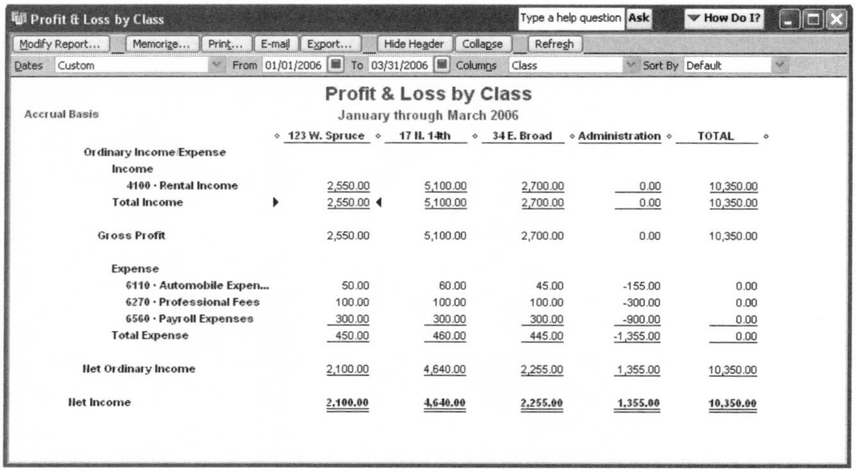

	123 W. Spruce	17 N. 14th	34 E. Broad	Administration	TOTAL
Ordinary Income/Expense					
Income					
4100 · Rental Income	2,550.00	5,100.00	2,700.00	0.00	10,350.00
Total Income	2,550.00	5,100.00	2,700.00	0.00	10,350.00
Gross Profit	2,550.00	5,100.00	2,700.00	0.00	10,350.00
Expense					
6110 · Automobile Expen...	50.00	60.00	45.00	-155.00	0.00
6270 · Professional Fees	100.00	100.00	100.00	-300.00	0.00
6560 · Payroll Expenses	300.00	300.00	300.00	-900.00	0.00
Total Expense	450.00	460.00	445.00	-1,355.00	0.00
Net Ordinary Income	2,100.00	4,640.00	2,255.00	1,355.00	10,350.00
Net Income	2,100.00	4,640.00	2,255.00	1,355.00	10,350.00

Figure C-6: Track net income for all properties

To create a separate report for each property, modify the report by going to the Filters tab and select Class from the Filter list. Select one class (property) and memorize the report. Repeat for each class. Name the memorized reports with the property address.

Property Management Companies

If the client is a property management company and manages properties for multiple owners (customers), you need to be able to report on the profit for each customer, as well as for each property owned by that customer.

Use the guidelines described here, but in addition to creating the owners as customers, create a class for each owner, and create a subclass for each property.

Create a customer for each tenant, but as tenants move and are replaced, make the old tenants inactive customers. On the other hand, you can create a generic customer named Tenant and keep information on the tenant (telephone, employer information, etc.) outside of QuickBooks.

Payroll Issues

Payroll causes more angst, confusion, and panic calls to accountants than any other element involved in running a business. Whether the client does payroll in-house, or has a payroll service, questions and problems abound.

Separate Vendors For Liabilities

Businesses that remit their own payroll liabilities often have to go through some difficult maneuvers to create the liability checks properly. In many businesses the 941 and 940 liabilities are paid to the bank, and the state payroll taxes, UC and SDI payments are all paid to the same state agency (e.g. Department of Revenue).

The business owner or bookkeeper (or even the accountant) sets up the bank as a vendor, and sets up the state revenue department as a vendor. When it's time to remit liabilities, all the liabilities are selected, and QuickBooks creates one check for each vendor.

This doesn't work, because there are always forms or coupons attached to each individual liability payment, and the vendor won't accept one large check with multiple coupons or reports.

What's the solution? There are two solutions; one is a pain, the other is easy. At CPA911, we presented this topic as a puzzle (our newsletter readers can vie for prizes by answering our puzzles), and only a couple of respondents presented the easy solution, everyone else was using the "painful" solution.

The painful solution is to select each liability, one at a time, in the Pay Liabilities window. Create the check, print the check, attach the appropriate paperwork, and return to the Pay Liabilities window to process the next check for the same vendor.

That's real work, and I'm far too lazy to do that. Besides, I'd probably lose track and cut the same check twice.

The easy solution is to take advantage of the fact that QuickBooks presents a "Print On Check As" field in each vendor record, so you can have separate vendors with the same payee name.

For the federal deposits, create one vendor named 940 and another vendor named 941. Both vendors have the same bank name in the Print On Check As field. For the state, create separate vendors for each separate liability (payroll taxes, UC, SDI, etc.). Enter the appropriate payee name in the Print On Check As field (possibly the same text for all vendors).

TIP: I name all my payroll liability vendors with the form name: 940, 941, PA501 (the form number for remitting payroll taxes in Pennsylvania), PAUC (the form name for UC), and so on. I enter the appropriate payee name for each vendor.

Edit your payroll items list to reflect the vendor names (not the payee text). After you've completed this one-time-only setup chore, paying liabilities is a snap. Select all the liabilities that are due and click Create. QuickBooks creates separate checks for each liability payment.

This system works well for garnishments, too. If you have employees with garnishments for child support, tax liens, etc. and the money is all sent to the same government agency, you can't send one check for all garnishments.

Re-issuing a Lost Paycheck

You can't manage the replacement of paychecks the same way you manage the replacement of lost or destroyed vendor checks. It's more complicated than that, but if you follow these step-by-step instructions, it's easy to accomplish this task.

1. Do NOT void the original paycheck.
2. Create the employee as an Other Name. You have to use a variation of the name in the Name field, because you can't have duplicate names in your company file (add or remove a middle initial).

3. Use the Write Checks function to write a check for the NET amount to the Other Name entry. Post the check to any expense account (e.g. Misc).
4. Print the check, write down the check number, and give it to the employee.
5. Open the bank register and find the original check (the one that was lost). Write down the check number. Edit that original check so it has the same check number as the one you just issued. When QuickBooks asks if it's OK to have duplicate check numbers, say Yes.
6. Edit the check you just wrote to the Other Name. Change its number to the old check number (the check that was lost or destroyed).
7. Now that the new check has the old number, void it.

Your records show the correct check number for the voided check, the correct check number for the check that the employee will deposit, your liabilities haven't changed, the W-2 will be correct, the Other Name listing and the expense account you used do not show a balance for this transaction.

Payroll Deductions for Employee Purchases

If you do your own payroll, and you permit employees to purchase goods, and then pay for those goods with a payroll deduction, here's how to set up and use that function.

You can use the same paradigm presented here to track and repay employee loans and advances.

Configuring Your Company File for Employee Purchases

Before you can create transactions for employee purchases, you have to set up the list components you'll need, which are the following:

- A customer record for the employee. You cannot duplicate the name you use in the employee record. Use a nickname, or use the format "employee name-cust", such as SmithJ-Cust.

- An account to track employee purchases. The account is of the type Other Current Asset. Name the account Employee Purchases (or something similar).
- An Item of the type Discount, which you can name Employee Purchase. The item is non-taxable, has a default amount of $0.00, and is linked to the Other Current Asset account named Employee Purchases.
- A Payroll Item that is a Payroll Deduction, named Employee Purchases. Link the payroll liability account for this item to the Other Current Asset account named Employee Purchases. Apply the item to Net pay (not Gross).

Creating an Employee Purchase Transaction

Here's how to create an invoice that will be paid from the employee's paycheck:

1. Create an invoice for the employee/customer.
2. Enter the services or items purchased by the employee/customer on the invoice, using the pricing structure for employees (which may be the same as for other customers).
3. In the next item line, enter the discount item you created for employee purchases.
4. Enter an amount equal to the total of the employee's purchases.

The balance of the invoice is now $0.00. However, the Employee Purchases Other Current Asset account has been increased by the amount for the discount item.

Deducting Payment from the Paycheck

When you create a paycheck for the employee, add the Employee Purchases payroll deduction item in the Other Payroll Items area of the Preview Paycheck window. Either enter the full amount owed, or a partial amount (and deduct the rest from subsequent paychecks).

If the full amount is deducted, the Employee Purchases Other Current Asset account has no balance. If a partial payment is deducted, the remaining balance equals the balance in that account.

Tracking Multiple Employee Purchase Accounts

If multiple employees make purchases that are deducted from paychecks, you don't have to set up separate asset account for each employee. Instead, you can track each employee's current balance by creating and memorizing a report, as follows:

1. Choose Reports, Custom Transaction Detail Report.
2. In the Date Range field, select All
3. Click Modify Report.
4. In the Display tab, select Sort by Customer.
5. In the Filters tab, select the Employee Purchases account.
6. Memorize the report (the name Employee Purchases seems appropriate).

The report provides a breakdown of employee indebtedness on an employee-by-employee basis. Run this report on payday so you know how much should be deducted from each paycheck.

Tracking Classes with Employee Timesheets

A newsletter reader wrote with a problem that was driving her crazy. She had configured her company file for classes, and enabled the option Prompt For Classes. In addition, she applied payroll by class to track separate locations.

Her e-mail message included, "When I save the timesheet I get a message that says, 'One or more items have not been assigned a class.' But there is no class column on the timesheet."

I made some interesting discoveries as I tried to duplicate her problem.

When you first open a timesheet window, no class column exists. As soon as you fill in a name at the top of the window, a class column appears - *unless* the name you select is an employee whose payroll record is configured to track time to create the payroll. (On the Payroll Info tab of the employee record, there's an option labeled Use Time Data To Create Paychecks.)

Unfortunately, even though QuickBooks doesn't provide a class column if the employee is configured for time tracking, it **does** pay attention to your Preference to warn if classes aren't assigned. So you see that Warning dialog, and you have no choice except to select Save Anyway because you can't assign a class in the absence of a Class column.

Here's the workaround I finally came up with. I deselected the option to track employee time for the paycheck in the employee records. When I entered that employee's name in the Timesheet window, QuickBooks issued a message telling me this employee is not configured for time tracking, and asking if I wanted to turn on time tracking for this employee. I clicked No (and QB remembered the answer in subsequent timesheets and never asked again).

The Class column magically appeared in the timesheet window! I filled in the timesheets, ran timesheet reports, and created the employee paychecks by entering the data manually.

I've reported this to QuickBooks, but haven't yet seen a solution/correction. Until this changes, you can track classes for payroll expenses or you can use timesheets to pay employees automatically—you can't do both.

Outside Sales Reps

I think the reason I'm asked so often about managing commissions for outside sales reps is the lack of an automatic commission calculator in QuickBooks. Some accounting applications let you enter the commission rate in the rep's record, and then automatically calculate the commission (and some of the automatically create the checks). QuickBooks doesn't, which makes the issue of sales reps and commissions seem more complicated than it is.

In this section, I'm not covering the processes involved in setting up employees for commissions. It isn't difficult; you just make the employee a rep, create commissions as payroll items, and then apply the commissions to pay checks.

Configuring QuickBooks to Track Reps

In order to track sales for which outside reps receive commission, you must create sales reps, and enter the rep on every affected sales transaction. (Chapter 4 covers setting up sales reps).

To enter the reps when you're creating transactions, you have to add the Sales Rep field to all the sales transaction templates you use (Sales Orders, Invoices, Sales Receipts, etc.). Some of the industry-specific Premier editions provide a sales order template with the rep field included. Make sure all the templates you use have a Rep field.

When a sales rep is linked to a customer, the rep's initials are automatically placed in the Rep field when that customer is selected in a sales transaction template. However, even if the rep is linked to that customer, if you use a transaction template without a Rep field, the transaction is not linked back to the rep.

WARNING: *You cannot split a sales transaction among multiple reps. If you need to pay commissions to more than one rep, you must create a separate transaction for each rep.*

Sales Transactions and Sales Rep Commissions

Most of the time, all the items (services and products) in a sales transaction can be posted to the sales rep's record, so the rep gets a commission on the total sale. QuickBooks does not include sales tax amounts in the sales total posted for commission tracking.

However, if the sales transaction includes reimbursement items, you may not want to include that total as a commissionable amount. When a sales transaction includes reimbursements, QuickBooks separates that total from regular sales items when it posts to the sales rep account for commission tracking. This action lets you decide whether you want to include that total in the commissionable total.

Sales Reports for Outside Reps

To create a report on sales by rep, choose Reports → Sales and then select one of the following reports:

- Sales By Rep Summary, which displays the total amount of sales credited to each rep for the period selected in the report.
- Sales By Rep Detail, which displays every sales transaction for each rep, totaled for each rep. In addition, reimbursement items are listed separately (see Figure C-7).

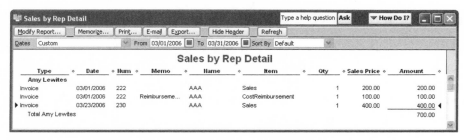

Figure C-7: Two detail lines have the same invoice number because the reimbursement items are separated from sales items.

You can use a calculator to add the amounts (omitting reimbursement amounts if you wish), and multiply by the commission rate. If you have a lot of sales reps and a lot of sales, export the report to Excel and perform your calculations there.

Write the commission check, posting the amount to the account you set up for that purpose (usually an expense account, but sometimes a COG account). For sales reps that receive 1099 forms, use an expense account that you've configured as a 1099 account.

Paying Reps Who Collect Payments

Some reps deliver invoices (when they deliver goods), and collect payments from some customers. The reps want to deduct their commissions from the total collection, and remit the balance to the business owner.

That's a common situation, and it's not difficult to manage it in QuickBooks, as long as you understand the two basic rules:

- The customer's invoice must be totally paid off in QuickBooks.
- The reps must have their commissions tracked (especially if they're 1099 recipients).

When you receive the money from the rep, open the Receive Payments window, enter the customer's name, select the appropriate invoice, and indicate the full amount of the invoice as the amount received.

You must deposit the money to Undeposited Funds, not directly to a bank; otherwise you cannot deduct the commission the rep already took.

Open the Make Deposits window, select this payment for deposit, and click OK. In the next Make Deposits window, make the following entries in the row below the deposit listing:

- Select the Rep's name in the Received From column.
- Select the account you use for posting commissions in the From Account column (this account is linked to 1099 payments if the Rep gets a 1099).
- Optionally, enter a comment in the Memo column (e.g. Commission on Inv1234).
- Skip the Check Number column.
- Optionally, choose Cash in the Payment Method column (it's not essential, but you may want to track this as cash).
- Assign a class in the Class Column (if you're tracking classes).
- Enter the amount the Rep kept as a negative amount in the Amount column.

The net amount is transferred to the bank account as a deposit. Your customer's record are accurate, your rep's records are accurate, and your 1099's will be accurate.

Sales Tax Complications

Could sales tax get more complicated than it already is? Unfortunately, the answer is yes. In addition to all the complications involved in tracking, reporting on, and remitting sales tax amounts for multiple tax jurisdictions and multiple tax rates, some states have an even more complicated twist: they impose different tax rates for different types of items.

I've found that this annoying paradigm is most prevalent in the hotel and restaurant industries, but I wouldn't be surprised if the practice spread to other types of products and services, and will eventually affect many types of businesses.

Managing Sales Tax Rates that Differ by Item

Suppose your client offers several products or services in a state that imposes one tax rate for some products and another tax rate for other products? The taxes are remitted to the same tax authority, this isn't a matter of "one rate for residents of X and another rate for residents of Y".

In the hotel and restaurant industry, some states impose one tax rate for alcoholic beverages, another tax rate for food, and yet another tax rate for hotel rooms. Your state may have different rate structures for another set of products and services.

If you sell items or services that have different sales tax rates, it's not an easy task to prepare a single sales transaction (Invoice or Cash Receipt) for a customer who is purchasing items that have differing tax rates.

Chapter 3 discusses the way to set up sales tax items, and sales tax groups for those taxes that include two tax rates and sometimes two tax authorities. However, for tax rates based on an item, creating a Tax Group doesn't work, because a Tax Group represents the total of differing rates, and that's not what's needed in this case. The workaround for this complicated situation has two parts:

- Creating the items you need.
- Leaning how to enter those items on an Invoice or Sales Receipt.

If you follow the instructions in this section, your sales tax remittances work properly.

Creating Items for Item-Based Tax Rates

You have to create multiple items to be able to apply different tax rates in the same sales transaction. Obviously, you have to create an item for each tax rate, but you also have to create two other items:

- A subtotal item (which you may already have) that enables you to create a subtotal for all items that bear the same tax rate.
- A fake tax item to satisfy the QuickBooks need for a tax rate for the entire invoice (the field appears at the bottom of the invoice).

Creating the Tax Items

You need to create a tax item for each tax rate. Open the Item List and press Ctrl-N to create a new item, using the following guidelines:

- The Item Type is Sales Tax Item
- The Tax Name is the specific tax, e.g. Food Tax
- The Description should be specific, such as Food Tax. Don't leave the Description field blank, because you want the customer to see what the line item tax is (remember, there won't be a single item named "Tax").
- In the Tax Rate field, enter the appropriate rate (QuickBooks adds the % character if you don't bother to type it).
- In the Tax Agency field, enter the name of the tax authority to whom you remit this tax. Make sure the tax authority is set up as a vendor.

Creating a Placeholder Tax Item

When you want to enter taxes as line items, QuickBooks throws up two impediments:

- It continues to tax the sale at the rate of the default tax item, which is displayed at the bottom of the transaction form.
- It won't let you enter a line item tax if that tax is already assigned to the customer or item, and is automatically listed at the bottom of the sales transaction (e.g. Food Tax).

The solution is to have a tax item that has a zero percent rate, and has a description that the customer will understand. Here's how I created the item:

- The Item Type is Sales Tax
- The Item Name is Placeholder
- The Tax Rate is zero percent
- The Description is "Other Sales Tax" (which is the only description that made sense when I printed the transaction)
- The Tax Agency is a vendor I invented named "No Tax", and the vendor has no address or other information, just the name.

TIP: The vendor named No Tax will appear on all sales tax reports, but since no money is involved, it won't affect your numbers, nor will a check print when you pay your sales tax.

Creating a Subtotal Item

In order to apply taxes as line items properly, you need a subtotal for each set of taxable line items. You have two ways to do this:

You can create one item of the type Subtotal, named Subtotal (which may already exist in your Item List). Then, when you prepare a sales transaction, you can type in the description, such as "Total Taxable Food" before applying the applicable tax (in this case, the food tax).

You can create one item for each subtotal you need, such as Subtotal-Food, and enter an appropriate description, such as "Total Taxable Food", which saves you the effort of entering the description when you prepare the sales transaction.

I use the second choice, because I'm always willing to do a little extra work once to save work on a daily basis.

Creating the Sales Transaction

In the Invoice or Sales Receipt transaction window, enter the Customer Name, and then change the Tax field at the bottom of the line item section to the Placeholder tax item you created. Then, take the following steps:

1. Enter all the line items that are subject to one of the taxes.
2. Enter a subtotal item to create a total of the previous items. You must enter a subtotal item even if you only had one item in this group.
3. Enter the appropriate tax item. QuickBooks will calculate the tax based on the amount of the subtotal (which is why you must enter a subtotal even if you only had one item).
4. Enter the line items that are subject to the next tax.
5. Enter a subtotal item for these items.
6. Enter the appropriate tax item for this subtotal.
7. Continue to enter items, subtotals, and tax.

Your invoice should resemble Figure C-8.

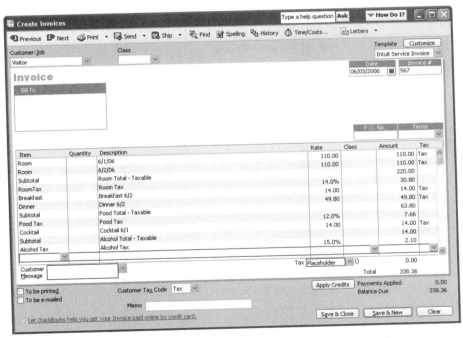

Figure C-8: When all the items you need are configured properly, creating the transaction is easy.

> *TIP*: You can make the printed version easier to read by inserting blank lines after each tax line (to separate the sections). To insert a blank line, place your cursor on the line below the place where you want the blank line, and press *Ctrl-Ins* (or *Ctrl-Insert*, depending on your keyboard's text).

When you print the Invoice or Sales Receipt, you'll see that QuickBooks has printed the "default" tax. Because you changed the default tax to the placeholder tax, using the description "Other Sales Tax", and a value of zero, this shouldn't confuse your customer.

When you save the transaction, QuickBooks asks if you want to change the tax item you inserted in the Tax field (the placeholder) on this customer's record. Say Yes until all your existing customers have had their items changed (which is easier than opening every customer record and changing the tax ahead of time).

Index

172–177
and build disassembly, 212
in centers windows, 26, 28
custom fields, 109
default settings, 72–73, 79
escrow, 480
hiding, 156–157
limits on numbers of, 164
preferences settings, 70–74
QuickBooks types, 227–228
and Retained Earnings Account, 65
and sales tax issues, 606–608
template options in window, 105
troubleshooting vendor, 590–592
voided, 176–177, 222, 590–591
trial balances, Accountant Edition, 348
Type field, import files, 54, 58

U

UCOA (Unified Chart of Accounts), 434–436
unbillable time, tracking, 457
Undeposited Funds account, 91–92, 382, 464–466
Unified Chart of Accounts (UCOA), 434–436
unrestricted vs. restricted funds for nonprofits, 439, 441–442
updating existing files during setup, 5–6
upfront deposits for services, 472–479, 497–499
users. *See also* My Preferences tabs
administrator, 10
importance of login procedures, 226
permissions for, 311–312
profiles in Remote Access, 305

V

Vehicle List, 121
Vendor Center, overview, 26–27
Vendor List, 125–126

vendors
and assembly items, 205
Contractor Edition, 376–377
credits/refunds for paid bills, 427–428
importing lists, 125–126, 545–548, 559, 566–567
preferences settings, 85–87
Professional Services Edition, 457–458
and purchase order creation, 200
returning products to, 426–428
transaction troubleshooting on, 590–592
types of, 118
versions of software, 2–3, 48, 336, 342
viewing options
Access Anywhere, 287–288, 298–300
and PDF files, 174, 177, 251, 365
previous reconciliation reports, 172–177
QuickBooks windows, 16–28
Remote Access, 312–314
and report templates, 215
virtual bank accounts
customer deposits, 379–385, 473–474
retainers, 461, 463–469
voided transactions, 176–177, 222, 590–591
vouchers (check stubs), options for, 79–80

W

WebEx, 280, 293, 304–305
WIP (work-in-process) inventory, 585–588
Word, Microsoft, 422–423, 447
word processing software and business plan write-up, 252
work-in-process (WIP) inventory, 585–588
workers compensation, 405